D0629868

LIGHT FOR MY LIFE

LIGHT FOR MY LIFE

Desmond B. Hills

This book is published in
collaboration with the Youth Department
as an enrichment of the
Morning Watch devotional plan.

Review and Herald Publishing Association
Washington, D.C.

Copyright © 1981 by
Review and Herald Publishing Association

Editor: Bobbie Jane Van Dolson
Cover Design: Kaaren Kinzer

Library of Congress Cataloging in Publication Data

Hills, Desmond B., 1932-
   Light for my life.

   Summary: Readings for each day of the year, each focusing on facts
and stories about Jesus, based on various Scriptural texts.
   1. Children—Prayer-books and devotions—English. 2. Devotional
calendars—Seventh-Day Adventists—Juvenile literature. [1. Prayer
books and devotions. 2. Devotional calendars—Seventh-Day Advent-
ists]
I. Title.
BV4870.H44   242'.2   81-2556
ISBN 0-8280-0041-7   AACR2

Printed in U.S.A.

INTRODUCTION

Leads readers to look to Jesus each day.

Is a follow-up to *Catch the Bright Dawn,* by Jan Doward.

Gets readers interested in the complete Bible story.

Has many stories from around the world.

Teaches most of the doctrines of the Bible.

Follows a monthly theme—person, power, plan, et cetera.

Organized to use 365 chapters and most of the Bible books.

Really is interesting for both junior and senior youth.

Meets a need for specific information about the Bible.

Yields inspiration for each day of the year.

Leads to answers to questions juniors and youth are asking.

Includes a brand-new and challenging daily Bible reading plan.

Features many Bible characters and modern heroes of faith.

Enlightens, and is a book to treasure for reference.

The story is told of a man in Carnarvonshire, Wales. Walking one stormy night on the mountain, he became so cold that he put his lantern under his cloak to get its warmth. The moon was shining dimly, and he thought he could trace his way without the lantern.

Suddenly a gust of wind blew aside his cloak, and the light revealed that he stood on the edge of a deep slate quarry. In another instant, he would have plunged over the precipice. He retraced his steps, and you may be sure he did not again cover his lantern.

Light for My Life is like a lantern. Its messages can stop us from falling and hurting ourselves. Heeding these messages can help us make wise decisions.

This Morning Watch book features three important words—*light, love,* and *life*. They summarize God's character, Christ's life and work, the gospel message, and the teachings of Scripture. They also are three of our basic needs.

● We need God's *light* to see through spiritual and moral darkness.

● We need God's *love* to live peaceably in a world of hate.

• We need God's *life* to live and to obtain eternal life.

The divine light *illuminates,* the divine love *inspires,* and the divine life *ensures* us of eternal life.

It has been an exciting adventure and spiritually rewarding for me to write this Morning Watch book. Now it is my prayer that those who read it will find spiritual help to enter into a closer walk with the Lord Jesus Christ, to follow Him in the paths of service, and then be caught up in the clouds to meet Him in the air when He returns very soon.

Desmond B. Hills

DEDICATION
To my wife, Ruth, son,
Allan, and daughter,
Neroli, who have
strengthened my ministry
by their love and loyalty,
and by their patience and
prayers.

Unless otherwise stated, the Bible texts at the beginning of each reading are from the Revised Standard Version of the Bible, copyrighted 1946 and 1952 by the Division of Christian Education of the National Council of Churches of Christ in the U.S.A. Published by Thomas Nelson & Sons, New York.

Unless otherwise stated, texts used in the readings throughout are from the King James Version.

Texts credited to R.S.V. are from the Revised Standard Version.

Texts credited to K.J.V. are from the King James Version.

Texts credited to N.E.B. are from *The New English Bible*. © The Delegates of the Oxford University Press and the Syndics of the Cambridge University Press 1961, 1970. Reprinted by permission.

Texts credited to N.I.V. are from *The Holy Bible, New International Version*. Copyright © 1978 by the New York International Bible Society. Used by permission of Zondervan Bible Publishers.

Texts credited to Phillips are from J. B. Phillips: *The New Testament in Modern English,* Revised Edition. © J. B. Phillips 1958, 1960, 1972. Used by permission of Macmillan Publishing Co., Inc.

Verses marked T.L.B. are taken from *The Living Bible,* copyright 1971 by Tyndale House Publishers, Wheaton, Ill. Used by permission.

JANUARY	Pattern	Matthew
FEBRUARY	Power	Acts
MARCH	Plan	Genesis
APRIL	Purpose	Exodus to Deuteronomy
MAY	Promises	Romans to Galatians
JUNE	Prophecies	Daniel, Revelation
JULY	Person	Mark, Isaiah, Jeremiah
AUGUST	Perfection	Luke, Job
SEPTEMBER	Providence	Judges to Esther
OCTOBER	Praises	Psalms, Proverbs
NOVEMBER	Peace	Ephesians to Jude
DECEMBER	Proof	Ruth, Jonah, John

PATTERN
Matthew 1

MAN OF THE YEAR

Jacob the father of Joseph the husband of Mary, of whom
Jesus was born, who is called Christ. Matthew 1:16.

Each year *Time* magazine features a Man of the Year. A
photograph of the one selected is printed on the front cover, and
several pages are devoted to an appraisal of the chosen one. The
first person to be given this title was Charles Lindbergh, and
others have included John F. Kennedy, Martin Luther King,
Jr., and Ronald Reagan. Sometimes a woman is selected, as
when the title Woman of the Year was given to Queen Elizabeth
II.

In 1950 Winston Churchill was selected as Man of the Half
Century. If time and *Time* last, someone special will be selected
in the year 2000 and titled Man of the Century. No one can
predict who the man of the century will be, but we know who the
Man of All Ages is. There is One who stands above all men of all
time, and someday everyone will sing His praises. Jesus Christ
holds undisputed claim to this title and very soon He will be
proclaimed "King of kings, and Lord of lords."

Nineteen centuries have proved Jesus to be the greatest Man
who ever lived. Every time we date a letter, a check, or a
document, we testify to the birth of Christ, for time is reckoned
as before Christ or after Christ. There are more songs composed,
more pictures painted, and more books written about Him than
about anyone else. Surely Jesus Christ is the master character
of the century. History is centered on Him, all time is divided by
Him (B.C.-A.D.), and our future is dependent upon Him.

The Man of All Ages is the main *Person* of the Bible. The first
and last verses of the New Testament mention His name, and
He is the focal point of all sixty-six books. As we begin reading
this mini one-volume Morning Watch Bible story, there is no
better place to start than with a book that has many pen pictures
of the Person of the whole Bible. Each of this month's daily
readings has inspiring and interesting facts and stories about
the Man of All Ages. Those who read the twenty-eight chapters
of Matthew can say, "This is *light* for my *life*."

PATTERN
Matthew 2

MAN OF ALL AGES

And he went and dwelt in a city called Nazareth, that what was spoken by the prophets might be fulfilled, "He shall be called a Nazarene." Matthew 2:23.

"Here is a man who was born in an obscure village, the child of a peasant woman. He grew up in another village. He worked in a carpenter shop until He was 30, and for three years He was an itinerant preacher. He never wrote a book. He never held an office. He never owned a house. He never had a family. He never went to college. He never put His feet inside a big city. He never traveled two hundred miles from the place where He was born. He never did any of the things that usually accompany greatness. He had no credentials but Himself. While still a young man, the tide of popular opinion turned against Him. His friends ran away. One of them denied Him. He was turned over to His enemies. He went through the mockery of a trial. He was nailed upon a Roman cross between two thieves. While He was dying, His executioners gambled for the only piece of property He had on earth . . . His robe. When He was dead, He was taken down and laid in a borrowed grave through the pity of a friend.

"Nineteen wide centuries have come and gone, and today He is the centerpiece of the human race and the leader of the column of progress. I am far within the mark when I say that all the armies that ever marched and all the navies that were ever built, and all the parliaments that ever sat and all the kings that ever reigned, put together, have not affected the life of man upon this earth as did that one solitary Life." *

This summary of the Person of the Bible shows us again that Jesus has influenced rich and poor, youth and aged, saints and sinners.

Although it takes only eighty-four hours to read the Bible through, many never read the 1,189 chapters, or 31,173 verses. On the other hand, if we hop, skip, and jump, reading favorite passages without any definite plan, we may never learn to know the Person of the Bible. *Light for My Life* gives us an exciting new way to discover the Man of All Ages.

---

* Credited to Phillips Brooks.

PATTERN
Matthew 3

THE THREE CHOICES

"Repent, for the kingdom of heaven is at hand." Matthew 3:2.

The beating drums at daybreak announced a wedding feast. Everyone in the village was excited. The weeping and wailing did not mean that the bride-to-be was unhappy, for this was the custom among the village people. However, some trouble began that turned the crocodile tears into real ones. The old man who had ferried the bride across the lake the day before told the village chiefs that a storm had almost destroyed them. This was considered a bad omen, since possibly the girl had been responsible for this evil.

After a meeting of the tribal council, the announcement was made as to what the gods required. The girl was to be given three choices: (1) she would be poisoned; (2) she would be sent to the forest to live alone; or (3) she would be allowed to marry as planned. She was to make her choice by selecting one of three boxes placed before her.

The first box was an imported chest with beautiful paintings and ornaments all over it. On a card were the words "Whosoever chooses me shall have all that her heart desires." The second box was equally attractive and had the words "Whosoever chooses me will have all the riches desirable." The words on these two boxes were promising, but she knew that one of them could contain dried bones, which would be her death sentence. The third box was not as attractive as the first two, and on it were the words "Whosoever chooses me will have that which the great god hath prepared for her."

The longer the maiden stood before the boxes, the more she trembled. There were three choices before her, and she longed for wisdom to make the right decision. With trembling hands she finally touched the third box. Gathering courage, she opened the lid, and, to her delight, inside were the wedding garments.

There are important choices facing every one of us today. First we must choose to accept or reject Jesus. If we choose to accept Him, we will follow His example and be baptized. Matthew shows that we need not only to choose to repent, or to turn from our sins, but also to choose to be filled with the Holy Spirit.

PATTERN
Matthew 4

AN EXPENSIVE BOOK

Then Jesus said to him, "Begone, Satan! for it is written . . ."
Matthew 4:10.

Two million dollars is the highest price ever paid for a book. The book was sold at a New York City auction in only thirty seconds. Bidding began at half a million dollars, and within ten seconds it had reached a million. In just another twenty seconds the sale was complete.

And what was this book that brought such a fabulous price? Yes, it was a copy of God's Holy Word. As you could guess, there is something special about this two-volume Bible. It is more than 500 years old, and one of only twenty-one complete copies of this Latin Bible still in existence. It was printed by the German printer Johann Gutenberg, and is one of the first books ever printed by movable type.

It is interesting to know that old Bibles are so valuable. We can be thankful that we do not have to pay large sums of money to obtain a copy. When Jesus was living in Palestine, there were only hand-copied Old Testaments available. However, it is evident that He knew the Scriptures very well.

Jesus was tempted three times in the wilderness, and He was able to give a scriptural answer to resist each temptation. If we would gain the victory in our lives, we must also be able to say with authority, "Begone, Satan! for it is written . . ."

As we study this pen picture of Jesus in the wilderness, we realize that He was subject to temptation just as we are. He did not exercise divine power, but defeated the devil as a human being could do. This should be an encouragement to us. Jesus was tempted to use His divine power to satisfy His hunger after forty days without food. He was challenged to throw Himself from a tall mountain to see whether the angels would care for Him. He was then promised all the kingdoms of this world if He would worship Satan. In order to entice Jesus to fall, Satan misquoted Scripture.

We can't believe everyone who says, "It is written." We must discover for ourselves the truths of the Word of God. Then, no matter what the price, we must not "sell" our beliefs.

PATTERN
Matthew 5

LAMPLIGHTERS

"You are the light of the world. A city set on a hill cannot be hid." Matthew 5:14.

Jennie loved to listen to the stories Grandma told. One evening as the sun was setting, they were sitting together on the garden seat. As the golden sun set and the stars began to blink, Jennie said, "Wasn't that a beautiful sunset, Grandma?"

"Yes, Jennie. I have watched many sunsets and I have never seen two alike. Tonight as the stars came out one by one, they made me think of the lamplighter."

Jennie had not heard of the lamplighter, and she said, "What did he light, Grandma? Tell me about him."

Grandma replied, "The lamplighter lighted the gas lamps on the posts in the streets of the little town where I grew up. When I was very young, there were no streetlights, and on dark nights people carried lanterns when they went out. Next came wonderful gaslights. My home was on top of a hill, and I could see over most of the town. About sunset each night the lamplighter started on his rounds. He carried a long stick with a hook on the end. With the hook he turned on the gas jets in the lamps high upon the post and then early each morning he turned them off again."

Jennie was surprised when Grandma asked, "Have you ever thought that you are one of God's lamplighters?"

"What do you mean, Grandma?" she questioned in reply. "There aren't any lamps that I could light."

"I am not talking about kerosene or gas lamps, Jennie," said Grandma. "If you are happy and cheerful and do what you can to help others, if you are loving and kind, sweet-tempered and good, you will surely light a lamp that will comfort and help someone who is finding life dark and difficult. If you are truthful and honest, you will light the way for others who may be stumbling along, not knowing which way to go. We are all God's lamplighters, Jennie, and we must make sure the lamps are bright so that those who are confused can take the right track. When Jesus preached His sermon on the mountainside, He said, 'Ye are the light of the world.'"

15

PATTERN
Matthew 6

BLANK COLUMNS

"And forgive us our debts as we forgive our debtors." Matthew 6:12, K.J.V.

Tex Wilson owned a weekly newspaper. During the second year of his editorship an edition appeared with a blank column on the second page. After that, perhaps twice a year, other blank columns would appear. Once there was even one on the front page.

The mystery of the blank columns in the newspaper was often talked about in the little country town. One day at the grocery store, old Pete Moody heard a rumor that Tex was being paid to keep stories out of his paper. As soon as Pete heard this, he jumped to his feet and cried, "It isn't so! Tex never took a penny in his life to keep stories out of his paper. What he did was out of the greatness of his heart. I know because . . . because . . . I was one of those columns!" Pete then hesitatingly related the story of how four years previously, at the age of 70, he knew he would soon be replaced by a younger man. So he took an expensive tool from the company where he worked and sold it. He had stolen one each week for a month or so when his employer caught him.

The day Pete was taken to the sheriff's office, Tex Wilson was there looking for news. The sheriff pleaded that Pete and his wife were a fine couple and that Molly Moody did not deserve the disgrace. After listening to the story, the newspaper editor announced that Pete was to be given another chance, with the understanding that he must pay back in money the value of the tools he had stolen.

Tex told Pete, "Normally I would run the story of your thefts in the newspaper. As a warning to you, I am going to run the column anyway, but it will be blank. If you ever let Molly down again, I'll publish the story." Tex ran eleven blank columns in the newspaper before he died, and to this day eight of them remain mysteries.

Those blank columns remind us of God's forgiveness and our need to forgive others. Let us pray the Lord's Prayer often and ask for "blank columns" in the record books of heaven.

16

PATTERN
Matthew 7

COLLECT CALL

"Ask, and it will be given you; seek, and you will find; knock, and it will be opened to you." Matthew 7:7.

As I lifted the phone in my home in Maryland, an operator with a British accent said, "London calling. Collect call from Neroli Hills [our daughter] for anyone. Do you accept the call?" Immediately I said Yes, and soon my wife, son, and I were talking with Neroli, who was at Newbold College near London.

It is amazing that it is possible to make a telephone call from almost anywhere in the world. Radio telephones are now available in cars, ships, and airplanes. Since Alexander Graham Bell invented the telephone a little more than one hundred years ago, phones have become so popular that today there are about 300 million of them.

To send a message round the world requires powerful electronic facilities. However, God has placed something in this world that exceeds the speed and power of radio and telephones and requires no facilities. Prayer is God's communication system, and its messages travel faster than radio—faster than seven and one-half times round the world in one second!

Although billions of prayers may ascend to Heaven's switchboard at the same time, everyone can get through immediately. We do not have to wait until the line is clear; it is always open. All we have to do is to reach out by faith, for "prayer is the key in the hand of faith to unlock heaven's storehouse."—*Steps to Christ*, p. 94.

When we make telephone calls, there is a charge; if the call is collect, there is an additional charge. The only calls Heaven's switchboard knows are "collect calls," and there are no charges. But we can get through only because the price of opening communication lines between heaven and earth has already been paid by Jesus.

Let's be sure that we dial Heaven every day. You will never get a busy signal, and the lines are always open. The Holy Spirit is the operator, and your heavenly Father and Elder Brother are waiting for you to make a "collect call" home.

PATTERN
Matthew 8

THE DOLPHINS' GIRL

"What sort of man is this, that even winds and sea obey him?"
Matthew 8:27.

Yvonne Vladislavich, along with four others, boarded a motorboat for the return voyage from Inaca Island to Lourenço Marques, capital city of Mozambique. About twenty miles out in the Indian Ocean the eighty-horsepower Mercury outboard motor stopped and the inboard six-cylinder Volvo motor would not start. The seas became rough, and the waves were twenty feet high. The party had spent twenty hours praying and bailing water when three huge waves hit the boat and sank it.

During their first five hours in the water the sea claimed two lives. It was then decided that someone would have to swim for help. Being a good swimmer and having a bronze medal for life-saving, Yvonne was the natural choice. After swimming for six and a half hours, she saw black shadows around her. "I thought they were sharks," Yvonne said. "When I looked around, my fears were justified. . . . I closed my eyes and said, 'Dear Lord, if this is the way I must die, please let it be quick.'" When she opened her eyes she noticed two fins coming toward her. To her relief, they belonged to dolphins, who guarded her from the sharks.

Yvonne told me that additional miracles took place. "A dolphin lifted me out of the water when I fainted. Soon I noticed a shipping buoy. With the strength that could come only from a loving God, I swam and caught onto a hook that the buoy had on its side. After seeing a ship go by without stopping, I decided I must get onto the buoy. The dolphins helped me get onto the buoy, for it was thirty feet high." Five minutes later a ship stopped. After swimming approximately seventy kilometers, she was rescued and taken back to South Africa.

Yvonne, who is a lawyer, told reporters, "If anyone tells you there is no God, send him to me. How can anyone try to explain away my experience? How now is it possible for me not to believe?"

Yes, the dolphins, winds, and sea obey God the Son. He is a wonderful and powerful person, and we have many reasons for believing in Him.

PATTERN
Matthew 9

"FOLLOW ME"

*As Jesus passed on from there, he saw a man called Matthew
sitting at the tax office; and he said to him, "Follow me." And he
rose and followed him. Matthew 9:9.*

The city of London was noted for fog so thick that it has been
described as "pea soup." At times the fog was so dense that you
could see only a few yards in front of you.

A businessman became lost in the fog when he could not see
the street signs. As he was wondering what to do, he saw the
shadowy form of a man who evidently knew where he was going.
The lost man called out to the stranger, "I say, can you help me
find my way?"

He told the man the building he was looking for, and the
stranger said, "I'll take you there. Follow me."

The businessman followed block after block, wondering how
his guide could be so sure of his way in the dense fog.

The stranger stopped in front of a large building and said,
"Here, sir, is the building you are looking for."

"How could you find it in this dense fog?" To which the
stranger replied, "Oh, the fog doesn't bother me. I am blind."

Matthew, also called Levi, was lost in a fog of worldliness
when the Stranger of Galilee said, "Follow me." Jesus knew all
about Matthew's shady dealing in tax collecting. However,
Jesus looked deeper and saw a disciple, the author of the New
Testament book, and a candidate for the kingdom of heaven.
This short, dramatic story, which took place on a busy street in
Capernaum, tells us a lot about Jesus and also a lot about
Matthew.

The Stranger of Galilee who called twelve men to follow Him
as His disciples was not blind like the stranger in the fog. In
contrast, Matthew saw that Jesus had the power to give sight to
the blind. In this chapter we have not only the miracle of giving
sight to two blind men but also of giving a dumb man back his
power of speech, healing a woman of disease, and raising a girl
from the dead.

Jesus also invites us to follow Him. This is our privilege and
responsibility, and as we follow we will experience joy and
satisfaction.

PATTERN
Matthew 10

THE KING'S MEN

And he called to him his twelve disciples and gave them authority over unclean spirits, to cast them out, and to heal every disease and every infirmity. Matthew 10:1.

The Cocos or Keeling Islands are in the Indian Ocean about halfway between Australia and Sri Lanka. There are twenty-seven islands in this group, and one of them is used to refuel airplanes on international flights. Before the large jetliners stopped regularly, the only contact the people of these flat coral islands had with the outside world was ships that came in about three times a year.

Rita Snowden in her book *Listen Children* tells of twenty-six Englishmen who were looking after a cable radio station on one of these remote islands. Rita was a passenger on the ship *Orion,* which was too big to come in close to the island, so the men came out in small boats. They brought letters sealed in a barrel to keep the water out. The captain of the ship arranged for another barrel of food and magazines to be put into the sea for the lonely men on these remote islands.

"But just before we sailed away from each other once more, a great big man from the island—he looked just like what I think Robinson Crusoe must have looked, with a bright-brown beard and a red handkerchief tied around his neck—stood up in his tiny boat and waved a goodbye to our ship. Then he called out loudly for all of us to hear . . . , 'Give my love to King George.'" *

Like the man on Cocos Island, we are living a long way from our King, and we should send our love to Him each day. Our King expects us to serve as faithfully as did the twelve disciples, and to tell others about the kingdom of heaven.

In the book of Matthew we will discover some ways to tell others the good news about the heavenly realm. The main message of the book is that Jesus is king and that He will soon set up His kingdom. The word *kingdom* is used fifty-five times and the phrase "kingdom of heaven" thirty-two times. There are twenty parables in Matthew, given to help us learn more about the kingdom and how to help others become its subjects.

---

* Rita W. Snowden, *Listen Children* (London: Epworth Press, 1952).

PATTERN
Matthew 11

THE GREATEST PROPHET

"'Behold, I send my messenger before thy face, who shall prepare thy way before thee.'" Matthew 11:10.

We could not select the greatest prophet who ever lived. Our ideas of greatness are different from God's because He sees the heart and we judge on outward appearances. However, Jesus stated that John the Baptist was the greatest of the prophets. No doubt one reason John is called the greatest is that he was the ambassador who announced the first advent of Jesus.

Then, too, in order to be the messenger who was to prepare the way for Jesus, John would need to be a holy person. As we study his character, we note that he did have strong convictions and was a faithful messenger.

"Therefore it would be necessary for him to control the appetites and passions. He must be able to so control all his powers that he could stand among men as unmoved by surrounding circumstances as the rocks and mountains of the wilderness."—*The Desire of Ages,* p. 100.

John did not make any predictions that we know of, and this helps us to understand that a prophet is also a messenger. If a true prophet does make predictions, all these prophecies must come true. But it is not necessary for a prophet to make predictions to be a true prophet.

How wonderful it is to know that we are the personal ambassadors of Jesus before His second advent! If we have characters like John, we can be God's messengers and prepare the way for Jesus to come again.

The statement that John was the greatest prophet who ever lived would have been an encouragement to him and his disciples. At the time it was given, John was in prison. It was his disciples and not John himself who raised questions as to whether Jesus was the Messiah. To help confirm the faith of these men, he sent them to have an interview with Jesus.

When we are tempted to think that Jesus has forgotten us in the "prisons" that we get into, we need to think of John's faith in the face of death, and like those doubting disciples, we need to have an interview with Jesus. We can speak to Him in prayer and we can be sure He will answer us.

21

PATTERN
Matthew 12

A MODERN JONAH

"For as Jonah was three days and three nights in the belly of the whale, so will the Son of man be three days and three nights in the heart of the earth." Matthew 12:40.

James Bartley was only 20 years old when he signed on board the whaling ship *Star of the East.* In August of 1891, when James was 35, he was sailing on the ship in the South Atlantic east of the Falkland Islands.

The lookout cried "Thar she blows" as he sighted a whale spouting water, and all hands came on deck to launch the small boats. The harpooner sighted the whale and threw his weapon. The rope that was tied to the harpoon rushed from the barrel as the whale dived. It pulled down eight hundred feet of rope and then slackened. The sailors waited in silence.

Suddenly the boat was flung into the air as the whale surfaced under it. As James was thrown from the smashed boat, he felt the cold water, then experienced darkness, sliding, and terrible pain as he lost consciousness.

Hours later the whale lay dying on the surface. The sailors launched longboats again and towed the carcass to the ship. By the light of lanterns they began cutting it up in order to take the meat on board. Suddenly one of them discovered a human foot protruding from the whale's stomach. Cutting further, they discovered James Bartley, unconscious but alive after nearly fifteen hours inside the whale.

James lay near death for two weeks and suffered from loss of memory. His hair dropped out and his skin changed to an unnatural white. Many scientists and medical men traveled to his home in Gloucester, England, to examine him. "When he died, a tombstone giving an account of his experience was erected above the grave. It has a footnote that reads, 'James Bartley, 1856-1909. . . . A modern Jonah.'"

Jesus made reference to the story of Jonah in response to the request "Teacher, we wish to see a sign from You." The people had just seen a blind and dumb devil-possessed man healed, so they did not need another sign. What are some of the signs that we have had to help us believe the Bible is the Word of God and Jesus is the King of the universe?

PATTERN
Matthew 13

SECRET STORIES

Then the disciples came and said to him, "Why do you speak to them in parables?" And he answered them, "To you it has been given to know the secrets of the kingdom of heaven, but to them it has not been given." Matthew 13:10, 11.

There are at least forty secret stories told by Jesus and recorded in the books of Matthew, Mark, Luke, and John.

These secret stories are called parables, and Jesus was so fond of telling them that Mark says that when He taught the people, "he did not speak to them without a parable" (chap. 4:34, R.S.V.). The parables that Jesus told were earthly stories with heavenly meanings.

When the disciples asked Him, " 'Why do you speak to them in parables?' " He explained that those who wanted to know truth could find it by studying the parables. He also said there was no point in giving truth to those who would rather not hear it. By using this secret-story method of teaching, Jesus was able to say many things that He couldn't say openly. There were those who sought to kill Him and who were looking for evidence to condemn Him. By speaking in parables, Jesus foiled these evil people.

The secret stories that Jesus told were generally based on things or people that were familiar to everyone. Nature was often the center of these stories.

In the parables in today's chapter, Jesus tells about the gospel and the kingdom of heaven. The seed that the sower sows is the gospel. Some people accept it, others reject it, and some are indifferent to it.

From the stories of the tares and the fish we learn that everyone is not going to be converted. Also, there are going to be true Christians and false Christians in the church up to the time when Jesus comes.

The stories of the mustard seed and the leaven encourage us, for they show that from a small beginning Christ's kingdom will go to the ends of the earth. The hidden treasure and the goodly pearl teach that it is worth giving up everything in order to find Jesus as our personal Saviour. Actually, when we find Jesus, we lose only those things that are not helpful to us.

23

PATTERN
Matthew 14

WHITE MA OF CALABAR

As he went ashore he saw a great throng; and he had compassion on them, and healed their sick. Matthew 14:14.

"In loving memory of Mary Mitchell Slessor, born at Aberdeen, Scotland, second of December, 1848, died in use at Calabar, Nigeria, the thirteenth of January, 1915. For thirty-eight years heroic and devoted missionary chiefly among the upriver tribes of this land."

These words, written on Mary Slessor's grave, were copied down to share with the readers of this Morning Watch book. The grave is located on a hill overlooking Calabar, a seaport town in Nigeria. As I stood by the grave and reflected on the life of this woman, I realized that there was only one reason she risked her life and lived alone here for thirty-eight years. Like Jesus, she had compassion for the people.

At 11 years of age Mary worked as a weaver in a textile factory, for ten long hours a day. She had no opportunity to go to school, but she read the Bible going to and from work, and it had a tremendous influence on her life. Her father was a drunkard and sometimes forced her out of the house even at night. Despite these and many other sad experiences in her childhood, Mary early developed a loving spirit and sympathy for others.

At 27 she volunteered to serve as a missionary, and sailed for Calabar the following year. In those days many white people died of disease in Calabar. Mary did not stay in the city, but ventured into the more dangerous, unknown interior. She knew she could be killed by entering these new territories, but she continued her pioneer missionary work.

Mary's work included preaching, teaching the people to care for themselves and their homes, nursing, and speaking against alcohol and pagan customs. People in one area believed that twins brought evil to the family and so abandoned them at birth to wild beasts. Mary helped stop this practice. Her well-marked Bible told of her confidence in God, and her life showed her love for the African people. The compassion for the people that the "White Ma of Calabar" felt is the same compassion that we need to have in our hearts. This love for people will give them *light* for their *lives*.

PATTERN
Matthew 15

FOOD FOR 18,000

Then Jesus called his disciples to him and said, "I have compassion on the crowd, because they have been with me now three days, and have nothing to eat; and I am unwilling to send them away hungry, lest they faint on the way." Matthew 15:32.

When you read today's title, did you think the printer had made a mistake? We all know that Jesus fed 5,000 people with five loaves and two fish, but did you know that on another occasion, just a few weeks later, He fed 4,000 people? Although some people think this was the same event, a study of the two accounts shows there were two different times when Jesus fed multitudes from loaves and fish. There are some points of similarity in the stories, but there are also a number of differences.

Now, I can hear some of you saying that the total is still only 9,000, even though the heading says 18,000. And maybe you are right. But as you read both accounts, you will notice that they say 5,000 men and 4,000 men, "beside women and children." It is therefore reasonable to believe that at least 18,000 were fed on these two occasions.

Jesus fed the large multitudes for the same reason that He healed the sick, gave sight to the blind, opened the ears of the deaf, and raised the dead. This reason is stated in today's text: "'I have compassion on the crowd'" (R.S.V.). It is wonderful to know that Jesus can perform miracles not only to heal us but also to feed us. The fact that vegetables grow in the ground and fruit on trees is a miracle. Jesus was able to make grape juice instantly at the wedding feast, but the grapevine turning water by which it is irrigated into grape juice is also a miracle. In all ways, Jesus provides for us.

One reason there is not enough food in this world today is that men are selfish. God has supplied the soil, seed, rain, and sunshine, and has given man the knowledge and ability to sow and harvest. If all were to work and share, despite disease and disaster there would be food for everyone.

Some of the 18,000 people were interested only in the food. They missed learning of the bread of life that Jesus gave to the multitudes. We need physical and spiritual food each day.

25

PATTERN
Matthew 16

WHO IS JESUS TO YOU?

"Who do men say that the Son of man is?" Matthew 16:13.

To the *architect* He is the Chief Cornerstone.
To the *artist* He is the One Altogether Lovely.
To the *astronomer* He is the Bright and Morning Star.
To the *baker* He is the Bread of Life.
To the *banker* He is the Redeemer.
To the *biologist* He is the Life.
To the *builder* He is the Sure Foundation.
To the *carpenter* He is the Door.
To the *doctor* He is the Great Physician.
To the *educator* He is the Great Teacher.
To the *farmer* He is the Lord of Harvest.
To the *florist* He is the the Lily of the Valley.
To the *geologist* He is the Rock of Ages.
To the *lawyer* He is the Lawgiver.
To the *newspaperman* He is the Glad Tidings of Great Joy.
To the *orphan* He is the everlasting Father.
To the *philanthropist* He is the Unspeakable Gift.
To the *philosopher* He is the Wisdom of God.
To the *preacher* He is the Word of God.
To the *rancher* He is the Good Shepherd.
To the *servant* He is the Good Master.
To the *student* He is the Incarnate Truth.
To the *tourist* He is the Map to Heaven.
To the *traveler* He is the Way.
To the *weary* He is the Giver of Rest.

But Jesus is more than what is included in these twenty-five descriptions.

To *Simon Peter* He was "the Christ, the Son of the living God."

To the *sinner* He is "Saviour, Counselor, and Mediator."

To *His disciples today* He is "King of kings, and Lord of lords."

To the *church member* He is the Rock on which the church is founded.

To *you and me,* Jesus is everything. He is "Light for my life."

PATTERN
Matthew 17

MONEY IN A FISH

"Go to the sea and cast a hook." Matthew 17:27.

How do you think the former fisherman felt when Jesus told him to go catch a fish that would have a silver coin in its mouth? I wonder whether Peter argued with Jesus, or whether he had seen enough miracles to go and do what Jesus told him. There were many people who saw the miracles that Jesus did but who did not believe. There are some today who say that the miracles did not really happen.

Matthew is the only one who records this dramatic story, and he does not tell how it ended. However, we assume that Peter caught the fish and paid the Temple tax. Otherwise, Jesus and Peter would have been in trouble with the authorities.

The miracle of the coin was performed to strengthen the faith of Peter and to silence the people, including the tax collectors, who were criticizing Jesus. Those who were collecting the Temple tax had no right to ask Jesus for the money, but the Lord did not argue with them about rights. He paid the money to avoid controversy, teaching us that we should not always demand our rights but should try to live at peace and do what we can to avoid conflict with others. However, just as Jesus never compromised, so we should not do wrong just to please other people.

This is the only time in the New Testament where a fishhook is mentioned, as Peter and his friends fished with a net. Here is another example of Jesus' using an experience with which everyone was familiar in order to teach a lesson.

We must be prepared to do exactly what Jesus asks, even though we may not be able to see why He has asked us to do it. Jesus could have asked someone for the money or even produced the money out of nothing. But He chose to use Peter in order to perform the miracle.

I want to be available for Jesus to use me to help others find truth, don't you? I am glad we have this opportunity. Jesus could have written the truths He wanted us to follow in the clouds or He could have sent angels to teach on this planet. But instead He chose us to give the Word. We can all be instruments of God to show others the *light* they need for their *lives*.

PATTERN
Matthew 18

A HAND ON MY SHOULDER

"Whoever receives one such child in my name receives me."
Matthew 18:5.

Ever had a bad day? A bad week? Let me tell you about Ben, who had a bad *two* weeks when he was 16. He got into one spot of trouble after another, and it climaxed the day he wrecked his father's day-old Plymouth. He didn't want to go home, nor did he want to face any of the church members, who were already talking about the escapades of the preacher's son.

Ben made up his mind that he was not going to church and said to himself, "I can tell you, twenty-five wild horses are not going to drag me into church on Sabbath." But Mom had a better idea. She held firm, and with a smile persisted, until Ben found himself trudging across the Mount Vernon Academy campus to church. "Walking down the long corridor that led to the chapel was debilitating to my soul. I looked at no one, talked with no one. As I came to the door that led to the chapel, I felt a hand on my shoulder. It was the local elder. He spoke and said to me in words that I shall never forget, 'Ben, I think a lot of you; in fact, someday I believe you are going to be a preacher, and a good one!' He restored my dignity; he gave me courage and hope. And I can still feel his hand on my shoulder."

The elder's prediction came true, for Ben E. Leach did become a preacher, and at this writing is a union president. Young people—and older folks—never forget how they are treated when they are in trouble. The elder's kind words were the turning point, although he didn't really know what the future held for the boy.

> Nobody knows what a boy is worth,
>   A boy at his work or play,
> A boy who whistles around the place,
>   Or laughs in an artless way.
>
> Nobody knows what a boy is worth,
>   And the world must wait and see,
> For every man in an honored place
>   Is a boy that used to be.

> *—Author Unknown*

PATTERN
Matthew 19

LACKING BUT LOVE

Jesus said to him, "If you would be perfect, go, sell what you possess and give to the poor, and you will have treasure in heaven; and come, follow me." Matthew 19:21.

On January 8, 1956, the Auca Indians of the Amazon jungle speared five missionaries to death. These five men had landed their little plane in the jungle in order to tell the Aucas of God's love for them.

The wives of these five men did not believe that the work among the Indians should end with this tragedy. Missionary planes passed over the Auca villages dropping gifts, and on October 8, 1958, the wives of two of the men, Rachel Saint and Betty Elliot, and Mrs. Elliot's young daughter, accompanied by friendly Auca women, left for the valley of death where the missionaries had been killed. As a result, an entire tribe of Auca Indians was converted to Christianity. Rachel Saint learned the Auca language and translated portions of Scripture. The Indians who worked with her in translating the Bible called it "God's carving." Some of those who had killed the five missionaries have now become Christian leaders and have helped to build churches, called "God's speaking house."

Jim Elliot, one of the dead missionaries, once wrote in his diary, "He is no fool who gives what he cannot keep to gain what he cannot lose."

The rich young ruler who came to Jesus was not prepared to give what he could not keep in order to gain what he could not lose. This young man came to the right Person, asked the right question, and received the correct answers, but did the wrong thing. Many people today act like that rich young ruler.

Jesus loved this young man in spite of what he lacked, and told him the one thing that he needed to do in order to obtain eternal life. Jesus did not ask every rich man to give away his money. However, this young man stated that he had kept all the commandments, and Jesus was testing him on the first, which says, "Thou shalt have no other gods before me." We can be thankful that Jesus loves us even though we are lacking. But we must do something about what we lack if we are to have eternal life.

29

PATTERN
Matthew 20

FIRST WILL BE LAST

"So the last will be first, and the first last." Matthew 20:16.

The unusual statement that " 'the last will be first, and the first last' " (R.S.V.) was made by Jesus. This is not the first time He said it. He used it fairly often. It is also recorded in Mark and Luke, so it must have an important teaching.

The rich young ruler who came to Jesus apparently was one whom everyone thought should be first. At least he seemed to believe that he was a number one candidate for heaven. However, Jesus revealed that he lacked love in his life, and he is not heard of again in the New Testament. So we presume that he did not even run the Christian race.

The twelve disciples who had been selected by Jesus prior to the experience of the rich young ruler did not seem to be promising workers, but they, with one exception, will be among those who cross the finish line into the kingdom of heaven.

It is natural to expect those who win a race or a contest to be given a prize; this is the way we have always been taught. However, this is not the way God measures people.

And as you think of it, the first-place measurement may not always be a good one. The person who finishes second may be only a split second behind and may be just as good a runner. Likewise, some people win because they have cheated or because the others who competed did not have a very high standard of performance. And very often people are rewarded simply for defeating others.

After the visit of the rich young ruler, Jesus had a discussion with His disciples about riches. The disciples did not have any money and they had left their trades, so Peter asked, "What do we get out of this?" It was in answer to this question that Jesus assured the disciples that all who had forsaken relatives or property would receive a reward. It was then that He said, "But many that are first shall be last; and the last shall be first" (Matt. 19:30).

This statement also highlights the fact that the quality of anything is more important than the quantity. It is not only the number of hours we put into a thing that counts, but also the spirit and motive behind the service.

PATTERN
Matthew 21

A ROYAL WELCOME

And the crowds that went before him and that followed him shouted, "Hosanna to the Son of David! Blessed be he who comes in the name of the Lord! Hosanna in the highest!" Matthew 21:9.

One hundred and sixty-eight planes flew over London in salute.

Crowds of people up to one hundred deep lined the streets, while others paid one hundred pounds (more than two hundred dollars) for a seat.

So far as possible all soldiers, sailors, airmen, civil servants, and palace guards were released from regular duty to march in the procession or line the processional route.

It was June 2, 1953, the coronation day of Queen Elizabeth II.

The soon-to-be-crowned monarch and her husband, His Royal Highness Prince Phillip, rode in the royal golden carriage pulled by beautiful horses. Guards in colorful uniforms escorted the carriage on horseback.

The small parade on the day Jesus rode into Jerusalem cannot be compared to processions at coronations of rulers such as Queen Elizabeth. However, the people there were apparently just as excited, because they thought Jesus would become king and deliver them from Roman bondage. They tore branches from palm and olive trees and made a green carpet. There were no horses or golden carriages, for Jesus rode on a donkey. Five hundred years before His birth, a prophet had predicted that Jesus would enter Jerusalem in this way.

The whole city of Jerusalem was stirred by this entry. Jesus had never allowed such adoration before. He was not calling attention to Himself, but to His mission. For the triumphant procession pointed to the tragedy of the cross. And after His crucifixion, it led many to discover from the Scriptures that Jesus was the rightful ruler of this world.

One day the triumphant procession will be completed as it should be. Jesus will be given a royal welcome into the New Jerusalem, and His subjects will crown Him "King of kings, and Lord of lords."

PATTERN
Matthew 22

BOOMERANGS

Then the Pharisees went and took counsel how to entangle him in his talk. Matthew 22:15.

A boomerang is a specially curved flat piece of wood. There are two kinds of boomerangs, those that, when thrown, return to the thrower and those that do not. The original boomerangs were made by the aborigines of Australia, and were used for hunting. I have seen an aborigine throw a boomerang and have it come back and land at his feet.

From this term has come the phrase "boomerang question." These are questions that are asked in order to trap someone, but often they return to ensnare the one who has asked them. Sometimes, rather than to argue, it is best just to ask another question. But however we respond, it should be done with a loving spirit.

After the triumphal procession, the religious leaders were jealous of Jesus and tried to arrest Him (Matt. 21:46). They were also upset by the authority He exercised in driving out those who were buying and selling in the Temple. And no doubt some had discovered the meaning of some of His secret stories.

So the Pharisees decided to engage Jesus in conversation so that they could trick Him into condemning Himself, and then they could have Him arrested. They asked Him several crafty, difficult questions. But the three attempts to make Jesus condemn Himself failed, and now it was necessary for Him to send out a nonreturning boomerang question. He asked them if the Messiah was the Son of God. Because of their wrong teachings concerning the Messiah, they were so confused that they could not answer. Jesus was not asking them to say that *He* was the Messiah; He just wanted them to see that they did not know the Scriptures, which clearly taught that the Messiah is the Son of God.

There are those who would try to trip you up on your beliefs. You and I need to know our Bibles so well and have the same control of ourselves as Jesus had in order to give logical and convincing answers. This is not in order to show our wisdom, but in order to help others find the truth as centered in the *Person* of the Scriptures—Jesus.

PATTERN
Matthew 23

FROZEN ALIVE

"Whoever exalts himself will be humbled, and whoever humbles himself will be exalted." Matthew 23:12.

In 1775 the captain of a Greenland whaling vessel was alarmed to discover that during the night his ship had been surrounded by giant icebergs. He expected the wooden ship to be broken to pieces at any moment. As the morning light appeared, he was delighted to see another ship. But when he hailed it, there was no answer.

The captain ordered a small boat lowered, and some of the crewmen rowed to the ship. As they drew near, they saw a man sitting at a table as though he were writing in the logbook. The sailors called out, but there was no answer. When they boarded the vessel, they found that the man had frozen to death. The logbook was dated 1762.

For thirteen years the vessel had floated among the icebergs, the sailors frozen in their hammocks. For thirteen years this ship had carried its burden of corpses over the icy waters. The Captain of our salvation, Jesus, described the condition of the religious leaders of His day as "like unto whited sepulchres, which indeed appear beautiful outward, but are within full of dead men's bones" (Matt. 23:27).

This was only one of eight descriptions Jesus gave of the scribes and Pharisees. Each of these portrayals is preceded by the word *woe,* a term of grief and reproof.

The ship with its frozen crew on board had been on the water for only thirteen years; the religious leaders of Israel had been frozen alive for hundreds of years. They had become spiritually dead because they had accepted the *traditions* of men rather than the *truths* of the Scriptures. They had substituted obedience to the *law* in place of obedience to the Lawgiver, Jesus. They had *memorized* the Scriptures, but had *forgotten* that they applied to the Person, Jesus.

Amid these woes Jesus appeals to the leaders to humble themselves. If they had done this and accepted Him as Messiah, they would not have crucified Him. Today, as we journey on the gospel ship to the harbor of heaven, we must keep our eyes on the Captain.

PATTERN
Matthew 24

TRACKING THE TRAIL

As he sat on the Mount of Olives, the disciples came to him privately, saying, "Tell us, when will this be, and what will be the sign of your coming and of the close of the age?" Matthew 24:3.

The Indians of North America are experts at tracking the trails of animals and people. They look carefully not only for footprints but also for disturbed leaves, broken branches, and other clues left by the bird, animal, or person they are tracking. Some of them can actually tell from feeling and examining the footprint how long ago the object of the search was there.

The trail the Christian is following leads to heaven. The Bible not only outlines how we are to follow that trail but has given us signs to look for along the way so that we can know when we are getting close to our destination. Note ten signs of the Second Advent:

Advent signs given by Jesus.
Deadly pestilences, earthquakes, and disease (Matt. 24:7).
Very many false christs and prophets (verses 4, 5).
Everyone afraid of what is happening (Luke 21:26).
Notable famines in many areas (Matt. 24:7).
The gospel preached in all the world (verse 14).

Signs in sun, moon, and stars (Luke 21:25).
Increase in wickedness, loss of love (Matt. 24:10-12).
God's true people persecuted (verses 8, 9).
Noticeable increase in earthquakes in many places (verse 7).
Several international wars and rumors of wars (verse 7).

As we read the signs of Christ's coming listed in Matthew 24, we should also read the parables of the ten virgins, the talents, and the sheep and goats, recorded in chapter 25. These parables were given to help us prepare for Christ's second coming. In both chapters we are instructed to "watch," since those who do not watch will not be prepared.

Christians are to track the events that appear on our trail to the kingdom of heaven. We have been warned that "in such an hour as ye think not the Son of man cometh" (chap. 24:44).

PATTERN
Matthew 25

TICKETS, PLEASE

"Watch therefore, for you know neither the day nor the hour."
Matthew 25:13.

Austria is a beautiful country. The snow-clad Alps, the Danube River, and historic buildings help to make it popular with tourists. The capital, Vienna, has a very good public transportation system consisting of streetcars, buses, and electric trains.

On my first visit to Austria I was interested to note that it is possible to ride on the public transportation without paying. However, most of the people do not do this because they know that they are on their honor. Yes, the commercial company trusts the people of Vienna and tourists to purchase tickets and pay for their rides. Because there are people who would take advantage of the honor system, occasionally a ticket inspector will board and ask to see tickets.

A minister who was traveling on a train when an inspector came aboard noted that everyone in the carriage with the exception of one man was able to show a ticket. The officer waited patiently as the man fumbled in his briefcase. Finally the inspector took out his pad and pen and began writing. The man frantically searched in his pockets and briefcase, and the officer kept writing. At the next station the inspector took the man off the train while the passenger continued searching. There is a heavy fine levied against anyone who uses the transportation system without a ticket.

Our journey to the New Jerusalem can be likened to a railway journey. God has appointed the church to be the train on which His people are to travel. However, before we board we need to have a "ticket" stamped at the station called Calvary. And we need to keep it properly dated by continued confession of sin and daily surrender of our lives to Jesus.

We do not know when the examiner will come and ask for our ticket. The Bible teaches us that at the close of probation it will be too late to purchase a ticket. Just as there was a day when the doors of the ark were closed by angels, so there is a time when Jesus will complete His work of judgment, just prior to His second coming.

PATTERN
Matthew 26

THE LAST SUPPER

"I tell you I shall not drink again of this fruit of the vine until that day when I drink it new with you in my Father's kingdom."
Matthew 26:29.

One hot day a horse-drawn carriage stopped at a humble home alongside a road in England. The poor widow who lived in the cottage went out, and the lady in the carriage asked her for a drink of water. The widow took a cup and filled it with cool, pure water.

Imagine the widow's astonishment when she learned that the lady in the carriage was Queen Victoria! The cup became a very precious possession to her, and she placed it on a shelf and covered it with a glass bowl. Many people came to see the cup and to hear again the story of how she had given a drink of water to the queen of England.

The cup on the widow's shelf reminded her of the queen's visit; the cup used in the communion service is to remind us of our Saviour's sacrifice. It also brings back to our minds the promise recorded in our Morning Watch verse.

As we drink the fruit of the vine from the communion cup, it shows our acceptance of the salvation offered by Jesus and keeps vivid in our minds the hope of the Second Coming. The communion cup links the first and second advents of Jesus.

Just as Jesus celebrated Communion before His departure from this world, so when we take part in that service we recognize that we are living in the time before His return. This is the time of the end, and each time we have Communion may be the last supper.

Our communion cup must not be just of historic value, as was the widow's cup. As we eat the bread it reminds us of the broken body of Jesus; as we drink the grape juice it teaches us that His blood was spilt on our behalf. It is a privilege to partake of the communion service, and all who have accepted Jesus as their personal Saviour may do so. The Bible does not teach that one has to be a member in order to celebrate Communion in a particular church.

PATTERN
Matthew 27

CROWN AND CROSS

And plaiting a crown of thorns they put it on his head, and put a reed in his right hand. And kneeling before him they mocked him, saying, "Hail, King of the Jews!" Matthew 27:29.

"They borrowed a bed to lay His head
  When Christ the Lord came down;
They borrowed the ass in the mountain pass
  For Him to ride to town;
But the crown that He wore and the cross that He bore
  Were His own—the cross was His own.

"They borrowed the bread when the crowd He fed
  On the grassy mountainside;
He borrowed the dish of broken fish
  With which He satisfied;
But the crown that He wore and the cross that He bore
  Were His own—the cross was His own.

"He borrowed the ship in which to sit
  To teach the multitude;
He borrowed a nest in which to rest;
  He had never a home so rude;
But the crown that He wore and the cross that He bore
  Were His own—the cross was His own.

"He borrowed a room on His way to the tomb,
  The Passover lamb to eat;
They borrowed a cave for Him a grave,
  They borrowed a winding sheet;
But the crown that He wore and the cross that He bore
  Were His own—the cross was His own."

—Author Unknown

This month we have noted some things that were borrowed for Jesus to use. Now we see that the crown and the cross were "His own."

The soldiers who mocked Jesus, saying, "Hail, King of the Jews," will one day acknowledge Him as King of the universe. After the earthquake that accompanied Jesus' death, one Roman soldier said, "Truly this was the Son of God." I hope he accepted the Son of God as his personal Saviour and that you have too.

PATTERN
Matthew 27

CROWN OR CROSS

Pilate said to them, "Then what shall I do with Jesus who is called Christ?" They all said, "Let him be crucified." Matthew 27:22.

We do not have the complete story of the *Person* of Jesus in any one of the four Gospels, and each one is silent as to His early years in Nazareth. However, each Gospel presents a particular phase of Jesus' life, and as we read all four, the picture grows in beauty. Even now, from reading Matthew, we have found *light* for our *lives* and we can choose to crown Jesus king.

"I stood alone at the bar of God,
    In the hush of the twilight dim,
And faced the question that pierced my heart:
    'What will you do with Him?
Crowned or crucified—which shall it be?'
    No other choice was offered to me.

"I looked on the face so marred with tears
    That were shed in His agony.
The look in His kind eyes broke my heart—
    'Twas full of love for me.
'The crown or the cross,' it seemed to say;
    'For or against Me—choose thou today.'

"He held out His loving hands to me,
    While He pleadingly said, 'Obey.
Make Me thy choice, for I love thee so';
    And I could not say Him nay.
Crowned, not crucified—this must it be;
    No other way was open to me.

"I knelt in tears at the feet of Christ,
    In the hush of the twilight dim,
And all that I was, or hoped, or thought,
    Surrendered unto Him.
Crowned, not crucified—my heart shall know
    No king but Christ, who loveth me so."

                                        —Florence E. Johnson

PATTERN
Matthew 28

GO QUICKLY!

"Then go quickly and tell his disciples that he has risen from the dead, and behold, he is going before you to Galilee; there you will see him. Lo, I have told you." Matthew 28:7.

Waterloo was one of the most significant battles in history. The two commanders were the Duke of Wellington, leading the English armies, and Napoleon Bonaparte, leading the French. The people of England waited for news of the battle, which was sent by ship to the southern coast of England and relayed by semaphore to the top of Winchester Cathedral. From the cathedral it was sent again by semaphore to London.

The message began coming through from the sailing vessel, "W-E-L-L-I-N-G-T-O-N D-E-F-E-A-T-E-D . . ." But a dense fog settled over the harbor, making it impossible to receive any further information. The incomplete message was sent by semaphore to London; the people were very upset and pledged to defend their country against the French. But then the fog lifted, and the semaphore signals began to come through again. W-E-L-L-I-N-G-T-O-N D-E-F-E-A-T-E-D T-H-E E-N-E-M-Y. You can imagine the excitement when the complete message was received.

After the crucifixion of Jesus, His followers were crushed with despair. Because they did not fully understand the mission of Jesus, to them the message of the cross spelled J-E-S-U-S D-E-F-E-A-T-E-D.

No doubt they felt that way all during the Sabbath as Jesus rested in the tomb. However, on Sunday morning, an earthquake announced that the message was not complete. An angel, whose appearance is described as "like lightning . . . and white as snow," appeared before the women who had come to the tomb and gave the entire message—J-E-S-U-S D-E-F-E-A-T-E-D D-E-A-T-H. They were then told to "go quickly" and tell His disciples that He had risen from the dead.

Today we are to "go quickly" to tell our neighbors, relatives, and friends that Jesus is risen from the dead and wants to meet them in the clouds of heaven. We are to go with the full message that after He rose, Christ returned to heaven to be our mediator, high priest, and judge.

PATTERN
Matthew 28

FIND MY WORLD

"Go therefore and make disciples of all nations, baptizing them in the name of the Father and of the Son and of the Holy Spirit, teaching them to observe all that I have commanded you; and lo, I am with you always, to the close of the age." Matthew 28:19, 20.

David Livingstone, the explorer and missionary, was at one time believed to be lost in Africa. Many people wanted news of his whereabouts, and James Bennett, the owner of the New York *Herald,* finally decided to find out where Livingstone was and what he was doing. So while he was visiting Paris he cabled one of his correspondents, Henry Stanley, who was stationed at Gibraltar, to come to Paris.

Stanley set off immediately and arrived one night at midnight. After James Bennett greeted him, Stanley asked why he had been sent for. The reply was delivered in two words: "Find Livingstone." When asked how much money was available for the expedition, Stanley was told, "Fifty thousand dollars or a larger sum. Never mind the money; find Livingstone."

It took Stanley two years to arrive in Africa, and he risked his life walking through the jungles to find David Livingstone. Then one day the two men met in an African village and Stanley said simply, "Dr. Livingstone, I presume."

At one time it looked as though this world was lost. Many had been sent by the Creator to find it, and finally it became necessary for God to send His own Son, who explored ways of finding the world for thirty-three years. By dying on the cross, He won it back for the Father. After His resurrection Jesus left the world in the care of His followers—first His disciples and then the Christian church.

Today He is sending to the church the same message that He gave the disciples. "Find My world and bring it back. Never mind the expense of money and of lives, for I gave My life for this world. Find My world and win it back."

Go ye is our *invitation* and *command.* Go ye and teach is our *privilege.* Go ye and teach all things is our *responsibility.* Go ye and teach all things to all nations is our *duty.*

PATTERN
Matthew 1

THE FORTIETH BOOK

The book of the genealogy of Jesus Christ, the son of David, the son of Abraham. Matthew 1:1.

In your Bible and mine the book of Matthew is the fortieth book, coming after the thirty-nine books of the Old Testament. The sixty-six books of the Bible were written by forty authors, each one telling about Jesus. As we observe the Morning Watch during the next eleven months, we will have further *light* for our *lives*.

The title of the book we have studied this month is "The Gospel According to Matthew." Why do you think Jesus let Matthew, Mark, Luke, and John write His life story? Wouldn't it have been better if Jesus Himself had written it? Most people who claim to have something to say to the world write a book so that their message can live on after they die. As we read the Gospels, we see that there is only one record of Jesus ever writing. He did not write on paper that time, but on the ground, and we do not know exactly what He wrote.

If Jesus had written His own story, the book itself would probably have been worshiped. Also, He knew that you and I would understand His *Person* better if we read what those who knew Him personally wrote about Him. As we read the four Gospels, we do not find a dry, boring story, but we sense that the men who wrote the accounts loved Jesus very much.

Yes, we can get to know the *Person* of Jesus by reading the books of the Bible. However, it is sad that many people who read and even learn parts of the Bible by memory still do not discover a personal relationship with Jesus. As has often been said, the religion of Jesus is *caught,* not *taught.* As we read the Bible, pray, fellowship with God's people, witness, study nature, go through life's experiences, we can enter into a personal relationship with Jesus Christ.

The kingdom of heaven, which is the theme of the book of Matthew, is concerned with the inward life. If the heart is right, all things are right. The lamp of faith burns brightly in the lives of those who are daily charged by the light of the world. I need this kind of *light for my life,* don't you?

POWER
Acts 1

ONCE UPON A TIME

"But you shall receive power when the Holy Spirit has come upon you; and you shall be my witnesses in Jerusalem and in all Judea and Samaria and to the end of the earth." Acts 1:8.

Once upon a time, so an old legend goes, three horsemen were riding in the darkness across the desert. As they crossed a dry riverbed about midnight, a commanding voice called, "Halt!" They obeyed.

They were told to dismount, pick up a handful of pebbles, put them in their pockets, and remount. Again they obeyed.

As they were about to continue their journey, they heard the voice again: "You have done as I commanded. At sunrise tomorrow you will be both glad and sorry."

At sunrise the men took the pebbles out of their pockets, and to their amazement saw diamonds, rubies, and other precious gems glinting in the morning sun. And they were both glad and sorry—glad they had taken some, sorry they hadn't taken more!

Once upon a time, almost two thousand years ago, Jesus told His disciples to stop their activities. He told them to wait to receive the precious power that the Father wanted to give them. They obeyed and waited, and were amazed. Those who emptied their lives entirely of self were glad they had. Those who could not receive the full measure of the Holy Spirit because of self in their lives were very sorry.

The promise of the Holy Spirit was given to the disciples, and it is also for us today. We may not fully understand the ministry of the Holy Spirit, but we would be wise to pause at the beginning of each day and pray that He will fill us with His power.

The book of Acts is exciting to read. It tells of supernatural things done by ordinary men and women who were filled with the Holy Spirit. It begins with the preaching of the gospel to the Jews in Jerusalem and closes with Paul's preaching to the Gentiles in Rome.

The Morning Watch text for today is the key to the book of Acts. During this month we shall see that this prophecy that the disciples were to witness "'to the end of the earth'" (R.S.V.) was dramatically fulfilled.

POWER
Acts 2

WHIRLWIND AND WONDER

When the day of Pentecost had come, they were all together in one place. And suddenly a sound came from heaven like the rush of a mighty wind, and it filled all the house where they were sitting. Acts 2:1, 2.

One of the most unique caves in the world is located in the Black Hills of South Dakota. The cave has very few of the stalagmites and stalactites for which many caves are famous. Instead it has beautiful formations that have been called boxwork and frostwork formations. Boxworks are crystal structures made up of beautiful colors ranging from bright yellow, pink, brown, and deep blue. In contrast, frostwork formations are composed of tiny white crystals aligning the ceilings and walls of the caves.

The cave is also noted for the strange, strong wind currents that blow into it when the temperature drops and rush out when the temperature rises. It is this feature that has given it the name Wind Cave. Wind Cave was discovered in 1881 by Tom Bingham when he heard the wind whistling as it passed in and out of a small opening in the rock wall of the cave.

The God of nature who made the wind used it to announce the arrival of the Holy Spirit in the upper room where the disciples were gathered on the day of Pentecost. The wind symbolized the power of the Holy Spirit, and the "tongues of fire" represented the purity of the Holy Spirit. When those assembled were filled with the Holy Spirit, they were able to proclaim the gospel in a remarkable way.

All Jerusalem heard about the wind and the fire. Three thousand were converted in one day as a result of a sermon preached by Peter in the power of the Holy Spirit. One of the wonders was that people from many countries, each speaking a different language, understood Peter when he preached.

The book of Acts, written by Luke, records the spread of Christianity from the descent of the Holy Spirit on the day of Pentecost until Paul's preaching in Caesar's palace in Rome. In his Gospel Luke records what Christ "began to do and teach" (Acts 1:1). In Acts he records what Christ continued to do by the Holy Spirit through men like Peter and Saul.

POWER
Acts 3

A BOOK OF MIRACLES

But Peter said, "I have no silver and gold, but I give you what I have; in the name of Jesus Christ of Nazareth, walk." Acts 3:6.

"It was the most exciting day of my life. I shall never forget it as long as I live, and I must tell everybody about it. It was nothing new for me to go to the Temple gates. And that day I went the same as always, carried on a stretcher by friends. All the gates were beautiful, and I don't think those of you living in 1982 have ever seen gates like them. They were made of brass and were covered with gold and silver.

"People didn't like to look at me, as I was dressed in rags and hopelessly deformed. In my 40 years of life I had not known a day without pain. However, I did have friends who carried me to the Temple gate so that I could beg for alms.

"A little hope came into my life when I heard about a Physician whom people said had actually healed cripples like me. However, although I desired with all my heart to see Him, I was too far away from where He was working. And my hopes were crushed when I heard that He had been put to a very cruel death. Then, as I was pitying myself, it happened, without any fanfare! Two men who looked like ordinary passers-by were going to the Temple. I simply held out my beggar's cup and asked them for money. The one who looked like a fisherman said, 'Look at us.'

"I had nothing to lose, so I looked up, expecting to receive a coin. Once again my hopes were dashed when all I saw was a look of compassion. He said, 'I have no silver and gold . . .' I had heard this before, and wondered where I was going to get money for food. Then the man, whom I found out later was called Peter, uttered words that changed the whole course of my life: 'But I give you what I have; in the name of Jesus Christ of Nazareth, walk.'

"You don't know my name. Just remember me as the lame man at the Gate Beautiful who was healed of my deformity and found eternal life by accepting Jesus Christ. And I can assure you that all who accept Jesus will find new meaning to life."

44

POWER
Acts 4

THE SECRET OF POWER

Now when they saw the boldness of Peter and John, and perceived that they were uneducated, common men, they wondered; and they recognized that they had been with Jesus. Acts 4:13.

A young lady 17 years of age swam an icy river to a country where she had freedom to worship God. She eagerly accepted the teachings of the Bible and rejoiced in her consecration to the Lord Jesus Christ. Those she worshiped with could not believe their ears when she announced that she was going to swim back to her country and share what she had learned from the Bible with her relatives and friends. They admired her courage and today pray that many will be in the kingdom of heaven as a result of her witness.

This young lady's love and courage is the same brand as that demonstrated by Peter and John after their arrest. They were the first of the disciples to be taken into custody, and it seems as though there were several reasons, or at least excuses, for their arrest. The priests were no doubt jealous of their influence with the people. There was also fear that they would stir up the multitude and bring trouble with the Romans. Also the Sadducees, who did not believe in the resurrection, would try to silence their authoritative preaching that Christ had risen from the dead.

When we speak with boldness and authority about Jesus, we can be sure there will be opposition, if not persecution. Satan does not worry when we are just religious. But when we really give a strong testimony about salvation through Jesus Christ and announce that He is coming to this earth again, Satan endeavors to silence us. At these times the Spirit gives us power to witness.

The secret of the great power of the apostles is summarized in one small phrase of the Morning Watch text for today: "And they recognized that they had been with Jesus" (R.S.V.). When we spend time with Jesus, when we love and obey Him, we will also have the courage to live the Christian life. Our testimony will be used by the Holy Spirit to help others discover the way to eternal life.

POWER
Acts 5

ESCAPE FROM PRISON

They arrested the apostles and put them in the common prison. But at night an angel of the Lord opened the prison doors and brought them out and said, "Go and stand in the temple and speak to the people all the words of this Life." Acts 5:18-20.

The tall, handsome Solomon Island pastor had been arrested and flogged with a pliable piece of cane while bent over a gasoline drum. Later he was sentenced to be shot.

Kata Ragoso, a civilian, now faced an army firing squad. The officer said, "I'll count three. At three, fire!" He began to count. "One! Two! Th—!" But he could not say three. He tried again. He tried two more times. Not only could he not say the word *three,* but for more than a day he could not speak at all. The barefoot pastor had to be put back in prison with another minister, Lundi.

As in the days of the early church, members in the Solomon Islands prayed for the release of their leaders. The dramatic answer to their prayer is recorded by A. W. Spalding in the book *Christ's Last Legion:*

"And just as the moon rose over the mountain, a tall man with a bunch of keys walked to the prison compound, put the key in the padlock, and opened the gate. Standing there in the light of the moon, he called in a loud voice, 'Ragoso! Lundi!'

"'Yes, sir,' came the reply.

"'Come here.'

"When the two men were together at the gate, the tall man reached in, took each by the arm, and pulled them out. He then shut the gate and locked it. Then he led them down the path toward the beach. As they came within sight of the water he paused and said to them, 'Go on down to the beach and there you will find a canoe. Take it and go home.'"

At least one angel has a master key that will unlock any prison door. And it was also used to release Peter and John from jail. In both escapes the prisoners were led past the guards without being seen. These ministers were rescued because God had more work for them to do.

46

POWER
Acts 6

ARITHMETIC IN ACTS

"Therefore, brethren, pick out from among you seven men of good repute, full of the Spirit and of wisdom, whom we may appoint to this duty." Acts 6:3.

Previously Luke had used the word *added* to describe the church's rapid growth. Now, in Acts 6:1, for the first time he uses new arithmetic and a word that is normally translated "multiplied." This conveys the idea of rapid increase. The power of God had been so manifested through the lives of the apostles and early church members that there was very rapid growth.

Church growth is very exciting to observe, but it sometimes has problems associated with it. As we grow, we must adapt to the new situations that result. So the young church had to adapt. The Holy Spirit prompted the apostles to meet the problems that came with growth. In order for the ministers to have more time to preach the Word of God, they asked the members to select seven deacons to care for the church's day-by-day activities.

We do not know why the number *seven* was selected, although it is certainly a significant number in Bible arithmetic. The first two deacons, Stephen and Philip, both became evangelists.

As you look forward to serving the church as a lay officer or a full-time worker, you can learn a lot about what God expects from the qualifications required for deacons and elders. A full list of these is given in 1 Timothy 3:1-14 and Titus 1:5-11, but here is a three-point summary:

The officers of the church are to be of good reputation. They are to be spiritual and "full of the Spirit" (R.S.V.). They are also to be practical and "full . . . of wisdom" (R.S.V.)

Soon after I started writing this book, I had the privilege of participating in the ordination of two teen-agers and one young man just out of his teens as deacons. Our church today needs young men like Howard Bankes, Steven Davis, and Allan Hills to serve the church. We should pray just as earnestly for the modern Stephens as the early church did for their Stephen, one of the first deacons.

POWER
Acts 7

WHO SAW HEAVEN OPENED?

And he said, "Behold, I see the heavens opened, and the Son of man standing at the right hand of God." Acts 7:56.

Who had this privilege of seeing right into heaven itself and looking at Jesus standing by the side of God? Yes, his name was Stephen, and he was "full of the Holy Ghost" (Acts 7:55). Also God knew that Stephen needed this encouragement, as he was the first Christian to die because of his faith in Jesus.

It is interesting to note from this chapter that it was after Stephen had given a clear statement of his faith that he saw the heavens opened. His is an eloquent sermon and is the main content of our Morning Watch chapter for today. He reminds the council of God's leading during Old Testament times and rebukes the people for murdering Jesus. In the face of death he was not ashamed to make a full confession of his faith.

Stephen saw the heavens opened when he was at a time of apparent defeat. He had done everything he could, but what he said only enraged the people. When we have done our best we can rest our case with God and He will, as He did in Stephen's case, encourage us and turn our apparent defeat into victory.

Another question we should ask is, What happened to Stephen as a result of his seeing the heavens opened? It gave him the necessary courage to endure the terrible death by stoning that was to follow. It enabled him to say these words, similar to those of Jesus on the cross: "Lord, lay not this sin to their charge."

Stephen's name means "wreath of victory," and his life gives us inspiration to witness for the Lord and to be true no matter what happens to us. We have a record of the last day in the life of Stephen. It was a day of victory for Stephen, but it was a day of defeat for the Jewish nation. By stoning Stephen they symbolized their final rejection of God. On Stephen's last day he saw heaven opened, but the Jews as a nation saw heaven closed. We will soon see heaven "split open" if, like Stephen, we are "full of faith and of the Holy Ghost" (chap. 6:5).

POWER
Acts 8

VANISHING VISITORS

And he commanded the chariot to stop, and they both went down into the water, Philip and the eunuch, and he baptized him. Acts 8:38.

At the beginning of this century an Ethiopian named Zechariah was on a trip. During this time he was visited by three men. One of his visitors said he wanted Zechariah to teach his people about Jesus and the prophets.

After the visitors left, Zechariah was too frightened to speak, but the next day he loaded up his mules and continued on his journey. That night he had a dream, and the same man who had appeared to him in Asmara said to him, "Are you running away? Stop. Go back and give the message." Zechariah obeyed this time, and some of the people he preached to were baptized.

The emperor made a proclamation that Zechariah had freedom to preach, and he was given a bodyguard of one hundred men. This story, which is written on an old manuscript, was told to me by a man whose father had been one of the guards.

Some of those who opposed Zechariah's teachings asked him which was the correct method of baptism. He stated that it was his responsibility only to teach certain truths. He said that later some people who spoke another language and had a different color skin would come to Ethiopia and preach the same message in three languages. Soon after Zechariah was baptized by immersion, he died.

One of Zechariah's followers discovered from the Bible that he should be baptized by immersion and that he should worship on the seventh day. As he was reading his Bible a man came to him and said that he would take him to another place in Asmara where he could find a group teaching the truths that he believed.

The next Saturday the stranger took this man to church with him. It was 1907, and three white-skinned men came onto the platform. The preacher spoke in English, the second man translated into Swedish, and the third translated into the local language.

The Holy Spirit, who directed Philip to baptize the Ethiopian, also led Zechariah and his followers to learn about the Advent message.

POWER
Acts 9

RIGHT MAN, TIME, PLACE

But the Lord said to him, "Go, for he is a chosen instrument of mine to carry my name before the Gentiles and kings and the sons of Israel." Acts 9:15.

Capt. George Vancouver was a British explorer who sailed with Captain Cook for fifteen years. He had entered the Navy as a midshipman when just a boy of 13. His ships were noted for their cleanliness, fresh air below decks, and for the balanced diet that was provided for the sailors.

In 1791 he was ordered to sail to the northwest coast of North America. His boat was called the *Discovery,* and he followed the same route as Captain Cook, surveying the coast as he journeyed. On April 17, 1792, he anchored at Nootka Sound on a large island off the coast of what is now Vancouver, British Columbia, Canada.

Some of this information concerning Captain Vancouver is on a plaque attached to a portion of a replica of the H.M.S. *Discovery* in a museum on Vancouver Island. The tribute ends with this statement: "At 33 years of age he arrived at Nootka and was the right man at the time for the right place."

The book of Acts has interesting stories of three men who were God's men at the right time for the right place. The first was the young man named Saul of Tarsus, who had been profoundly influenced by the stoning of Stephen. When God spoke to him, Saul was ready to do what He wanted him to, and Saul the persecutor became Paul the preacher.

The second man was a disciple at Damascus named Ananias. This disciple must have trembled when God asked him to go to Saul the persecutor, but he obeyed.

The third right man was Barnabas. His name means "son of encouragement," and this was appropriate, for it was Barnabas who encouraged the Christians to accept Paul as a disciple of Jesus.

It was also difficult for Saul, Ananias, and Barnabas to do their work. However, they were God's chosen instruments. When we are God's people at the right time and in the right place, we will also be God's chosen instruments.

POWER
Acts 10

ANGELS HELP US

"Cornelius, a centurion, an upright and God-fearing man, who is well spoken of by the whole Jewish nation, was directed by a holy angel to send for you to come to his house, and to hear what you have to say." Acts 10:22.

Cornelius was a Roman officer stationed at Caesarea, the Roman capital of Palestine. The city was situated on the seacoast about fifty miles northwest of Jerusalem and was near Joppa, where Peter was staying.

A few years after the church in Jerusalem was founded, God sent an angel to Cornelius, who already was looking for the Messiah to come. Cornelius became the first Gentile Christian. This was not the first time heavenly agencies had visited Joppa, however, for eight hundred years before, a special submarine had come to take Jonah to preach to the Gentiles at Nineveh.

Both men and angels were used to help Cornelius become a Christian. An angel told him to go to Peter, and the same angel was sent to that disciple to prepare his heart to present the message of salvation to the Gentiles. This was done when Peter was given a dream of a net full of many living creatures. Some have misinterpreted this to mean that we can eat anything we want, but Peter gives the true meaning of the vision when he says, " 'Truly I perceive that God shows no partiality, but in every nation any one who fears him and does what is right is acceptable to him'" (Acts 10:34, 35, R.S.V.).

If Cornelius had refused to obey the angel's instruction, he would not have discovered divine light and power. If Peter had not obeyed his instructions, he would not have received and baptized this Gentile.

"In the tenth chapter of Acts we have still another instance of the ministration of heavenly angels. . . . In . . . [chapters 8-10] we see that heaven is much nearer to the Christian who is engaged in the work of soul saving than many suppose. We should learn through them also the lesson of God's regard for every human being, and that each should treat his fellow man as one of the Lord's instrumentalities for the accomplishment of His work in the earth."—*The Seventh-day Adventist Bible Commentary*, Ellen G. White Comments, on Acts 10, p. 1059.

POWER
Acts 11

QUEEN OF THE EAST

And the hand of the Lord was with them, and a great number that believed turned to the Lord. News of this came to the ears of the church in Jerusalem, and they sent Barnabas to Antioch. Acts 11:21, 22.

Antioch was one of the largest cities of the Roman Empire. It had been beautified by several nations, and thus was called the Queen of the East. However, it was also a throne of heathen gods, and the people there were very wicked. The fact that the Christian church became strong in Antioch was a miracle, and once again the result of a demonstration of God's power.

After the martyrdom of Stephen the Christians were persecuted, and as a result scattered to many regions, including Antioch and Syria. When the mother church at Jerusalem heard about this, they selected Barnabas, "a good man, full of the Holy Spirit"—the same qualifications that Stephen had had—to go to Antioch to strengthen the church. We need to pray that we will be "full of the Holy Ghost and of faith" so that we can be called "good" by God as well as by the church members. The fact that Barnabas took Paul with him indicates that he was confident Paul was the right person to aid in the evangelization at Antioch.

Did you ever wonder why the name *Christian* was given to the disciples of Jesus? Many were called followers of the way, because Jesus had said, "I am the way, the truth, and the life." The disciples in Antioch lived so close to the Lord that the people of this heathen city called them Christians—followers of Christ (Acts 11:26). The challenge is for us to live so close to Jesus that the people in our community will call us Christian.

"It was God who gave them the name of Christian. This is a royal name, given to all who join themselves to Christ."—*The Acts of the Apostles,* p. 157.

A Christian has been defined by F. A. Noble as

—a *mind* through which Christ *thinks,*

—a *heart* through which Christ *lives,*

—a *voice* through which Christ *speaks,*

—a *hand* through which Christ *helps.*

POWER
Acts 12

SUFFERING AND SUCCESS

About that time Herod the king laid violent hands upon some who belonged to the church. He killed James the brother of John with the sword; and when he saw that it pleased the Jews, he proceeded to arrest Peter also. Acts 12:1-3.

"If you are *succeeding* without *suffering,* someone else who preceded you has *suffered.* If you have *suffered* without *succeeding,* someone else who follows you will *succeed.*"

These statements were made by the son of Adoniram Judson, missionary to Burma. I heard them over my car radio when I was traveling in Queensland, Australia, in 1967. I have kept them in my file to share with young people who are looking for power in their lives.

The members of the early Christian church at the time James was killed and Peter imprisoned no doubt thought they were "suffering without succeeding." They were also perplexed, as are many people today, as to why God allows one Christian to die prematurely or tragically and delivers others from the same fate.

James was the first of the twelve disciples to die, but to this day the example of his faith is used to lead many to find power for their lives now and eternal life hereafter. Although Peter was miraculously delivered from prison instead of being executed after the Jewish passover, years later he also died a martyr's death. But James and Peter did not suffer without succeeding; only in heaven will we know the full result of their witness.

God is not the author of suffering and death, but because He knows the end from the beginning, He allows some things to happen that may not make sense to us at this stage in our lives. However, if we are faithful, one day we will understand. This statement from Ellen White amplifies the Bible teaching that God is love and that He knows best:

"God has a purpose in sending trial to His children. He never leads them otherwise than they would choose to be led if they could see the end from the beginning, and discern the glory of the purpose that they are fulfilling."—*Prophets and Kings,* p. 578.

POWER
Acts 13

A TALE OF TWO CITIES

And when the Gentiles heard this, they were glad and glorified the word of God; and as many as were ordained to eternal life believed. And the word of the Lord spread throughout all the region. Acts 13:48, 49.

The dramatic story of the Christian church as recorded in Acts has been summarized as "The Tale of Two Cities." During the first years, recorded in Acts 1 through 12, the church was directed from Jerusalem. In Acts 13 through 28 we learn that Antioch became the new church headquarters. This change might not have been necessary if God's first plan had been accepted by the Jewish nation, for they would have evangelized from Jerusalem. However, after the death of Stephen, God implemented His second plan, which included scattering the Christians. As we have discovered, some located in Antioch, and the work spread rapidly under the ministry of Paul and Barnabas.

Peter was the leader of the Jerusalem-based church, and is the outstanding person of power in the first twelve chapters of Acts. The real power for our lives, the Holy Spirit, was demonstrated many times in Peter's life. That power enabled him to overcome racial prejudice and pave the way for the work of Paul, the apostle to the Gentiles. The last mention of Peter in the book of Acts is in connection with the church council held at Jerusalem. After that, we will not study him again until we read his Epistles of peace in the month of November.

The remaining sixteen chapters of Acts focus on Paul's three missionary journeys from Antioch and his trip to Rome. Paul had been a Christian for twelve or fourteen years by this time, and was a leader of the Antioch church. As he returned from his missionary trips, stories of God's power in other parts of the world thrilled the believers just as they inspire us today.

"The Tale of Two Cities" is more than the acts of the apostles. It is the acts of the Holy Spirit, or of Jesus. What was done by the apostles in Jerusalem, Antioch, and other cities was the work of God. Ordinary people can do extraordinary things when they are controlled from above. I want to do extraordinary acts for God, don't you?

54

POWER
Acts 14

DOWN BUT NOT OUT

And from there they sailed to Antioch, where they had been commended to the grace of God for the work which they had fulfilled. And when they arrived, they gathered the church together and declared all that God had done with them, and how he had opened a door of faith to the Gentiles. Acts 14:26, 27.

"It is better to fail in a cause destined to win than to succeed in a cause destined to fail." The life of Paul illustrates the truthfulness of this statement. He seemed to fail at times, but now we can see that he was successful.

Paul's first missionary journey took him about three hundred miles northwest from Antioch during the years A.D. 45 to 47. He sailed with Barnabas to the island of Cyprus and then on to Asia Minor, which is now the country of Turkey. He preached in several cities, was persecuted, stoned, and left for dead, but people were converted and churches were organized as a result of his work.

Paul is an example of men and women who, by God's grace, keep pressing on in spite of opposition. As Paul put it in one of his letters, "We may be knocked down but we are never knocked out!" (2 Cor. 4:9, Phillips).

> Keep pressing on,
> Though you may feel like stopping;
> Keep pressing on,
> Though you feel more like dropping.
> Keep pressing on,
> No race is won by sitting;
> Keep pressing on,
> No goal is reached by quitting.
> Sing while you're pressing on;
> If you can't sing it—hum it.
> Trust while you're pressing on,
> Each mountain has a summit.
> Pray while you're pressing on,
> For your rewards come later;
> Smile while you're pressing on,
> Rewards will be the greater!
>
> —*Author Unknown*

POWER
Acts 15

TROUBLE IN CHURCH

Peter rose and said to them, "Brethren, you know that in the early days God made choice among you, that by my mouth the Gentiles should hear the word of the gospel and believe." Acts 15:7.

Trouble arose in the Christian church about twenty years after it was established. Those responsible were apparently former members of a strict group of Pharisees who had recently become Christians. A delegation of these members traveled from Jerusalem to Antioch, stating that they had been sent by the mother church. However, a runner took a letter to the church stating that this was not so.

Whenever there are problems in a local church, it is best to seek counsel from the church organization, and this church in the first century appealed to the headquarters at Jerusalem to decide whether the Gentiles must keep the Jewish laws before they could become Christians.

The council was chaired by a man named James, a noted leader of the church in Jerusalem. It is possible that he was the brother of Jesus (see Gal. 1:19). Paul also refers to him as one of the "pillars" of the church (see Gal. 2:9).

After a lot of debate, Peter made a closing statement and urged that it was only the grace of Jesus that saved a person, and not obedience to laws. His words reechoed what he had stated in his first sermon—"There is none other name under heaven given among men, whereby we must be saved" (Acts 4:12). He pointed to the very heart of Christianity, Jesus Christ, and made it clear that salvation is by faith in Him. However, all did not see clearly that the laws dealing with ceremonies pointed to Jesus and were fulfilled in Him, and for many years Jewish Christians continued to take part in certain rituals.

The Holy Spirit was leading the church step by step into truth. Even Martin Luther, who was used by God centuries later to rediscover the principle that "the just shall live by faith," did not discover all the verities in God's Word. The church at Luther's time had suffered persecution, and God was leading it through a tunnel into full light. Jesus promised that the Holy Spirit would guide into all truth.

POWER
Acts 16

THE GOSPEL TO EUROPE

And a vision appeared to Paul in the night: a man of Macedonia was standing beseeching him and saying, "Come over to Macedonia and help us." Acts 16:9.

Have you ever stopped to think that if Paul and his companions had traveled east instead of west, Europe and America might have adopted religions that were not Christian? On the other hand, those living in lands where Buddha, Confucius, and Mohammed were predominantly worshiped might now be Christians. The whole course of the world was influenced by Paul's decision to answer the call of the man of Greece whom he saw in vision.

This introduced the gospel to Europe, and Europe became the home base for Christian missions. A German monk, Martin Luther, translated the Bible from Latin into German; an Englishman, William Tyndale, translated it into English.

It was in England that the first foreign mission society was founded in 1872. William Carey, one of the founders, went as the first missionary to the non-Christian world. And it was from Europe that the Pilgrim Fathers sailed to America, bringing Christianity to the New World.

The first convert in Europe mentioned by name was not a king, neither was she influential or highly educated. She was, according to the book of Acts, a businesswoman, a seller of purple-dyed garments. What was her name?

"God's Spirit can only enlighten the understanding of those who are willing to be enlightened. We read that God opened the ears of Lydia, so that she attended to the message spoken by Paul. To declare the whole counsel of God and all that was essential for Lydia to receive—this was the part Paul was to act in her conversion; and then the God of all grace exercised His power, leading the soul in the right way. God and the human agent cooperated, and the work was wholly successful."—*The SDA Bible Commentary,* Ellen G. White Comments, on Acts 16:14, p. 1062.

Paul first met Lydia when he spoke to a group of women near the river. As a result of this contact, on Sabbath the Lord opened her heart, and Lydia believed and was baptized.

POWER
Acts 17

TELLING THE WORLD

"These men who have turned the world upside down have come here also." Acts 17:6.

Do you think 3 million Seventh-day Adventists could turn the world upside down with their teachings? Yes. If the membership of the church were to double every year, there would be more than 6 billion members by the year 1993! According to estimates based on present population growth, there will be 6.4 billion people living in the world in 1982. (In English and French numbering systems, on which the above figures are based, 1,000 million equals 1 billion.) Sometimes it's good to think in terms of big numbers, isn't it? But this raises the question, How is it possible for the membership of the church to double each year?

The secret of doubling church membership is outlined in the New Testament. God's plan is that church members will be converted Christians, and that under the power of the Holy Spirit they will share their faith each day.

God wants to use people like you and me to influence hundreds or thousands of people to become Christians. He has planned for us to move the world in this generation, too. "If Christians were to act in concert, moving forward as one, under the direction of one Power, for the accomplishment of one purpose, they would move the world."—*Testimonies,* vol. 9, p. 221.

It is a part of God's plan that everyone have the opportunity to accept Jesus Christ and to have eternal life. That is why Jesus died. God has provided the power for Christians to be witnesses in this world. With the power of the Holy Spirit in our lives, we can be used to influence men and women to choose the abundant life now and eternal life hereafter. God's plan, followed through with God's power, could result in millions of people being converted in a very short space of time.

We should also note the theme of the disciples' preaching. It is summarized in Acts 17:18—"Jesus, and the resurrection." Today the world needs to know about the Jesus who lived, died, and rose to be our mediator, and who is coming again as king.

POWER
Acts 18

SPACE TRAVEL AHEAD

Now a Jew named Apollos, a native of Alexandria, came to Ephesus. He was an eloquent man, well versed in the scriptures. Acts 18:24.

The Apollo 11 lunar module landed on the moon July 20, 1969, and Neil Armstrong and Edwin Aldrin stepped from the "Eagle" onto the flat, rocky surface of the Sea of Tranquillity. Astronaut Armstrong's words were heard all around the world: "It's one small step for man, one giant leap for mankind." Another statement, on a plaque attached to the landing portion of the spacecraft that was left on the moon, says: "Here men from the planet earth first set foot upon the moon July, 1969, A.D. We came in peace for all mankind."

Although only two men actually set foot on the moon that day, three names appear on the plaque. The third is Michael Collins, the pilot of the command module with which Apollo 11 had to link.

Although we may never walk on the moon, we can look forward to traveling in space past the moon to heaven itself. In the meantime we are to help people take that "small step" now that will ensure them of taking that "giant leap" into space. The small step is accepting Jesus as our personal Saviour. Those who take that step will one day land on heaven's Sea of Tranquillity.

We have noted that such men as Peter and Paul were mighty ministers whom God used to help many people reserve their place for space travel. However, just as there was a third astronaut piloting the Apollo command module, so there were many others who helped the apostles with their work. One of these was Apollos, who was baptized by John the Baptist.

The ministry of this little-known man was very important, as he has given us an example of how we can answer the question "How can I be sure that Jesus Christ is my Saviour, that He forgives my sins and gives me eternal life?" This preacher who worked behind the scenes showed from the Old Testament scriptures that Jesus Christ is the Saviour (see Acts 18:28).

POWER
Acts 19

A BIG BONFIRE

And a number of those who practiced magic arts brought their books together and burned them in the sight of all; and they counted the value of them and found it came to fifty thousand pieces of silver. Acts 19:19.

One piece of silver was a day's wages for most people in Paul's day. Fifty thousand pieces of silver, which were possibly Greek drachmas, was the value of the books that were burned in the big bonfire as a result of the preaching about Jesus in Ephesus.

Burning these books not only cost the people money but lost them the income they would have received from practicing their magic. They could have sold the books, but they were so convicted of the truth of Christianity that they did not want others to become involved in the magic arts.

Our decision to follow the Lord Jesus must also be accompanied by bonfires. We need to "burn" all those things that would foster love of the world and stop us from drawing nearer to Jesus. If we do not "burn" these things, we are making provision to return to what has separated us from God in the past. The monetary cost of destroying books, music, photographs, and drugs should not be considered, for if we had been following God's plan for our lives we would not have purchased them to begin with. Sometimes it is not a *thing* that needs to be burned, but a *desire,* a *habit,* or a *friendship* that must be stopped in order for us to progress in the Christian life.

When the people of Ephesus destroyed their books on magic and their silver idols, it meant that they were turning from their old lives and beginning again. And just as the silversmiths stirred up a riot in which Paul was almost killed, so we can be sure that Satan will make things difficult for us when we put him off the throne of our lives and give it back to its rightful owner, Jesus Christ.

Paul stayed in this second-largest city of the Roman Empire for three years. He not only taught but worked as a tentmaker to support himself and wrote the first letter to the Corinthians from there. The account of this, Paul's third tour, is recorded in Acts 18:23 through Acts 21:17.

POWER
Acts 20

"I AM . . . A LITTLE PENCIL"

"But I do not account my life of any value nor as precious to myself, if only I may accomplish my course and the ministry which I received from the Lord Jesus, to testify to the gospel of the grace of God." Acts 20:24.

The Swedish chemist who invented dynamite became very rich. Before he died, however, he became concerned that dynamite would be used in wars. Since this was not his intention, he formulated a plan to encourage peace. He established a fund of about $9 million and stipulated that the interest on this fund was to be used to award annual prizes for people who promoted peace among the nations. The scientist was Alfred Bernhard Nobel, who died in 1896. And the prize he established is known as the Nobel Prize.

In 1979 this coveted prize was awarded to a five-foot, 69-year-old Yugoslavian woman, the daughter of a grocer. She was the first Roman Catholic ever to receive this award, and her name is now known by people in most countries of the world.

The $192,000 award and medal were presented to Mother Teresa, a humble nun, in recognition of her work in the slums of Calcutta, India, and her supervision of her missionaries and charities. These missionaries—1,800 nuns, 275 brothers, and 120,000 volunteers—minister to the poor, sick, and dying in 31 countries. One of Mother Teresa's missions has been to establish a home for the dying. She has rescued hundreds of people from the streets and given them love and attention in a rest home. The Nobel Prize money, along with the funds that would have been spent on a banquet in her honor, has been given to her work.

Mother Teresa shuns publicity and does not seek credit. A summary of her life reminds us of the words of Paul in our text today. This modern missionary says, "No one thinks of the pen while reading a letter. They only want to know the mind of the person who wrote the letter. That's exactly what I am in God's hands, a little pencil. God is writing His love letter to the world in this way through works of love."

God wants us to be "little pencils" in His hand too. If we place our lives in His hand, there is no limit to our usefulness.

POWER
Acts 21

PURE, KIND, AND TRUE

Then Paul answered, "What are you doing, weeping and breaking my heart? For I am ready not only to be imprisoned but even to die at Jerusalem for the name of the Lord Jesus." Acts 21:13.

Angelina lives in the tiny mountainous country of Lesotho. Her home village is Mokhotlong, but I first met her at the Maluti Mission Hospital near the South African border. She was baptized January 24, 1970, and, despite difficulties, told me, "I want to do God's will no matter what others say. I want to have courage no matter what comes my way. In spite of all the difficulties I may have, I want to be a true Christian."

This nurse's beautiful statement of loyalty reminds me of Paul's statement of steadfast purpose that is our Morning Watch verse for today. Paul's statement was similar to the one made by Peter before his denial of Jesus, " 'Though they all fall away because of you, I will never fall away' " (Matt. 26:33, R.S.V.). However, there was a difference, because Peter's boast was that of self-assurance, whereas Paul's came from the depth of experience. Paul had already proved that he could bear things for the Lord Jesus. He had been imprisoned for his faith and had been stoned by a mob and left for dead. Both Peter and Paul loved the Master, but Peter, at that stage of his life, was talking from feeling rather than from conviction. If like Paul we have fully submitted our lives to the Lord Jesus, we too will be true.

Paul's third missionary journey must have been a trying experience for him, for at every place when he said farewell to his friends, he knew it was the last time he would see them. The closing part of his tour took him from Greece to Troas and back to Ephesus. After he had preached to the elders at Ephesus (Acts 20:18-35), they "wept and embraced Paul and kissed him" (verse 37, R.S.V.). Sailing across the blue Mediterranean, he arrived at Caesarea, where he stayed in the house of Philip the evangelist. These were Paul's last days of freedom.

Like Mother Teresa in our reading for yesterday, Paul was literally "a little pencil" in God's hand. During this missionary tour he wrote 1 Corinthians at Ephesus, 2 Corinthians at Macedonia, and Galatians and Romans at Corinth.

POWER
Acts 22

AMBASSADOR ARRESTED

" 'The God of our fathers appointed you to know his will, to see the Just One and to hear a voice from his mouth.' " Acts 22:14.

The ambassador was arrested. However, he reminded the guard who rescued him from the mob that he was a citizen of Rome and asked to talk to the people from the steps of the Roman castle where Pilate had condemned Jesus just twenty-eight years before. He told them the story of Jesus in eloquent words, and when they heard him speaking in the Hebrew language they listened carefully.

Prior to his conversion Paul had been ignorant of God's will for his life. He had been a religious man, but he had not given his life into God's hands. The statement recorded in the text for today shows that on the Damascus road, Paul saw Jesus and accepted the invitation to be His ambassador. An ambassador is one who represents his king or president in another country, and that is just what Paul did.

Today we have the privilege of being ambassadors for Jesus on this earth, and we need to have the same courage of our convictions that Paul demonstrated.

The mob listened to Paul intently until he declared that the gospel was to go to the Gentiles. They couldn't accept that people other than Jews could find salvation, and they regarded Paul as a traitor.

The next day Paul was taken by the Roman soldiers to the Jewish council that had voted to crucify Jesus. He had once been a member of this council, and some of its current members knew him very well. Now he stood before them in chains. At this moment he no doubt remembered the promise that he had made at Caesarea, "For I am ready not to be bound only, but also to die at Jerusalem for the name of the Lord Jesus."

As Paul stood before his former associates, he had peace because before he became a prisoner of the Romans he had become a voluntary prisoner of the Lord.

As strange as it may seem, it is true that when we become prisoners of the Lord, we have freedom; when we surrender our lives to Jesus, we are victorious.

POWER
Acts 23

QUEER-RELIGION MAN

And Paul, looking intently at the council, said, "Brethren, I have lived before God in all good conscience up to this day." Acts 23:1.

Only one of three thousand youth at the first mass meeting refused to sign the oath stating that he would "kill, kill, kill the enemy." Although he stood alone, he also refused to work on Sabbath. So he was locked in a cold, damp prison room with no food or blankets. He wrote, "Though my stomach cramped from hunger and my body was numb from cold, I was able to feel glorious inside by singing praises to my Maker."

Although there were many attempts to break his faith, he, like Paul, remained true to his beliefs. This young man was the first Seventh-day Adventist youth in his country to be drafted into the army. He was tall, athletic, and a very good student. From prison he wrote to two pastors, who visited the commanding officer of the military camp. Their conversation with him went something like this:

"Why did you lock this boy up? Is he a bad boy?" "No, he is a good boy."

"How is his deportment?" "Perfect."

"How are his drills on the parade ground?" "The best."

"How are his grades?" "The highest."

"Does he get along with others?" "The men like him."

"You yourself have said what a fine person he is. Why do you treat him like a criminal for refusing to violate his conscience?"

The commanding officer finally asked the boy, who had no rank, whether it would be all right for him to stay in the barracks over Sabbath with food and a Bible.

Later this young man wrote, "Two nicknames were given to me—Sabbath Warrior and Queer-Religion Man. . . .

"Finally came graduation exercises, and the son of the president of the country was present to make the awards. Before the audience of three thousand people he pinned the highest medal of honor on my breast for the best grades. Those who looked on me with scorn now held a child of God in high esteem! Praise our unfailing Father in heaven."

64

POWER
Acts 24

BUILT-IN RADAR!

"So I always take pains to have a clear conscience toward God and toward men." Acts 24:16.

Radar devices send out pulses of radio waves that travel at 186,282 miles per second. The electronic equipment measures the time of the radio wave post to go out to an object and return as an echo. We use light waves to see, but radar uses radio waves. Radar can therefore "see" through rain, snow, clouds, and darkness, enabling planes to land even in storms or at night. The name *radar* comes from the phrase Radio, Detection, and Ranging.

You and I have a built-in radar called conscience. Prayer and Bible study enable us to send out "radio waves" and receive an "echo" back from heaven. The conscience is a safety device whereby we can "see" through the darkness and know what God wants us to do. One writer describes this sense of right and wrong this way: "Conscience is a sharp, three-cornered thing inside me. When I do wrong, it turns around and hurts me. But if I keep doing wrong, it will turn so much that the corners become worn off, and it doesn't hurt anymore."

Paul told the council that he had a good conscience. This was a very bold claim, but Paul knew that by God's power he had lived according to His revealed will. In his writings Paul often refers to the conscience. In today's text he claimed he had a "clean conscience."

In the New Testament (K.J.V.) the word *conscience* appears thirty-one times. We can find out more about conscience by studying the texts where the word is used. You can find a list of these in a concordance.

The book *The Acts of the Apostles,* by Ellen G. White, a commentary on the book of Acts, includes this statement: "In the great crisis through which they are soon to pass, the faithful servants of God will encounter the same hardness of heart, the same cruel determination, the same unyielding hatred. All who in that evil day would fearlessly serve God according to the dictates of conscience, will need courage, firmness, and a knowledge of God and His word; for those who are true to God will be persecuted."—Page 431.

POWER
Acts 25

"KEEP A LEVEL EYE"

Paul said in his defense, "Neither against the law of the Jews, nor against the temple, nor against Caesar have I offended at all." Acts 25:8.

Johnny stood at the gate longing to go in and see the film all the boys had been talking about. A man noticed and said, "If you would like to go in, I will pay for you." Johnny replied that his father had told him he could not go to see this particular film. The man then told Johnny that he would go in with him, and his father would not know anything about it. The boy's conscience would not allow him to go in, and in a simple, childlike way he said, "If I go in, I shall not be able to look my father in the face tonight." This is a good test of our conscience—Are we able to look God and man in the face?

Paul, at his second trial, once again stated that he had a clear conscience. This time, as stated in our text, he had not done anything against the law of the Jews, the house of worship, or the Roman Empire. He was able to look them in the eye and declare his innocence of the charges that they had brought against him in all three areas. This statement concerning his conscience was made under trying circumstances. He had been a prisoner for two years, and this second trial was before the new governor, Festus.

Festus was convinced of Paul's innocence, but he still planned to give him to the Jews to be put to death. It was at this point that Paul stated, "I appeal to Caesar." This meant that, as a Roman citizen, he would go to Rome to be tried.

Everyone who claims to be a Christian should be able, with Paul, to say that he or she has a clear conscience toward God and toward men. As we repeat the phrase in the Pathfinder Law that says "Keep a level eye," we are reminded of the example of Paul and pray for the power that enabled him to have a clear conscience.

"There are only a few things heavier than lead, and one of them is a guilty conscience." God has provided the power so that we don't have to carry that weight. We can always be confident that all is right between ourselves and God and others. We can "keep a level eye."

POWER
Acts 26

THE PREACHER IN CHAINS

"I would to God that not only you but also all who hear me this day might become such as I am—except for these chains." Acts 26:29.

The trumpet sounded and the royal guests entered, dressed in brightly colored robes adorned with gold, silver, and precious stones. The soldiers' weapons glistened in the sunlight as the king took his place on the throne and all bowed to him.

In front of this group of important people stood a small, aged prisoner in worn clothes. There were shackles on his feet, and his right arm was chained to the arm of a soldier. It was evident that he had suffered privation, but his face showed that he had an inner peace.

The king on the throne was Herod Agrippa II, the last of the Herods. Sixteen years earlier his father had killed the disciple James; before that, his great-uncle had killed John the Baptist and mocked Jesus; and his great-grandfather had slaughtered the children at the birth of Jesus.

In reply to Agrippa's statement "Almost thou persuadest me to be a Christian" (Acts 26:28), Paul made his last appeal, which is our text for today. The wicked king had been deeply affected by Paul's conversion story and personal plea, and for a moment he even considered becoming a Christian.

Paul's reply to Agrippa is one of the most beautiful statements in Scripture. The love of Paul stands in sharp contrast to the lust of Agrippa, Bernice, and Festus. He prays not only that they would accept Christ, but that everyone in the courtroom would choose eternal life.

Perhaps only two other scenes in the New Testament are more touching to the human heart than is this one. They are both similar in setting—Christ standing before Herod and later before Pilate. In these three scenes in Roman judgment halls we see Christianity at its finest. We see that the Christian life has far more to offer than does all the pomp, power, and pleasure of this world.

Let us also determine to be true Christians. And let us pray for the power to reveal the light of the Christian life.

POWER
Acts 27

PREACHER IN A STORM

There a centurion found a ship of Alexandria sailing for Italy, and put us on board. Acts 27:6.

Every ship's captain keeps a record of daily events in what is known as a logbook. It would certainly be interesting to read the logbooks of the ships on which Paul sailed on his voyage to Rome, beginning in A.D. 60. However, Acts 27 and 28 contain a record of the journey that, in many parts, reads like a ship's logbook.

The captain of the large Alexandrian ship on which Paul sailed for the final stage of his voyage decided not to stay in Fair Havens, but to continue the journey. Winter was approaching, and Paul, when asked for his opinion, told the officers that if they were to go on, the ship would sink.

As soon as the south winds began to blow, however, the ship sailed out into the Mediterranean Sea and along the coast of Crete. Soon a fierce storm arose, and they had to throw cargo overboard to stay afloat. No one could rest, for all available hands had to work the pumps. There was no means for cooking, and food had been washed overboard. The men were soon very hungry in their slowly sinking ship.

After fourteen days of this, there was a lull in the storm, and Paul announced that God had shown him that, although the ship was going to sink, there would be no loss of life. You can imagine the shouts of joy, for the men respected Paul's word. Paul too was pleased, for he wanted to have the opportunity of presenting Jesus Christ at Rome.

The ship finally ran aground on the island of Malta. Those in charge wanted to kill the prisoners so they would not escape. However, Julius, the centurion, knew that Paul had helped them in the emergency, so the prisoners were allowed to swim to shore.

Paul and the others were on Malta for three months. During that time he had many opportunities to preach, and as a result the Christian faith was introduced on the island. Again we see that if we are true to God, all things will "work together for good." God can take the shipwrecks of our lives and make them into blessings.

POWER
Acts 28

THE UNFINISHED BOOK

And he lived there two whole years at his own expense, and welcomed all who came to him, preaching the kingdom of God and teaching about the Lord Jesus Christ quite openly and unhindered. Acts 28:30, 31.

Acts is the only unfinished book in the Bible. The last two verses, which are our text for today, reveal how abruptly it ends. Luke did not record what happened to Paul during his two years in Rome. However, there are references to those years in Epistles written by the apostle—Ephesians, Philippians, Colossians, and Philemon. Although at first Paul had freedom to preach, we find from his writings that he also suffered.

Many of Paul's former companions, including Luke, were with him. Others mentioned are Timothy, Tychicus, Demas, and Mark. Paul was not able to visit the churches as he had done previously. However, while awaiting trial he influenced many for the kingdom, including some in Nero's palace (see Phil. 1:13). "Not by Paul's sermons, but by his bonds, was the attention of the court attracted to Christianity. . . . Paul's patience and cheerfulness during his long and unjust imprisonment, his courage and faith, were a continual sermon."—*The Acts of the Apostles, p. 464.*

The main reason why the book of Acts is incomplete is not because Luke did not finish writing the story. It is an unfinished book because it is the story of a Person who is still alive. The power of the apostles' preaching was the resurrection of Christ. And that prevented anyone from finishing the book of Acts.

A Christian stood among thousands of people who were watching the burial of the bones of one of the leaders of an Eastern religion. He turned to the person next to him and said, "If they could find the bones of Jesus Christ, Christianity would die." No one can find the bones of our Saviour, for Jesus was resurrected and ascended to heaven. He is our mediator and judge, and soon He is coming back as our king.

The book of Acts, like all the books of the Bible, is centered in a *Person*—God the Son. He has given to His church *power*—God the Holy Spirit. With that power the followers of Jesus are to take the Advent message to all the world in this generation.

69

PLAN
Genesis 1

BOOK OF BEGINNINGS

In the beginning God created the heavens and the earth.
Genesis 1:1.

The title of the first book of the Bible—Genesis—in the Greek means "origin" or "source." Genesis is the first book that records God's revelation to mankind. Jews and Christians believe that Moses, guided by the Spirit of God, wrote the book of Genesis. It is written in narrative, or story, style, and as you read the whole book or selected chapters according to the Bible Reading Plan listed in the contents of this book, it will inspire and confirm your faith.

Genesis falls naturally into two main divisions. Part one (chapters 1-11) is a very brief but comprehensive history of the world from Creation to the Tower of Babel, and part two (chapters 12-50) outlines the story of Abraham and his descendants, to the death of his great-grandson Joseph. The beginnings that are covered in the Book of Beginnings include: The world, the human race, the Sabbath, marriage, sin and death, grace, man-made civilizations, nations of the world, and the Hebrew race.

Genesis covers at least two thousand years of history, but it is not intended as a comprehensive history and we must not get lost in its details. It is intended to help us believe in God. You will note that there are only two chapters that deal with the account of the creation of the world and of man. It is significant to note that there are only two alternatives for the origins of this world and its inhabitants. One explanation is stated in the first four words of the Bible, "In the beginning God." The other alternative, although not stated in these words, can also be summarized in four words: "In the beginning nothing." Both explanations of the origin of the world require faith, but it takes less faith to believe "In the beginning God."

Although Adam and Eve sinned and were unable to stay in the beautiful Garden of Eden, God's love is such that He gave them a second chance and has made provision for us to live in a restored Eden. In Genesis there is a record of many things lost, but praise God, in Revelation they are all restored to those who choose to love and obey God.

70

PLAN
Genesis 2

ROOTS

Then the Lord God formed man of dust from the ground, and breathed into his nostrils the breath of life; and man became a living being. Genesis 2:7.

Alex Haley's book *Roots* became a best seller soon after it was released. It is the story of a man's search to learn about his family. After years of seeking, this American black found a remote village in Gambia that had been the home of his great-grandparents. The story of his search was also made into a fourteen-hour television film. It is estimated that 130 million people in America watched "Roots" in 1977.

I have been interested in, and have searched for, information on my roots. Thus far I have traced my family back to Dalzell Castle in Scotland. It was exciting to go through the rooms of this large, uninhabited castle, and to learn of the underground tunnel that connects it with another edifice.

Most people are interested in their ancestors, and some have drawn family trees showing relationships that go back hundreds of years. When we discover an ancestor who was famous, we like to tell people about that person. However, when we find a pirate or someone who spent time in jail, we are not so eager to speak of our roots.

It seems strange that some people today, known as evolutionists, seem eager to prove that their roots go back to animals or blobs of life. An internationally known magazine recently published a story on man that did not include any reference to Adam and Eve. The authors explained that they did not think children would miss Adam and Eve, since churches have little to say about them anyway.

Your roots and mine are clearly stated in the Book of Beginnings. Adam, the first man, was created when God gave him the breath of life. Eve was created from a rib taken from Adam's side during the first operation.

God could have created Adam and Eve in other ways, but this method has special significance. In the first chapter of Genesis, we note that we were created "in the image of God." This is exciting because it shows that our roots go back to our heavenly Father.

PLAN
Genesis 3

TWELVE FEET TALL

"I will put enmity between you and the woman, and between your seed and her seed; he shall bruise your head, and you shall bruise his heel." Genesis 3:15.

Can you imagine a man who was more than twice as tall as men now living on the earth and very well-proportioned? Can you imagine a woman whose head reached a little above this man's shoulders? These are descriptions of Adam and Eve as given in the book *The Story of Redemption,* by Ellen White.

Adam lived with his beautiful companion in a perfect environment and communed with God face to face. Despite this, he failed what we believe to be the very first test of obedience that came to him. Jesus, who has been called "the second Adam," came to this world and was subjected to the sin, death, and disease of thousands of years, yet lived victoriously. Jesus endured temptation by the devil in the wilderness, and was conqueror.

A comparison of the two Adams reveals to us that we cannot blame our heredity or our environment for our actions. It is possible for us, through the strength of Jesus Christ, to be victorious. We must not hide behind excuses as Adam and Eve did. When tempted, we need to say, as Jesus did, "It is written." This is why we need to know the person, purposes, plan, power, promises, and prophecies of the Bible. This is why we need to observe the Morning Watch and each day read at least one chapter. Someone has said that an apple a day keeps the doctor away; a minister has added to this, "A chapter a day keeps the devil away!"

The first Messianic prophecy is recorded in Genesis 3:15. It simply means that from that day on, there would be a separation between the devil, who is described as the serpent, and God's church, which is described as a woman. There would also be a conflict between the followers of Satan and the members of the church down through the ages. However, there would be victory because Christ, although wounded on the heel at the cross, would ultimately destroy Satan by crushing his head. This is the first of thirty-seven prophecies that I know of, written hundreds of years in advance, stating that Jesus would be the Redeemer of this world.

PLAN
Genesis 4

COME BY CHANCE

To Seth also a son was born, and he called his name Enosh. At that time men began to call upon the name of the Lord. Genesis 4:26.

While serving as dean of men at Avondale College in Australia, I traveled through the outback of western New South Wales with a group of young men, collecting funds for missions. We camped out under the stars, saw lots of kangaroos and emus, and bathed in warm mineral springs.

One day as we studied the map we noticed that we were approaching a place called Come by Chance. The name aroused our curiosity, so we inquired about its origin. It appears that in the early days when the area was being settled, there was a rush for land. Two families without claims came by chance to this part of the country and both settled here.

As I drove out of the settlement, I thought about the name and the story behind it. Several lessons came to my mind. Although we may "come by chance" on land and possessions in this life, it is certain that we cannot secure for ourselves a place in God's kingdom in this way. The heavenly land is a prepared place for a prepared people, and we have to do our preparing right now. Briefly stated, in order to enter the kingdom of God we have to "call upon the name of the Lord." This means we need to choose to believe as did the sons of Seth.

Those who discovered the unsettled area around the township of Come by Chance were pleased with their find. They considered themselves fortunate to have come by chance on land suitable for farming. Likewise, junior youth who have chosen Christ rejoice in the discovery of a heavenly land that is prepared for them. The Scriptures reveal this to be a place far better than anyone could imagine or describe.

The settlers of Come by Chance were traveling when they made their discovery. Had they settled down and given up hope of finding land, they never would have improved their lot. So we need to remember that we are pilgrims bound for a better land. We are not to settle down to the pleasures and pastimes of this world but, like Abraham, we are to seek "a city . . . whose builder and maker is God."

HE LIVED 969 YEARS

This is the book of the generations of Adam. When God created man, he made him in the likeness of God. Genesis 5:1.

How would you like to live on this earth for 969 years? Can you name the man who did, and also his father? The father must have been a very godly man, because in two verses of Genesis 5 it says that he "walked with God." "The generations of Adam" record the names of the first son, or patriarch, of each family, and the age when each had his first son.

There are ten patriarchs listed here. It would be good for you to learn their names and the order in which they were born: Adam, Seth, Enos, Cainan, Mahalaleel, Jared, Enoch, Methuselah, Lamech, and Noah. The man who is recorded as having "walked with God" was seventh from Adam, and he was translated to heaven at 365 years of age. His son lived the longest of any man on earth. However, you'll notice that there were six others mentioned who lived for more than 900 years, including Adam and Noah.

Would you like to do some Bible mathematics and discover an important date? If so, let's go! Write down the names of the ten patriarchs in order, and then from the information supplied, write down the age of each when his first son was born. If you add up that list it should come to 1,556. That is the number of years from Creation to the birth of Noah's first son. Now let's find out how many years it was from Creation to the Flood. If we follow the Bible principle of comparing scripture with scripture, we will find the answer. In Genesis 7:6 it says that Noah was 600 years old at the time of the Flood. That means that if we add 100 years to our total, we will find the number of years from the Creation to the Flood.

Although not everyone likes math as such, many enjoy Bible mathematics. From these lists of genealogies we can learn facts that will help us to understand God's plan. However, we must not get lost in details. It is more important to "walk with God" than to calculate dates or the age of the earth. If we walk with God, we will live more than 969 years. That's exciting to think about, isn't it?

PLAN
Genesis 6

7,000 ANIMALS ABOARD

These are the generations of Noah. Noah was a righteous man, blameless in his generation; Noah walked with God. Genesis 6:9.

Someone has estimated from the information given in the Bible that there was enough space in Noah's ark for about seven thousand animals, besides the thousands of birds, reptiles, and insects. It was certainly one of the largest ancient cargo ships of which we have record. The dimensions as given in today's chapter are 515 feet long, 86 feet wide, and 52 feet high.

Although it is interesting to know these facts and figures about the ark, it is more important to know why God sent the Flood on the earth and what lessons we can learn from this event. The reason for the Flood is summarized in Genesis 6:5: "And God saw that the wickedness of man was great in the earth, and that every imagination of the thoughts of his heart was only evil continually." In the preceding verses it says that there were two distinct classes of people. There were the sons of God, the descendants of Seth, and the daughters of men, the descendants of the godless Cain.

Naturally, God was very displeased that His people were marrying godless people. The people had forgotten God, and there were very few righteous ones remaining. It was God's plan to give the human race another chance, so He cleansed the world with a flood.

Just as God warned the people before the Flood, so He has warned us about what is going to happen. Jesus Himself predicted that just before He comes the second time, wickedness would be so bad in this world that it would be like the days of Noah (Matt. 24:37-39).

We are living in those days when even the imaginations of people's minds are evil and they have hardly any restraints. No longer is God revered, even in countries that claim to be Christian. However, there are those in each land who, like Noah, have "found favor in the eyes of the Lord" (Gen. 6:8, R.S.V.). You'll notice that Noah, like Enoch, "walked with God" (verse 9). This is why he was saved with his household, who also repented. We need to be sure that we are walking with God.

PLAN
Genesis 7

THE DOOR TO LIFE

They went into the ark with Noah, two and two of all flesh in which there was the breath of life. And they that entered, male and female of all flesh, went in as God had commanded him; and the Lord shut him in. Genesis 7:15, 16.

For 120 years Noah had invited people to enter the ark when it should be completed. There was only one door, and all who wanted to live had to enter through it. Noah's ark is a perfect example of Jesus, who is our ark of safety. The ark was God's plan for the people who wanted to start life again, and the cross of Calvary is God's plan for those of us who want an abundant life now and eternal life hereafter. Jesus was represented not only by the ark but also by the door. He said, "'I am the door; if any one enters by me, he will be saved'" (John 10:9, R.S.V.).

Can you imagine Noah, who was by then 600 years old, and his sons and their wives helping in the last-minute preparations to get the thousands of animals, birds, reptiles, and insects aboard? Obeying God's command, the animals were guided by angels into the ark. He also has planted in men and women a desire for eternal life, but He has left them the power of choice. And all except eight of those living at the time of the Flood then chose to reject the invitation to go "into the ark."

The statement that "the Lord shut him in" tells us again that God was in control of this whole operation. The closing of the door meant that the time of invitation had ended and those who were outside would be destroyed. On the eighth day after the door was closed, heavy rains began to fall and water burst from the earth and covered the entire surface of the earth. The ark was saved from destruction in the storm because of Christ's work for those who believed in Him. "It was Christ who kept the ark safe amid the roaring, seething billows, because its inmates had faith in His power to preserve them."—*The SDA Bible Commentary,* Ellen G. White Comments, on Gen. 7:21-23, p. 1091.

The fact that the ark was saved is more important than the details of the Flood, for it shows us once again God's constant care for those who trust in Him. However, we must realize that He can save only those who choose to be saved.

76

PLAN
Genesis 8

NOAH'S AAA

But God remembered Noah and all the beasts and all the
cattle that were with him in the ark.... The ark came to rest upon
the mountains of Ararat. Genesis 8:1-4.
Then Noah built an altar to the Lord. Verse 20.

When those of you who live in the United States see the
letters AAA, you probably think of the American Automobile
Association. However, there were three important *A*'s in Noah's
life that had nothing to do with cars. They are mentioned in our
texts today—ark, Ararat, and altar.

Many people today do not believe that the first ship we have
any record of was Noah's ark. However, the Bible contains the
story of the Flood, mentioning it in both the Old and New
Testaments (see 2 Peter 3:5-7; Luke 17:26). Then, too, we find
the story of Noah's ark in the history of many nations and areas,
including India, China, and South America.

The Chinese language uses pictures to represent words. The
picture for ship is a boat with eight mouths on the side, each
symbolizing a person. Remember, there were eight people in
Noah's ark.

There is a mountain called Ararat that is between the Black
and Caspian seas and overlooks Turkey, Iran, and Russia. It is
difficult to climb because it is almost 17,000 feet high and is
always covered with snow. It is also difficult to get permission to
explore in that area. Several attempts have been made to climb
Mount Ararat to see whether Noah's ark is there, and some
explorers and evangelists claim that they have seen the outline
of a big boat under the snow.

The day the ark settled on dry ground on the mountains of
Ararat must have been exciting for Noah and his family. They
were probably eager to explore their new home, but the first
thing Noah did when he put his feet on the soil was to build "an
altar unto the Lord." And the first thing we need to do as we put
our feet on the floor each morning is to pray. Just as Noah
worshiped the Lord at his first opportunity, so we need to seize
every occasion we can to worship God. We also need to establish
family altars in our homes.

77

PLAN
Genesis 9

THE FIRST RAINBOW

"I set my bow in the cloud, and it shall be a sign of the covenant between me and the earth." Genesis 9:13.

How many colors are there in a rainbow? Can you name them? A rainbow has violet, indigo blue, green, yellow, orange, and red all blended together. There are lots of stories about pots of gold being at the end of rainbows, but we know that no matter how fast we were to run or how far we were to fly, we could never find the end of the rainbow.

The very first rainbow to appear in the sky was the one that Noah and his family saw after they left the ark and were standing on the dry ground of Mount Ararat. They had been in the ark a year and ten days, a long time to spend on board a ship. After they worshiped at an altar that Noah built, the Lord told them the earth would never again be destroyed by water, and as a reminder of this promise, He gave them the rainbow.

However, the rainbow is more than just a promise, for it represents God's love, which is felt in every part of the world at all times. In some parts of Central Europe a rainbow is called "the bridge of the Holy Spirit." When we see the rainbow, we can remember that, just as a bridge links places together, so the Holy Spirit is the bridge that links God and man.

A little more than 70 percent of the surface of our globe is covered with water. It has been calculated that if the surface of the earth were leveled out, our world would be completely covered with water more than one and one-half miles deep. Think of it! Nine thousand feet of water over the entire surface of the earth! That certainly is enough for a flood, isn't it?

Although there is enough water to have another worldwide flood, God has said that there will not be another one. He has also stated that the earth will be cleansed by fire after the Second Advent. This is so that all traces of sin can be removed and we can live again on this earth in a perfect state. We will read about these events when we study the prophecies during the month of June.

78

PLAN
Genesis 10

6 BILLION FROM 6

*These are the generations of the sons of Noah, Shem, Ham,
and Japheth; sons were born to them after the flood. Genesis 10:1.*

It is estimated that there will be more than 6 billion people in
the world by the year 2000. Nobody but God knows how many
have lived on the earth since the Flood, which happened 1,656
years after Creation. However, we do know that these billions
and trillions of people are all descendants of six people.
Everyone who has lived since the days of Noah will one day be
able to trace his or her roots back to one of Noah's three sons. I'm
eager to trace my family back to Noah, aren't you?

Shem, Ham, and Japheth were born before the Flood, and
their names have special meaning. Japheth's name means
"beauty" or "expansion." His descendants expanded their
territories, and his seven sons and their descendants moved
north of Palestine and Asia Minor into what is now known as
Europe.

Shem's name means "fame." He did become famous, because
his descendants were the Hebrews and Jesus was born into this
line.

The name of the youngest son, Ham, means "hot." Ham had
four sons, and from his son Cush came Nimrod, who is especially
mentioned as "the first on earth to be a mighty man." One thing
Nimrod did was to build the first city after the Flood.

This list of descendants and where they settled may seem dry
to you, however, there are important lessons for us to learn from
it. Noah's sons were commanded to repopulate the world. As
long as they followed the Lord, they lived together peaceably.
But bloodshed and division came soon after some tribes forgot
God.

Although new races appeared, along with different-colored
skin and different physical features, Genesis 10 clearly teaches
that no tribe or nation is superior to another. As we read this
chapter we are reminded that we are all of one family, for we
have all descended from the family of Noah. This is an
important truth found in Scripture.

PLAN
Genesis 11

BEGINNING OF NATIONS

Therefore its name was called Babel, because there the Lord confused the language of all the earth; and from there the Lord scattered them abroad over the face of all the earth. Genesis 11:9.

It is sad to read in the Bible that very soon after the earth was repopulated, most of its inhabitants did not walk with God. Instead of building altars and worshiping their Creator, they built a great Tower of Babel to show their rebellion against Him. The first two large cities, Nineveh and Babylon, were founded by a man named Nimrod. But there are other cities also mentioned in Genesis 10. Egypt was occupied and named by one of Ham's descendants soon after the Flood.

Prior to the building of the Tower of Babel, "the whole earth was of one language" (Gen. 11:1); but it did not have one God. In God's mercy, however, He did not immediately destroy the wicked again. "So the Lord scattered them abroad from there over the face of all the earth, and they left off building the city." Because they could not understand one another, the people had to divide into smaller groups.

As a result, everyone scattered, and the people began to speak new languages and dialects. Today there are more than three thousand of them. Many men and women have attempted to unite the nations, but they will never be united again until Jesus is crowned King of kings and Lord of lords after His second advent.

In the remaining part of chapter 11 are other interesting listings of generations. More Bible math shows us that one of God's special men was born 2,008 years after Creation. Yes, twenty generations after Creation God found a man who was willing to follow His plan and do His will. This man's name was first Abram, later changed to Abraham, and he was to become the father of a mighty nation.

Ever since Adam's day God has had men and women who were prepared to love and serve Him fully. Conditions today are similar to those that led to the destruction of the earth by water and to the apostasy at the Tower of Babel. However, there are still those on every continent and on many islands who let the *light, love,* and *life* of Jesus flow through in blessing to others.

80

PLAN
Genesis 12

ABRAHAM LEAVES HOME

Now the Lord said to Abram, "Go from your country and your kindred and your father's house to the land that I will show you. And I will make of you a great nation, and I will bless you, and make your name great, so that you will be a blessing." Genesis 12:1, 2.

When Abraham was 75 years of age, God asked him to leave his home and his country and everything that was familiar to him. Adding 75 years to 2,008, we see that this happened 2,083 years from Creation. Abraham's act of faith must have been a real joy to God, who centered the master plan of redemption on this man. There is a sevenfold promise given to Abraham, but the key statement is "and in thee shall all families of the earth be blessed" (Gen. 12:3). Not only does this statement promise that Abraham was to be the first Israelite, the leader of a great nation whose heirs were to inherit the land of Canaan, but it recalls the promise made to Adam and Eve in the Garden of Eden that one day the Messiah would come.

As we turn to the genealogies of the New Testament, we see that Jesus did come through the line of the twenty patriarchs and Abraham and his descendants. After leaving Ur of the Chaldees, Abraham traveled six hundred miles northwest and stopped at Haran. He then traveled on into the land of Canaan. Like Noah, the first thing he did was to build an altar to God and worship Him. Just as these men of the Old Testament worshiped God morning and evening, so His followers should do the same today. This is how we keep in touch with Him, renew our decision to serve Him, and give praise and thanks.

A famine in the land of Canaan forced Abraham to go down into Egypt, where he was given a severe test of faith. Although he failed the test of complete honesty in his statements to the Pharaoh, God overruled so that He could still work out His plan through Abraham. Into the lives of each of us come experiences where we must go "down into Egypt" to be tested. We note from the experience of Abraham that we must not tell half-truths. We must be sure that every statement we make to God and to others is completely correct. Time has proved that "honesty is the best policy."

PLAN
Genesis 13

LOT'S UNWISE CHOICE

The Lord said to Abram, after Lot had separated from him,
"Lift up your eyes, and look from the place where you are, . . . for
all the land which you see I will give to you. . . . I will make your
descendants as the dust of the earth." Genesis 13:14-16.

Do you think you would have made the same choice that
Abraham's nephew Lot did? He had traveled with his uncle from
Ur, and now there was a problem because food and water were
scarce for their animals, and their herdsmen quarreled about it.
Abraham first made an appeal for peace, saying, "Let there be
no strife, I pray thee, between me and thee, and between my
herdmen and thy herdmen; for we be brethren" (Gen. 13:8).
Even though we may have certain "rights," we should, like
Abraham, do all that we can to have peace.

Uncle Abraham gave Lot his choice of living either on the
plain of Jordan, which was very fertile and well watered, or in
the land of Canaan. Lot's choice, the best for himself, proved
unwise. In the first place he did not show the respect he should
have to his uncle, who had provided for him on the journey. It
was also unwise for him to separate from Abraham, as we will
see in our story tomorrow. Then, too, he made a very bad
mistake in moving toward the wicked cities of Sodom and
Gomorrah.

Each day we should pray for God's guidance in making wise
decisions. Lot was not a careless man; he was a good man. But he
did not take everything into account when he chose the best
pastures for himself. We must learn that in all decisions of life,
such as choosing our friends, our lifework, et cetera, we are
making decisions that affect the future. Lot did not gain
happiness from his choice. Instead, he reaped terrible consequences within his family.

Perhaps we could summarize his choice in the statement "All
that glitters is not gold." In other words, we must not make
decisions purely on the basis of present appearance. Rather, we
must examine every decision carefully and make it in the light
of its effect on our future life. Remember, little choices
determine habits, which mold character and influence our big
decisions.

82

PLAN
Genesis 14

THE RESCUE OF LOT

But Abram said to the king of Sodom, "I have sworn to the Lord God Most High, maker of heaven and earth." Genesis 14:22.

Remember that Lot selfishly chose the best land near the cities of Sodom and Gomorrah and left his uncle the poorer pastures. So it is amazing to note that Abraham rescued him when he was taken captive. If you had been Abraham, would you have rescued Lot? If the love of the Lord was in your heart, as it was in Abraham's, you would have. It is also significant to note that Abraham would not take any of the spoil. He told the king of Sodom that he would not even take a shoelace, because it did not belong to him.

This man of God also paid a tenth of his increase as a tithe (Gen. 14:20). This is one of the first references to tithe paying, which God had instituted long before there was a nation, in order that the priests, or ministers, might be able to work full time for the Lord. The priest to whom Abraham paid his tithe, Melchizedek, was also a king. His name means "king of righteousness," "king of Salem," and "king of peace."

Salem is probably an abbreviated form of Jerusalem. So this man was both king of Jerusalem and priest of God. Since he had this dual office and his life was apparently one that revealed the light and love of God, he is set forth as a type of Christ. Jesus is declared to be a priest after the order of Melchizedek. (See Ps. 110:4; Heb. 5:10; 6:20-7:3.)

The Bible and the Spirit of Prophecy teach that the Melchizedek order of the priesthood was not to be superseded by another. This is why Jesus Christ, our High Priest, is represented as being a high priest after the order of Melchizedek. It is wonderful to know that we have such a "high priest, who is set on the right hand of the throne of the Majesty in the heavens" (Heb. 8:1). We can rejoice in knowing that Jesus was not only the lamb but also the priest, and that He daily ministers in the courts of heaven. As we progress through the Scriptures, we will discover that there is no need for us to be concerned about our sins that have been confessed to Jesus. Every day we can begin with a new page through the grace of our Lord Jesus Christ.

PLAN
Genesis 15

THE BIBLE'S THEME

And he believed the Lord; and he reckoned it to him as righteousness. Genesis 15:6.

This is one of the key Bible texts; it shows the unity and inspiration of the Scriptures. Although there are sixty-six books written by forty authors, covering a period of about sixteen hundred years, there is a unity of thought that proves that the Bible is inspired by God. Here in the first book is a clear statement of the plan of salvation, which is quoted in the New Testament and is the basis of the book of Romans.

This is the first time that these great words, *faith* and *righteousness,* appear linked together in the Bible. It is a wonderful tribute to Abraham and simply says that he believed in God and because he accepted God's plan of salvation he was declared to be a good man. And because of what God was going to do through Jesus at Calvary, Abraham would be saved. Abraham did not earn this righteousness and salvation, but as stated in the King James Version of the Bible, God "counted it to him." We too can be counted righteous and have the assurance of salvation.

"If you give yourself to Him, and accept Him as your Saviour, then sinful as your life may have been, for His sake you are accounted righteous. Christ's character stands in place of your character, and you are accepted before God just as if you had not sinned."—*Steps to Christ,* p. 62.

These very important words of the Bible were spoken to Abraham under the stars. God had communicated with him for the fourth time, this time in a vision. Abraham was no doubt a little concerned about the kings that he had defeated in battle while rescuing Lot, but God said to him, "I am thy shield." When we are concerned about being overcome by the fiery darts of temptation we can, with Abraham, claim God as our shield. The Lord also renewed His promise to Abraham that he would have children and that his descendants would be as numerous as the stars of heaven that Abraham was looking at that night. God's promises are unlimited. Someone who has proved God's promises true said, "Tarry at the promises till God meets you there. He always returns by way of His promises."

84

PLAN
Genesis 18

GUESTS IN DISGUISE

And the Lord appeared to him by the oaks of Mamre.... And behold, three men stood in front of him. When he saw them, he ran from the tent door to meet them, and bowed himself to the earth. Genesis 18:1, 2.

It was a very hot day, and Abraham had perhaps eaten his midday meal and was resting in the shade of the tent. In those days people enjoyed having guests, and Abraham was delighted when he noticed three people approaching his tent. However, he was very surprised when he greeted them, for he recognized one of them as the Lord Jesus and immediately said, "My Lord." In the first verse of the next chapter we are told that the other two visitors were angels.

God was so impressed by Abraham's act of courtesy that it was recorded in the New Testament with instruction from Paul, "Do not neglect to show hospitality to strangers, for thereby some have entertained angels unawares" (Heb. 13:2).

The three heavenly messengers came to Abraham to tell him that God had remembered His promise that Abraham's wife, Sarah, would have a son who was to be the beginning of Abraham's descendants, who would be as numberless as the sands of the sea. Because they had heard this promise for 25 years, and because Sarah thought she was now too old to have children, she laughed. The statement made by Jesus in the tent on the plains of Mamre is one that we should always remember. Nothing is too hard for the Lord.

The visitors also revealed to Abraham that they were going to destroy Sodom and Gomorrah. Abraham was moved to plead that the inhabitants of Sodom and Gomorrah be spared not only because his nephew Lot and his family were living there but because of his concern for all the people. His request to save the people is one of the most beautiful prayers of intercession recorded in the Scriptures.

Some Christians today become so wrapped up in the cares of this life and their own comfort that they do not have the kind of compassion for people that was demonstrated by Abraham. Remember, our example, Jesus, was often moved with compassion when He saw people in need.

PLAN
Genesis 19

THE LADY LOOKED BACK

Then the Lord rained on Sodom and Gomorrah brimstone and fire from the Lord out of heaven. . . . But Lot's wife behind him looked back, and she became a pillar of salt. Genesis 19:24-26.

Many times Lot and his family failed to recognize God's purpose for their lives. His story is one of the saddest in the Bible, and the final record of his life and his wife's death is a tragedy. It is a pity that he did not follow the godly example of his uncle, of whom God said, "For I know him, that he will command his children and his household after him, and they shall keep the way of the Lord, to do justice and judgment" (Gen. 18:19).

What more could God do to save a family in a wicked city than to send His own Son and two angels to warn them personally and give them explicit instructions on how to be saved from the fire and brimstone? However, we note that Lot and his family were reluctant to leave Sodom. No doubt they had a lot invested there. The choice that Lot made to live near the wicked city had been a very unwise one. Now his family did not want to leave. The Lord in His mercy allowed the family to flee to another city, but this also proved too big a temptation.

One of the specific instructions, which is good advice to all who are fleeing from sin, was to "escape for thy life; look not behind thee, neither stay thou in the plain; escape to the mountain, lest thou be consumed" (chap. 19:17). Apparently Lot's wife was convinced to flee, but she was not fully converted. This reminds us that if we think we are nearly saved, we can be completely lost. The fate of Lot's wife teaches us that we should never delay when we hear a clear instruction from the Lord, but that we must always obey. Unfortunately, there are many today who, like Lot's wife, are awakened by the call of the gospel but look back to the pleasures of sin and thus lose life now and eternal life later. In order to be sure that we do not look back to the world, we need to "keep looking to Jesus." He is able to help us, for He is "the pioneer and perfecter of our faith, who for the joy that was set before him endured the cross, despising the shame, and is seated at the right hand of the throne of God" (Heb. 12:2, R.S.V.).

PLAN
Genesis 22

TWO MOUNTAINS

And Isaac said to his father Abraham, "My father!" And he said, "Here am I, my son." He said, "Behold, the fire and the wood; but where is the lamb for a burnt offering?" Genesis 22:7.

It didn't pay to be pretty in the rose-red city of Petra because pretty young ladies were prepared for the sacrifices for the sun god. Apparently the night before, they were kept in a building near the rock of sacrifice. They were kept near the altar rock so that they could be offered to the sun at sunrise.

The city of human sacrifice was the ancient desert kingdom of Edom. It is mentioned in the Bible, and Obadiah records that the people lived in the rocks. It is called Petra because this word in the Greek language means rock. Many of the ruins of Petra are still standing, but it is difficult to visit the site because it is isolated in the Arabian Desert.

A young man named Isaac was asked to be a sacrifice. This was not just to be a human sacrifice on a heathen altar, but a test of a father's and a son's faith in the true God. This sacrifice was scheduled to take place on Mount Moriah. Another sacrifice, a demonstration of God's love for us, did take place on Mount Calvary.

In the records of Moriah and Calvary, we have a mountain of sacrifice, a loving father, an obedient son, a three-day journey, an instrument of death, and a lamb. Mount Moriah is certainly Mount Calvary in miniature. Isaac's question, "Where is the lamb?" points forward to the statement of John the Baptist, "Behold the Lamb of God, which taketh away the sin of the world" (John 1:29).

The story of Isaac is not just another interesting story; this is the gospel in miniature. It was a preview of what would happen on Calvary. Once again we see that one of the purposes of the Bible is to reveal the plan of salvation.

"This act of faith in Abraham is recorded for our benefit. It teaches us the great lesson of confidence in the requirements of God, however close and cutting they may be; and it teaches children perfect submission to their parents and to God. By Abraham's obedience we are taught that nothing is too precious for us to give to God."—*Testimonies*, vol. 3, p. 368.

87

PLAN
Genesis 24

THE CAMELS ARE COMING

And Isaac went out to meditate in the field in the evening; and he lifted up his eyes and looked, and behold, there were camels coming. Genesis 24:63.

Isaac's name means "laughter." He was so named because his parents were filled with joy at his birth. His mother was 90 years old, and his birth was a miracle. When Isaac was a young man, he was willing to be sacrificed, but again a miracle was performed, and a ram, representing Jesus, was offered instead. When he was 40 years of age, Isaac showed the same obedience by allowing his father to select a wife for him.

The trusted family servant, Eliezer, took ten camels and journeyed five hundred miles from Beer-sheba, near the Dead Sea, to the city of Nahor. Eliezer obviously had been influenced by living in the household of Abraham, and he prayed for God's guidance. The story of his finding Rebekah at the well and the discussions with Laban is very interesting. When asked, "Will you go with this man?" Rebekah said, "I will go." Her decision to go with the stranger to a foreign land to marry a man she had never seen is a beautiful picture of Jesus, the bridegroom of the church, who was willing to leave heaven and come to a strange land in order to reunite heaven and earth.

Although Isaac is not as prominent a character as either his father, Abraham, or his son, Jacob, he is mentioned in twenty other books of the Old and New Testaments. The statement in our text that Isaac "went out to meditate in the field in the evening" (R.S.V.) summarizes his devotion. Meditation lights spiritual fires within our lives, and we, like Isaac, need to spend time meditating in a quiet place. What a thrilling moment it must have been when Rebekah got down from the camel and met her future husband. It is also wonderful to note that Isaac "loved her" and that they had a happy marriage.

"What a contrast between the course of Isaac and that pursued by the youth of our time, even among professed Christians! Young people too often feel that the bestowal of their affections is a matter in which self alone should be consulted—a matter that neither God nor their parents should in any wise control."—*Patriarchs and Prophets*, p. 175.

PLAN
Genesis 27

TROUBLED TWINS

"Let peoples serve you, and nations bow down to you." Genesis 27:29.

The drama in Isaac's household, as recorded in Genesis 27, took place when he was about 137 years of age. Esau was a cunning hunter. However, he was not clever enough to know that the birthright blessing was very valuable; he sold it to his brother, Jacob, for a bowl of pottage.

"Esau represents those who have not tasted of the privileges which are theirs, purchased for them at infinite cost, but have sold their birthright for some gratification of appetite, or for the love of gain."—*The SDA Bible Commentary,* Ellen G. White Comments, on Gen. 25:29-34, p. 1095.

In the closing years of Isaac's life Jacob became involved in trickery. With the help of his mother he deceived Isaac, who was now blind, into pronouncing on him, Jacob, the blessing that really belonged to the firstborn, Esau. The trouble that followed is an example of what happens when people run ahead of the Lord. Rebekah and Jacob should have waited for God to bring to pass the prediction that the elder should serve the younger.

The prediction made by Isaac, quoted in part in today's text, was obviously inspired by God. The descendants of Jacob did become the stronger nation, and it was through them that Christ was born.

It is clear from this story that those who deceive others are often deceived themselves. Jesus, through Paul, stated it in these words: "Be not deceived; God is not mocked: for whatsoever a man soweth, that shall he also reap" (Gal. 6:7).

Jacob reaped lots of trouble and sorrow from his seeds of deception, and Esau paid a high price for his disobedience to God. As a result of her part in the birthright deception, Rebekah never saw her beloved son Jacob again.

Jacob had to flee from his brother, who threatened to kill him, and he spent many years in exile. "In one short hour he had made work for a lifelong repentance."—*Patriarchs and Prophets,* p. 180. However, he did repent of his sin against God, his father, his brother, and himself. And on his return home he was reunited with his brother Esau.

PLAN
Genesis 28

THE DREAM LADDER

*And he dreamed that there was a ladder set up on the earth,
and the top of it reached to heaven; and behold, the angels of God
were ascending and descending on it! Genesis 28:12.*

Who dreamed of a ladder with its base resting on the earth
and its top rounds reaching the highest heavens? Who or what
does the ladder represent? And what was the effect of the dream
on the man who saw it? The answers to these questions are
found in Genesis 28. If you have not read that chapter, why not
read it now and discover the answer to these questions.

Yes, the man who had the dream had his name changed to
Israel, a prince who had "power with God" (Gen. 32:28). He had
twelve sons, who became the heads of the twelve tribes of Israel.
We can read about them in Genesis 49. The characteristics of the
sons are recorded in that chapter. They have special significance
to us because the names of these sons of Israel are inscribed on
the twelve gates of the New Jerusalem.

"Christ is the ladder that Jacob saw, the base resting on the
earth, and the topmost round reaching to the gate of heaven, to
the very threshold of glory. If that ladder had failed by a single
step of reaching the earth, we should have been lost. But Christ
reaches us where we are. He took our nature and overcame, that
we through taking His nature might overcome."—*The Desire of
Ages,* pp. 311, 312.

Even the dreams recorded in the Bible have special
significance, and we need to know why they are recorded. We
cannot gain this understanding by a superficial reading. We
need to follow the basic principles of understanding Scripture,
one of which is to compare verse with verse.

The effect of the dream on Jacob was that he declared "the
Lord is in this place; and I knew it not" (chap. 28:16). He called
the name of the place Bethel, which means "the house of God."
He also made a very solemn vow to the Lord. It is interesting to
note that in addition to committing his life fully to the Lord, he
also determined to be a faithful steward by giving a tithe to the
Lord as Abraham had done.

90

PLAN
Genesis 29

REAPING WHAT WAS SOWN

Jacob said to them, "My brothers, where do you come from?" They said, "We are from Haran." He said to them, "Do you know Laban the son of Nahor?" They said, "We know him." Genesis 29:4, 5.

Jacob spent the first seventy-seven years of his life in Canaan, then traveled five hundred miles northeast to Haran. Before returning to Canaan to live for thirty-three more years and to Egypt to live for seventeen years, Jacob had to stay in Haran twenty years because Laban deceived him. So we see that Jacob, the one who deceived his brother to gain their father's blessing, was now reaping what he had sowed.

Laban offered to pay Jacob for his work with the flocks, but Jacob chose instead to work for seven years without wages in order to have Laban's daughter Rachel as his wife. As is still the custom in some countries, it was the practice in these Old Testament times for a man to work for a wife or to give the father a large present. Jacob had fled from home because of the anger of his brother, and he did not have any money, goods, or animals to offer as a gift. After he had worked the seven years for Rachel, however, Laban deceived Jacob by giving him Leah, Rachel's older sister. Jacob did not discover the deception until after the wedding, since a bride in those days always wore a heavy veil over her face. Jacob's mother, Rebekah, had veiled her face when she got down from the camel and came to meet Isaac.

Jacob was determined to have Rachel as his wife, however, so he worked for Laban another seven years, though he became very dissatisfied with Laban's schemes. However, because of his love for Rachel, the additional seven years passed quickly.

Laban's greed was first mentioned when Abraham's servant, Eliezer, came seeking a wife for Isaac. Laban had been impressed then by the gold that he saw. This time he saw fourteen years of free labor, and he took advantage of this young man who was on the run hiding from his brother. As a result of Laban's scheming, when Jacob eventually left Haran, it was the end of "all trace of connection between the children of Abraham and the dwellers in Mesopotamia" *(Patriarchs and Prophets,* p. 194).

PLAN
Genesis 32

WHAT IS YOUR NAME?

Then he said, "Your name shall no more be called Jacob, but Israel, for you have . . . prevailed." Genesis 32:28.

Children in parts of Vietnam are given names of things that actually exist. Some interesting names include Moon, Tree, and Flower. These boys and girls are also called by a number, in the order of their birth into the family. The first child is always called Number 2, however, because the parents believe the devil wants to destroy the first child.

Number 4 in a certain family was called Turtle because turtles live a very long time. One day Number 2 died and Number 3 got very sick, so Father and Mother took Turtle to the witch doctor. The witch doctor told the parents to take Turtle down to the river and look for a stone with moss on it. They were then to kill a chicken and let the blood run onto the moss. He also said that if Turtle was to keep well they would have to call him Girl. As you can imagine, Turtle was very unhappy to be called Girl.

When Turtle was 17, he went with his parents to some Bible lectures, and they all accepted Jesus as their Saviour. On the day of his baptism the pastor asked Girl whether he would like to have a new name. The family was delighted, because they did not believe in pagan superstitions anymore. The pastor and parents decided that Number 4—Turtle (Girl)—should be called Friend. And Friend was happy with his new name.

Many people in the Bible had their names changed, indicating a change in their natures. Abram was changed to Abraham, Simon was changed to Peter, and Saul became Paul.

Today we discover that Jacob had his name changed by God to Israel. He was no doubt happy to have his name changed from "deceiver" to "he strives with God." His new name meant that he was a prince of God. As this new prince returned to his home in Canaan, "the angels of God met him," and because of his change in nature and God's blessings he had a wonderful reunion with his brother, Esau.

You and I will soon have new names. And as we approach our heavenly home the angels of God will meet us, too. That's light for my life.

92

PLAN
Genesis 35

GO UP TO BETHEL

"Then let us arise and go up to Bethel, that I may make there an altar to the God who answered me in the day of my distress and has been with me wherever I have gone." Genesis 35:3.

It is hard to imagine anyone who loves flowers and does not believe in God. However, there was a man who loved to work in his flower garden but who kept telling himself and others that he did not believe in God. One year he planted a bed of flowers to spell out the words "God is nowhere."

Many people visited the man's gardens, and one day a little girl who was looking over the fence asked, "May I come in? I just love flowers!" The man opened his gate and watched as the little girl looked at the various flowers so beautifully arranged.

At last she came to the flower bed with the words "God is nowhere." She turned to the man and said, "That is beautiful!" The man was surprised and said, "Do you really think so?" Then he asked, "Can you read?" To which the girl replied, "Oh, yes, I can read." However, the little girl could pronounce only one-syllable words, and she slowly spelled out the words "God is now here."

Although some people may say that "God is nowhere," the truth is that "God is now here." Those of us who read our Bibles and pray know that God is with us. Jacob made this discovery when he was a pilgrim at Bethel. At that time he made vows to God (see Gen. 28:20-22).

Twenty years had gone by since Jacob built the altar at Bethel, and he had not always kept his vows. His decision to return was prompted by God. It is good that even though we sometimes forget the vows we make the Lord reminds us. Those who are baptized take vows that need to be continually renewed.

Bethel means "house of God." As we go to the house of the Lord each Sabbath, it can be a Bethel experience for us. Before we go, we need to follow Jacob's example and "put away the strange gods" (Gen. 35:2). If we do put aside things that separate us from God, we will have the same sense of God's presence that Jacob had at Bethel. Then we will be able to say, This is light for my life.

PLAN
Genesis 37

SOLD AS A SLAVE

Then Midianite traders passed by; and they drew Joseph up and lifted him out of the pit, and sold him to the Ishmaelites for twenty shekels of silver; and they took Joseph to Egypt. Genesis 37:28.

The remainder of Genesis tells the story of Joseph. Of Jacob's twelve sons, Joseph was the most prominent. We do not know anything about him until he was 17 years of age, but his life from then on is one of the most interesting stories in the Bible.

There are three basic reasons why Joseph's older brothers did not like him. First of all, he told his father some of the bad things his brothers were doing. Also they were jealous because Jacob showed Joseph more love. The third reason the brothers were jealous was because of two dreams Joseph had about sheaves of wheat and the sun, moon, and stars. These dreams, given to him by God, revealed to Joseph that he was to be the leader of the family.

One day when Joseph was a long way from home and was looking for his brothers, they saw him coming and decided to put him into a big pit in the ground and later kill him. As the brothers were eating their evening meal, however, they noticed a long line of camels coming over the mountains. It was a caravan of traders who were going to Egypt, so they decided to sell Joseph to them as a slave.

Joseph must have been horrified at what his brothers were doing. As he started on his journey as a prisoner, he no doubt saw his father's tents in the distance and cried, wishing he could run home.

"One day's experience had been the turning point in Joseph's life. Its terrible calamity had transformed him from a petted child to a man, thoughtful, courageous, and self-possessed."—*Patriarchs and Prophets,* p. 214. Joseph's brothers changed too; the years that followed were filled with the results of their sins.

After walking the fifty miles back to their father's tents, they handed Jacob Joseph's coat, which they had deceitfully dipped in the blood of a goat. The old man was grief-stricken as he looked at the coat of many colors, stained with what he thought to be the blood of his son Joseph.

94

PLAN
Genesis 39

THE SLAVE PROMOTED

The Lord was with Joseph, and he became a successful man; and he was in the house of his master the Egyptian, and his master saw that the Lord was with him, and that the Lord caused all that he did to prosper in his hands. Genesis 39:2, 3.

In Egypt, Joseph was assigned to work for Potiphar, the captain of the soldiers who guarded the king. Joseph did his work so well that he was soon made manager of Potiphar's large house and of all the other servants.

By about 27 years of age, Joseph had become a very handsome young man. And it was at this time that he was tempted by Potiphar's wife. If he had given in to the temptation, he would have broken the seventh commandment, which says, "Thou shalt not commit adultery." He reminded Potiphar's wife that he was loyal to her husband, and also stated that he was loyal to God. His reply is one that we can all remember when we are tempted, "How then can I do this great wickedness, and sin against God?" (Gen. 39:9).

"Joseph carried his religion everywhere, and this was the secret of his unwavering fidelity."—Manuscript 59, 1897. Religion for him was not just something he practiced one day a week or during his daily prayers; it was a part of his daily life. He had such a love relationship with God that he would not allow anything to sever it.

Sometimes when we stand for right we are punished by those who try to involve us in sin. Potiphar's wife gave a false report about Joseph, and he was put into prison. It was not long, however, before he was put in charge of all the prisoners. It was also said of him that whatever he did "the Lord made it to prosper" (verse 23).

Here are some pointers on how we can prosper:

*P*ut God first, *O*thers next, *Y*ourself last.

*R*esolve to do right no matter what others think.

*O*ffer to help others even when you don't feel like it.

*S*eek to do your best at all times.

*P*ray every day for strength to live victoriously.

*E*mulate Christ's life of humility.

*R*ead the Bible to discover God's way of doing things.

PLAN
Genesis 41

SLAVE BECOMES RULER

So Pharaoh said to Joseph, "Since God has shown you all this, there is none so discreet and wise as you are; you shall be over my house, and all my people shall order themselves as you command; only as regards the throne will I be greater than you." Genesis 41:39, 40.

Pharaoh's chief butler and chief baker, both in prison with Joseph, each had a dream that Joseph interpreted. The butler was very pleased when Joseph predicted that he would be restored to his position in the palace.

But afterward the butler forgot about Joseph, and Joseph had to wait two more years before he got out of prison. Then one night Pharaoh dreamed that he was standing by the great Nile River, where seven thin cows and seven fat cows fed on the grass. Suddenly the thin cows ate the fat cows, and with that Pharaoh awoke.

The magicians of Egypt were unable to interpret the king's dream, and at this point the butler remembered the prisoner who had interpreted his dream. Imagine Joseph's joy when a messenger came and told him that he was to prepare to appear before Pharaoh. Like Daniel, Joseph said, "'It is not in me; God will give Pharaoh a favorable answer'" (Gen. 41:16, R.S.V.). Joseph then told Pharaoh that there were to be seven years of plenty followed by seven years of famine in Egypt and that he should store grain during the seven years of plenty. When he was asked for a suggestion as to how this should be done, Joseph told Pharaoh that he should look for a wise man to supervise the work.

Joseph must have been quite surprised when Pharaoh selected him to be this ruler. And you can imagine how the people talked when they saw this slave and former prisoner made second in command in all the land of Egypt!

Just as God blessed Joseph in Pharaoh's house and also in prison, so the Lord blessed his work as prime minister in Egypt. At the end of the first seven years there were full storehouses all over the country and "all the earth came to Egypt to Joseph to buy grain, because the famine was severe over all the earth" (chap. 41:57, R.S.V.).

PLAN
Genesis 42

DREAMS COME TRUE

Now Joseph was governor over the land; he it was who sold to all the people of the land. And Joseph's brothers came, and bowed themselves before him with their faces to the ground. . . . Thus Joseph knew his brothers, but they did not know him. Genesis 42:6-8.

Joseph was now 38 years old and looked like an Egyptian. He was shaved and he was dressed in the beautiful robes of a ruler. He also spoke the Egyptian language. When the ten sons of Jacob stood before him, they had no idea that they were bowing to their own brother, as predicted in the dream given to Joseph when he was just 17 years of age. They had been sent to Egypt to buy corn because the famine was in the land of Canaan, too.

The dramatic story of how Joseph tested his brothers as to their loyalty and love for God, their father, and their lost brother is one of the most beautiful in all the Bible. There was much drama as Joseph hid first money and then treasure in their sacks of grain as they went back to Canaan. It was Judah, the brother who had actually suggested selling Joseph into slavery, who offered to remain in Benjamin's stead when the cup was found in the younger brother's sack.

Up to that time Joseph had experienced one trial after another. He had remained true to God, however, and now his brothers were on trial. Jacob was also tested when he was asked to let Benjamin go to Egypt.

The seven years of plenty and seven years of famine were a part of God's plan to carry out His promise to Abraham, " 'Know of a surety that your descendants will be sojourners in a land that is not theirs, and will be slaves there, and they will be oppressed for four hundred years; but I will bring judgment on the nation which they serve, and afterward they shall come out with great possessions' " (Gen. 15:13, 14, R.S.V.).

One reason God took the children of Israel to Egypt was so they could develop into a strong nation that would trust Him, and so they could take possession of Canaan. Had they never left the land of Canaan, the children of Israel would have become like the pagan nations around them.

PLAN
Genesis 45

RULER REVEALS NAME

And he wept aloud, so that the Egyptians heard it. . . . And Joseph said to his brothers, "I am Joseph; is my father still alive?" But his brothers could not answer him, for they were dismayed at his presence. Genesis 45:2, 3.

Before Joseph revealed himself to his brothers, the men were given one more test. After they left for home, they were pursued by Egyptian soldiers on horseback. Despite their protest that they did not have the silver cup from the ruler's house, their bags were searched.

The brothers were so sure that the cup was not with them that they said, "With whomsoever of thy servants it be found, both let him die, and we also will be my lord's bondmen" (Gen. 44:9). And when the cup was found in Benjamin's sack, they despaired and tore their clothes.

Back in the palace they again fell to the ground before Joseph. And when he questioned them, they told him the story of their father and the grief he had suffered as a result of the one brother who was dead and of having to part with Benjamin. Judah then pleaded with the ruler to let them take Benjamin back home with them.

After Joseph saw their love for their father and their loyalty to one another, he asked for all his servants and soldiers to leave the room. He then cried so loudly that people in other rooms heard it, and through uncontrollable tears he said, "I am Joseph."

Joseph then assured his frightened brothers that they were forgiven and told them that it was God's plan for him to save the people from starvation and lead them into Egypt. Pharaoh granted Joseph permission to invite his family, with their flocks and herds, to live in Egypt. You can imagine the joy when the ten brothers returned home and said, "Joseph is yet alive, and he is governor over all the land of Egypt"!

As Jacob left the land of Canaan, God assured him that his descendants would return as a great nation someday. Including the family of Joseph, seventy people entered Egypt. And from this small number there grew a nation that numbered several million when they left that country years later.

PLAN
Genesis 49

THE TWELVE TRIBES

All these are the twelve tribes of Israel; and this is what their father said to them as he blessed them, blessing each with the blessing suitable to him. Genesis 49:28.

What a wonderful reunion Jacob had with his son Joseph! The children of Israel were given a section of Egypt called Goshen, which was suitable for their flocks and herds.

After living in Egypt for seventeen years, Jacob was now 147 years of age and knew that he was soon to die. So he called his twelve sons together and gave them a spiritual blessing in the form of a poem. Moses, the author of Genesis, tells us that it is more than just a prediction concerning the twelve sons; it is a prophecy concerning the twelve tribes (see Gen. 49:28).

The statement in Genesis 49:18, "I have waited for thy salvation, O Lord," is the midpoint of the poem. There are seven sons mentioned before that statement and five after. In the first group the most outstanding prediction is that Jesus would come through the line of Judah. " 'The scepter shall not depart from Judah, nor the ruler's staff from between his feet, until he comes to whom it belongs; and to him shall be the obedience of the peoples'" (verse 10, R.S.V.). In the second list Joseph is highlighted and described as "a fruitful bow."

Judah and Joseph received the most prominent of Jacob's blessings. These normally would have gone to the firstborn, Reuben, but he forfeited them because of his sin. Instead, Joseph received the double portion of his father's wealth and Judah was designated as leader of the twelve tribes.

As predicted, the kingly scepter remained in the tribe of Judah until it was given to the One to whom it really belonged—Jesus. From the tribe of Judah came David, and in God's plan Jesus was born through the royal line of King David. The lion, emblem for the tribe of Judah, is a symbol of strength and is usually associated with royalty. One of the names of Jesus is Lion of the tribe of Judah.

The names of the twelve tribes of Israel are still important, as they are on the twelve gates of the New Jerusalem.

PLAN
Genesis 50

JOSEPH AND JESUS

"As for you, you meant evil against me; but God meant it for good, to bring it about that many people should be kept alive, as they are today." Genesis 50:20.

Joseph's life is one of the most perfect illustrations given in the Bible of God's overruling providence. Although men may propose evil things, God can bring good out of them. It is still true that "all things work together for good to them that love God" (Rom. 8:28).

In reading the story of Joseph, we must not look at just the drama of a 17-year-old boy being sold into slavery, put into prison, becoming prime minister of a foreign country, and being next to the king. Many claim that no other person's life so closely parallels the life of the Lord Jesus as does Joseph's. I suggest you count the number of parallels.

"The life of Joseph illustrates the life of Christ. It was envy that moved the brothers of Joseph to sell him as a slave; they hoped to prevent him from becoming greater than themselves. . . . So the Jewish priests and elders were jealous of Christ, fearing that He would attract the attention of the people from them. They put Him to death, to prevent Him from becoming king, but they were thus bringing about this very result.

"Joseph, through his bondage in Egypt, became a savior to his father's family; yet this fact did not lessen the guilt of his brothers. So the crucifixion of Christ by His enemies made Him the Redeemer of mankind. . . .

"As Joseph was sold to the heathen by his own brothers, so Christ was sold to His bitterest enemies by one of His disciples. Joseph was falsely accused and thrust into prison because of his virtue; so Christ was despised and rejected because His righteous, self-denying life was a rebuke to sin; and though guilty of no wrong, He was condemned upon the testimony of false witnesses. And Joseph's patience and meekness under injustice and oppression, his ready forgiveness and noble benevolence toward his unnatural brothers, represents the Saviour's uncomplaining endurance of the malice and abuse of wicked men."—*Patriarchs and Prophets,* pp. 239, 240.

100

PURPOSE
Exodus 1

THE PLAN OF THE BIBLE

So they made the people of Israel serve with rigor, and made their lives bitter with hard service, in mortar and brick, and in all kinds of work in the field; in all their work they made them serve with rigor. Exodus 1:13, 14.

Although there is a gap of more than one hundred years between Genesis and Exodus, covering the period of time from the death of Joseph to the birth of Moses, Exodus is the planned follow-up book. Without Genesis, the book of Exodus would not have the meaning that it does. The first book of the Bible tells of the failure of man under testing conditions and introduces God's plan for salvation. The second book is the wonderful story of God's hastening to the rescue of the fallen race.

The word *exodus* comes from two Greek words meaning "the way out" or "the going out." It begins with slavery and ends with salvation. It begins with God's people being enslaved, but ends with them on the way to occupying the Promised Land. The chosen people, in hopeless bondage in the land of Egypt, have no power to deliver themselves. But God says, "I am come down to deliver them." So Exodus is the book of redemption in the Old Testament and thus it reveals the plan of the Scriptures.

God is ever in sympathy with the oppressed and against their oppressors. Everyone who has studied God's character as revealed in the Bible confirms this truth. His compassion is declared by His words, confirmed by His deeds, and demonstrated by the cross. Sometimes we ask why God allows something to happen, but we can be assured that one day everything will be made plain. The sovereignty and sympathy of God have been confirmed. Wherever possible He intervenes on behalf of His people who are oppressed or in slavery of any kind.

When a ship, airplane, or car is being designed, a pattern or plan has to be made. Our salvation from sin and its effects was designed by God before the foundation of the world, and that plan is clearly outlined in the book of Exodus. The story of Exodus is repeated in the life of everyone who seeks deliverance from the slavery of sin. We have many promises that God's plan will deliver us and change us from slaves into saints.

PURPOSE
Exodus 2

SOMEBODY OR NOBODY

And the child grew, and she brought him to Pharaoh's daughter, and he became her son; and she named him Moses, for she said, "Because I drew him out of the water." Exodus 2:10.

Did you ever feel that you were a nobody? Perhaps people have told you that you will never amount to anything. There is no need to accept what they say as a fact, but neither should a person think that he or she is a somebody.

The book of Exodus tells the story of a man who was a nobody when the princess' servant found him in the bulrushes. Moses, at the age of 40, after having graduated from the University of Egypt and its finest military college and knowing that he was heir to the throne, no doubt thought that he was somebody. His authority as a prince and a judge apparently went to his head, and in Exodus 2 we read of a mistake he made that caused him to flee out of Egypt. During the next forty years he was to learn in the University of Hard Knocks that he was a nobody. His first class was minding sheep in the wilderness. Moses had to make some pretty big adjustments from the luxuries of Pharaoh's palace to the privations of the wilderness.

"Shut in by the bulwarks of the mountains, Moses was alone with God. The magnificent temples of Egypt no longer impressed his mind with their superstition and falsehood. . . . Everywhere the Creator's name was written. Moses seemed to stand in His presence, and to be overshadowed by His power. Here his pride and self-sufficiency were swept away. In the stern simplicity of his wilderness life, the results of the ease and luxury of Egypt disappeared. Moses became patient, reverent, and humble, 'very meek, above all the men which were upon the face of the earth' (Numbers 12:3), yet strong in faith in the mighty God of Jacob."—*Patriarchs and Prophets,* pp. 248, 249.

In the last forty years of his life, Moses discovered what God could do with a nobody. A tribute to his greatness is recorded in Hebrews 11. There is no reason why every Christian young person cannot, by the grace of Jesus, make the same discovery that Moses did, and like Moses choose rather "to suffer affliction with the people of God, than to enjoy the pleasures of sin for a season" (Heb. 11:25).

PURPOSE
Exodus 3

THE BURNING BUSH

Now Moses was keeping the flock of his father-in-law, Jethro, the priest of Midian. . . . And the angel of the Lord appeared to him in a flame of fire out of the midst of a bush; and he looked, and lo, the bush was burning, yet it was not consumed. Exodus 3:1, 2.

During the years that Moses cared for the sheep amid the mountains in solitary places, he was alone with God. He thought often about the children of Israel in slavery in Egypt, and recounted the promise made to Abraham, "I will make of thee a great nation." It is interesting to note in the book *Patriarchs and Prophets* that it was while attending sheep in Midian that "under the inspiration of the Holy Spirit, he wrote the book of Genesis" (p. 251). Moses' first book presents a view of God's people from Creation to the close of the patriarchal age, a period of many centuries. The first two chapters of Exodus, which are a continuation of Genesis, cover about eighty years. The remainder of the book of Exodus covers only a few years of time.

One day while near Mount Horeb, "the mountain of God," Moses saw a burning bush. He drew near, and as he stood there he heard a voice calling his name. God's first words to Moses were to advise him that he was on holy ground.

"Humility and reverence should characterize the deportment of all who come into the presence of God. In the name of Jesus we may come before Him with confidence, but we must not approach Him with the boldness of presumption, as though He were on a level with ourselves. There are those who address the great and all-powerful and holy God . . . as they would address an equal, or even an inferior. There are those who conduct themselves in His house as they would not presume to do in the audience chamber of an earthly ruler. These should remember that they are in His sight whom seraphim adore, before whom angels veil their faces."—*Ibid.*, p. 252.

With face covered but with his ears wide open, Moses stood before God and learned His will. God not only called him to a particular work but revealed to him why he was called, exactly what he was to do, and the main issues involved. It was necessary for God to demonstrate to Moses by miraculous signs that those He calls He empowers.

PURPOSE
Exodus 4

WHAT IS IN YOUR HAND?

The Lord said to him, "What is that in your hand?" He said,
"A rod." Exodus 4:2.

Have you ever thought that when talents were given out you
were overlooked? When asked to take part in a church program
or to do something in the community, do you feel unable? Do you
make excuses and refuse? If you answer Yes to these questions,
then you know how Moses felt when God asked him to lead
Israel out of Egypt. Even after God spoke to him in the burning
bush, he made all sorts of excuses for not answering the call.

God gave three signs to remind Moses that when He calls
someone to work He gives the power to do that work. First He
changed Moses' walking stick into a snake. When Moses picked
it up by the tail, the snake became a rod again. God told Moses
that these and other miracles would convince the people that he
was to lead them out of Egypt.

God does not always silence our excuses for not working for
Him, nor convince people that they should believe us. However,
He does bless what is in our hands so that we can accomplish the
task He has given us. We all have talents and abilities, and God
can use these in His service. After forty years of leadership
training in the desert, God asked Moses, "What is in your
hand?" Moses had only a rod, but it became a symbol of his call.
Today God is asking, "What is that in your hand?"

What is that in your hand, O friend of mine,
In the bustle and din near the end of time?
Is it hammer or pen or typewriting skill,
A spanner, a spade, a voice that can thrill? . . .
Of this rest assured: whate'er it may be,
'Twas God put it there, He planned it for thee.
Thy part in His work depends on the use
Of His gifts to thee; pray do not refuse,
But joyfully yield what is there in thy hand
To the good of His cause—spread His love o'er the land.
Thy skill will increase, thy faith grow more strong,
Thy name will be blessed by souls saved from wrong,
And miracles too will be seen in our day
If o'er that in thine hand Jesus has the full sway.
—W. R. Veitch

PURPOSE
Exodus 5

LET MY PEOPLE GO

*"Thus says the Lord, the God of Israel, 'Let my people go. . . .'"
But Pharaoh said, "Who is the Lord, that I should heed his voice
and let Israel go?" Exodus 5:1, 2.*

Pharaoh was the title of the ruler of Egypt. This is the
English word for an Egyptian term that meant "the great
house." Each Pharaoh, or king, had three titles and two names,
so it was easy to refer to him as "the great house." Today we note
that when news is released by the President of the United
States, it is often introduced by "The White House says . . ." The
White House has become a symbol of the President, just as "the
great house" meant the king of Egypt.

It must have been an exciting day for Moses when he
returned to Pharaoh's palace. As a prince of Egypt he had often
been through the gates and walked down the corridors and
through the reception rooms. But now, after forty years as a
sheepherder in the wilderness, he must have been awed by the
splendor of the palace. Accompanied by Aaron, he entered the
audience chamber of Pharaoh and in the name of Jehovah said,
"Let my people go!"

Pharaoh was ignorant about Jehovah, or at least pretended
to be. Apparently he had heard about the true God, for he asked,
"Why am I to obey His voice?" He actually said to Moses, "He
may be your God, but He is not mine. In Egypt *I* am worshiped as
a god."

And Moses, the man who claimed that he was "slow of
speech," now boldly challenged the Pharaoh of Egypt and
proceeded to explain that Jehovah was not only the God of the
Hebrews but the *only* true God.

Pharaoh made no reply to this appeal, but commanded the
slavemasters to make the Hebrews work harder. They would
now have to gather their own straw for the bricks they made.

Although it appeared that the interview with Pharaoh was a
failure, it was God's purpose for them to repeat their request
until eventually Pharaoh was forced to let the people go.
Remember, it is possible to lose a battle and yet to win the war.
We must not give up, for if we are doing God's work in His way,
the work will succeed.

PURPOSE
Exodus 7

RIVER TURNED TO BLOOD

Moses and Aaron did as the Lord commanded; in the sight of Pharaoh and in the sight of his servants, he lifted up the rod and struck the water that was in the Nile, and all the water that was in the Nile turned to blood. Exodus 7:20.

The second time Moses and Aaron went to see the mighty Pharaoh, Aaron cast down his rod, and it became a serpent. The Egyptian magicians, however, copied this miracle, and Pharaoh was delighted. Even today on the streets of Cairo, Egypt, magicians practice this trick. The deadly Egyptian cobra can, under certain circumstances, become as stiff as a cane or rod. Then when it is thrown to the ground, the snake recovers, an apparent miracle. Since Pharaoh was not convinced by the second appeal accompanied by the sign, the Lord sent the first of the ten plagues.

The waters were turned to blood because the Nile River was one of the Egyptian gods. This certainly gave proof of the power of Jehovah over the gods of Egypt. The fish in the river died, and the people were not able to drink the water. The water changed to blood in all the streams, canals, ponds, and reservoirs, and even that stored in wooden and stone jars was affected. Once again, however, Pharaoh was pleased when the magicians of Egypt claimed that they had also duplicated this miracle.

There are always people who believe what they want to believe. Although they have evidence that God made the world in six literal days, some choose to believe that it evolved over a period of millions of years. The devil's master plan is to counterfeit everything God has done. We must test every claim, every miracle of healing, every teaching, to see whether it is God's genuine article or Satan's substitute.

It is also a sad fact that when people once reject the truths of God's Word, it is much harder for them to change their minds. God wants you to keep your mind open and your heart soft for the leading of the Holy Spirit. It is dangerous to harden your heart, to reject truth, or to become indifferent to the call of the Lord for you to change your conduct. Also, sometimes God does not reveal additional truths to those who do not act on the knowledge they have.

PURPOSE
Exodus 11

NINE MORE PLAGUES

And the Lord gave the people favor in the sight of the Egyptians. Moreover, the man Moses was very great in the land of Egypt, in the sight of Pharaoh's servants and in the sight of the people. Exodus 11:3.

Plague means "lashing," "torment," or "suffering." The ten plagues that fell on Egypt are described in the Bible as wonders, signs, and judgments. The first nine were calamities with which the Egyptians were familiar, but the tenth was not like anything they had ever heard of.

The ten plagues of Egypt were: the rivers turning to blood, swarms of frogs, invasion by lice and flies, diseases affecting animals and people, hail, swarms of locusts, and supernatural darkness. The tenth plague was the death of the first child in each Egyptian family.

The plagues in the natural world involved things that the people worshiped, such as frogs. Egyptians would not kill the frogs, so the creatures invaded the homes freely. Can you imagine Pharaoh being annoyed because there were hundreds of frogs in his bed? The sun refusing to shine was a defeat for the worshipers of the Egyptian sun god Ra.

The first nine plagues can be divided into three groups of three. Pharaoh was warned about the first two of each group, but the third came unannounced. During each plague we see Pharaoh pleading for mercy, but every time the Lord showed pity, the king reaffirmed his decision to keep the Hebrew people in Egypt. Thus it became necessary for God to send ten plagues.

Besides forcing Pharaoh to let Israel go, the plagues taught the children of Israel valuable lessons. As we study these results of stubbornness, we can see justice mixed with mercy, and thus our faith in God is strengthened.

Although the ten plagues of Egypt seem a long way away from our time, we must remember that before Jesus comes, seven great plagues are going to fall on this earth. Some of us may be living when these plagues come, and we need to learn as much as we can about how we can be sheltered from them. When we come to prophecy month, we will study more about the seven last plagues described in Revelation.

107

PURPOSE
Exodus 12

THE PASSOVER

"And when your children say to you, 'What do you mean by this service?' you shall say, 'It is the sacrifice of the Lord's passover, for he passed over the houses of the people of Israel in Egypt, when he slew the Egyptians but spared our houses.'" And the people bowed their heads and worshiped. Exodus 12:26, 27.

The clearest picture given in the Old Testament of our personal salvation through faith in the shed blood of Jesus Christ is in the story of the Passover. This service portrays the plan for Jesus to be the Lamb of God and our Redeemer.

In order for Pharaoh to let God's people leave Egypt, it was necessary for God to send ten plagues on the land. The last plague was the slaying of the firstborn. This was a terrible thing, brought about by Pharaoh's hardened heart. However, all those who sprinkled the blood of the lamb on the doorpost were saved from death.

Every part of the Passover service has special significance and further reveals God's plan for our salvation. It would be well for us now to study in detail all the particular parts of the Passover service, because they have special significance and point to Christ. Let's note just some of them.

The slain lamb without blemish was a beautiful representation of the Lamb of God, who died for our sins. It was not sufficient to kill the lamb; the blood must be applied. So today, it is not enough for us to know that Jesus Christ died for our sins; we must accept His sacrifice by daily giving our lives to Him.

After the blood was applied to the doorpost, there was direction for the nourishment of those who were about to travel. As we prepare for our journey to the heavenly kingdom, we need the nourishment provided by Christian fellowship, worship, and service.

The people were to eat while they were standing because they did not know at what moment they would have to leave. We must remember that we are pilgrims, and we must not become entrenched in this world and unprepared for the close of probation, which precedes translation.

Although we no longer celebrate the Passover, we are to claim "Christ our passover" Lamb each day (1 Cor. 5:7).

PURPOSE
Exodus 13

REMEMBER THIS DAY

And Moses said to the people, "Remember this day, in which you came out from Egypt, out of the house of bondage, for by strength of hand the Lord brought you out from this place; no leavened bread shall be eaten." Exodus 13:3.

Only about seventy people went down into Egypt, but at the time of the Exodus they had increased to between 2 and 3 million (see Num. 1:46). The growth from seventy to more than 2 million people in 215 years means the population doubled every fourteen to fifteen years.

Our text today reminds us that after the death of Joseph there was a change in the rulership of Egypt, and the children of Israel became a race of slaves. We have no account of what happened during the long period of silence between the books of Genesis and Exodus. Apparently the Israelites' growth and prosperity were reasons that led to their becoming slaves. It was hard for these people, who had lived with many evidences of God's blessing, to become bondsmen. While they were working under the lash of the slavemaster's whip, the promise of God that the descendants of Abraham would become a great nation was very hard for them to understand.

The reference to unleavened bread refers to the practice specified by God that only bread made without yeast would be eaten for a period of seven days following the Passover meal. Exodus 12 gives the details of the Passover, and we will look at its spiritual significance again when we study the book of Corinthians.

The exhortation "Remember this day" can also be applied to Christians today. We are to remember that we have been rescued from the house of bondage. Egypt represents the world, and we need to ask ourselves today, Have we really come out from the bondage of sin? Jesus has made provision whereby we can be "free indeed." Christians certainly need to remember the great things that God has done for them. Just as the Israelites celebrated the Passover, so we are to celebrate the Lord's Supper as a memorial of our deliverance. Baptism is another way in which we can remember God's deliverance from the bondage of sin.

PURPOSE
Exodus 14

THROUGH THE SEA

Then Moses stretched out his hand over the sea; and the Lord drove the sea back by a strong east wind all night, and made the sea dry land, and the waters were divided. And the people of Israel went into the midst of the sea on dry ground, the waters being a wall to them on their right hand and on their left. Exodus 14:21, 22.

The Passover sealed God's people. Likewise, today we are to be sealed as born-again Christians. The passage through the Red Sea followed the Passover. When we have truly passed over sin by claiming Christ's sacrifice and mediation, we can look forward to our passage to the sea of glass.

This is one of the greatest events in Old Testament history and is certainly a dramatic story of God's deliverance. There were 2 to 3 million people, unarmed and unorganized, including women, children, and the aged, in what seemed to be a hopeless condition. The sea lay to the east, the hills to the north and south, and to the west stretched an open valley along which perhaps a thousand Egyptian chariots with armed soldiers would soon appear. However, God led them this way. He did not take them by Philistia or by the caravan road round the mouth of the western arm of the Red Sea, but directly to this position of extreme danger with the sea roaring in their ears. It was possibly seven days between the Passover and the song that was sung on the eastern shore of the sea. This gave the Egyptians plenty of time to pursue.

On the fourteenth day of the month, on the night of the Passover, Israel had become a nation. On the morning of the twenty-first, the nation became free. If Moses had not said, "Forward," as God commanded, the children of Israel would never have become a nation. What a thrill it must have been to the people to see Moses stretch out his hand and then see the sea divide, with dry ground for them to walk on between the walls of water.

With our human reasoning we often think that any opening is God's plan for ourselves. Just as God took the children of Israel on what seemed to be a dead-end road, so we must remember that seemingly hopeless situations can be turned into times of triumph if we place our complete confidence in the Lord.

PURPOSE
Exodus 15

THE SONG OF TRIUMPH

"Thou hast led in thy steadfast love the people whom thou hast redeemed, thou hast guided them by thy strength to thy holy abode." Exodus 15:13.

It was natural and appropriate for the children of Israel to sing a song of deliverance on the morning after the Red Sea experience. Although Moses is not named as the author, the structure and content have led people to call it the Song of Moses. This song of triumph is composed of three stanzas. Each one begins with praising God and ends with a reference to the overthrow of the Egyptians in the Red Sea.

"Their emotion found utterance in songs of praise. The Spirit of God rested upon Moses, and he led the people in a triumphant anthem of thanksgiving, the earliest and one of the most sublime that are known to man."—*Patriarchs and Prophets,* p. 288.

In our verse for today, which is a part of that song, we once again have reference to the theme of the Bible, the plan of redemption. God's people are said to be redeemed, or purchased, and the deliverance at the Red Sea is the second time that God purchased Israel. They were also redeemed the night they were delivered from Egypt. As we trace the story of *light, love,* and *life* through the Scriptures, we will note that God is ever ready to redeem His people.

A small boy made a boat, fitted it with a sail made from a handkerchief, and set it out on the lake. The wind caught the sail, and the boat floated quickly out of his reach. The boy was very upset, and although his father tried to console him with the thought that he could make another one, he wanted that boat back. One day as he was walking with his father past a shop that sold secondhand goods, he noticed his boat in the window. His father agreed that it was his boat, so they went in and explained this to the shopkeeper. But he said that he had purchased it from another boy, and therefore it now belonged to him. There was only one way for the little boy to get the boat back, and that was to buy it. The boy held the boat close to him and said, "Now you are twice mine—first because I made you and second because I have bought you back." God has not only made us; He has redeemed us.

PURPOSE
Exodus 15

WHAT SHALL WE DRINK?

Then they came to Elim, where there were twelve springs of water and seventy palm trees; and they encamped there by the water. Exodus 15:27.

Before arriving at Elim, a beautiful oasis in the desert, the children of Israel first stopped at Marah. They had journeyed from the Red Sea after singing the Song of Moses, and they had run out of water. At Marah they were sorely disappointed because the water was bitter. However, the Lord performed a miracle, and when Moses cast a tree into the water, it was made sweet. We all have many Marah experiences because of failures, detours, or disappointments. We must remember that everyone has these trials, and just as God turned the bitter waters sweet for the children of Israel, so He will help us in our Marah experiences. When we are discouraged, we should be careful, because we cannot make wise decisions when we are at Marah.

The children of Israel traveled seven miles south and camped next to Elim. Even today this is one of the principal stopping places between Suez and Sinai because of its springs and vegetation. There are many Elims in our life's pilgrimage to heavenly Canaan also, including the weekly day of rest, the church, the home, the beauty spots of earth, and Christian service. God has been good to provide these Elims where we can have spiritual refreshment.

However, whatever outer lights may be in this land of our pilgrimage, we must remember that we are only camping. We must continue our journey and interest others in traveling to the city whose builder and maker is God. God has something better in store than the Elims of this life, and we will have the privilege of singing the Song of Moses and the Lamb.

The Song of Moses, found in the first eighteen verses of Exodus 15, is a song of victory. Ellen White states that it is "one of the most sublime [anthems] that are known to man" *(Patriarchs and Prophets,* p. 288). However, the Song of Moses and the Lamb that will be sung by the redeemed in the kingdom of heaven will be more sublime than even the song sung on the banks of the Red Sea.

PURPOSE
Exodus 16

WHAT IS IT?

And the people of Israel ate the manna forty years, till they came to a habitable land; they ate the manna, till they came to the border of the land of Canaan. Exodus 16:35.

Have you ever sat down at the dinner table and looked at the food and asked, What is it? Those of us who travel to different countries often see new foods and ask that question. It is interesting to taste foods that we have never seen before. No doubt in the new earth we are going to have many delicious foods to eat, and we will ask, What is it?

One day when the children of Israel were very hungry and some of them were longing for the familiar foods of Egypt, God told Moses, "I will rain bread from heaven" (Ex. 16:4). As the people rushed out to gather it, they asked, "What is it?" and their question has been translated in the Bible as the name of the food—"manna" (verse 15).

As you read Exodus 16, you'll notice that the manna came down from heaven six days a week, but on the seventh day it did not fall. Some people went out to gather it on the seventh day, but they could not find any. The only way they could have food for the Sabbath was to gather it on Friday. But if they tried to save food overnight on any other day, it would not keep. I believe that even if there had been refrigerators it would have gone bad, because God was teaching His people a very important lesson on Sabbathkeeping. He wants us to know how to prepare for and keep the Sabbath too.

This experience took place one month before the Ten Commandments were given to Moses on Mount Sinai. However, when God gave the manna, He stated that it would fall on six days, but not on the seventh day. He was teaching them that the seventh day is holy. When people went out to gather manna on the seventh day, the Lord said to Moses, "How long refuse ye to keep my commandments and my laws?" (verse 28). It is evident from this verse and the whole experience that the Ten Commandments were known from the time of Creation to Mount Sinai, and were simply given in written form at that time.

113

PURPOSE
Exodus 17

WHAT SHALL I DO?

And he called the name of the place Massah and Meribah, because of the faultfinding of the children of Israel, and because they put the Lord to the proof by saying, "Is the Lord among us or not?" Exodus 17:7.

It was a long way from the Red Sea to the land of Canaan, and the children of Israel had to find campsites where there was water. After they left the wilderness of Sin, where the manna fell for the first time, they pitched camp at Rephidim, where there was no water. Just as the people had demanded food, now they demanded water. And Moses did not know what to do, so he cried out to the Lord, "What shall I do?" There are many Bible examples of Moses turning to the Lord. This is God's plan for us when we come to troublesome situations. Moses was really in a difficult place this time, because the people were ready to stone him.

God, in His love and mercy, provided water by performing a miracle. The Lord had promised to help Moses, and He did so by allowing him to take part in the miracle. Moses was commanded to strike the rock with his staff, and when he did so, water flowed out. If the leaders who witnessed the miracle had any doubt about Moses being the Lord's appointed leader for the nation, it was settled at this time.

The place where the rock stood in Horeb was given names that mean "temptation" and "murmuring." These are mentioned in our text today. They would remind the children of Israel that they should never doubt God's power to provide or murmur against His appointed leaders. It is interesting to note that reference is made to this experience in the Psalms (78:20; 95:8; 105:41).

It is better to endure discomfort and to be continually doing God's will and sensing His presence than to try to escape discomfort if it means disobeying God, murmuring, and thus removing ourselves from His presence. We have every reason to trust God, and just as He provided water from a rock for the children of Israel, so He can provide for all our needs.

114

PURPOSE
Exodus 18

FAMILY REUNION

And Jethro, Moses' father-in-law, came with his sons and his wife to Moses in the wilderness where he was encamped at the mountain of God. Exodus 18:5.

Up to this time Jethro is known only as a relative of Moses, but now he stands forth as a spiritual giant who gave good advice to Moses on how to govern the people. Moses received his counsel as graciously as he received Jethro upon his arrival (Ex. 18:7). Zipporah, Moses' wife, is not mentioned often in the Bible. Her name means "bird." She was one of Jethro's seven daughters, and first met Moses when she was caring for her father's flocks as Moses fled from Egypt.

Moses' sons' names have interesting meanings, which are explained in verses 3 and 4. They are reminders to Moses of lessons learned during his stay in Midian. Gershom recalled his human weakness, and Eliezer reminded him of God's deliverance in time of need. The elder son's name recollected his loneliness in a strange land, and the younger caused him to remember that God was his refuge and strength in times of trouble and loneliness.

This beautiful family reunion in the wilderness took place at the encampment of the children of Israel "at the mount of God." This was Mount Horeb, in the area where Moses had stood before the burning bush and later supplied water from the rock for the people. Imagine the excitement of the sons of Moses as they approached this memorable spot! Gershom probably had never seen as many sheep as he saw in the flocks of the children of Israel. Never before would he have seen so many tents. It would be like someone in your country coming from a mountain home into a very large city. Gershom would be introduced to an aunt and uncle whom he had never seen before, who would tell him many stories about Egypt and the journey through the wilderness. But most of all he would be delighted to see his father again.

Like the sons of Moses, we are about to have a family reunion "at the mount of God." We are going to see all of God's people, from Adam down to those living in our time. We are going to meet our relatives in the Lord. But above all we will have the joy of a new relationship with our heavenly Father and His Son, our Elder Brother, Jesus.

PURPOSE
Exodus 19

THE BIRTH OF A NATION

"And you shall be to me a kingdom of priests and a holy nation." Exodus 19:6.

How would you feel if you had to walk through a wilderness each day and camp in it each night for about six weeks? This is what the boys and girls who marched with the children of Israel had to do. There must have been a lot of dust from the tramping of millions of feet, both human and animal. Finally, though, they arrived at Mount Sinai, where they were to remain for more than eleven months.

All of us need time to rest, as Jesus advised (see Mark 6:31). Just as God had special things planned for the children of Israel at Mount Sinai, so He has times of quietness and solitude planned for us when we can enter into a close relationship with Him. It was His plan at Mount Sinai that the children of Israel would pledge to love and obey Him, and He wants us to say sincerely, "All that the Lord has spoken, we will do." How sad the Lord must have been when the people did not keep the covenant that they had made. He is also very sad when we fail to ask Him for strength to do the things that we say we want to do for Him.

The wilderness of Sinai, about two miles long and a mile wide, has sufficient space for a large number of people to camp. There are rocky mountains on either side, forming a natural amphitheater. Moses and Aaron and some of the leaders were allowed to go up the mountain, but the people were to watch God's presence from a distance. Thus far God had revealed Himself to them as a deliverer, but now they were to see Him as lawgiver and ruler of the universe. To Elijah on the mountain He spoke in a "still small voice." But to these people who had murmured and questioned His leadership, He appeared in a very dramatic way. After specific instructions as to how they should prepare themselves spiritually and physically, on the third day there were thunderings and lightnings, followed by a thick cloud on the mountain and the sound of a trumpet that was so loud everybody trembled. Next there was smoke and fire, and the whole mountain shook. At Mount Sinai one of the most significant events in the history of the children of Israel took place when Israel was organized into a nation ruled directly by God.

PURPOSE
Exodus 20

GOD SPOKE

And God spoke all these words, saying, "I am the Lord your God, who brought you out of the land of Egypt, out of the house of bondage." Exodus 20:1, 2.

The Ten Commandments form a summary of our duties and responsibilities toward God and man. When we love God supremely and unselfishly, we will not let anything or anyone come between us. We will not make graven images or take our Maker's name in vain, and we will delight to keep the seventh-day Sabbath as a memorial of Creation. When we love people as God loves them, we will honor our parents, and refrain from killing, committing adultery, stealing, bearing false witness, and coveting.

When we study the New Testament, we will see that Jesus summarized the commandments in one word—*love*. He stated that the commandments simply mean that we are to love God and other people unconditionally. One of the major causes for unhappiness is that we tend to want God and other people to love us unconditionally while we, in turn, attach strings to our love for God and others.

Our Morning Watch text today, which is the preface to the Ten Commandments, emphasizes the fact that these laws are applicable to all mankind. We can rejoice that God still says, "I am the Lord thy God." Just as Israel had been redeemed from Egypt, so we have been delivered from the bondage of sin. It is significant to note that the Ten Commandments were proclaimed at Mount Sinai rather than in Palestine, which further emphasizes that they are for all people. This beautiful law, to ensure the happiness of the human race, crosses all cultures and civilizations.

The introduction to the Ten Commandments has been beautifully put into verse by Isaac Watts:

"I am the Lord, 'tis I proclaim that glorious and that fearful name,

"Thy God and king; 'tis I that broke thy bondage and the Egyptian yoke;

"Mine is the right to speak My will; and thine the duty to fulfill."

PURPOSE
Exodus 24

FORTY DAYS WITH GOD

And Moses entered the cloud, and went up on the mountain. And Moses was on the mountain forty days and forty nights. Exodus 24:18.

What a wonderful privilege it was for Moses to spend forty days and forty nights on the mountain with God. He was completely alone with Him, for Aaron and his sons and the forty elders were not invited into God's immediate presence. The glory of the Lord, described as being "like devouring fire," was seen by all the people, however.

Before Moses could enjoy communion with God alone, though, there had to be a six-day preparation period. We also need to prepare our lives before we come into the presence of God. Secret prayer is just as necessary for the Christian today as it was for Moses on Mount Sinai. The time of prayer should be accompanied by meditation. We must not only speak to God but we must allow Him to speak to us through His Word.

A small boy was standing on tiptoe trying to reach the doorbell of a house near the sidewalk of a busy London street. A man came along and, feeling sorry for the boy, lifted him up so that he could reach the bell. The little fellow pressed the button and said, "All right, mister, now let's scoot!"

This boy was just playing a game that would eventually get him into trouble. His game reminds us of what we sometimes do in our prayers. We kneel down and reach up by the hand of faith, asking the Lord many things. But before He can answer, we scoot off. We need to spend time with the Lord in secret prayer and allow Him to speak to us through His Word.

Moses' time on Mount Sinai also reminds us of the work of Jesus as our mediator. He has ascended into heaven and one day soon will be coming back to His people. Although the heavens may be covered with clouds and we may think that our prayers do not ascend any higher than the mists, we can rest assured that our Mediator hears our prayers. The signs of the Second Coming are all around us, reminding us that very soon our Maker will return as King of kings and Lord of lords. When that day comes, we will begin eternity with God.

PURPOSE
Exodus 31

BY GOD'S FINGER

And he gave to Moses, when he had made an end of speaking with him upon Mount Sinai, the two tables of the testimony, tables of stone, written with the finger of God. Exodus 31:18.

The Ten Commandments were not only spoken so that all the children of Israel could hear every word, they were also miraculously written on tables of stone by the finger of God. One of the reasons that Moses was invited to the mountaintop was so that he might receive the commandments, engraved on the two tables of stone. It is interesting to note that they are called tables of "testimony," for this is one of the words that is used in the Old Testament to describe the Ten Commandments. The fact that God wrote the commandments originally with His own finger indicated their importance, and Jesus reaffirmed in the New Testament that they will always be binding and should never be changed in any detail (see Matt. 5:18).

Do you know what the word *law* means? It comes from the verb "to lay," and literally means "something laid down." The Ten Commandments, given by God to Moses, have been laid down for us to obey, not to spoil our happiness, but to ensure that we are happy. There are three reasons why it is best to obey what God has said. The first is that it gives us security in what we have to do. The law also outlines what we can and cannot do, and this direction shows that God loves us. Finally, it is pleasant to obey God because we are practicing for heaven, which is a perfect, peaceful place where everyone is delighted to obey the Lord.

While Moses was up in the mountain, he was also given instructions on building a portable church, which was called a tabernacle or sanctuary (Ex. 25:8). All the details concerning the materials to be used, the construction, and the plans were given to Moses. These are recorded in Exodus and Leviticus. God even named certain men, such as Bezalel, who was a skilled craftsman, to take charge of building the sanctuary. God has given skills for secular work that can be just as valuable to Him as are spiritual gifts, if they are fully consecrated to the Lord. Today God needs Bezalels as well as Pauls to extend the boundaries of the kingdom of heaven.

PURPOSE
Exodus 32

PEER PRESSURE

Then Moses stood in the gate of the camp, and said, "Who is on the Lord's side? Come to me." And all the sons of Levi gathered themselves together to him. Exodus 32:26.

In all the years that Aaron had been associated with Moses, his brother, in leadership, he had not learned to stand for the right when it meant standing alone. Aaron gave in to the pressures of the people and actually led out in the erection of a golden image. This was in direct defiance to the words of God that had been spoken on Mount Sinai. Although the people actually began their celebration by worshiping God, the mob spirit took over, and they soon bowed down before the golden calf and engaged in other terrible sins.

There were perhaps two reasons why the people requested Aaron to have a molten god. One was the delay of Moses' return from the mountain, and the other was that they did not have a heart religion. They had given mental assent by saying, "All that the Lord hath said, will we do" (Ex. 24:7). But it was not a real experience with the God of heaven. Today there are professed Christians who say, "My Lord delayeth his coming," and make an excuse to indulge in things that God, for our good, has forbidden.

Aaron's sin was that of compromise. Then, as in the case of Adam, he made weak excuses for his actions. However, there was a bright side to this story. And that is that Moses demonstrated strong leadership no matter what the personal consequences might be. Seeing the acts of idolatry and immorality, this great leader broke the tables of stone, indicating that the people had broken their covenant with God. Then he had the courage to stand before the people and call for allegiance to God.

The newly formed nation deserved to be destroyed, but God did not annihilate the people, because of the mediation of Moses and his willingness to be blotted out of the book of life in order to save them. Once again we see the plan of redemption in operation as Moses offers to do what Jesus did do, and that was to die for the people. God could not accept Moses' sacrifice, but He did accept the future atonement of Jesus Christ.

PURPOSE
Exodus 33

PROMISED REST

And he said, "My presence will go with you, and I will give you rest." Exodus 33:14.

As we study the Bible records carefully, we see in all God's words and acts a master plan of which every part is designed to help people develop characters fit for the kingdom of heaven. In order for the children of Israel to develop spiritually, they had to learn the dangers of yielding to sin. As a result of worshiping the golden calf, three thousand people were slain and a plague broke out in the camp. God also declared that rather than accompanying them Himself, He could send only an angel with them as they entered the Promised Land. However, as they showed true repentance He instructed Moses to make a temporary tabernacle outside the camp, where Moses talked with God and the people saw the glory of His presence.

Moses once again interceded on behalf of the people and himself, and God declared, "My presence shall go with thee, and I will give thee rest." Once again we see the mercy and love of God to a wayward people. Moses asked for personal contact again with God, and he was assured that God knew his name. God also directed Moses to a cleft in a rock, where, covered by God's hand, he saw the divine glory pass by. This was one of the closest encounters that any human being has ever had with God.

Chapter 33 begins with the people discouraged because they were separated from God, but it closes with a promise of God's rest and a demonstration of His presence.

This promise is ours today, too. We can always have the sense of God's presence as long as we are connected to Him. God does not move away. Even though we may not feel that our prayers go any higher than the ceiling, God has declared that His presence is always with us and that we can have rest in the midst of tempest. When we think of rest, we must not think only of some hallowed feeling that comes over us as we sit in church. As a matter of fact, we can enjoy God's rest without any overwhelming feelings. We can be assured that when we have God's presence with us we also have His peace in our lives. This assurance is based on the fact that Jesus is the Prince of Peace.

PURPOSE
Exodus 34

ON THE MOUNT AGAIN

And he was there with the Lord forty days and forty nights; he neither ate bread nor drank water. And he wrote upon the tables the words of the covenant, the ten commandments. Exodus 34:28.

It is interesting to note that Moses was allowed to spend another forty days and forty nights in the presence of God on Mount Sinai. During this time God had to teach Moses and the children of Israel lessons that we need to learn also.

Inasmuch as Moses had broken the first set of tablets, he had to make the second set to take up into the mountain. So it is with us—if we willfully break the law, we need to restore and to go to the mount to seek the Lord's pardon. If we steal something, we need to return it. If we say something that is unkind about someone, we need to make an apology. When we have made things right with those we have wronged, we must confess our sins to the Lord.

Although Moses literally broke the stone on which the Ten Commandments were written, the law was actually broken by the people when they disobeyed God. They, along with Moses, had lessons to learn, and in addition they had to be tested to see whether they would remain true to God during another six weeks without their spiritual leader. We may not have access to a church or the help of a pastor, and perhaps we are not even able to fellowship with believers, but this is no excuse for failing to serve God. We need to be strong enough Christians that we can be true to God, independent of circumstances. We have many examples in the Bible of boys and girls, young people and adults, who were true to the Lord although they were separated from their loved ones or their country and its religious freedom. Can you name some of these people?

Another blessing that came from Moses' going into the mountain the second time was that the Lord revealed to him again six beautiful characteristics of His character. These are listed in Exodus 34:6, 7.

After Moses had spent time with the Lord, his face was aglow. Do you want to have a radiant face? If so, don't think about it, but spend time in communion with God. When we forget self and reflect on the character of God, our faces will be truly radiant.

PURPOSE
Exodus 35

READY TO BUILD

Moses assembled all the congregation of the people of Israel, and said to them, "These are the things which the Lord has commanded you to do." Exodus 35:1.

There was excitement in the camp of Israel when Moses gathered the people together and told them that they could begin building the sanctuary. Between the two visits of Moses to the mountain there was a delay in construction. This was because of the people's rebellion. Time was also needed to renew the covenant or agreement that God had made with them that He would be their God and they would be His people.

The detailed description that God gave for the construction of the sanctuary shows its importance in the plan of salvation. As we will discover when we read the book of Hebrews, every article of furniture pointed to Jesus. Since each piece had special significance, it had to be carefully constructed. There were very detailed instructions about the manufacture, about the materials, and about even such seemingly small things as the number of curtain loops. The tabernacle itself was forty-five feet long, fifteen feet wide, and fifteen feet high. There was also a courtyard around it, surrounded by a curtain.

The last chapter of Exodus contains a description of the completion of the tabernacle and of what happened on the day it was finished. One of the most significant events was that a cloud "covered the tent of the congregation, and the glory of the Lord filled the tabernacle" (verse 34). Then, too, "fire was on it by night" (verse 38).

You'll remember that the book of Exodus begins with a description of darkness and gloom, but because of God's *light, love,* and *life,* it ends in glory. In the first part of the book we learned that God came down in grace to deliver slaves from captivity, and the closing chapters show how He came down in glory to dwell with the people who had been redeemed. Now that we have reviewed God's plan for redeeming His people from the Red Sea and Egypt and from destruction at Mount Sinai, we need to make sure that He has redeemed us. If we have been redeemed, we will rejoice in the *light, love,* and *life* offered by the gospel of Christ, and know that God's protecting cloud by day and pillar of fire by night will accompany us as we journey to the Promised Land.

PURPOSE
Leviticus 1

ANIMALS TO CHURCH?

And the Lord called unto Moses, and spake unto him out of the tabernacle of the congregation, saying, Speak unto the children of Israel, and say unto them, If any man of you bring an offering unto the Lord, ye shall bring your offering of the cattle, even of the herd, and of the flock. Leviticus 1:1, 2, K.J.V.

Can you imagine what it would look and smell like to have thousands of animals and birds in the parking lot of your church? Imagine bullocks, sheep, goats, and little lambs and kids. There would also be doves and pigeons by the hundreds in cages. This is what you would have seen if you had lived back in the days when the people brought animals as offerings instead of money. There would have been a great number of animals and birds, because there were 2 to 3 million people in Israel and sometimes it was necessary for a family to bring an offering once or twice a day.

The offerings were part of the sanctuary services, and each pointed to Jesus, "the Lamb of God, which taketh away the sin of the world" (John 1:29). God instituted these offerings as a part of His plan to teach the people what sin really was. The five offerings, all of which pointed to Jesus' sacrifice for sin, were called by these names: burnt, meal, peace, sin, and trespass. These offerings are described in the first seven chapters of the book of Leviticus.

You'll notice that the book of Leviticus begins with the word *and,* which suggests that it is a continuation of the book of Exodus. Exodus ended with the record of the building of the sanctuary, and Leviticus and Numbers outline the services, including the work of the priest from the tribe of Levi. The book gets its name from the fact that it chiefly deals with the priesthood. The children of Israel remained at Sinai for the thirty-day period covered by the book of Leviticus.

Although we are not suggesting that you read the book of Leviticus at this stage, it is one that Christians should study, for it helps us to understand the New Testament. It is evident that the author of the book of Hebrews understood the book of Leviticus.

PURPOSE
Leviticus 11

THINGS THAT CREEP

For I am the Lord your God: ye shall therefore sanctify yourselves, and ye shall be holy; for I am holy: neither shall ye defile yourselves with any manner of creeping thing that creepeth upon the earth. Leviticus 11:44, K.J.V.

We certainly do not like unclean "creeping things that creepeth," and God has told us that we must not defile ourselves with them. There are clean "creeping things that creepeth," so we have to learn what clean and unclean creeping things are all about. When Noah brought the animals into the ark, he took seven pairs of clean animals and birds and only two pairs of unclean. Moses, under instruction from God. put into writing the distinction between these two classes of creatures, and this is recorded in Leviticus 11.

The principles outlined in this chapter are given to protect people from eating food that would be harmful to their bodies. Some people think everything that is written in the books of Moses concerning laws has been dispensed with, but this is not true. These health laws, outlined more than 3,500 years ago, are still applicable today. Some of the unclean animals mentioned are scavengers, and their flesh is not to be eaten at all.

You'll no doubt be interested in studying the characteristics of the clean and unclean creatures. You'll discover that only animals that chew their cud and have a divided hoof and fish that have fins and scales are clean. Among the unclean are the camel, hare, pig, eagle, owl, swan, and pelican.

Many people do not eat any flesh foods. They are known as vegetarians. God intended for us to be vegetarians, for this is the diet that He gave at Creation. All who go to heaven will be vegetarians, because animals and birds will not be killed there. Nothing is going to die in the new earth.

There is a deeper reason why God gave the law of clean and unclean animals. This precept is designed to teach that God is holy and that we are to be holy too. God wants His people to know that holiness, which is the main lesson of the book of Leviticus, also relates to our physical being.

PURPOSE
Leviticus 16

DESERT PASSION PLAY

And he shall make an atonement for the holy sanctuary, and he shall make an atonement for the tabernacle of the congregation, and for the altar, and he shall make an atonement for the priests, and for all the people of the congregation. Leviticus 16:33, K.J.V.

A Passion play is a dramatic portrayal of the crucifixion of Jesus. The most famous Passion play is performed every ten years in Oberammergau, in southern Germany. This eight-hour drama is presented by more than one thousand people as a result of a vow made in 1633 when a terrible plague ended.

God planned the first Passion play in the desert near Mount Sinai. There were between 2 and 3 million men, women, and children living in tents set out in orderly rows. The stage for the play was the sanctuary, which was the focal point of the canvas encampment. The play might have been entitled *The Day of Atonement,* and was held on the tenth day of the seventh month. The main "actor" in the play was the high priest, who, dressed in beautifully embroidered, spotlessly white garments, represented our High Priest, Jesus. All the people watched in reverence as this chosen man took the blood of the animal that had been offered in the courtyard, and sprinkled it in the holy place. This signified the blood of Jesus, shed for repentant sinners. The climactic act in the play came when the high priest entered the Most Holy Place, which he did only once a year.

There was silence in the camp as the people listened for the tinkle of the bells on the priestly robes. If all sins had not been confessed and forsaken, the priest would die as he entered the presence of God. The act of going into the Most Holy Place represented Jesus' beginning the work of judgment in the heavenly sanctuary. We will study this in Daniel's prophecies.

This sacred service was a part of God's plan to reveal how we are to be saved. We need to know about the Day of Atonement and the cleansing of the heavenly sanctuary in order to appreciate fully what Jesus is doing. Leviticus 16 is one of the great chapters of the Bible. Hidden within its 34 verses is one of the most important truths of the Bible. This is summarized in the next chapter—"For the life of the flesh is in the blood" (verse 11).

126

PURPOSE
Numbers 10

TWO SILVER TRUMPETS

The Lord said to Moses, "Make two silver trumpets; of hammered work you shall make them; and you shall use them for summoning the congregation, and for breaking camp." Numbers 10:1, 2.

It's interesting to note that God is interested even in small details. He specified to Moses that he was to make two trumpets and that each one was to be constructed of one piece of silver. These trumpets were not only for calling the assembly together and for commencing and signaling the start and finish of a day's march, but they were also used on special occasions and to commence a battle. God actually promised that when the trumpet was blown in times of battle, He would deliver the people from their enemies (Num. 10:9).

The blowing of the silver trumpets is a figure of prayer. The trumpets of jubilee mentioned in the book of Leviticus were a symbol of the preaching of the gospel. We can rest assured that when we pray, the Lord remembers us and delivers us from the assaults of Satan and his wicked angels. Just as a trumpet emits a ringing, joyful sound, so our prayers should contain not only requests but also joyful praise to God for His goodness.

The two silver trumpets were first used to start the children of Israel on their journey out of the wilderness of Sinai. It was God's plan that they travel by way of Kadesh straight to the land of Canaan. But because of their disobedience, they had to wander in the wilderness for forty years. By that time almost all the adults who came out of Egypt were dead. Only the two faithful spies, Joshua and Caleb, were alive to go into the Promised Land. Even Moses was not allowed to enter. However, he was resurrected from the dead and is in heaven today (see Matt. 17:3).

"The Lord spake," "God said," and similar expressions are used more than five hundred times in the first five books of the Bible, and God expects us to heed His instructions.

The sound of the silver trumpets could be heard throughout the camp of Israel, and when the people heard it, they were to obey. Likewise, we need to obey the voice of the Lord when He speaks to us through His Word and in prayer.

PURPOSE
Numbers 11

BOOK OF MURMURINGS

And the people complained in the hearing of the Lord about their misfortunes; and when the Lord heard it, his anger was kindled, and the fire of the Lord burned among them, and consumed some outlying parts of the camp. Numbers 11:1.

Grandma Brown was sitting in her rocking chair one beautiful spring day, her green parrot perched on the chair enjoying the motion as she rocked back and forth. But Grandma Brown was not happy. She was soon to go to a home for the aged, and she would have to give her parrot away.

Andrew, Mary Ann, and Johnny had each asked to have the beautiful bird. So before deciding who could keep it, Grandma Brown was going to let each of the children take the parrot home for one week.

At the end of the first week when Andrew brought it back the parrot said, "I don't want to chop wood. I don't want to chop wood . . ." When the parrot came back from Mary Ann's home the next week, it said, "Oh, do I have to do homework? Oh, do I have to take the dog for a walk?" And when it came back from Johnny's home the parrot said, "OK, Mother, I'll rake the leaves." "Yes, Mother, I'll go to bed now."

Grandma Brown gave the parrot to Johnny. From Andrew and Mary Ann it learned only words of murmuring, and Grandma did not like that.

Are you a murmurer? For more than forty years the children of Israel, after leaving Mount Sinai, seemed to specialize in complaining. Their grumblings are not mimicked by parrots, but are recorded in the book of Numbers. It is the record of their wanderings from the mountain where they met the Lord to the Land of Promise where they should have dwelt with the Lord.

Just as we do not like people who murmur about all they have to do, neither does the Lord. After listening to the Israelites' complaining for many years, one day God checked their grumblings by consuming parts of the camp with fire. Today some of us need the fire of the Holy Spirit to take selfishness from our lives so that we will not murmur. It would be good for us to pray for cleansing by the Holy Spirit each day.

PURPOSE
Numbers 23

WHAT HATH GOD WROUGHT!

"For there is no enchantment against Jacob, no divination against Israel; now it shall be said of Jacob and Israel, 'What has God wrought!'" Numbers 23:23.

Samuel was on the ship *Sully,* traveling from Europe to the United States in 1832. One day while having dinner, he heard that it was now possible to send electricity through a piece of wire. He was a famous artist with an interest in electrical and chemical experiments. While on the ship he thought of sending a message through the wires. As he left the ship, he said, "Well, Captain, should you hear of the telegraph one of these days, as the wonder of the world, remember the discovery was made on the good ship *Sully.*"

Samuel Morse experimented for many years, but he lacked funds to complete his work. However, in 1843 the United States Congress voted $30,000 to test the telegraph. What happened on May 24, 1844, is now history, for Samuel Morse tapped out the famous message "What hath God wrought!"

The statement "What hath God wrought!" was first made by Balaam to Balak, king of the Moabites. The children of Israel were now in Moabite territory, and Balak had bribed Balaam to curse them. Balaam was noted for unusual powers, but he was no longer a true prophet. However, under the influence of the Holy Spirit, he did prophesy of the Messiah: "There shall come a Star out of Jacob" (Num. 24:17).

We have discovered that God has many ways of calling people back to true worship. Numbers 22 records the dramatic story of a donkey talking to Balaam. The animal sat down in the middle of the road because it had seen an angel. When Balaam struck the donkey, it said, "What have I done unto thee, that thou hast smitten me these three times?" (verse 28). After the donkey spoke a second time, Balaam saw the angel with a drawn sword in his hand. He recognized his sin, but did not fully repent. He was later killed in battle.

Yes, God is leading in the lives of individuals as well as in the events of nations. We can be thankful for what He has wrought despite the effects of sin in this world.

PURPOSE
Deuteronomy 18

JESUS' FAVORITE BOOK

"The Lord your God will raise up for you a prophet like me from among you, from your brethren—him you shall heed." Deuteronomy 18:15.

More books have been written about Jesus than about any other person, according to the Library of Congress of the United States. Their list of books written about famous people is as follows: Jesus Christ, 5,152; William Shakespeare, 3,172; Abraham Lincoln, 2,319; George Washington, 1,755; and Napoleon, 1,735.

Although we may learn of and read books that have been written about Jesus, it is interesting to consider that our Saviour read books too. When He was a young man just entering His teens, only the Old Testament had been written, and there were not many copies of each of its thirty-nine books available. These books were read on Sabbath in the synagogue, and we have record of at least one occasion when Jesus read in the synagogue from the book of Isaiah.

If someone were to ask us what other books Jesus quoted from, we would no doubt say the Psalms and other prophets. However, many who have studied the Bible carefully have concluded that the book of Deuteronomy was one of Jesus' favorites. He often quoted from it and adopted its teachings as a guide for His life. The answers He gave the devil in the wilderness come from the book of Deuteronomy (see Deut. 8:3; 6:13, 16; 10:20).

Some of the reasons this book was a favorite with Jesus were that it tells what God expects of us, and shows how to live a life of obedience and the blessings that result from doing God's will. The book of Deuteronomy also has strong appeals for us to live the Christian life through the power that God has provided.

Deuteronomy is quoted at least ninety times in the New Testament. It climaxes with the statement about Jesus recorded in our text for today.

"The book of Deuteronomy should be carefully studied by those living on earth today."—*The SDA Bible Commentary*, Ellen G. White Comments, on Deut. 1:1, p. 1117. Although we have not been able to list the book of Deuteronomy to be read this year, we recommend that you read it in a single sitting as soon as possible.

PROMISES
Romans 1

5,891 PROMISES

Paul, a servant of Jesus Christ, called to be an apostle, set apart for the gospel of God which he promised beforehand through his prophets in the holy scriptures. Romans 1:1, 2.

The boy had suffered with malaria for nine weeks. The year was 1848, and because of the lack of medicine, he almost died. As soon as he was strong enough to walk, however, John Norton Loughborough, 16 years of age and with one dollar and patched clothes, determined to fulfill his vow to preach. When a family friend heard of his decision, he said, "This is just what I have expected you to do. When you were 2 years old your father said to me, 'That little fellow is going to help blow the gospel trumpet.'" The friend gave him an additional two dollars, and John set off.

In New York he heard John Andrews preach, and joined him in spreading the third angel's message. Sixteen years later, with Pastor D. T. Bourdeau, he answered the call to open the work in California. There was no transcontinental railroad, so the two men sailed to Panama, crossed the narrow isthmus, and sailed north, taking a tent and books. Soon a church was started in California, and a camp meeting was conducted in 1872.

John Loughborough felt "set apart for the gospel of God," and preached till he died at 92. Among other things, he is remembered for his book *The Great Second Advent Movement*.

This pioneer Seventh-day Adventist preacher read the Scriptures through at least seventy times. In the flyleaf of one of his Bibles, written in his own hand, is this:

"There are in the Old Testament 2,253 promises for the present.

"There are in the Old Testament 791 promises for the future.

"There are in the New Testament 274 promises for the present.

"There are in the New Testament 2,573 promises for the future.

"Total of 5,891 promises in the Bible."

This month we shall discover in Paul's writings thirty-one promises and statements that can help us live the Christian life. It would be good to underline these assurances. Also, let's see whether, like J. N. Loughborough, we can discover thousands of promises in the Bible.

PROMISES
Romans 2

WEALTH FOR YOU!

Or do you think lightly of his wealth of kindness, of tolerance, and of patience, without recognizing that God's kindness is meant to lead you to a change of heart? Romans 2:4, N.E.B.

For thousands of years the sign of wealth has been a bright, yellow metal called gold. At the time this book was written, gold was selling at more than $600 an ounce. The majority of the world's gold is now mined in South Africa and Russia. If a country has a lot of gold in storage, its money is considered valuable.

While visiting a gold mine in South Africa, I was given the opportunity of trying to lift a gold brick. The brick weighed about thirty-five pounds, and the visitors were told that whoever could lift it with one hand could have it. However, it was slanted so that it was wider at the bottom than at the top, making it very difficult even to grasp with one hand, much less lift it. That brick of gold would now be worth about $336,000.

When we think of wealth or riches, it is natural for us to think of gold. However, there are other kinds of wealth, and the most valuable thing that you and I can possess is our character. Our entrance into the kingdom of heaven is not going to be determined by the amount of gold that we have, but by the golden character that we have obtained through the grace of the Lord Jesus Christ.

Not only does God want us to be wealthy in character but He has promised that we can be. Paul's writings remind us of these promises. The purpose of the opening chapters of the book of Romans is to show to us that the world needs the character and salvation that is offered through Jesus.

It is wonderful to know that even though we are not always good Christians, God continues to show us kindness, tolerance, and patience. However, these beautiful character qualities should lead us to "a change of heart." If we were given a brick of gold, we would not be able to buy things with it if we kept it in a cupboard. Likewise, it is not enough for us to receive God's "goodness and forbearance and longsuffering." These things will only help us as they lead us to a "change of heart."

PROMISES
Romans 3

SET FREE

For all alike have sinned, and are deprived of the divine splendour, and all are justified by God's free grace alone. Romans 3:23, 24, N.E.B.

It is a sad fact that ever since there have been nations, there have been slaves. We read in the Bible of people who were captured in battle and taken to other countries to work. Under these circumstances they lost their freedom and had to do exactly what their masters told them, without being paid for their efforts. Large sailing ships took people as slaves from one country to another. Many people from Africa were brought to America in this capacity.

The slaves in North America were given their freedom when Abraham Lincoln signed the Emancipation Proclamation. Some years later an artist wrote the Emancipation Proclamation in such a way that at first glance it looks like a picture of Abraham Lincoln. However, as you look more closely you can read the declaration that freed the slaves. As we read the books of the Bible, we may see only stories of people and events and teachings and prophecies. However, as we look closer we will see in every part of the Scriptures a declaration of freedom from the slavery of sin.

Last month we saw God's *purposes* as He guided His people from slavery to salvation through Jesus Christ. This month we will examine the *promises* and see that God has assured us that we are to be set free.

Yes, we all have sinned and are in slavery of sin until we are set free by Jesus. This is declared as "an act of liberation." When a slave or country is freed from an oppressor, it is liberated. When we are set free from sin, we are liberated and can praise God for this freedom.

In our promise today, as it reads in other versions, we are told that when we are set free it is a "gift." We cannot buy it even with bricks of gold. Our lives belong to God, and as we give them back to Him we are set free. When we experience this, we will rejoice because we will be able to live a happy life now and have eternal life hereafter. This is *light for my life.*

PROMISES
Romans 4

THE PROMISES ARE SURE

And never doubted God's promise in unbelief, but, strong in faith, gave honour to God, in the firm conviction of his power to do what he had promised. And that is why Abraham's faith was "counted to him as righteousness." Romans 4:20-22, N.E.B.

Ropes used in the British Navy have a scarlet strand interwoven in them. This distinguishes them from other ropes and shows clearly that they belong to Her Majesty's Navy. In a similar way there is a scarlet thread of salvation to be seen in every book of the Bible. When that salvation becomes a part of our lives, everybody knows that we belong to Jesus—the One responsible for the lifeline between heaven and earth.

We have already discovered from Romans how we can become Christians. And in the next few chapters Paul elaborates on this and clarifies the relationship of the place of faith and works in our lives. Paul anticipates that someone in his day might say that people such as Abraham and David were saved by their own merits. These men certainly did great things for God, and some of these deeds are recorded in Romans 4. But they were not saved by their own works.

Paul also shows from the life of Abraham that the gospel is clearly seen in Genesis. Abraham's good life and good works were the result of his faith. Abraham obtained three things by faith: righteousness, an inheritance, and many descendants. The birth of Isaac was a miracle, for Abraham was 100 and his wife, Sarah, was 90 before the promise of a son was fulfilled.

Abraham's promise of an inheritance included the birth of Jesus among his descendants. Abraham lived thousands of years before Jesus, but the genealogy of Christ, recorded in Matthew 1, shows that He was "the son of David, the son of Abraham." Once again we see that the promises of God are sure.

Later this month we will see that the promises are conditional on obedience. We cannot expect to disobey God and still receive the promised blessings. Also, as stated in our Morning Watch text today, in order to claim the promises of God we must be "strong in faith."

PROMISES
Romans 5

REASONS TO REJOICE

More than this: let us even exult in our present sufferings, because we know that suffering trains us to endure, and endurance brings proof that we have stood the test, and this proof is the ground of hope. Romans 5:3, 4, N.E.B.

The heading "Brain Pacemaker Has Made His Life a Joy" was in large type across six columns of the *Rhodesian Herald,* November 6, 1974. The feature story was about a Seventh-day Adventist man who was the first person in Africa to have an electronic pacemaker placed in his brain.

Douglas Mattheys realized that he had only a fifty-fifty chance of success. But he had suffered from blackouts for years, and the last time had experienced a severe concussion as he fell. When told of the odds, he said, "I thought about it and talked it over with my wife. I was no asset to my family as I was. I was ill and depressed and I couldn't enjoy my three boys. So what had I to lose?"

The craniotomy involved an incision requiring fifty-five stitches. Electrons were inserted above each ear, and a cut was made at the nape of his neck in order to put in an electronic brain pacemaker. Wires from the pacemaker were placed under his skin past the shoulders to the chest. Two transmitters were inserted just below the collarbone, leaving little round bumps on his chest.

The battery-operated regulator was connected to the transmitters; ten volts of electric current activated the electrodes in the brain. The electronic brain pacemaker, electrodes, and transmitters, connected to the regulator, controlled the faulty circuit that had caused the suffering over the years.

Douglas Mattheys knows what it is to suffer. During his extensive tests and operations, his "ground of hope" was his God. The six reasons for rejoicing listed in Romans 5 have also been cause for rejoicing for Mr. Mattheys. As you read this chapter in Romans, you will note that these reasons can be summarized as follows:

—Pardon (verse 1), peace (verse 1), patience (verses 3, 4);
—Power (verse 5), passion (verse 8), promise (verse 2).

PROMISES
Romans 6

A NEW PATH

By baptism we were buried with him, and lay dead, in order that, as Christ was raised from the dead in the splendour of the Father, so also we might set our feet upon the new path of life. Romans 6:4, N.E.B.

The British Museum in London contains some of the world's most priceless treasures. One of these is a tiny face of a king cut in amethyst with the point of a diamond. This small work of art is worth millions of dollars. Another irreplaceable object is a carved head of Emperor Caesar Augustus, who ruled the Roman Empire when Jesus was born. It is crowned with a diadem of gold and precious stones and could not be purchased for any amount of money.

One of the most precious of the museum's treasures is a fabulous vase, known as the Portland Vase, after the British family that purchased it. This vase was discovered in the 1600's in a long-forgotten tomb near Rome. It is as blue as the sky, transparent, with inlaid flowers and human forms whiter than snow.

For many years no one could tell what the vase was made of. This mystery was solved, however, under tragic circumstances when someone, no doubt mentally disturbed, smashed the priceless vessel with a stone that he had concealed in his pocket. The discovery that this ancient vase was made of glass enhanced its value.

Art lovers were shocked by this act of vandalism, and a search was made to find someone who could put the pieces back together. The restoration has been declared to be the most perfect of its kind the world has ever known.

The Portland Vase was created perfect and unmarred. It was shattered by the hand of a madman, a fool. But the fragments were gathered together, and it was made completely whole by another master craftsman.

The story of the Portland Vase reminds us that we were created in the image of God. We were crushed and broken by an enemy out to destroy the beautiful works of God's creation. We should be thankful that the Master Himself made provision whereby we could be re-created and restored to the image of God. Through Jesus Christ we can discover a new path and find new life.

PROMISES
Romans 7

NO NEED TO HIDE

Miserable creature that I am, who is there to rescue me out of this body doomed to death? God alone, through Jesus Christ our Lord! Romans 7:24, 25, N.E.B.

Twenty-nine years after the close of World War II, Second Lieutenant Hiroo Onoda, an intelligence officer of Japan's Imperial Army, formally surrendered, ending twenty-nine years of needless hiding in the jungle. Lt. Onoda emerged from the jungle of Lubang Island in the Philippines only after his wartime commander sent him a copy of Emperor Hirohito's 1945 surrender order. When Onoda was fully convinced that the war was over, he returned to his hideout and brought back his sword, which he surrendered to a major general of the Philippine Air Force. The event took place on his fifty-second birthday.

Lt. Onoda was discovered by a Japanese student who was camping on Lubang Island. Onoda said he would surrender only if his commanding officer ordered him to do so. In 1944 that officer had ordered the lieutenant to stay on the island and spy out the enemy "no matter what." In 1972 Philippine soldiers killed one Japanese war straggler in a clash, and another—presumably Lt. Onoda—fled. When his parents were notified of their son's whereabouts they burst into tears.

Although the differences are many, Lt. Onoda's experience in some ways parallels that of many professed Christians. They join the Christian army, but get cut off from headquarters. They miserably continue fighting sin, "no matter what," but in their own strength. They are so busy fighting and hiding from the enemy that no one can find them to tell them that the war between good and evil was won by Jesus, and when they surrender to Him they are victorious. There is no need to keep on fighting; they just need to claim the victory. With Paul they can say, "Thanks be unto God"!

We may be obedient to commands, but if we don't know the Emperor and all His declarations, we are still lost in the jungle of the old nature of sin. We do things we should not do and fail to do things we should do. The way out of this power struggle is outlined in Romans 7 and 8.

PROMISES
Romans 8

LIVING WITH A KING

For all who are moved by the Spirit of God are sons of God.
Romans 8:14, N.E.B.

William, a brilliant young musician in the military band of Hanover, Germany, was often asked to play before the king. When war broke out, he was drafted, but instead of serving in the army, he deserted and fled to England. Desertion was punishable by death, but William was not caught. In his new country he established himself as an astronomer. In 1781 he discovered a new planet, *Georgium sidus* (later named Uranus), which made him famous in the scientific world.

One day William was summoned to the palace of King George III of England, formerly King George of Germany. William feared that he would be confronted with desertion from the German army. However, he decided to confess his crime.

When William came before the king, he began to make his confession. But before he could do so, a sealed envelope was handed to him. He imagined it to be his death sentence, so you can imagine his relief when he discovered that it contained a pardon.

King George said, "And now we can talk. You must come to the castle. From henceforth you shall be known as Sir William." So William, formerly Friedrich Wilhelm, became the king's private astronomer. The deserter was given a new status and a new home.

In Romans 8 we discover again that we have been given a royal pardon that entitles us to a new status and guarantees that we can live with the King of kings. This is possible only when we put aside self and make room for the working of the Holy Spirit.

William was invited to live with the king, but never became heir to the throne of England. Not only have we been pardoned but we have been promised that we will be heirs of Christ's kingdom (Rom. 8:17).

We have not only the assurance of an abundant life now but the promise of eternal life to come. We are heirs because we are children of God. Our adoption has been made possible by the death of Jesus and the power of the Holy Spirit. The promise is sure: "For as many as are led by the Spirit of God, they are the sons of God."

138

PROMISES
Romans 9

WE ALL NEED IT!

What shall we say to that? Is God to be charged with injustice? By no means. For he says to Moses, "Where I show mercy, I will show mercy, and where I pity, I will pity." Romans 9:14, 15, N.E.B.

"The pen of inspiration, true to its task, tells us of the sins that overcame Noah, Lot, Moses, Abraham, David, and Solomon, and that even Elijah's strong spirit sank under temptation during his fearful trial. Jonah's disobedience and Israel's idolatry are faithfully recorded. Peter's denial of Christ, the sharp contention of Paul and Barnabas, the failings and infirmities of the prophets and apostles, are all laid bare by the Holy Ghost, who lifts the veil from the human heart. There before us lie the lives of the believers, with all their faults and follies, which are intended as a lesson to all the generations following them. If they had been without foible they would have been more than human, and our sinful natures would despair of ever reaching such a point of excellence. But seeing where they struggled and fell, where they took heart again and conquered through the grace of God, we are encouraged, and led to press over the obstacles that degenerate nature places in our way. . . .

"We need just such lessons as the Bible gives us, for with the revelation of sin is recorded the retribution which follows. The sorrow and penitence of the guilty, and the wailing of the sin-sick soul, come to us from the past, telling us that man was then, as now, in need of the pardoning mercy of God. It teaches us that while He is a punisher of crime, He pities and forgives the repenting sinner."—*Testimonies,* vol. 4, p. 12.

It is certainly encouraging to know that men and women who are regarded as heroes of faith made mistakes, repented, received God's mercy, and were forgiven. It is also assuring to know that God's "pardoning mercy" and pity are just as freely given to us.

As we taste the mercy and forgiveness of God, it should lead us to a new relationship with the people with whom we associate. We should show mercy and pity and forgiveness. We should remember that God hates sin but loves the sinner. Although we may not like what people do to us, we should continue to love them and pray that they will receive God's mercy.

PROMISES
Romans 10

THE BIBLE GIRL

If on your lips is the confession, "Jesus is Lord," and in your heart the faith that God raised him from the dead, then you will find salvation. Romans 10:9, N.E.B.

At 9 years of age Shaji began attending a Christian Sunday school at a neighbor's home. One day the teacher asked the students to prepare a talk on the joy of salvation. Shaji's mother was a Hindu, but she helped her daughter by saying, "Just tell them what you know about Jesus."

So when Shaji's turn came the next week, she told how she had committed her life to Jesus and how she had become a better girl and God had blessed her in her studies. She was given a Bible for her presentation, and this inspired her to tell her parents and friends about her new-found faith.

"Christ has become the Lord of our home," Shaji says. "My father was a drunkard. We prayed for him for several years. Now he is a transformed person altogether."

At the time of this writing Shaji is 15 and attends a Hindu high school. When the representatives of the Bible Society of India visited her, they were able to locate her because most of the other students knew "The Bible Girl." Every day, despite opposition, she reads a portion of Scripture to her fellow students and leads a prayer group out under the rubber trees near the school.*

"The Bible Girl" is doing what Paul and others have advised all Christians to do.

"Strive to arouse men and women from their spiritual insensibility. Tell them how you found Jesus and how blessed you have been since you gained an experience in His service.

"Tell them what blessing comes to you as you sit at the feet of Jesus and learn precious lessons from His word. Tell them of the gladness and joy that there is in the Christian life.

"Your warm, fervent words will convince them that you have found the pearl of great price. Let your cheerful, encouraging words show that you have . . . found the higher way. This is genuine missionary work, and as it is done, many will awake as from a dream."—*Testimonies,* vol. 9, pp. 38, 39.

---

* American Bible Society *Record,* March, 1980.

PROMISES
Romans 11

TRUST GOD'S WORD

Observe the kindness and the severity of God—severity to those who fell away, divine kindness to you, if only you remain within its scope. Romans 11:22, N.E.B.

"In 1885 the first group of Seventh-day Adventist missionaries, led by Elder S. N. Haskell, went to Australia. They settled in Melbourne and immediately began to plan for the work there. In November of that same year, while waiting for some printing machinery to arrive, Elder Haskell went to New Zealand to spy out the land. 'Can you recommend a boarding house in Auckland run by some religious person?' he inquired of one of the seamen during the trip. 'Yes,' said the seaman. 'Go to the house of Edward Hare; he has rooms.'

"So Elder Haskell went to Edward Hare's house as soon as he arrived. 'Yes, I have a room you may have,' said Edward Hare.

"It wasn't long, however, before the man in the room next to Mr. Haskell came downstairs and said, 'That new man is crazy! He's talking to himself all the time! . . .'

"Mr. Hare went upstairs and listened. . . . He realized Mr. Haskell was praying! 'O God, help me to win this good man to the message. Help me to——'

"Edward Hare . . . went downstairs and said to his wife, 'That man's not crazy; that man is praying for us!' And it was only a few days until Edward Hare had accepted the message. He took Elder Haskell two hundred miles north to Kaeo, where Edward's father, Joseph Hare, and five of his brothers lived. In a few more days they all had accepted the third angel's message and were keeping the Sabbath. Edward Hare was my uncle, and my father was one of his brothers who accepted this message in Kaeo! That's the way God's Word began to prosper in New Zealand. You can put your faith in every promise and in every prophecy foretold in the Word of God." *

The fact that we can trust God's Word is highlighted by Paul in Romans 9 through 11. Our verse today shows that God's promises are conditional on obedience, and that only those who continue to love and serve God will be saved.

---

* Eric B. Hare, *Make God First* (Washington, D.C.: Review and Herald, 1964), p. 139.

PROMISES
Romans 12

LET YOUR LIGHT SHINE

Adapt yourselves no longer to the pattern of this present world, but let your minds be remade and your whole nature thus transformed. Then you will be able to discern the will of God, and to know what is good, acceptable, and perfect. Romans 12:2, N.E.B.

Martin Luther is well known as one of the leaders of the Protestant Reformation. In October, 1517, he nailed ninety-five statements of belief to the door of a castle in Wittenberg, Germany, marking the beginning of his contribution to the Reformation. He later translated the Bible into German and wrote several hymns, including "A Mighty Fortress Is Our God."

Another Martin lived in Basel, Switzerland, during this time. He also became acquainted with the great truth of righteousness by faith. He also wrote what he believed, and here is a selection from his writings: "O Merciful Christ, I know that I can be saved only through the merits of Thy blood. Holy Jesus, I recognize Thy sufferings for me. I love Thee. I love Thee."

But Martin of Basel, also a monk, placed this tribute to Jesus behind a stone in the wall of his cell. It was later plastered over, and the piece of paper was not discovered until a hundred years later when the old monastery was demolished. It was Martin Luther who is remembered for his tribute to Jesus and his declaration of righteousness by faith, because he nailed his beliefs to the church door and publicly proclaimed them at the risk of his life.

There is a great need today for Seventh-day Adventist Christians to take the light that they have concerning righteousness by faith, the mediation of Jesus in the heavenly sanctuary, the judgment, the Second Coming, and other truths, and proclaim them in every way that they can. It is not in God's plan that we should be silent or write our confessions of faith in books that are hidden away on shelves or distributed only to those who already know these truths.

Martin Luther's life was "transformed" by the reading of the book of Romans. He not only discovered the great truths of righteousness by faith but he also shared his faith. He let his light shine.

PROMISES
Romans 13

WORLD CITIZEN

Every person must submit to the supreme authorities. There is no authority but by act of God, and the existing authorities are instituted by him. Romans 13:1, N.E.B.

More than thirty years ago a resident of the United States denounced his citizenship and declared himself to be a "world citizen." Up to that time he had been a loyal subject of the United States, serving in the Air Force during World War II.

In 1953 Gary Davis established the World Citizen Government in the State of Maine. The organization claims a membership of 800,000 "citizens of the world," who have each paid a thirty-two-dollar fee. In one year recently the organization issued five thousand passports. However, when Gary Davis arrived at Dulles International Airport in May, 1977, his World Passport was rejected by immigration authorities. Since that time the World Citizen Government and its passports have been discussed in the courts.

There is a day coming when we will all be "world citizens," and that day will be when Jesus returns to this earth as King of kings and Lord of lords. In the meantime it is His plan that "every person must submit to the supreme authorities." We are not to establish our own government, but we are to submit to the authority of the laws of the country in which we live.

God has given governments the power to rule, and they are responsible to Him for their actions. If the leaders force people to do things that are contrary to the government of heaven, they will one day have to answer for their deeds. In God's plan, governments are to protect life and property, repress crime, and encourage good behavior (see Rom. 13:3).

Most rulers repeat their oath of office with a hand placed on a Bible. The Queen of England is often described as "Queen of England by the grace of God." Those in positions of responsibility are responsible to God for their actions. They are to govern with justice, mercy, and love.

In this world some people have dual citizenship. However, soon there will be only one kingdom, and the subjects will be pleased to give full allegiance to King Jesus.

PROMISES
Romans 14

NEXT WORLD RULER

For Scripture says, "As I live, says the Lord, to me every knee shall bow and every tongue acknowledge God." Romans 14:11, N.E.B.

While living in Zimbabwe, Africa, I received a letter from a man who signed himself "Acting King of the World." The letter was marked with a rubber stamp, the seal of office of the "Acting King of the World." This man wanted me to help him bring peace in Africa.

The only person who is worthy to be called King of the world is Jesus. His right to reign is based on the fact that He is our Creator and also the One who died to save the human race from destruction.

One day "we shall all stand before the judgment seat of God," when the words of Isaiah, quoted by Paul, will be fulfilled. At that time "every knee shall bow and every tongue acknowledge God." At the present time there are many people who do not acknowledge Jesus as the next world ruler. However, since we have discovered that every *prophecy* and *promise* of the Bible is true, we can be sure that this one is true also.

The only people who are going to be subjects of the King of kings are those who proclaim Him as King of their hearts now. Paul also reminds us that we are to give an account of our lives and that we must live each day knowing that all we do is subject to judgment. However, Jesus is not only king to those who choose to be His subjects, but He is also our advocate or lawyer. He is the One who is going to stand for us in the judgment and ask for us to be pardoned and allowed the privilege of living forever in the new earth.

All will one day acknowledge Jesus as world ruler, for He not only created the world but also purchased it back after Adam and Eve sinned and Satan became prince of this world. Since the beginning of sin there has been a great controversy raging between Christ and Satan as to whom this world really belongs to. When Jesus died on the cross as a sacrifice for sin He won back His right to be the world's ruler.

There will be tremendous rejoicing on the day that Jesus is crowned King of the world. The millions of angels will join with the saved of earth in singing tribute to the rightful world Ruler.

PROMISES
Romans 15

WE HAVE THIS HOPE

And may the God of hope fill you with all joy and peace by your faith in him, until, by the power of the Holy Spirit, you overflow with hope. Romans 15:13, N.E.B.

Norwegian explorer and scientist Fridtjof Nansen led two expeditions to the North Pole. One of these covered a period of three years, from 1893 to 1896. During the months when there was little or no sunlight Nansen and his fellow explorers lived in ice huts. One day he wrote a message to his wife and put it into a little capsule. He tied it to a homing pigeon and released the bird.

The pigeon circled three times and then, following the instinct implanted in it by God, headed in the right direction for its long journey south. The bird flew more than 2,000 miles, carrying Nansen's message, until one day, to Mrs. Nansen's delight, it reached home. When she discovered the message, she knew that all was well with her husband, and this gave her new hope for his safe return from the long expedition.

Christians should be full of hope that Jesus will return soon from heaven. Our Lord has sent many messages to assure us that He is coming soon. Also, He has given us the Holy Spirit. As the third person of the Godhead comes into our lives, we are filled with "joy and peace," leading us to "overflow with hope."

The second coming of Jesus, referred to as the "blessed hope," has been the confidence of Christians in all ages. "We Have This Hope" was the theme song used for the fifty-first General Conference session held in Austria in 1975.

"We have this hope that burns within our hearts,
  Hope in the coming of the Lord.
We have this faith that Christ alone imparts,
  Faith in the promise of His Word.
We believe the time is here when the nations far and near
  Shall awake, and shout, and sing—Hallelujah! Christ is King!
We have this hope that burns within our hearts,
  Hope in the coming of the Lord."

—Wayne Hooper

145

PROMISES
Romans 16

THE CHOICE IS OURS

And the God of peace will soon crush Satan beneath your feet.
The grace of our Lord Jesus be with you! Romans 16:20, N.E.B.

The choice is ours—endless hope or a hopeless end. If we choose to serve the God of peace we will have endless hope; if we choose to ignore or reject His love we will have a hopeless end. There are only two options, and no neutral position. Jesus Himself said that if we do not choose Him, then we are against Him.

It is obvious that many young people and adults think there is neutral ground between those who are saved and those who are lost. They do not believe they are saved, but neither will they admit that they are lost. When they are in this position, the devil, the great deceiver, cheats them out of the blessings of the believer and denies them even the fleeting pleasures of sin.

Yes, there are only two alternatives: We are either Christians or we are not. If we are Christians we have experienced the new birth and will have peace in our hearts; if we are not Christians we will have a hopeless end.

Although it sometimes seems that the wicked are prospering and Satan is gaining many followers, the promise is sure that "the God of peace will soon crush Satan beneath your feet." This is a repetition of the promise made in Genesis 3:15. Here we discovered that although Satan may bruise the heel of Jesus, which he did when Christ died on the cross, one day the God of peace will crush Satan's head. Truth will finally triumph, and Christ will be the victor in the great controversy between good and evil.

Yesterday we talked about a homing pigeon that flew two thousand miles from the North Pole to Norway. Another pigeon flew seven thousand miles from Saigon, Vietnam, to Paris, France. Long, accurate flights by these birds are not unusual.

The God of peace has given you and me a far greater power for finding our way back home than He has given even to the homing pigeons. He has given us the heavenly dove of peace, and if we give our lives to Jesus, we can have endless hope and find our way to our heavenly home.

PROMISES
1 Corinthians 1

GIVING GIFTS

There is . . . no single gift you lack, while you wait expectantly for our Lord Jesus Christ to reveal himself. 1 Corinthians 1:7, N.E.B.

Rosemary's home country is Zimbabwe, and as a child in Sabbath school she heard stories of the victims of leprosy who came to the Malamulo Hospital in Malawi. She was particularly interested in the children of the lepers, and was sad to learn that some of these boys and girls also contracted the disease. Many of the leper children had very little food and hardly any clothes. About all the income the parents had was what they earned from weaving baskets or mats. At times these were difficult to sell, for some people will not buy things made by lepers.

Even though Rosemary was not quite 6 years old, she wished that she could do something. After thinking for some time, she had a bright idea. Soon she was going to have a birthday party, so she asked her mother whether her friends could bring gifts for the leper children. Her mother readily agreed, and the invitations read something like this: "Instead of bringing me a present, please bring a toy or article of clothing for the leper children."

About thirty people came to this different kind of birthday party, and the response was tremendous. The children brought brand-new khaki suits, beautifully knitted sweaters, and toys and books.

This was the happiest birthday party Rosemary and her friends had ever attended. Then, together with their parents, they had such fun packing the boxes to send to Malamulo. Rosemary could have gotten gifts for herself, but she decided to make others happy instead.

God has promised us spiritual gifts so that we can help others rejoice in salvation. See how many spiritual gifts you can discover in Romans 12, 1 Corinthians 12, and Ephesians 4.

Rosemary also made the angels of heaven happy when she gave her heart completely to Jesus, and it was my privilege to baptize her. She graduated from Helderberg College and in her first work was able to use her gifts, serving as a secretary in the Trans-Africa Division youth department.

PROMISES
1 Corinthians 2

YOU CAN'T IMAGINE

But, in the words of Scripture, "Things beyond our seeing, things beyond our hearing, things beyond our imagining, all prepared by God for those who love him." 1 Corinthians 2:9, N.E.B.

Thirty-one people agreed to test a new drug to help relieve anxiety and tension. After taking the tablets for some time, about one third of the patients reported that they felt better when they took the tablets than when they used other medicines they had tried for the same problem. About half the people said they did not feel any change, and the rest reported nauseous feelings and pounding hearts. One patient even said that he got a bad skin rash as a result of taking the medicine.

After the test had been completed, the doctors who conducted the experiment gathered the patients together and surprised many of them with what they announced. Some of the patients had actually been given the new drug, while others had been given tablets that looked the same but were made of sugar. Some of those who had been taking the sugar tablets let their imaginations run away with them, for they were the ones who reported the bad results. It has been proved, as stated in the Spirit of Prophecy writings, that many of the diseases from which people suffer begin in their minds.

Your imagination and mine can play tricks on us. But when it comes to imagining what heaven and the new earth are going to be like, thoughts fail us. God knows our minds, and He has declared that we cannot imagine how wonderful it will be. He has also promised that it will be better than we could ever have dreamed.

The statements that it is beyond our seeing, hearing, and imagining are from the prophet Isaiah. Other descriptions of the new earth tell us that it is a place where we will build houses and plant gardens. It is not as many people imagine, a place where we will sit on clouds and strum harps all day. Heaven is a real land, and we can rejoice that it is wonderful beyond our imagination.

PROMISES
1 Corinthians 3

"I WAS REALLY HOOKED"

Surely you know that you are God's temple, where the Spirit of God dwells. Anyone who destroys God's temple will himself be destroyed. 1 Corinthians 3:16, 17, N.E.B.

A teen-ager who did not realize that his body was the "temple of the Holy Ghost" tried drugs. He later wrote of his experience in a letter, and here is what he said:

"When I was 15 a 'friend' introduced me to pot. It gave me a lift and a chance to escape from reality for a little while. I enjoyed the high and happy feeling it gave me, but the trouble started when I kept wanting that feeling more and more often. Finally the same 'friend' got me to try heroin. That was the greatest! Total escape! By the time I was 17 I was really hooked. And I mean really hooked.

"I won't tell you how low I sank to get the stuff, but you'd better believe it was *low*. It was expensive, and I needed more and more as time went on. I had to involve other kids to go my route, which is something I will never be able to forgive myself for.

"Then I realized all I could think about was getting the stuff, and I tried to kick the habit, but couldn't. I attempted suicide. I failed, and woke up in a hospital, where I spent many months in the psychiatric ward. That saved my life, because there I started to learn all about what my problem was and why I couldn't relate to society."

It is still true that an ounce of prevention is worth a ton of cure, so we must know the facts concerning those things that destroy the body. Those who have experimented and have been rescued from being hooked would advise us to "touch not and taste not."

If you have ever visited an Eastern temple, you know that the buildings are kept spotlessly clean. Many of them require visitors to remove their shoes before entering. If men are so careful about caring for temples of marble and stone, how much more should we care for the temples of the Holy Ghost! We sing, "Live out Thy life within me, O Jesus, King of kings," but we also need to prepare our body temples for the King to come into them.

PROMISES
1 Corinthians 7

NO MORE TIME

What I mean, my friends, is this. The time we live in will not last long. . . . For the whole frame of this world is passing away. 1 Corinthians 7:29-31, N.E.B.

We all can no doubt remember sitting in a room during a test when the teacher announced, "No more time. Pass your papers in." Also, those who have played or watched ball games are acquainted with the buzzer or gun signaling the end of the game. On these occasions, although people wish for more time, there is no point in arguing. There are rules that have to be followed.

In some respects this world is like a ball game. The different nations comprise the teams, and they are all playing for first place. Just as there is a set time for many ball games, so there is for those who live on this planet. This was not God's original plan, for He had intended for us to live forever. But because of sin, there had to be a time limit; otherwise the world would eventually destroy itself. As predicted, soon Jesus will stand up in the courts of heaven and say, "It is finished. No more time."

As we read the newspapers and hear news reports, we realize that "the time we live in will not last long." Man is not, as evolutionists predict, getting better. Hundreds of thousands of human beings are killed because of people's desire for power and money. While I was living in Africa, there were wars in several countries. These were barely reported in the newspapers, but I knew that hundreds of thousands of people were killed. Also, accidents and disease take the lives of many. It is certainly time for God to intervene and take us to a land free of sickness, death, and pain.

Scientists confirm the Bible statement that "the whole frame of this world is passing away." We are living in a time of the predicted calamities such as earthquakes, which cannot be explained or controlled.

Those who realize that at any time the Master Teacher may say, "No more time," live in a state of continual readiness for His coming. Yesterday I read a timely message on a car bumper sticker: "Prepare for the finals—read your Bible!"

150

PROMISES
1 Corinthians 10

A WAY OUT

So far you have faced no trial beyond what man can bear. 1 Corinthians 10:13, N.E.B.

One of my work assignments as a student at Avondale College was to stoke the old steam boiler with wood and coal. The hot water built up tremendous pressure, and we had to keep close watch on the pressure dial. Should the pressure increase so that the boiler was in danger of blowing up, we pulled the lever and released some of the steam.

Our lives are like a steam boiler. As we fuel them with work, study, and play, we get into situations of tremendous strain. Sometimes we may not sense the pressure building up. There are also various kinds of tests that come to us, and we need strength in order to pass them successfully. We do not want to give in to the temptations to do wrong, so we need power to resist.

God has made provision for His children to live as Christians in this world of sin, so there is no need for us to be overcome by pressure and to yield to temptation. The Bible is full of promises like the one in our Morning Watch text today. God keeps faith and will not allow us to be tested above our powers. He has assured us that He will provide a way out.

We should notice that the promise is not that we will be taken away from enticement, or that we will not meet it. The promise is that when we are tested and tempted we will be able to bear it.

Jesus has also provided us with an example of how to overcome temptations and to be victorious. Peter states that Christ has left us "an example" and that we should "follow his steps" (1 Peter 2:21). If we heed this advice we will find a "way out" of every problem, trial, and temptation. Here is how to find the way out.

W atch and pray, that ye enter not into temptation.
A sk—"What would Jesus do?"
Y ield your will to Jesus every morning.

O ccupy yourself with "doing good," as Jesus did.
U nite with other Christians for prayer and fellowship.
T ake time to read the Bible every day.

PROMISES
1 Corinthians 13

TRUE LOVE DEFINED

In a word, there are three things that last for ever: faith, hope, and love; but the greatest of them all is love. 1 Corinthians 13:13, N.E.B.

"The Lord desires me to call the attention of His people to the thirteenth chapter of First Corinthians. Read this chapter every day, and from it obtain comfort and strength. Learn from it the value that God places on sanctified, heaven-born love, and let the lesson that it teaches come home to your hearts. Learn that Christlike love is of heavenly birth, and that without it all other qualifications are worthless."—*The SDA Bible Commentary,* Ellen G. White Comments, on 1 Corinthians 13, p. 1091

"I may speak in tongues of men or of angels, but if I am without love, I am a sounding gong or a clanging cymbal. I may have the gift of prophecy, and know every hidden truth; I may have faith strong enough to move mountains; but if I have no love, I am nothing. I may dole out all I possess, or even give my body to be burnt, but if I have no love, I am none the better.

"Love is patient; love is kind and envies no one. Love is never boastful, nor conceited, nor rude; never selfish, not quick to take offence. Love keeps no score of wrongs; does not gloat over other men's sins, but delights in the truth. There is nothing love cannot face; there is no limit to its faith, its hope, and its endurance.

"Love will never come to an end. Are there prophets? their work will be over. Are there tongues of ecstasy? they will cease. Is there knowledge? it will vanish away; for our knowledge and our prophecy alike are partial, and the partial vanishes when wholeness comes.

"When I was a child, my speech, my outlook, and my thoughts were all childish. When I grew up, I had finished with childish things. Now we see only puzzling reflections in a mirror, but then we shall see face to face. My knowledge now is partial; then it will be whole, like God's knowledge of me. In a word, there are three things that last for ever: faith, hope, and love; but the greatest of them all is love" (1 Corinthians 13, N.E.B.).

PROMISES
1 Corinthians 15

STAND FIRM

Therefore, my beloved brothers, stand firm and immovable, and work for the Lord always, work without limit, since you know that in the Lord your labour cannot be lost. 1 Corinthians 15:58, N.E.B.

One of the world's most famous trees is a twisted, deformed Jeffrey pine. This centuries-old tree is on top of the 8,117-foot Sentinel Dome in Yosemite National Park, California.

This old tree has defied nature's laws, setting its roots down into solid granite. Somehow it is able to get the nutrients necessary to live and stand firm against the icy winds. The National Park Service has placed at its base a plaque with these words: "Jeffrey pine—this gnarled, wind-swept tree has clung tenaciously to life in spite of great odds."

Here is our pattern for living in this difficult age when there are winds of strife, fear, doubt, perplexity, and apathy blowing on every hand. A tree lives and thrives because its roots are firmly and deeply anchored in the rock. Likewise, in these times in which we live we may anchor our lives firmly in Jesus Christ, the Rock of Ages.

We are assured that when we work for the Lord, our "labour cannot be lost," so we have every reason to "stand firm and immovable." When we are rooted in the living Word and feed on the Written Word, we will be as firm as the old Jeffrey pine.

There is another reason for hanging on in spite of great odds, and that is the promise of translation or resurrection when Jesus comes. The closing verses of 1 Corinthians 15 are among the most beautiful in all Scripture:

"Listen! I will unfold a mystery: we shall not all die, but we shall all be changed in a flash, in the twinkling of an eye, at the last trumpet-call. For the trumpet will sound, and the dead will rise immortal, and we shall be changed. . . . 'O Death, where is your victory? O Death, where is your sting?' . . . God be praised, he gives us the victory through our Lord Jesus Christ" (verses 51-57, N.E.B.).

PROMISES
2 Corinthians 1

CURE FOR THE BLUES

Praise be to the God and Father of our Lord Jesus Christ, the all-merciful Father, the God whose consolation never fails us! He comforts us in all our troubles, so that we in turn may be able to comfort others in any trouble of theirs and to share with them the consolation we ourselves receive from God. 2 Corinthians 1:3, 4, N.E.B.

Charles Wesley wrote more than six thousand hymns, which have been a source of comfort and encouragement to Christians for more than two hundred years. It is interesting to note, however, that this godly man also had times of discouragement.

One day as Wesley was sitting at his desk brooding over his troubles, a small bird flew in through the open window, hit him in the chest, and scrambled under the lapel of his coat. The man could feel the bird's fast-beating heart, and he quickly placed his hand over the frightened creature. He then went to the window to look for the reason for the bird's fear. He saw a large hawk circling overhead, and immediately knew why the little thing was seeking safety.

As Wesley held the bird, he thought of his own experience and realized that He could find refuge in God. He then wrote the following words:

> "Jesus, lover of my soul,
> Let me to Thy bosom fly.
> While the billows near me roll,
> While the tempest still is high;
> Hide me, O my Saviour, hide!
> Till the storm of life is past;
> Safe into the haven guide,
> O receive my soul at last!"
> —*The Church Hymnal,* No. 401.

Those who find the comfort that God offers should comfort others. A recent public-opinion poll asked what methods people used to cheer themselves. Some of those surveyed mentioned that they turned to television, entertainment, or hobbies; a large percentage said they did nothing. Some said they prayed and read their Bibles. But no one said that they helped others, a sure cure for the blues.

154

PROMISES
2 Corinthians 2

IN THE PROCESSION

But thanks be to God, who continually leads us about, captives in Christ's triumphal procession, and everywhere uses us to reveal and spread abroad the fragrance of the knowledge of himself! 2 Corinthians 2:14, N.E.B.

Jim accepted Jesus as his personal Saviour when he was 11. Over the years he continued to grow in the Christian life, and his faith was deepened and his prayer experience enriched after he was in a plane crash in 1961. After serving some years in the United States Air Force, Jim was given the chance of a lifetime—to join the National Aeronautics and Space Administration (NASA). Promotions followed, and as Col. James B. Irwin he was the lunar module command pilot on *Apollo 15*.

Colonel Irwin planted a United States flag in the dust of the moon, and then saluted it. In 1973 he visited Southwestern Adventist College and presented a color picture of himself saluting the flag on the moon.

Colonel Irwin explained that for him the lunar trip had been spiritual, as well as scientific; it had quickened in him a spiritual awakening. "I felt God on the moon as I had never felt Him before in my life," he said. "Something happened to me there that I felt I must share with everyone on earth."

Jim Irwin was given a hero's welcome on his return to earth. He is also a part of Christ's triumphal procession when he testifies of his love for God. Before large audiences around the world he has told the story of planting his country's flag on the moon and of his allegiance to the King of kings.

Jesus Christ has also given us the privilege of being a part of His triumphal process. By our lives and deeds we are to reveal the fragrant beauty of Jesus. According to the apostle Paul, we are "ambassadors for Christ," and we must unfurl our colors. Our flag has a cross on it, a symbol of the kingdom we represent. As we uplift Christ on the cross, men and women will have the opportunity of accepting Him and thus will be assured of going beyond the moon to the kingdom of heaven at His second coming.

PROMISES
2 Corinthians 4

TRIAL BAY

Hard-pressed on every side, we are never hemmed in; bewildered, we are never at our wits' end. 2 Corinthians 4:8, N.E.B.

The historic and abandoned jail with its unfinished breakwater at Trial Bay, New South Wales, Australia, attracts thousands of visitors each year. Although the jail took ten years to build and cost a lot of money, it was occupied by prisoners for only about ten years and then used as an internment camp during World War I.

Trial Bay Gaol is named after the body of water on which it is situated. Before my visit there I concluded that the bay was named after the jail. But thanks to the Macleay River Historical Society, I discovered that Trial Bay was named after the brig *Trial,* which was wrecked there in 1816 after being stolen by escaping convicts. Since ships frequently used the bay, it was decided to construct a five-thousand-foot breakwater. This was to be built by prison labor, so the jail was constructed to accommodate prisoners.

The story of the naming of Trial Bay echoes some valuable life lessons for us. In the first place, all of us have to face our own Trial Bay sooner or later. Despite our efforts to shelter ourselves from the storms of life or to hide in the asphalt jungle, sometimes we find ourselves face to face with the shipwreck of our best plans.

To some, Trial Bay will be failure in the classroom. To others, it will mean physical handicaps or loss of loved ones. Trials are necessary for success in life, and by accepting that fact we are well on our way to a triumphant voyage over the seas of life.

Trial Bay also teaches us that there is no need to abandon our goals because of the Trial Bays in which we may find ourselves. Detours, failures, setbacks, and handicaps need not stop you from living a successful Christian life here and now, and obtaining eternal life hereafter. Remember, many have shared light despite personal trials. The poet Milton was blind when he wrote *Paradise Lost.* Louis Pasteur, partly paralyzed, carried on his ceaseless war against disease; and from a sickbed Florence Nightingale organized the hospitals of a nation.

156

PROMISES
2 Corinthians 5

A BRAND-NEW PERSON

When anyone is united to Christ, there is a new world; the old order has gone, and a new order has already begun. 2 Corinthians 5:17, N.E.B.

The engineers were searching for a base for one of the pillars for the new bridge. At the very spot where they wanted to put a pillar deep in the mud, they discovered an old barge full of bricks and stones. This had to be moved before the new bridge across a portion of New York Harbor could be built. In spite of many attempts, however, the barge remained firmly held in the muddy bed of the harbor.

One day one of the engineers had an idea. He asked for many boats to be brought to the spot where the old barge was resting. He then ordered chains to connect the boats on the surface to the sunken wreck. The chains were fastened at low tide, and people soon realized what the engineer had in mind. As the tide rose, the chains creaked and strained, and gradually the old boat emerged from the thick mud. It was raised not by the strength of man or machinery, but by the lift of the Atlantic Ocean.

Before a person finds the Lord Jesus, his life is like that old barge, full of bricks and stones. One who does not know Jesus is stuck in the mire of sin. His habits are hard to break, and a vicelike grip is holding him to this world. There is only one way for us to be lifted from the mire, and that is by the power of God's love.

The barge was removed to make way for a new construction. In order for us to become a new creation, old habits and sins have to be removed. When these are expelled, a brand-new person appears. We must not try merely to patch up the old life, but rather allow God to construct a new life for us. We let Him do this work by choosing each day to be Christians and claiming God's *promises* for *power* to live a victorious Christian life.

Our Morning Watch text is one of many promises that assure us that when we unite with Jesus we become changed. There is no limit to that change, for by His grace and power we can become brand-new persons.

PROMISES
2 Corinthians 9

PROMISED GIFTS

And it is in God's power to provide you richly with every good gift; thus you will have ample means in yourselves to meet each and every situation, with enough and to spare for every good cause. 2 Corinthians 9:8, N.E.B.

Carolyn, who was 13, lived in New York City with her mother and father. One day as she was walking home from school she glanced down onto the pavement, and there was a crisp, new $1,000 bank note!

Although she was excited about her find, Carolyn knew that the money was not hers to keep. She took it to the police station, and was delighted to learn that the law stated that if the money was unclaimed after thirty days, it would be hers. Each day she expected to receive a message from the police that the owner had come for the money. However, thirty days passed, and when Carolyn went to the police station, she signed some papers and was given the $1,000 bill.

As we know, there isn't much chance that any of us would find so large a sum of money. But God has promised us gifts that are worth far more than that. He who owns the silver and the gold, and the cattle on a thousand hills, is "able to provide you with every blessing in abundance" (2 Cor. 9:8, R.S.V.).

We must not expect God to provide us only with money, for we have greater needs than that. Our promise today says that He will provide us with "every good gift," or whatever is good for us. If it is to God's glory and for our good for us to have funds for something worthwhile, then we will receive the amount needed. Good health is another gift from God. And we need the peace and courage to live contentedly despite problems and handicaps that are part of living.

The verses before and after our Morning Watch text show that God has the ability, and is willing, to provide us with everything we need. These blessings are given to us in order that we might in turn give to others. One of the "good gifts" we need in order to help others find the kingdom of heaven is the Holy Spirit. Let's ask God for this "good gift."

PROMISES
Galatians 2

WE CAN BE CHRISTIANS

I have been crucified with Christ: the life I now live is not my life, but the life which Christ lives in me; and my present bodily life is lived by faith in the Son of God, who loved me and gave himself up for me. Galatians 2:20, N.E.B.

An 8-year-old boy in Innsbruck, Austria, had a wound that would not stop bleeding. He suffered from an affliction known as hemophilia, which means that his blood would not clot. His only hope was to have a certain serum given to him immediately.

At that time the serum was available only in the United States, 4,500 miles away. A telephone call was made, and soon the precious fluid was on its way to Austria. All the doctors and the child's parents could do was to wait and hope that it would arrive in time.

The serum was sent from the State health laboratory at Lansing, Michigan. Despite bad weather, it was flown to Austria. A jeep picked it up and sped over the snow-clad Alpine roads to deliver it to the hospital, where it was administered, and the boy's wound healed. A life was saved because of the concern of many people in two countries.

The wounds that we have received as a result of sin will not heal without the serum that is stored in the blood bank of heaven. Whenever a call goes up from Planet Earth, all heaven cooperates. However, only the divine Physician can apply the new life to those who claim His death to cover their sins.

As long as we live by faith in Jesus, we are able to be true Christians. It is not possible for us to live the Christian life in our own strength, but we are promised that we can "live by the faith of the Son of God."

The writings of the apostle Paul constitute almost half the New Testament. Of these, Galatians 2:20 is one of the most precious promises. It reminds us that if Jesus had not come to this earth, or had refused to die for us, we could not have eternal life. The reason He came from pure heaven to this sinful earth and died like a common criminal is also given in this text—He loves us.

PROMISES
Galatians 5

ORCHARD OR FACTORY?

But the harvest of the Spirit is love, joy, peace, patience, kindness, goodness, fidelity, gentleness, and self-control. There is no law dealing with such things as these. Galatians 5:22, 23.

If you had a choice between visiting a factory that manufactured nuts and bolts and an orchard in which the trees were loaded with fruit, which would you choose? No doubt many of you would prefer to visit the orchard and eat the cherries, apples, or peaches.

In Galatians 5 Paul tells Christians that they have a choice between the "works of the flesh" and the "fruit of the Spirit." In our verse for today the fruits of the Spirit are described as "the harvest of the Spirit."

These nine "fruits" should be possessed by all Christians. The first three—love, joy, and peace—are qualities that we should show in our relationship with God. In all our dealings with other people, by the grace of Jesus, we should demonstrate patience, kindness, and goodness. In our own lives there should be fidelity, or faithfulness, gentleness, and self-control.

"In newspaper English the passage would read something like this: The fruit of the Spirit is an affectionate, lovable disposition, a radiant spirit and a cheerful temper, a tranquil mind and a quiet manner, a forbearing patience in provoking circumstances and with trying people, a sympathetic insight and tactful helpfulness, generous judgment and a big-souled charity, loyalty and reliableness under all circumstances, humility that forgets self in the joy of others, in all things self-mastered and self-controlled, which is the final mark of perfection." *

We cannot manufacture fruit in the same way that nuts and bolts are made in a factory. Fruit grows on living trees and must be cultivated. We must be patient while waiting for it to grow. However, we can cultivate the "fruit trees" of the Spirit with prayer and Bible study. We must also ask God to destroy Satan's worms of sin that would rob us of our fruit.

We should ask God daily to give us these beautiful fruits of the Spirit.

---

* Samuel Chadwick, *The Way to Pentecost* (London: Hodder and Stoughton, 1951).

PROMISES
Galatians 6

SOWING AND REAPING

Make no mistake about this: God is not to be fooled; a man reaps what he sows. Galatians 6:7.

Do you have a promise box in your home? This is a box containing Bible promises printed on small pieces of paper or cards. The one in our home has the promises stacked in a plastic container that is shaped like a loaf of bread. On one side are the words "Bread of Life," which is exactly what these promises are.

As we come to the end of our study of the *promises* in three books of the Bible, we must remember that not all are for gifts and blessings. Some carry punishment, reproof, and counsel. We need these just as much as we need the pledges of His gifts. Today's promise can be taken as a gift or a punishment, depending on our decisions. If we sow well we will reap rewards; but if we sow bad deeds we will reap punishment.

A certain boy who lived on a farm did not like to do very much work. But he did love to swim in the swimming hole at the end of the farm. One day his father gave him some watermelon seeds to plant, and told him that when he had finished, he could go swimming. The boy was finished in a very short time, and his father was surprised.

Several weeks later the father asked the boy to come down to the garden. As they stood at the end of the patch, they both saw the large clumps of watermelon plants, rather than small groups of plants. In order to save time, the boy had put handfuls of seeds in a few places down the rows. The boy forgot that what we sow is what comes up. He was punished as he deserved. The rest of his life, though, he was careful about what he did, because he learned that with the passing of time, his actions would be revealed.

God wants us to sow the "fruit of the Spirit" in our lives so that we can have a harvest of *love, joy, peace, patience, kindness, goodness, fidelity, gentleness, self-control*. He knows that if we have this kind of harvest we will be happy Christians and He can take us to heaven. Only those who have the "fruit of the Spirit" can enter into that place of love, joy, and peace.

PROPHECIES
Daniel 1

THE CASE OF TWO BOYS

But Daniel resolved that he would not defile himself with the king's rich food, or with the wine which he drank; therefore he asked the chief of the eunuchs to allow him not to defile himself. Daniel 1:8.

Joseph and Meshach were Sabbathkeepers who lived in an African village in a remote part of Zambia. They enjoyed life but in their hearts was a deep yearning to go to school.

One day their dream came true, and they were enrolled in a church school. During their first few months at the school no one mentioned their absence from church on Sunday. But one day there was a stir as the children learned that an official was visiting the school. The case of the two boys who studied their Bibles under a tree on Saturday was brought to his attention.

He said, "You have come to school to learn, but you must also worship." The boys replied respectfully, "We do worship, sir, but on the Bible Sabbath."

After some consideration it was decided that a test would be placed before the boys. A special exam was scheduled for Saturday morning. The students were eager to know what these Seventh-day Adventist youths would do. When they did not go to the examination, the inspector said, "You must unite with us in worship or you must pack up your belongings and go home."

Joseph and Meshach immediately replied, "We came here for education, but we want to be true to the Lord." When the inspector asked them what they would do without an education, the boys replied, "The Lord will provide."

The head teacher of the school, impressed by the boys' faithfulness, said, "Let these boys alone."

Joseph and Meshach, named after Bible characters, when tested were as loyal to God as were Daniel, Shadrach, Meshach, and Abednego. Loyalty to God requires a firm decision to be true. It says in our text that Daniel "resolved." Resolution, or decision, is one of the first steps toward victory in the Christian life. As you pray, tell God that you have decided to be pure and kind and true!

PROPHECIES
Daniel 2

THE METALLIC MAN

"Blessed be the name of God for ever and ever. . . . He reveals deep and mysterious things; he knows what is in the darkness, and the light dwells with him." Daniel 2:20-22.

Nebuchadnezzar, the king, lay down on his royal couch for a night's rest. Before going to sleep, he thought of his capital city, Babylon, the wonder city of the ancient world. Within the sixty-mile-long wall surrounding the city there were beautiful palaces, temples, and gardens. In some places the wall was eighty feet thick and extended thirty-five feet below the ground so that the enemy could not tunnel under it.

However, the king had a dream that night that really troubled him. When his magicians were unable to explain it the next day, he ordered them executed. At this point Daniel, the young Jewish captive, was brought into the palace. He told the king, "There is a God in heaven that revealeth secrets" (Dan. 2:28).

As Daniel described the metallic man with the head of gold, breast and arms of silver, abdomen and thighs of bronze, legs of iron, and feet part of iron and part of clay, the king was delighted. He remembered that that was what he had dreamed, and asked Daniel for the interpretation. The young prophet revealed to the mighty king that the various metals represented the kingdoms of Babylon, Medo-Persia, Grecia, Rome, and the ten divisions of the Roman Empire. He also told him that the stone was the most important part of the dream because it represented the kingdom of God.

This amazing prophecy is the basis of all the prophecies in the book of Daniel. In about two hundred words the prophet summarizes world history twenty-five hundred years before it happened and answers the question asked by many people today, Will this world end in pieces or in peace?

In just six words, " 'But they will not hold together' " (verse 43, R.S.V.), Daniel tells why Louis XIV of France, Napoleon, the League of Nations, and the United Nations have not succeeded in uniting the nations of Europe. We can rejoice that "in the days of these kings [of Europe] shall the God of heaven set up a kingdom" (verse 44).

PROPHECIES
Daniel 3

TRIUMPH THROUGH TRIAL

*Did not we cast three men bound into the midst of the fire? ...
Lo, I see four men loose, walking in the midst of the fire, and they
have no hurt; and the form of the fourth is like the Son of God.
Daniel 3:24, 25, K.J.V.*

The royal orchestra of Babylon began to play. There were
horns, reed instruments, and a variety of strings, including a
harp. The music was the signal for everybody to fall down and
worship the ninety-foot image that had been erected on the
plain of Dura. Every eye was fixed on this huge golden idol as it
glistened in the sunlight.

This dedication of the golden image was to be one of
Babylon's great events. Officials from every nation ruled by the
great city-state and every province within Babylon itself were
on the plain. When they heard the music, all but three captive
Hebrews—Shadrach, Meshach, and Abednego—bowed low.
Their act of defiance was soon reported to the king, and they
were condemned to death.

It was the custom of the Babylonians to burn alive anyone
who insulted the gods or defied the king. The furnace was
probably a cone-shaped brick kiln. And in his anger against
these young men the king commanded that it be heated seven
times hotter than usual.

But after the three young men were thrown bound into the
fire, the king, watching from his royal seat, was terrified to see
four men loose in the fire. He knew that the fourth must be the
Son of God.

This divine deliverance was followed by royal repentance,
and the king decreed that everyone was to honor the God of
Shadrach, Meshach, and Abednego.

"As in the days of Shadrach, Meshach, and Abednego, so in
the closing period of earth's history the Lord will work mightily
in behalf of those who stand steadfastly for the right. He who
walked with the Hebrew worthies in the fiery furnace will be
with His followers wherever they are.... In the midst of the time
of trouble—trouble such as has not been since there was a
nation—His chosen ones will stand unmoved."—*Prophets and
Kings,* p. 513.

PROPHECIES
Daniel 4

THE KING DREAMS AGAIN

And I blessed the Most High, and praised and honored him who lives for ever; for his dominion is an everlasting dominion, and his kingdom endures from generation to generation. Daniel 4:34.

" 'I saw a very tall tree out in a field, growing higher and higher into the sky until it could be seen by everyone in all the world. Its leaves were fresh and green, and its branches were weighted down with fruit, enough for everyone to eat. Wild animals rested beneath its shade and birds sheltered in its branches, and all the world was fed from it.

" 'Then as I lay there dreaming, I saw one of God's angels coming down from heaven. He shouted, "Cut down the tree; lop off its branches; shake off its leaves, and scatter its fruit. Get the animals out from under it and the birds from its branches, but leave its stump and roots in the ground, banded with a chain of iron and brass, surrounded by the tender grass. Let the dews of heaven drench him and let him eat grass with the wild animals! For seven years let him have the mind of an animal instead of a man. For this has been decreed by the Watchers, demanded by the Holy Ones. The purpose of this decree is that all the world may understand that the Most High dominates the kingdoms of the world, and gives them to anyone he wants to, even the lowliest of men!" O Belteshazzar, that was my dream; now tell me what it means. For no one else can help me; all the wisest men of my kingdom have failed me. But you can tell me, for the spirit of the holy gods is in you' " (Dan. 4:10-19, T.L.B.).

Nebuchadnezzar was given this dream of the tree about ten years after he erected the golden image. However, the sentence was not carried out immediately, for God in His love gave the king a chance to reform. Then one day when Nebuchadnezzar was boasting about the great empire that he had built, he went mad and for seven years thought himself a beast. But the experience worked for good: "The once proud monarch had become a humble child of God; the tyrannical, overbearing ruler, a wise and compassionate king."—*Prophets and Kings,* p. 521.

PROPHECIES
Daniel 5

THE KING'S LAST FEAST

Then Belshazzar commanded, and Daniel was clothed with purple, a chain of gold was put about his neck, and proclamation was made concerning him, that he should be the third ruler in the kingdom. Daniel 5:29.

The dramatic events that resulted in the promotion of Daniel took place in the great banquet hall in Babylon. The king was Belshazzar, grandson of Nebuchadnezzar; Daniel, the prophet, was called Belteshazzar by the Babylonians.

At this great feast the young king of Babylon made several mistakes, which shows just how far he had wandered from the God of his grandfather. Belshazzar was drunk, and he ordered the gold and silver vessels that had been taken from the Temple in Jerusalem by his grandfather to be brought in; he and his guests then drank wine from the sacred containers. The revelers mocked God and praised their heathen gods of gold and silver.

The music and laughter stopped suddenly, however, as an unseen hand wrote on the walls in large letters the words "Mene, Mene, Tekel, Upharsin." The queen, who had not joined in the drunken party, advised Belshazzar to call Daniel.

After reminding the king that he had forgotten and defied the true God, Daniel told him the meaning of the words. With authority the prophet stated that the Babylonian kingdom had been weighed in the balances of heaven and had been found to be wanting in goodness. It was therefore to be given that night to the Medes and Persians. It must have taken a lot of courage for Daniel to deliver that message. We also need to have the courage to present God's truths.

Belshazzar did not question Daniel's interpretation, and he kept his promise by making Daniel the third ruler in his kingdom. But that very night, while the feast was at its height, Cyrus, the commanding chief of the Medes and Persians, skillfully and silently entered and captured the city.

Although it may seem at times that wicked men prosper and nations get away with defying God, we know that all are weighed in God's scales.

PROPHECIES
Daniel 6

THE LIONS' MOTEL

"I make a decree, that in all my royal dominion men tremble and fear before the God of Daniel. . . . He delivers and rescues, he works signs and wonders in heaven and on earth, he who has saved Daniel from the power of the lions." Daniel 6:26, 27.

During World War II a Seventh-day Adventist was captured, tried, and condemned to death by the enemy. As the time of execution approached, this faithful Christian was kneeling in prayer in his cell when the guard told him to get up. When the man did not immediately respond, the guard asked, "What are you doing?" The Christian replied, "I am praying to the God of heaven." The guard said, "You need not pray, for no one can save you from our hands."

Outside, the Christian knelt before an open grave, and the executioner lifted a great sword in the air, ready to bring it down on the neck of the doomed man. Suddenly, to his utter astonishment, the blade broke off, and he stood holding only the hilt. The prisoner heard the thud of the blade on the ground and waited calmly without turning to look. A guard approached, touched him on the shoulder, and said, "Arise!" The prisoner, so suddenly reprieved, was brought before an officer, who declared, "You are a free man. It is the rule of our country that if an instrument of death fails, the man shall be free." This loyal Christian, who had the courage of his convictions, was delivered by the hand of God and went forth to tell his story and to proclaim Christ to hundreds throughout the land.*

In every century God has demonstrated His ability to deliver and rescue and to perform "signs and wonders in heaven and in earth." An angel broke that executioner's sword, and an angel closed the mouths of the big cats in Lions' Motel, Main Street, Babylon. "God did not prevent Daniel's enemies from casting him into the lions' den; He permitted evil angels and wicked men thus far to accomplish their purpose; but it was that He might make the deliverance of His servant more marked, and the defeat of the enemies of truth and righteousness more complete."—*Prophets and Kings,* pp. 543, 544.

---

* A. W. Spalding, *Christ's Last Legion* (Washington, D.C.: Review and Herald, 1949).

PROPHECIES
Daniel 7

BIBLE CARTOON STRIPS

"'And the kingdom and the dominion and the greatness of the kingdoms under the whole heaven shall be given to the people of the saints of the Most High; their kingdom shall be an everlasting kingdom, and all dominions shall serve and obey them.'" Daniel 7:27.

Yes, there are cartoon strips in the Bible! A cartoon is a pictorial sketch, and that is exactly what we find in the seventh chapter of Daniel—four pen pictures of strange-looking animals. These animal cartoons were designed by God and have special meaning. They were shown to Daniel in a vision.

The first animal is "like a lion, and had eagle's wings." Some of its feathers are falling out, and this lion is not a king of beasts because it has the heart of a man. The second animal is "like to a bear" and is very hungry. It is pictured as having in its mouth three ribs dripping with blood. The third animal is "like a leopard," but it is a strange sight because it has four wings and four heads.

The fourth animal cannot be likened to any other animal on earth. It is described as dreadful and terrible, with iron teeth and ten horns on its head. Three of these horns are plucked out, and a "little horn," with eyes and a mouth, takes their place.

We are not left to guess what these beasts, heads, and horns represent. In Daniel 7:17 and 23, God says that the four beasts represent four kingdoms. Also, we know that this vision of Daniel's is related to the vision of the metallic man. When we compare these prophecies, we discover that the four beasts represent the kingdoms of Babylon, Medo-Persia, Grecia, and Rome. The ten toes of the metallic man and the ten horns of the fourth beast represent the nations of Europe. The little horn is a combined political and religious power that arose in the territory of the nations of Europe, and we will learn more about it when we study the book of Revelation.

While the countries of Europe and the little horn are reigning, God is engaged in a work of judgment in heaven. The best news of all is that after the judgment, Jesus Christ will set up His kingdom (verses 26, 27).

PROPHECIES
Daniel 8

MORE CARTOONS

*"As for the ram which you saw with the two horns, these are
the kings of Media and Persia. And the he-goat is the king of
Greece; and the great horn between his eyes is the first king."
Daniel 8:20, 21.*

A ram is a male sheep, and the one mentioned in our text had
two large horns that curved into half circles. Rams use their
horns for defense, and many animals flee when a ram charges
because they know they will be injured if the horns strike their
bodies. The he-goat in the vision also had horns and was a very
hairy animal.

In today's "cartoon" the he-goat is traveling so fast that
sometimes its feet do not even touch the ground. The goat is
angry and charges the ram, breaking its horns. It throws the
ram to the ground and jumps on it. This is a clear description of
the kingdom of Greece overthrowing the dual kingdoms of
Media and Persia. Alexander the Great was the Greek king who
accomplished this. He was the "first king" represented by a
"great horn."

This vision was given to Daniel two years after the vision of
the four strange animals of Daniel 7. Both were given during the
reign of King Belshazzar. The little-horn power that was
introduced in Daniel 7 is mentioned in Daniel 8. There are at
least ten identification points of this religious and political
power presented in these two chapters. It is referred to as
working against Christ, and in the book of 1 John is called the
antichrist.

Daniel was so concerned about the information he had
received that he actually became sick and fainted. He was also
upset that a power would arise claiming to do the work of Jesus
while persecuting God's people and substituting the traditions
of men for the truths of God's Word.

The devil is very cunning. He deceives by inventing
counterfeits and does everything he can to take attention away
from Jesus. Remember that Cain and Abel represented two
classes of Christians. One group relies on man-made systems of
worship; the other looks only to Jesus. Let us be sure that we
look only to Jesus for salvation.

PROPHECIES
Daniel 9

COUNTDOWN

"Seventy weeks of years are decreed concerning your people and your holy city, to finish the transgression, to put an end to sin, and to atone for iniquity, to bring in everlasting righteousness, to seal both vision and prophet, and to anoint a most holy place." Daniel 9:24.

10, 9, 8, 7, 6, 5, 4, 3, 2, 1, 0 . . . Liftoff!

This countdown was used for the manned-space-vehicle launches. And at the word *liftoff,* the spaceships sped skyward and soon reached speeds of many miles per minute. Without a countdown an accurate split-second timing for all systems could not be brought into operation.

A time prophecy in the Old Testament, known as the 2300 days, is one of God's divine countdowns. In Bible prophecy a day often stands for a year. The Inventor of time stated that at the end of a 2300-day (or year) period the sanctuary would be cleansed (see Dan. 8:14). This cleansing was known in Old Testament times as the Day of Atonement, and when used in reference to the heavenly sanctuary it refers to the beginning of the judgment.

God said that the first 70 weeks, or 490 years, of this countdown, which started in 457 B.C., were "determined," or cut off, for the Jewish people. As we see from today's text, six important events were to take place during that time. However, the most important part would be the last week. It was during this period that Jesus was to be crucified. It's easy to follow Bible math and to see that seven days equals seven years, that three and one-half years before the cross, Jesus was baptized, and that three and one-half years after the cross, Stephen was stoned. The stoning of Stephen determined the end of time for the Jewish people, as a nation, to be considered God's special people.

Jesus was baptized and died according to a time determined by God's great prophetic clock. The Bible also shows that He commenced His work of judgment on time, at the end of the 2300 years, in 1844. And He will come back on time. Since we do not know the day or hour of His return, we must be ready to meet Him each day.

PROPHECIES
Daniel 10

VIP

*And he said to me, "O Daniel, man greatly beloved, give heed
to the words that I speak to you, and stand upright, for now I have
been sent to you." While he was speaking this word to me, I stood
up trembling. Daniel 10:11.*

In some airport terminal buildings I have noticed a special
lounge in the arrival and departure areas labeled VIP. Do you
know what those letters stand for? Yes, they mean Very
Important Person. Heads of governments, churches, and
various organizations are invited to go into the VIP lounge.

Daniel was such a VIP that he was invited to go into heaven's
arrival lounge. No, he did not go there in body, but in vision it
seemed that he was actually in the presence of God. The angel
Gabriel was sent to escort the prophet on many occasions, and
the experience was so awesome that Daniel trembled.

After the vision of the 490-year prophecy, Daniel ate very
sparingly for three weeks so that he would be alert to God's voice
speaking to him. His last vision is recorded in chapters 10, 11,
and 12. Our chapter today reveals how the angels work among
the nations, combating forces of evil that would destroy God's
people.

The reason Daniel was a "very important person" is
summarized in today's text. In these verses he is referred to as
"greatly beloved" for the second time. This is one of the finest
compliments ever given to man, and would certainly have
reassured the prophet of God's love for him. This same love is
shown to us, and when we, like Daniel, stand "upright" for God,
we will also be known in heaven as "greatly beloved."

In the country of Zaire I met a church member whose name
meant "noble." He had been a very wicked man during most of
his life, and people had been fearful because of his drunken
rages. However, he responded to God's love and was baptized,
and soon twenty members of Noble's family also decided to love
and serve Jesus.

In every generation God's notable VIPs are a blessing to
other people. They introduce many to the most important
Person of all time—Jesus.

PROPHECIES
Daniel 11

FAITHFUL AND FEARLESS

But the people who know their God shall stand firm and take action. Daniel 11:32.

For a thousand years they hid in the mountains. They had secret caves with concealed entrances that hundreds of seeking soldiers could not find. They had only the bare necessities, and grew their food on steep mountain slopes. Their children were taught to endure hardship, to be ready at all times to go into hiding, and, if found, to die rather than betray others.

These people whom God had raised up to keep the flame of truth burning were the Waldenses. They lived in the mountains of France and Italy during what is known as the Middle Ages. "The Waldenses were among the first of the peoples of Europe to obtain a translation of the Holy Scriptures."—*The Great Controversy,* p. 65. Their teachers taught the Bible to the youth as the main subject in their mountain schools. I have sat at a stone table where portions of the Bible were once hand-copied by these people. These portions of the Bible were sealed in secret pockets in their clothing. They also memorized the Gospels of Matthew and John and many of the Epistles.

"The work of these missionaries began in the plains and valleys at the foot of their own mountains, but it extended far beyond these limits. With naked feet and in garments coarse and travel-stained as were those of their Master, they passed through great cities and penetrated to distant lands. Everywhere they scattered the precious seed. Churches sprang up in their path, and the blood of martyrs witnessed for the truth. The day of God will reveal a rich harvest of souls garnered by the labors of these faithful men."—*Ibid.,* pp. 71, 72.

As I stood in a dark cave that had been used as a church by the Waldenses, I was told that hundreds had died there as a result of betrayal. Hundreds of others chose to be true to God rather than to deny their faith.

What gave the Waldenses the ability to "stand firm and take action" (R.S.V.)? The answer is in our text—they were people who knew their God. Let's determine to know God and to be faithful, fervent, and fearless.

PROPHECIES
Daniel 12

COUNTDOWN TO LIFTOFF

"At that time shall arise Michael, the great prince who has charge of your people. And there shall be a time of trouble, such as never has been since there was a nation till that time; but at that time your people shall be delivered, every one whose name shall be found written in the book." Daniel 12:1.

Prior to the "liftoff," God's people will experience "a time of trouble, such as never was," preceded by Jesus' standing up in the heavenly sanctuary and saying, "Time has been cut off for everyone." This is to be the end of the judgment, and there will be no further opportunity for salvation. Just as the angel closed the door on Noah's ark, so when Michael stands up there will be no more mercy for those who do not want to know God.

At this time Satan and his evil angels will bring about the time of trouble. "Those who honor the law of God have been accused of bringing judgments upon the world, and they will be regarded as the cause of the fearful convulsions of nature and the strife and bloodshed among men that are filling the earth with woe."—*The Great Controversy*, p. 614.

The great controversy between Christ and Satan reaches a climax. However, "the people who know their God shall stand firm." The promise is that the plagues that afflict the world at that time will not touch God's people and that no Christian whose name is written in the book of life will be killed after Michael stands up and the judgment ceases.

It would be helpful for us to read the closing chapters of the book *The Great Controversy*, by Ellen White. They are entitled "The Impending Conflict," "The Scriptures a Safeguard," "The Final Warning," "The Time of Trouble," "God's People Delivered," "Desolation of the Earth," and "The Controversy Ended." In this commentary on the Scriptures we have information and inspiration to help us.

Daniel was instructed to seal his book until "the time of the end." We have discovered from the book of Daniel that this time in which we are living *is* the time of the end. We need to study in detail the book written by God through the man who recorded prophecies concerning the end of time.

PROPHECIES
Revelation 1

FREEDOM FOR EVERYONE

Blessed is he who reads aloud the words of the prophecy, and blessed are those who hear, and who keep what is written therein; for the time is near. Revelation 1:3.

Abraham Lincoln is regarded as one of the greatest of men. He was the sixteenth president of the United States of America, and his name is known in many countries of the world. One reason he is respected by people of many nations is that in 1863 he issued the Emancipation Proclamation, a document stating that the slaves were free.

The book of Revelation is an emancipation proclamation of even greater value, for it outlines the work of Jesus, who has freed everyone from the slavery of sin. When people look casually at the book of Revelation, it appears to be a riddle. Its twenty-two chapters contain more than three hundred symbols, and many people do not understand the meaning of the stars, beasts, horns, thunders, crowns, and trumpets. However, the Bible is its own interpreter, and each of these riddles has special meaning. The word *revelation* comes from the Greek word *apocalypse,* which means "disclosure" or "something revealed."

In the first verse of chapter 1 we read that it is "the revelation of Jesus Christ." John has written Revelation in such a way that we can see the beautiful face of Jesus in each of its prophecies. It is an unveiling of penned pictures about the Person who has freed us from sin.

Abraham Lincoln's life was cut short by someone who wanted to stop his work. He did not deserve to be shot like a criminal, for he was a good man.

Lincoln was buried on May 4, 1865, at Oak Ridge Cemetery in Springfield, Illinois. As the funeral procession moved along the street, thousands of people wept. A black woman lifted her small son to her shoulders so that he could see. And with tears in her eyes she said, "Take a long look, honey; he died for you."

As you read the prophecies of Revelation, look carefully and you will see Jesus. Yes, you should take a long look at Him, because He died for you.

174

PROPHECIES
Revelation 2

SEVEN IS SPECIAL

"To the angel of the church in Ephesus write: 'The words of him who holds the seven stars in his right hand, who walks among the seven golden lampstands.'" Revelation 2:1.

Of all Bible numbers, seven is the most significant. It stands for completeness and perfection. This fact was first demonstrated in Genesis, for God selected seven days as the basis for the week. The seventh day is special, for after six days of Creation God rested and He blessed and made holy the seventh day.

Most of the prophecies in the book of Revelation are centered upon the number seven. Some of the sevens in the Apocalypse are: seven churches, seals, trumpets, candlesticks, stars, angels, spirits, thunders, heads, crowns, mountains, kings, and plagues. There are also seven beatitudes. The first one, found in the third verse of chapter 1, promises us a blessing if we read the book of Revelation.

The seven churches mentioned in Revelation 2 and 3 were not the only churches in Asia. However, they were selected because they represented seven periods of the Christian church between Jesus' first and second advents. The actual churches were located on a Roman highway, and the order in which they are mentioned in Revelation is the order you would come to them as you traveled on that road. As you read the messages to the seven churches, you will notice that Jesus is revealed to each in a different way. He appears in the midst of the candlesticks, as the Resurrection, with a sharp sword, as the Son of God, having seven Spirits and seven stars, with the key of David, and as the faithful and true Witness. Five of the churches were given commendation and reproof; each one was given counsel and a promise.

The words of our text do seem to be a riddle, but the meaning of the symbols is stated in the preceding verse. Remember, there were no chapter divisions in the original Scriptures. When we read the book of Revelation as a complete letter, we can discover its main messages. Jesus is the One holding the seven stars, and He is "the morning star" that was promised to the church at Thyatira. If we let Him, He will be the morning star of our lives, too.

175

PROPHECIES
Revelation 3

THE LATCHLESS DOOR

" 'Behold, I stand at the door and knock; if any one hears my voice and opens the door, I will come in to him and eat with him, and he with me.' " Revelation 3:20.

Have you seen Holman Hunt's famous painting of Jesus knocking at the door? The artist put on canvas the picture described in today's text. If you look closely at the painting, you will notice that there is no latch on the door. Mr. Hunt left the latch off because he believed the door to our hearts has a handle only on the inside and that we must open the door. Jesus does not force His way into our lives; He comes only by invitation.

The picture shows that the door is closed. This was the condition of the Laodicean church then, and it is also the condition of the last-day or remnant church—the church to which we belong. The Laodiceans were neither cold nor hot, a condition that God cannot tolerate. At Laodicea, the "city of compromise," were lukewarm baths—neither cold nor hot. Today some members of the remnant church are neither hot in their love for Jesus nor are they entirely cold.

There are many things that can close the door of our hearts. John, who wrote the book of Revelation, warns us of these in his First Epistle—"the lust of the flesh, the lust of the eyes, and the pride of life" (chap. 2:16). Also, the Gospels tell us that the cares of this life can keep the door closed. We don't need to do anything deliberately wrong, but if we fail to do what is right, we keep the door of our heart closed. Jesus not only knocks at the door but also calls to us. Even though we may not voluntarily open the door, He is there pleading for admission.

One of the most wonderful promises of the Bible is that He will come into our lives and will fellowship with us. He says that not only will He share a meal with us but if we enter into this relationship with Him, He will one day let us share His throne in the kingdom of heaven.

Today as we pray let us tell Jesus that we have opened the door of our heart. Tell Him that He is welcome every day and that we want to help others open the door to their heart.

OPEN DOOR IN HEAVEN

After this I looked, and lo, in heaven an open door! And the first voice, which I had heard speaking to me like a trumpet, said, "Come up hither, and I will show you what must take place after this." Revelation 4:1.

Windsor Castle has been one of the homes of British royalty for about nine hundred years. It is the oldest royal residence in England that is still in use. Originally built as a fortress, the castle occupies fourteen acres and is near enough to London so that the monarch can visit often. When the reigning king or queen is residing at Windsor Castle, a special flag flies from the Round Tower.

There are many grand chambers in the castle besides the section used as the residence. The huge rooms are decorated with wood carvings, tapestries, beautiful rugs, chandeliers, and ornate furniture. As I stood at the end of the Garter throne room, I thought of the throne room in heaven that John was privileged to see through the open door. He was unable to describe adequately its beauty, but the brief description that we do have shows it to be beyond any throne room in any earthly castle.

Tourists at Windsor Castle always see the throne *empty*. However, by the grace of Jesus, we will be able to stand before the *occupied* throne in heaven. The most encouraging part of John's description of the high court of heaven is the fact that God is on His throne. Many today tell us that God is not the supreme ruler of the universe, but I believe He is and John confirms that belief.

John's description of the throne of God is similar to Daniel's description, which we read earlier this month. These prophets could say only that it was covered in a halo of clear, dazzling white and that around it were brilliant shades of red and green like a rainbow. Everything about the throne was spectacular.

Previously John has related to us things that have already happened, but now he is going to reveal to us things that "'must take place after this'" (R.S.V.). We are going to read not only about the trials but also about the final victory of the church.

PROPHECIES
Revelation 5

CLOSED BOOK IN HEAVEN

And they sang a new song, saying, "Worthy art thou to take the scroll and to open its seals, for thou wast slain and by thy blood didst ransom men for God from every tribe and tongue and people and nation." Revelation 5:9.

The book that John saw in God's hand was actually a scroll, such as those made from tall reeds that grew in the valley of the Nile River in Egypt.

This sealed book held the secrets of the future, and John wept because no one was able to open it. However, one of the twenty-four elders from around the throne told him not to cry. All the heavenly beings rejoiced when Jesus broke the seven seals and opened the scroll. It was certainly a "new song," for it could not be sung before Jesus had died on the cross. It was then that He provided salvation for every person.

Jesus is described both as a lion, representing a king, and as a lamb, representing a sacrifice. In the book of Revelation there are at least twenty-six references to Jesus as the Lamb. For more than fourteen hundred years He had been represented as the lamb in the Jewish Passover. And since the cross, for almost two thousand years, Christians have remembered Him as the Lamb of God every time they celebrate the Lord's Supper.

In the West Indies there is a tree with gold-colored fruit whose poisonous juice will blister the skin. However, there is another, called the whitewood tree, that has sap that will cure the blisters.

Many people have been blistered by sin, which is often attractive, like the gold-colored fruit. But these blisters of sin can be healed if the blood of Jesus is applied. The whitewood tree represents the cross on which the Lamb of God gave His blood to heal us.

Have you been blistered by sin? Have you made mistakes that have not been made right? You will find pardon, followed by a wonderful peace, if you put things right with God and your fellow men. This pardon and peace is ours because of Jesus' death on the cross. We can be healed of our spiritual sickness and find *light for our lives* by looking to Jesus.

178

MYSTERIOUS HORSES

And I saw, and behold, a white horse, and its rider had a bow; and a crown was given to him, and he went out conquering and to conquer. Revelation 6:2.

The best known of the world-famous Lippizaner horses are at the Spanish riding school in Vienna. Each year thousands of people come to see these horses perform. I have seen one of these beautiful animals stand almost upright on its back legs with a rider on its back. These white horses are able to do this because they have strong bones, short legs, and a thick, arched neck.

The Lippizaner horses, originally from Spain and Italy, were imported to Austria more than four hundred years ago. Partly because of their build, they are able to jump in a way that other horses cannot.

We would expect to see horses at a riding school, but while John was in vision he saw four mysterious horses in the sky. The first was white, and its rider was a conquering king. This is a picture of Jesus, and the church in the first century.

The second horse was red, representing the war and persecution that followed the first century. The black horse, whose rider carried a pair of balances, depicts a period of spiritual poverty and famine in the church. "Death," the rider of the pale horse, represents the period of church history known as the Dark Ages.

The four horses also denote the first four seals. The fifth seal represents a period of martyrdom in the Christian church, the sixth and seventh seals symbolize the terrible convulsions in the natural world. Great earthquakes, the Dark Day, and the stars falling from heaven like figs from a tree precede the second coming of Jesus.

The climax of all Bible prophecies is the advent of Christ. The information in the prophecies is not given to make us wise in earthly wisdom, but to prepare us for the coming of the Lord.

Those who are not ready for the last event in this world's history will cry, "Fall on us, and hide us from the face of him that sitteth on the throne" (Rev. 6:16). Those who are ready will say, with John, "Come, Lord Jesus."

PROPHECIES
Revelation 7

THEY CAN'T BE COUNTED

After this I looked, and behold, a great multitude which no man could number, from every nation, from all tribes and peoples and tongues, standing before the throne and before the Lamb, clothed in white robes, with palm branches in their hands. Revelation 7:9.

Lord Leicester invited Queen Victoria to visit his castle in the midlands of England. On the day the queen arrived, thousands of people waited to see her. Many came early so they could have a good position. As the queen approached in her royal carriage, the cry was passed along the lines of people, "The queen is coming." Lord Leicester was so pleased to have her visit his castle that he stopped the main clock the moment she crossed the threshold and ordered that it would not start again as a reminder of the moment the queen arrived.

Kings and queens have come and gone upon the stage of history, and our study of the prophecies indicates that the King of the universe is about to return to this earth. The moment He appears in the clouds of heaven, all clocks will stop forever. We will not need watches from that moment, because we will not be dealing in hours, days, and years, but in eternity.

As the people waited for the arrival of Queen Victoria, some noticed a cloud of dust in the distance as the horse-drawn carriage appeared on the horizon. Those who study the Word of God see many signs that Jesus is coming soon. In the last chapter we noted signs in the natural world. These signs, given by Jesus, are recorded in Matthew 24 and Luke 21.

Although we are interested in knowing when Jesus will come, the Bible does not give an exact time. However, we do have information to answer the question How many will go to heaven?

The people who will go to heaven cannot be numbered. They will come from every nation and will wear white robes because, by the grace of Jesus, they have been victorious.

They express their appreciation by singing " 'Salvation belongs to our God who sits upon the throne, and to the Lamb!' " (Rev. 7:10, R.S.V.).

PROPHECIES
Revelation 10

EATING A BOOK

And I took the little scroll from the hand of the angel and ate it; it was sweet as honey in my mouth, but when I had eaten it my stomach was made bitter. Revelation 10:10.

Goats like to eat paper and cloth, but I don't think you would like to have a book for breakfast. In our verse today, however, we see that John was told to eat the little book. He was also warned that although it would taste "sweet as honey," it would soon be "bitter."

The book of Revelation is full of mysteries such as this one. As we read Revelation and other books of the Bible, however, we will understand some of these mysteries better.

In the books of Jeremiah and Ezekiel we discover a little about what eating a book represents. When Jeremiah said that he ate the Word of God, he did not really mean that he had it for one of his meals. In the Bible, when a prophet talks about eating a book, he means he absorbed and understood the meaning of the message.

John is relating to us what he learned while he was in vision. The statements made in Revelation 10 describe the bitter experience that was to come to the people who were looking for the advent of Jesus in 1844. They studied Daniel's time prophecy of the 2300 days and came to the conclusion that Jesus was going to come in 1844. They were right about the time, but they were wrong about the event. It was a bitter experience for tens of thousands of Adventists in many church groups. (This occurred before the Seventh-day Adventist Church was formed.)

In the final verse of the chapter we note that after the bitter experience, those who were looking for the Advent were to "prophesy again." As they restudied the 2300-day prophecy, they realized that Jesus commenced His work of judgment in 1844. And as instructed, many went forth to proclaim the judgment-hour message to every nation. Today this church is preaching Jesus and all Bible truths in almost all of the more than two hundred nations listed by the United Nations organization.

PROPHECIES
Revelation 11

THE TWO WITNESSES

These are the two olive trees and the two lampstands which stand before the Lord of the earth. Revelation 11:4.

The New Testament contains at least 260 direct quotations from the Old Testament. The symbols of the olive trees and lampstands are first recorded in Zechariah 4. This Old Testament prophet says, "These are the two anointed ones, that stand by the Lord of the whole earth" (verse 14), a similar statement to that made by John.

Zechariah states that the olive branches supplied the oil for the lamps in the sanctuary. In the Psalms, David says that the Word of God is the light for all people.

In the verse before our Morning Watch text for today, we are told that the olive trees and lampstands are God's "two witnesses." A comparison of the prophecies of Zechariah and John leads us to the conclusion that the Old and New Testaments are His witnesses. Jesus also stated that "'the scriptures . . . bear witness to me'" (John 5:39, R.S.V.).

"The two witnesses represent the Scriptures of the Old and New Testament. Both are important testimonies to the origin and perpetuity of the law of God. Both are witnesses also to the plan of salvation. The types, sacrifices, and prophecies of the Old Testament point forward to a Saviour to come. The Gospels and Epistles of the New Testament tell of a Saviour who has come in the exact manner foretold by type and prophecy."—*The Great Controversy*, p. 267.

Now let's note ten ways in which the Scriptures witness.

S hows Christians truths to follow.
C omforts those who sorrow and suffer.
R eveals remarkable power to change lives.
I nspires people to be like Jesus.
P oints readers to eternal life.
T ells all how to be saved.
U sed as basis for songs, poems, films, and books.
R eminds us of God's love and protection.
E ach book testifies about Jesus.
S hows all how to grow in faith.

PROPHECIES
Revelation 13

A DRAGON IN CHURCH

So that no one can buy or sell unless he has the mark, that is, the name of the beast or the number of its name. Revelation 13:17.

A type of lizard known as the dragon of Komodo lives on the island of Komodo and other islands of Indonesia. This reptile is up to ten feet long and is the largest lizard known to exist on the earth today. However, every country has stories about dragons. The ancient Greeks believed that Hercules killed dragons, and the English talk about Saint George slaying the dragon. Although these creatures did not really exist, people have painted vivid descriptions of them, including green eyes, nostrils that breathe fire, and big wings.

These dragons from mythology represented evil and destruction, and they became symbols of sin. Perhaps these ideas are based on what John says in the book of Revelation where the prophet identifies the dragon as the origin of evil. Do you know who this dragon is? If you do not, you can find out by reading Revelation 20:2.

In today's chapter we discover that the dragon wants to go to church so he can destroy God's people. In Bible prophecy a woman in white represents the Christian church, with whom the dragon is at war. He wants to destroy those who are true to God, but is not worried about those who are worshiping false religious systems, because he has already conquered them. He wants to destroy those who have the shield of faith and the sword of the Spirit and can overcome dragons. The people who can destroy dragons are described as those who "keep the commandments of God and bear testimony to Jesus" (Rev. 12:17, R.S.V.).

In Revelation 19:10 we discover that the "testimony of Jesus is the spirit of prophecy." In other words, the dragon is trying to destroy the remnant church. By the "church" John means the true Christians, for they constitute the living church in the last part of this earth's history. Satan cannot destroy the remnant church, for Christ has promised that He will protect it. When the church meets in heaven, the dragon won't be anywhere near. We will soon discover where he will be at that time.

PROPHECIES
Revelation 13

A LAMBLIKE COUNTRY

Then I saw another beast which rose out of the earth; it had two horns like a lamb and it spoke like a dragon. Revelation 13:11.

On Liberty Island in New York Harbor stands the Statue of Liberty, a lady 305 feet tall. Her head is so big that thirty people can stand in it at once. One arm is stretched above her head, and in her hand is a torch of liberty large enough for twelve people to stand in. There are nineteen lamps inside the torch, and the light from these lamps can be seen for many miles. Her other hand is holding a large tablet with the inscription "July 4, 1776." It was on this day that the first step was taken to form a new nation.

The statue was made in France and was a gift to the United States. A broken chain lies at the feet of the woman, symbolizing that in the United States, everyone is to be free.

The real name of the statue is *Liberty Enlightening the World,* and the liberty lady has become a hallmark for the nation. Most people who have visited or live in America know about this symbol. However, many do not know that the Bible has another emblem for this country of more than 200 million people. We have discovered from the book of Daniel that God often uses animals to represent nations. Many students of the Bible believe the lamblike beast, mentioned in our text today, is God's symbol for the United States.

The beasts that Daniel saw representing kingdoms rose up out of the sea, which in Bible prophecy represents people. However, this lamblike beast came up out of the earth, which would indicate that it was not to rise among other nations. The time and manner of its rise, the character of its government, and its work also point to the United States.

A little girl who visited the Statue of Liberty was so excited that she could not sleep. She said, "Daddy, I am thinking about that lady with the lamp out there in the dark. She is all alone. Don't you think we should be helping Miss Liberty to hold up the lamp?" Yes, every Christian does have a duty to help hold up the lamp of liberty. Also, it is God's plan for every person to live in a land where the light of liberty will never go out.

184

PROPHECIES
Revelation 14

SPECIAL DELIVERY

Then I saw another angel flying in midheaven, with an eternal gospel to proclaim to those who dwell on earth, to every nation and tribe and tongue and people. Revelation 14:6.

One of the 290 species of pigeons, the homing pigeon, has the instinct to fly to its home loft from long distances. It can travel between fifty and sixty miles an hour and has been used to carry messages in small lightweight holders fixed to its leg. This bird was used to carry news of Olympic victories in ancient Greece. And since the days of the Roman army homing pigeons have been used to carry messages in times of war.

It would certainly be interesting to receive a message delivered by a bird. We would regard it as a special delivery.

God has sent three special messages to this world for Christians to read and to pass on. These messages, recorded in verses 6 to 12 of today's chapter, are so important that it would be good for us to memorize them. The first message states that the gospel will be taken to all the world. It declares that the hour of God's judgment has come. As we studied in the book of Daniel, the judgment commenced in 1844, so the statement that the "judgment is come" is in harmony with that prophecy. Jesus is engaged in a work of judgment in the heavenly sanctuary right now. This first angel's message also includes a call to worship the Creator, as we are told to do in the fourth commandment.

The second and third angels' messages focus on the fall of Babylon. We will see what Babylon represents when we read Revelation 17 and 18. The most severe warning ever given by God is contained in the third angel's message.

The conclusion of these messages makes it clear that the "saints" are those who love and obey Jesus. They are identified as those who "keep the commandments of God, *and* the faith of Jesus." When the word *saint* is used in the Bible, it means Christian believer. We see that the last-day "saints" not only love Jesus but also demonstrate their love by obeying Him.

185

ONE-HUNDRED-POUND HAILSTONES!

Then I heard a loud voice from the temple telling the seven angels, "Go and pour out on the earth the seven bowls of the wrath of God." Revelation 16:1.

Hailstones are lumps of ice and are as hard as stone. Those of you who live in cold climates may have seen hailstones as large as marbles. Some have been reported as big as golf balls and can cause a lot of damage to fruit trees and buildings. However, before Jesus comes there are going to be hailstones weighing from sixty to one hundred pounds.

Hail is one of the seven last plagues to be poured out on those who have turned their backs on God. The description of all seven plagues, in Revelation 15 and 16, causes people to tremble when they read it. However, there is no need for God's people to be afraid, since these plagues will fall only on the wicked.

The seven last plagues are punishments that fit the crimes committed against God and His people. Those who have turned their backs on their Maker and worshiped false gods will have sores that will not heal. Because blood of Christian people has been spilt, the second and third plagues cause the sea, the rivers, and fountains of water to be changed into blood. Under the fourth plague, those who have gone against God will be scorched by the heat of the sun. The fifth, sixth, and seventh plagues are directed against the powers of the Papacy, apostate Protestant churches, and spiritualism. The punishment, including darkness, will be so intense that people will not be able to bear it.

God is not punishing people to get even; He simply cannot continue to allow wicked men and false worship to go unchecked. As we have already seen from our study of the Bible, God is a God of love and mercy who always deals justly.

Prior to the announcement of the plagues, we have a picture of a large group of people who have been true to God singing a song of triumph. No one needs to receive the seven last plagues, because God has made provision whereby we can stand on the "sea of glass" and "sing the song of Moses servant of God, and the song of the Lamb."

PROPHECIES
Revelation 18

GOD'S LAST WARNING

"Fallen, fallen is Babylon the great! . . ." Then I heard another voice from heaven saying, "Come out of her, my people, lest you take part in her sins, lest you share in her plagues." Revelation 18:2-4.

When somebody says, "This is the last time I will warn you," we know what is going to happen next. There is something very serious about the "last warning," so we generally take note and try to avoid the promised results. Today we are reading about God's last warning. It is not a warning to the whole world, but to God's people who are in Babylon.

Can this refer to the kingdom of Babylon where Daniel was captive? No, that nation was destroyed hundreds of years before John wrote. As we compare scripture with scripture, we see that Babylon denotes confusion and opposition to Jesus.

Revelation 17 gives another detailed description of Babylon. Those who reject the truths of the Word of God as centered in Jesus are "in Babylon." Satan has organized his opposition to Jesus and has created counterfeit religions. The one counterfeit mentioned frequently in the book of Revelation is known as the Papacy. You can read more about it in the book *The Great Controversy,* by Ellen G. White.

God's people are "in Babylon" today if they are relying on salvation by works rather than salvation by faith. Any church or individual that offers another way of salvation than through Jesus is part of the last-day confusion the devil has organized. Like Cain, they may even bring a sacrifice to the Lord regularly. But sincerity is not enough. We must also do exactly what Jesus wants us to do.

Before God destroyed Sodom and Gomorrah, He called people out, and Lot and his family responded. Before God destroyed the earth with water, He called people out, and Noah and his family came. Before God destroys the world by fire, He is calling people out. A part of our responsibility as Christians is to pass on God's last warning, "Come out of her [Babylon], my people." Let us heed God's warning and pass it on to others.

ON WHITE HORSES

Then I saw heaven opened, and behold, a white horse! He who sat upon it is called Faithful and True, and in righteousness he judges and makes war. . . . On his robe and on his thigh he has a name inscribed, King of kings and Lord of lords. Revelation 19:11-16.

In old times white horses were often selected by kings and military leaders to ride in victory processions. Jesus is now proclaimed "King of kings and Lord of lords" and is pictured by John as riding on a beautiful white charger. White represents holiness of character, and the Rider is called "Faithful and True."

The angels who accompany Jesus to this earth are dressed in pure-white linen and appear to follow Him on white horses too. Imagine the beautiful sight of tens of thousands of holy angels coming with Jesus, who will be wearing sparkling royal crowns on His head!

This is one of the Bible's most spectacular descriptions of the Second Advent. John once again "saw heaven opened" and tried to describe the scene. The second coming of Jesus is the basic teaching of the book of Revelation. All the prophecies of Daniel and Revelation climax in this, the greatest event of all time.

Nowadays all eyes are fixed on the heavens, and people are wondering what the next great event will be. Man has walked on the moon and now wants to go to other planets. I do not know what the next great space event will be, but I do know what the grandest event of all will be. Soon you and I will look up and see heaven opened, and Jesus descending with all the armies of heaven arrayed in white. They will be coming to this earth to take those to heaven who have crowned Jesus "King of kings and Lord of lords" in their lives.

Then we will be caught up in the clouds to meet Jesus in the air. As much as He loves every person, Jesus cannot take those to heaven who have sin in their lives. If we want to march in the future triumphant procession to heaven, today we need to crown Jesus king of our lives.

PROPHECIES
Revelation 20

ONE THOUSAND YEARS OF PEACE

Blessed and holy is he who shares in the first resurrection!
Over such the second death has no power, but they shall be priests
of God and of Christ, and they shall reign with him a thousand
years. Revelation 20:6.

More than thirty years ago representatives of seventy-two
countries held special meetings in Paris, France, and Prague,
Czechoslovakia. These meetings comprised the first World
Peace Conference, and since that time the conference has
become a mass movement involving more than 130 countries.

Any committee that could guarantee one thousand years of
world peace would be extremely popular. But we know that as
long as there is sin in the heart of even one person, there will not
be peace on this earth. However, God has predicted and
guaranteed that there will be one thousand years of peace
sometime in the future. And more than that, there will be peace
forever in the new earth.

In the Bible this one thousand years is mentioned only in the
book of Revelation. It appears six times in our chapter for today.
We often refer to this time period as the millennium, which is
Latin for "one thousand years."

The "first resurrection" occurs at the second coming of Jesus.
The righteous dead are raised to join those who are translated
without seeing death, and spend the 1,000 years in heaven. The
earth is desolate during that time, but it will be restored to its
original beauty after it has been cleansed by fire at the end of
1,000 years. Then the righteous will inhabit the new earth.

At the beginning of the millennium, the devil will be bound
by a chain of circumstances to this earth. The wicked, slain with
the brightness of Christ's second coming, are raised from the
dead at the end of the one thousand years. Then, because of the
sin in their hearts and their attempt to overthrow the New
Jerusalem, they are destroyed with fire. This is the only fire
mentioned in the Bible as destroying the wicked. Nowhere does
it teach that there is a hell where people go when they die to
burn forever.

PROPHECIES
Revelation 21

HAPPILY EVER AFTER

"God himself . . . will wipe away every tear from their eyes, and death shall be no more, neither shall there be mourning nor crying nor pain any more, for the former things have passed away." Revelation 21:3, 4.

Have you ever read a story that ended, ". . . and they lived happily ever after"? That is the way we like all stories to end, but it is not always how life is on this earth. However, it is going to be true in the new earth that Jesus is preparing for us.

Can you imagine a country with more people than you can number and where no one ever cries? Those living there will have no need for tears because they will always be happy. There will be no pain, death, or separation from loved ones. Everyone will be in perfect health and will always be thankful. The capital of the new earth will be a city larger than any on earth today. Its foundations will be made of precious stones, and each gate will be made of a single pearl. The walls will be of diamonds, and the whole city is described as a "city of gold." We may even walk on streets of gold!

There will be exciting things to do, including visiting other worlds. And we won't need cars or airplanes to travel. We cannot imagine how it is possible to move through space without these inventions, but remember that when Jesus comes we will be "caught up together" (1 Thess. 4:17). The God who made the atom and holds the world in space is able to do things we have never dreamed of.

The best part of heaven, of course, is that we will have fellowship with the Father, the Son, and the Holy Spirit. We were created to have companionship with them, and we will not be perfectly happy until that fellowship is restored. I am looking forward to heaven, aren't you?

Everyone has the opportunity of going to heaven, but only those whose names are written in the book of life will be there. Our names are entered when we accept Jesus as our Saviour, and with His help become true Christians.

PROPHECIES
Revelation 22

A SPECIAL INVITATION

The Spirit and the Bride say, "Come." And let him who hears say, "Come." And let him who is thirsty come, let him who desires take the water of life without price. Revelation 22:17.

Do you like to receive an invitation to a birthday party? I remember that as a boy, I was always thrilled when I was invited to such affairs. As an adult I also like to get wedding announcements. Some of you may have received special invitations to visit VIPs. Generally those who have the opportunity of visiting the ruler of their country or state take photographs of such a meeting.

The best and most prized invitation is printed in our text for today. Jesus invites us to "come" to the New Jerusalem, which is represented as His bride. The Father, the Son, and the Holy Spirit all invite us to be present in heaven. We have found that we can respond to this invitation by giving our lives to Jesus, and then, from a heart full of love, doing what He wants us to do.

In verse 14 of today's chapter we are told that those who "wash their robes," or become righteous through Jesus, will "enter the city by the gates" (R.S.V.). Another meaning for "wash their robes" is "keep His commandments." If I love my father, I do what he wants me to; and those who love Jesus, by His strength, obey Him.

An evangelist preaching to an audience of about four thousand people asked everybody to stand up. Then he said, "Now, all of you who accepted Christ before you were twenty years old, take your seats." Hundreds of people sat down. The evangelist made another request: "All of you who took your stand for God after you were 40, sit down." Only five people were left standing. Then he said, "All of you who took your stand after you were 50, sit down." Now only two of the 4,000 people were standing.

This experience reminds us that the longer we wait to respond to the invitation to come to Jesus, the less chance there is that we will ever do it. Jesus says, " 'Surely I am coming soon' " (verse 20, R.S.V.). And in the light of this fact, we need to be able to say with assurance, "Come, Lord Jesus."

PERSON
Mark 1

GOOD NEWS

The beginning of the gospel of Jesus Christ, the Son of God.
Mark 1:1.

A visitor to a war cemetery noticed a man weeping beside a grave. He wanted to say something comforting, but he thought it best to leave the man alone. However, when he returned later and the man was still there, he spoke to him. "There are a lot of soldiers buried here."

"Yes, and this one died for me."

"They all died for all of us, so that we could have freedom."

"No, you don't understand. This one died for me."

"What do you mean?"

The man, who had been kneeling by the grave, stood up and said, "This one took my place. I was called to go into the army, and he offered to go instead. He said that he was single and that I had a family. He took my papers, bore my name, went overseas, and was killed. Can you now understand that he died for me?"

Someone—Jesus—died for you and me. We need to learn all we can about the One who died for us, and Mark gives us further details. The Gospel of Mark is the shortest of the four Gospels. It is also the most comprehensive, and lists events in order of time.

The author, John Mark, a citizen of Jerusalem, wrote the story of Jesus for non-Jews. He concentrates on what Jesus *did* rather than on what He *said*.

Mark makes no comment on the birth, boyhood, or first one and one-half years of Jesus' public ministry. However, in just 678 verses he gives us a digest of the gospel, the "good news" of salvation available through Jesus. The word *gospel* is used fifteen times in the books of Matthew, Mark, Luke, and John. Six of those are in Mark.

G ood news
O ffers pardon
S alvation
P eace
E ternal life
L asting joy

PERSON
Mark 2

TEACHER, DOCTOR, PASTOR?

And it was noised that he was in the house. Mark 2:1, K.J.V.

Many junior youth would like to be teachers, doctors, or pastors, but Jesus did the work of all these professions. After His baptism He began His work in Galilee, "preaching the gospel of the kingdom of God" (Mark 1:14). After calling the four fishermen to be disciples, He taught in the synagogue on the Sabbath day. On that same day, of which Jesus said He was Lord, He healed Peter's wife's mother, and later a leper. When He arrived back in His adopted hometown of Capernaum, the people crowded into Peter's house, and Jesus preached again. While He was telling them about the kingdom of God, four men tore open the roof and lowered their paralyzed friend, and Jesus healed him.

You can imagine the astonishment of the crowd as the roof was broken open and the crippled man was lowered on a stretcher. This tells us a lot about the man and his faith. It also tells us a lot about Jesus, who immediately understood what the man needed, and before healing him forgave his sins. All these miracles showed Jesus to be a servant, which is the message of the book of Mark, and also helped establish that He was the Son of God.

The Servant at work as a teacher gave *light* to those who listened. The Servant at work as a pastor revealed *love,* and the Servant at work as a doctor established that He could give *life.* As we hear reports of Jesus, we need to come to Him for the light, love, and life that He can give to us.

Just as "it was noised that he was in the house" at Capernaum, so His disciples today are to report that He is in the house of God—the church. We also need to invite others to church so that they may have the opportunity of hearing the good news. As we go into church, we should be reverent and pray that all will find spiritual and physical healing because of their contact with Jesus.

Our neighbors and friends also should be able to gather in our own houses because "it is noised that Jesus is in the house." When He is there, those who live in the house and those who visit will find light, love, and life.

PERSON
Mark 3

HOW THE CHURCH BEGAN

And he went up into the hills, and called to him those whom he desired; and they came to him. And he appointed twelve, to be with him, and to be sent out to preach. Mark 3:13, 14.

Did you ever wonder when the first church was organized? The beginning step in establishing the church came when Jesus called the twelve disciples to help Him. No, they did not have a church building. In many parts of the world today, people meet under the trees, by the river, or in somebody's house. We know that the church is the object of God's "supreme regard" (see *Testimonies to Ministers,* p. 15) and that Jesus not only established the church but loved it and "gave himself for it" (Eph. 5:25).

There were two other reasons why Jesus appointed twelve men to be His disciples. They needed "to be with him" (R.S.V.), and these men could not be qualified for service in any better way than to be companions with Jesus every day. However, they were not to spend all their time preparing; they were also to preach. They were to be not only disciples, which means "followers" or "learners," but also apostles, which means "someone who is sent" or "messengers." We too are to have fellowship with Jesus before preaching about Him. When we learn of Him, as disciples, we will want to be His messengers.

The disciples are listed in today's chapter, and it would be good to learn their names. Peter, James, and John were the closest to Jesus. Andrew, of Bethsaida, learned of Jesus from John the Baptist. Matthew, stationed at Capernaum, was a tax collector. When called to be a disciple, he immediately quit his job and followed Jesus.

Each of the apostles had his own personality, and they were far from perfect. It is a tremendous encouragement to us to know that Jesus accepts us just as we are. Also, if we stay close to Him, we will be changed in character. "He who called the fishermen of Galilee is still calling men to His service. And He is just as willing to manifest His power through us as through the first disciples. However imperfect and sinful we may be, the Lord holds out to us the offer of partnership with Himself, of apprenticeship to Christ."—*The Desire of Ages,* p. 297.

PERSON
Mark 4

ABOARD A SINKING BOAT

*And he awoke and rebuked the wind, and said to the sea,
"Peace! Be still!" And the wind ceased, and there was a great
calm. Mark 4:39.*

It must have been a bad storm to terrify brave fishermen who
knew the Sea of Galilee like the backs of their hands. It was
night, but these men had been in night storms before. The
rain-packed winds were lifting waves that crashed down on the
boat, but they had experienced that before. However, Mark
mentions something that the other Gospel writers do not—"the
boat was already filling" (Mark 4:37, R.S.V.). Then a flash of
lightning lit up the sky and revealed Jesus lying asleep. The
disciples, amazed at His seeming unconcern, uttered a desperate cry, " 'Teacher, do you not care if we perish?' " (verse 38,
R.S.V.). Our text for today dramatically states how Jesus
delivered the disciples who constituted the church at that time.

"How often the disciples' experience is ours! When the
tempests of temptation gather, and the fierce lightnings flash,
and the waves sweep over us, we battle with the storm alone,
forgetting that there is One who can help us. We trust to our own
strength till our hope is lost, and we are ready to perish. Then we
remember Jesus, and if we call upon Him to save us, we shall not
cry in vain. Though He sorrowfully reproves our unbelief and
self-confidence, He never fails to give us the help we need.
Whether on the land or on the sea, if we have the Saviour in our
hearts, there is no need of fear. Living faith in the Redeemer will
smooth the sea of life, and will deliver us from danger in the way
that He knows to be best."—*The Desire of Ages,* p. 336.

Just as the disciples were delivered on a troubled sea when
Jesus said, "Peace, be still," so disciples today on the sea of life in
an uncertain world can have peace amid the storm. Sometimes
it may seem that we are alone, but we can be assured that our
Saviour cares. If the disciples had remembered that Jesus was
with them and had demonstrated faith, they would not have
feared losing their lives. When we are afraid, Jesus has to ask as
He asked the twelve, " 'Why are you afraid? Have you no faith?' "
(verse 40, R.S.V.). Let us remember that

Faith ends when worry begins;
Worry ends when faith begins.

PERSON
Mark 5

WHO TOUCHED ME?

And he said to her, "Daughter, your faith has made you well; go in peace, and be healed of your disease." Mark 5:34.

Have you ever been in a crowd where there were so many people pressing against you that even if you lifted both your feet you would not fall down? Soon after Jesus cast the demons out of a man who behaved like a madman, He entered into a city where people pressed in on Him on all sides. Suddenly He paused in His slow walk, and asked, "Who touched my clothes?" Surrounded as they were by a huge crowd, the disciples thought it was a foolish question.

However, Jesus knew that the touch was one of faith by someone who had seized a golden opportunity to be cured. The woman who was healed by touching Jesus had suffered for twelve years from a disease that the doctors could not cure. The Lord made it clear that it was her faith and not just the contact with His garment that healed her of the disease.

There are many people who come in touch with Jesus through the church, through nature, and by studying the Bible, but never touch Him by faith and thus miss the help that they could obtain. We must not be like the multitude that thronged Jesus on His way to the house of Jairus. While we are on our way to our heavenly home, we must be like the woman who purposefully touched Him. It is good to be in the crowd that throngs Christ, but it is much better to be among the few who touch Him by faith. There are many who, like the rich young ruler, discover Jesus but never decide to become Christians.

To get nourishment from food, you must eat it; to appreciate the sweetness of music, you must listen to it; to enjoy the benefits of an electric light, you must touch the switch. Likewise, to know, enjoy, and share the light, love, and life of the gospel, we must exercise faith.

There are three parts to faith—*knowledge, belief,* and *action.* The woman in the crowd *knew* something about Jesus; she also *believed* that He could heal her. However, if she had not *acted* on that belief and knowledge, she would not have been healed.

We all have some knowledge of Jesus; we believe that He lived, died, rose from the dead, and is coming back to this earth. This knowledge and belief, plus action, is faith.

196

PERSON
Mark 6

HOMECOMING

And Jesus said to them, "A prophet is not without honor, except in his own country, and among his own kin, and in his own house." Mark 6:4.

The former village carpenter returned to Nazareth, the town of His birth. Jesus was probably excited about the trip, because He would have the opportunity of serving the needy Nazarenes. If there was any town that should have received Jesus, it was this one. These were the streets where He had played, and this was where He had worked as a carpenter. He had never done any act of unkindness or said anything to hurt anyone in this place where He had "increased in wisdom and stature, and in favour with God and man" (Luke 2:52).

On His first Sabbath back in Nazareth, Jesus taught in the synagogue, and that is where the jealousies and bad feelings of the people were expressed. The Lord marveled at their unbelief and quoted the proverb that is our Morning Watch text for today. When we talk about Jesus to those who know us, they may not listen as readily as do strangers. Our neighbors and even our relatives, who may know of our lack of formal training, may not think that we can explain the Scriptures.

It is interesting to note that Jesus' four brothers, James, Judas, Joses, and Simon, did not believe in Him at this time, but after His death and resurrection, they were converted. These conversions alone made the homecoming worthwhile, even though it seemed to be a failure at the time. We must never become discouraged because people do not receive the message that we have to give about the kingdom of heaven. We must continue to teach and pray that the One who fed the 5,000 people and walked on the water will be received by our loved ones and friends, too.

It is natural for us to look for "instant Christians," but we must remember that some people take longer than others to accept Christianity. Some plants and trees take longer to grow than others, and some fruit takes longer to ripen than does other fruit. You and I may not even see the results of our sowing of the gospel because someone else may have the privilege of helping those we influence make the final decision to love and obey Jesus.

PERSON
Mark 7

GOOD WORK

And they were astonished beyond measure, saying, "He has done all things well; he even makes the deaf hear and the dumb speak." Mark 7:37.

When we receive a test paper or an assignment back from the teacher, we like to see "good work" or a similar complimentary statement written on it. Jesus wants us to do very good work, and He gave us an example as He worked in the carpenter shop and when He served the people of Galilee. Although the citizens in His hometown of Nazareth did not recognize this, the heathen people who lived on the east side of the Sea of Galilee did. It was here a few weeks before the time of our text that they had tried to make Jesus king.

Although Jesus had come into Galilee in order to be alone with His disciples and to teach them, someone brought a deaf man with a speech impediment to Him to be healed. Although Mark records only twenty of the thirty-four miracles listed in the Gospels, he is the only one who records this healing. He says that Jesus looked up to heaven, sighed, and said, "Be opened." Christ's modern disciples who look to Him and who have sympathy for others can speak words of power to open people's senses to the gospel and, if necessary, perform physical miracles, too.

Two statements here remind us that Jesus was the Creator. "He hath done all things well" is similar to the statements made at the end of each day of Creation week—"And God saw that it was good." The authoritative words of Jesus, "Be opened," are similar to the words of the Creator, "Let there be light." Whatever Jesus does is "good work" and gives light.

The healing of the deaf man also reminds us of the process of salvation. In the crowd, the only person who was healed was the deaf man who stepped aside with Jesus. It was the touch of Jesus that restored his hearing, and it is that same touch that heals those who have the sickness of sin. Once again, without faith the man would not have received his hearing. Jesus still honors faith even among those who do not fully understand.

A little girl showed faith in God by taking an umbrella to a meeting called to pray for rain. If we expect a miracle, we need to act as though we believe it is going to happen.

198

PERSON
Mark 8

TO GAIN THE WORLD

For whosoever will save his life shall lose it; but whosoever shall lose his life for my sake and the gospel's, the same shall save it. For what shall it profit a man, if he shall gain the whole world, and lose his own soul? Mark 8:35, 36, K.J.V.

When Alexander was 16, he took his first step toward gaining the whole world. While his father was absent from the kingdom, the teen-ager was able, by his military planning, to stop a revolt. At 18 he fought in a famous battle, and two years later, when his father, Phillip II of Macedon, was killed, he became ruler. He destroyed the city of thieves and completed the uniting of Greece by defeating the Persians in 331 B.C. One military victory followed another, until most of the then-known world came under his control. His last project was the invasion of India, but the army refused to march farther with him, and he wept because there was "no other world for him to conquer." This great soldier was known as Alexander the Great, but he died at the age of 33.

There was another Person who died at 33, and the following poem contrasts the life of Jesus with that of Alexander:

Jesus and Alexander died at thirty-three.
One lived and died for self; one died for you and me.
The Greek died on a throne; the Jew died on a cross;
One's life a triumph seemed; the other but a loss.
One led vast armies forth; the other walked alone.
One shed a whole world's blood: the other gave His own.
One won the world in life and lost it all in death;
The other lost His life to win the whole world's faith.

Jesus and Alexander died at thirty-three.
The Greek made all men slaves; the Jew made all men free;
One built a throne on blood; the other built on love.
The one was born of earth; the other from above.
The one won all this earth, to lose all earth and heaven;
The other gave up all, that all to Him be given.
The Greek forever died; the Jew forever lives.
He loses all who gets; he wins all things who gives.

—Charles Ross Weede

PERSON
Mark 9

PREVIEW OF SALVATION

"The Son of man will be delivered into the hands of men, and they will kill him; and when he is killed, after three days he will rise." Mark 9:31.

It is rather exciting to think of previewing a film that has not yet been released to the public. And certainly it would be of particular interest if the film were shown at a place that nobody knew anything about. Although Jesus did not show the disciples a film, in today's chapter He did present before them for the second time what could be called *The Cradle to the Cross*. He had told them several times before that He would be killed but would rise again from the dead. But although He spoke plainly, they did not understand. One reason they could not believe was because they did not want to. Like everyone else, they wanted a king who would deliver them from the Romans.

One day as Jesus and the disciples walked to the city of Capernaum, the disciples hung behind, bickering with one another. Later, although He knew exactly what had gone on, the Lord asked what they had been talking about on the way. They were ashamed to tell Him, for they had been arguing about who would be the greatest in His kingdom. As Christ's disciples today, we must make sure that we are more concerned with service than we are with status. It would be a pity if, after spending many years as Christians, we, like the disciples, are still self-seeking. His words to the twelve need to be carefully heeded: "If any man desire to be first, the same shall be last of all, and servant of all" (Mark 9:35).

If we have selfish ambitions, we too will not be able to understand the teachings of Jesus concerning preparation for the Second Advent. While there is any rivalry in our hearts or lack of love for people, we will be unable to see in the prophetic pictures what we need to do to be ready for the establishment of the kingdom of heaven.

The disciples not only had a preview of the final events in the life of Jesus, but Peter, James, and John also saw Moses and Elijah and heard the voice of God. Surely this was one of the most wonderful experiences the three disciples ever had. Mark says that they were amazed at the glorious appearance of Jesus, so it should have convinced them that Jesus was the Son of God.

200

PERSON
Mark 10

THE CHILDREN'S FRIEND

"Let the children come to me, do not hinder them; for to such belongs the kingdom of God." Mark 10:14.

A man traveled to a far country and, after being away from home for more than thirty years, became very homesick. One reason He longed for His homeland was that none of the people He met in those years of sojourn in a foreign land could understand His words. He did all He could to help them, and even made special friends and shared personal concerns with twelve of them. He spoke to them plainly and performed miracles that amazed them, but they could not understand Him, and He longed to talk to someone who could.

One day this Traveler found someone who reminded Him of His homeland. This person was only a child, but in him the Traveler could see the qualities of innocence, purity, humility, and faith that reminded Him of His native country. Just as He was about to touch the child, His twelve closest friends told the little one to leave because their Friend did not have time for him. The Traveler reproved His friends, and to show how much He valued this reminder of His homeland, He took the child in His arms and said, " 'Let the children come to me.' "

The fact that Matthew, Mark, and Luke all recorded Jesus' encounter with the children is proof of the deep impression that it made on the early Christians and how important it was. This was Jesus' last journey with His disciples, and it was down a road that led to the cross. It was appropriate that on this last journey Jesus met a group of children and one had the privilege of sitting on His knee.

"In His work as a public teacher, Christ never lost sight of the children. When wearied with the bustle and confusion of the crowded city, tired of contact with crafty and hypocritical men, His spirit found rest and peace in the society of innocent little children. His presence never repelled them. His large heart of love could comprehend their trials and necessities, and find happiness in their simple joys; and He took them in His arms and blessed them."—*Counsels to Parents and Teachers,* p. 179.

PERSON
Mark 11

SERVANT AND KING

And those who went before and those who followed cried out, "Hosanna! Blessed be he who comes in the name of the Lord! Blessed be the kingdom of our father David that is coming! Hosanna in the highest!" Mark 11:9, 10.

It certainly must be interesting to be a king, but if one has no right to the throne and no kingdom to rule, he cannot be a king. A good king is one who has learned to be a good servant. A prince or princess must train for many years for this honor. At the beginning of the book of Mark we discovered that Jesus was a teacher, a doctor, and a pastor. Now we learn that He was also a servant and a king.

The Lord's service is summarized in Mark 10:45, the key verse for the entire book: "'For the Son of man also came not to be served, but to serve, and to give his life as a ransom for many'" (R.S.V.). The last six chapters of Mark portray the sacrifice of the Servant. When we think of the sacrifice of Jesus, we think of His death on the cross, the supreme offering. But He made other sacrifices also. Can you name some of them?

The last week of Jesus' life on this earth was extremely busy. It began with His triumphal entry into Jerusalem when the people shouted "Hosanna!" which means "Save, I pray." These words were uttered as a prayer that Israel would be saved through the Messiah. The Galileans to whom He had ministered and who were with Him at this time were ready to accept Jesus as the Messiah, but most of the Jews in Jerusalem rejected Him. More than five hundred years before Jesus lived on this earth, a prophet stated that the Promised One would enter Jerusalem triumphantly, riding on an ass (Zech. 9:9). The destiny of the nation of Israel was in the balance. Had the people accepted Jesus as their Messiah, Israel would have become a glorious nation.

Unfortunately, many today also are rejecting the Servant who gave His life to save them. Those who accept Jesus as king will have a place in His kingdom. However, before that takes place, they must follow His example and become servants.

PERSON
Mark 12

TRICKY QUESTIONS

"Have you not read this scripture: 'The very stone which the builders rejected has become the head of the corner; this was the Lord's doing, and it is marvelous in our eyes'?" Mark 12:10, 11.

Monday and Tuesday of Jesus' final week before His crucifixion were spent in the Temple. This was the center of all major activities of the Jewish nation and the place where the Messiah King should be crowned. The Temple rightfully belonged to Jesus, and in righteous anger He drove out the merchants who had made it a marketplace. On Tuesday morning He began teaching and was asked three trick questions by the religious leaders, who hoped to get evidence to condemn Him.

The first question concerned paying taxes. In response Jesus took a coin in His hand and asked them whose image was on it. When they said that it was the emperor's, Jesus gave a reply that is still a principle for His disciples: We should give to the government that which belongs to it, but to God the things that are His.

The second question concerned the resurrection, because there were different beliefs held by the two main religious groups. The Sadducees did not believe in the resurrection and were uncertain about the future. The Pharisees were more confident, for they believed in the resurrection.

The third question, asked by a young lawyer, concerned which was the most important commandment. Jesus told him that there are two all-inclusive commandments that are equally important—to love God and to love your fellow man. These summarize all the commandments. The young man was impressed by the replies of Jesus. After that, no one asked any more questions. He had silenced them, but their hearts were not yielded to Him. It is not enough to be convinced in our minds that Jesus is right; we must surrender our hearts to Him.

Jesus used a statement from the Psalms (Ps. 118:22, 23) and the parable of the vineyard keepers to declare that Israel was no longer a faithful steward of truth and that there would be a Gentile church. Today we must choose to be faithful stewards in the vineyard of the Lord and pray to have good fruits at the harvesttime.

PERSON
Mark 13

TEACHING THE TWELVE

"But of that day or that hour no one knows, not even the angels in heaven, nor the Son, but only the Father. Take heed, watch; for you do not know when the time will come." Mark. 13:32, 33.

As Jesus and the disciples were leaving the Temple, someone commented on the beautiful stones and buildings. Some of the stones were 30 feet long and 7½ feet high. Naturally the men were shocked when Jesus told them that the time would come when there would not be one left on top of another. When they arrived on the Mount of Olives, Peter, James, John, and Andrew asked Him to explain what He had meant and to tell them when Jerusalem would be destroyed. The answer Jesus gave is found in Mark 13 and, with a fuller description, in Matthew 24. This is a twofold prophecy, referring first to the destruction of Jerusalem and second to the end of the world. There are some signs that apply to both events and some that apply specifically to the second coming of Jesus.

Although it is good to know the signs of the Second Coming, it is more important to be prepared for that great event. Jesus emphasizes this by saying three times at the end of His discourse, "Watch."

"Few believe with heart and soul that we have a hell to shun and a heaven to win.

"The crisis is stealing gradually upon us. The sun shines in the heavens, passing over its usual round, and the heavens still declare the glory of God. Men are still eating and drinking, planting and building, marrying and giving in marriage. Merchants are still buying and selling. Men are jostling one against another, contending for the highest place. Pleasure lovers are still crowding to theaters, horse races, gambling hells. The highest excitement prevails, yet probation's hour is fast closing, and every case is about to be eternally decided. Satan sees that his time is short. He has set all his agencies at work that men may be deceived, deluded, occupied and entranced, until the day of probation shall be ended, and the door of mercy be forever shut."—*The Desire of Ages,* p. 636.

204

PLOT AND DENIAL

*And immediately, while he was still speaking, Judas came.
. . . And immediately the cock crowed a second time. And Peter
remembered. Mark 14:43-72.*

The words *immediately, straightway,* and *forthwith,* which
are all translated from the same Greek word *eutheos,* are used
nearly forty times in the Gospel of Mark. This book is full of
action, and these words remind us that we should be prompt and
enthusiastic in our obedience to the Lord Jesus Christ. It is sad,
however, that they are used in connection with the betrayal and
denial of Jesus.

Why did Judas betray his Master?

"No man can tell how far he may go in sin when once he
yields himself to the power of the great deceiver. Satan entered
into Judas Iscariot and induced him to betray his Lord."—*Testimonies,* vol. 5, p. 103.

"Judas was constantly planning to benefit self. In this he
represents a large class of professed Christians of today.
Therefore we need to study his case. We are as near to Christ as
he was."—*Ibid.,* vol. 6, p. 264.

Peter had stated that he would follow Jesus unto death.
Instead, he ran away and denied that he knew the Lord.
However, when Jesus looked on him, the disciple remembered
his boast. Like Peter, we may not always live up to the vows we
make, but we must be sure we keep looking to Jesus, and when
He speaks to us in any one of a variety of ways, we must
remember and return to Him.

"After he had denied his Lord, repented, and been converted,
all he needed to check his ardor and zeal was a mild caution from
John."—*Early Writings,* pp. 224, 225. Just as God used John to
check Peter, so He uses people to help us be the kind of
Christians we should be in order to do God's work in His way. We
need to learn to take counsel and reproof.

Jesus loved Judas and Peter when they were not loyal to
Him. Judas rejected that love and came to a hopeless end; Peter
accepted it and found endless hope.

Since we want endless hope, let us walk in the *light* of God's
Word, accept His *love,* and claim the promises of eternal *life.*
That is how to get *"light for my life."*

PERSON
Mark 15

TRIALS AND TRIUMPH

"Let the Christ, the King of Israel, come down now from the cross, that we may see and believe." "Truly this man was a son of God!" Mark 15:32, 39.

There were two trials that Jesus—the King, the Servant, the Son of God—was subjected to. The first one had three stages, as Christ appeared before Annas, the high priest, and the Sanhedrin. This trial was held at night, which made it illegal. The second trial was before Pilate, who was glad when he learned that Jesus was from Galilee, as this gave him an excuse to send the Prisoner on to Herod. Wicked Herod mocked the Saviour and sent Him back. Pilate obviously wanted to release Jesus, but was torn between the demand of the crowd for Barabbas and his wife's warning to let Jesus go.

"Pilate was startled. He had no correct idea of Christ and His mission; but he had an indistinct faith in God and in beings superior to humanity.... He questioned whether it might not be a divine being that stood before him, clad in the purple robe of mockery, and crowned with thorns."—*The Desire of Ages,* p. 736.

Pilate's question in the judgment hall was " 'Then what shall I do with this man whom you call the King of the Jews?' " (Mark 15:13, R.S.V.), a question that is still being answered by each of us. On this issue we cannot remain in a neutral position. Pilate failed to do what he inwardly believed he should—release Jesus. We must be sure that we do what we know we should do—receive Jesus.

One of the tragedies of this final day of Jesus' life was that Pilate lacked the courage of his convictions. Other tragedies followed: Jesus was scourged, mocked, and made to carry His cross. It was also a tragedy that the chief priest, who should have accepted Jesus as the Messiah, mocked Him.

However, there were triumphs on that fateful Friday: a Cyrenian had the privilege of carrying Jesus' cross; a criminal was converted; and a centurion declared that Jesus was the Son of God.

Like the Cyrenian, we are to carry the cross; like the criminal we should crucify sin and self daily; like the centurion, we should contemplate the cross and accept the Son of God as our Saviour.

PERSON
Mark 16

HE AROSE AND APPEARED

"Do not be amazed; you seek Jesus of Nazareth, who was crucified. He has risen, he is not here; see the place where they laid him. But go, tell his disciples and Peter that he is going before you to Galilee." Mark 16:6, 7.

It should be noted that the women were the last to leave the cross and the first to arrive at the tomb. As they approached it, one of them asked, " 'Who will roll away the stone for us from the door of the tomb?' " (Mark 16:3, R.S.V.). They knew that they could not manage, but there was no need to worry—an angel had already moved it. There is a lesson for the Christian in this experience. We should not be concerned about trying to solve future problems. Let us remember that there is no stone so great that Jesus cannot roll it away.

The disciple who denied Jesus must have been thrilled and grateful when told that he was mentioned by name in the message. Perhaps if Jesus had not mentioned Peter specifically, he might not have dared to go to Galilee. But Jesus knows us all by name and forgives us when we confess our sins. The disciples' appointment with Jesus in Galilee was one of several appearances after His resurrection. He first appeared to Mary Magdalene, and then to two disciples on a road to Emmaus. After His resurrection, Jesus was on earth forty days and, as we will see in other Gospels, appeared to other believers.

Prior to His ascension, Jesus gave clear instruction to all Christians that we are to take the gospel to all the world. The book of Mark opened with the words "The beginning of the gospel of Jesus Christ." At the end the Lord commissions His disciples to take the good news to the ends of the world.

Television has allowed thousands of people to watch the ascent of manned vehicles into space. These launchings were not as dramatic as seeing Jesus "taken up . . . into heaven" (Acts 1:11). This great event will be surpassed only by the heavens splitting open and millions of angels descending so that we can have the privilege of ascending into heaven. I want to be there on that ascension morning, don't you?

207

PERSON
Isaiah 1

THE MESSIANIC PROPHET

"Come now, let us reason together, says the Lord: though your sins are like scarlet, they shall be as white as snow; though they are red like crimson, they shall become like wool." Isaiah 1:18.

On several occasions Jesus stated that the prophets of the Old Testament had clearly testified of His birth, life, teachings, death, resurrection, mediation, judgment, and Second Advent. Isaiah is one of the Old Testament prophets who tells us a lot about the person of Jesus. John says that this prophet saw the glory of Christ, "and spake of him" (John 12:41). Because Isaiah spoke so much about Jesus, he is called the Messianic prophet and has often been called the greatest of the Old Testament prophets. He was a poet and an orator with a very large vocabulary. In the Hebrew Bible the book of Isaiah is the first of the seventeen prophetic books of the Old Testament.

Isaiah was a prince, was married, and had at least two sons, whose names are mentioned in his book. He served as a prophet for sixty years, during the reigns of four kings—Uzziah, Jotham, Ahaz, and Hezekiah. He lived more than seven hundred years before Christ, and the sixty-six chapters of his book contain more than twenty predictions about Jesus. All have been fulfilled.

It is significant to note that Isaiah's name means "salvation is of Jehovah." These words are actually a summary of the message of the book of Isaiah. In the first chapter, as recorded in our text for today, there is a declaration of salvation that is echoed in the New Testament. This proclamation that God is able to save to the uttermost has brought peace to millions of people. The deep colors, scarlet and red, stand out in contrast to the whiteness of snow, which depicts purity. This salvation is possible only through the Lord Jesus, and the transformation of our sins from scarlet to white takes place when we accept Him as our Saviour.

God's call for the children of Israel to "reason together" is preceded and followed by "a description of a people professedly serving God, but walking in forbidden paths" (Manuscript 29, 1911). When our feet wander, we need to look through Mark's and Isaiah's eyes to the person of Jesus, who saves to the uttermost (see Heb. 7:25).

208

A SONG OF WILD GRAPES

Let me sing for my beloved a love song concerning his vineyard. Isaiah 5:1.

The eight lines following our Morning Watch text are a song about wild grapes, which is really a parable similar to the story Jesus told of the vineyard (Mark 12:1-9). God had cared for His people just as carefully as the owner of a vineyard cares for his grapes. Because he had looked after it with such diligence, he expected a good crop of fruit, but it yielded wild grapes.

The "wild grapes" that Israel produced are summarized as covetousness, selfishness, drunkenness, skepticism, injustice, calling "evil good, and good evil" (Isa. 5:20), and being "wise in their own eyes" (verse 21). Each of these sins of God's people is preceded by a "woe," which implies that there will be punishment. This punishment, depicted as fire destroying dry grass, is described in verses 24 and 25.

At the time this message was given, the people had become as wicked as the inhabitants of Sodom and Gomorrah (chap. 1:9, 10). God is very long-suffering, but when those who know what is right act like the heathen, He must intervene.

In order to understand the book of Isaiah correctly, it is necessary to know that the Jewish nation was divided at this time. There was a northern kingdom of Israel, and a southern kingdom comprised of the tribes of Judah and Benjamin. The wild grapes mentioned by Isaiah refer to the sins of both Israel and Judah, but primarily they refer to Judah. The prophet also, in the course of delivering his messages, makes references to the surrounding nations of Syria, Assyria, Babylon, Philistia, Moab, Damascus, Ethiopia, Egypt, Edom, Arabia, and Tyre. God tried to bring Israel and Judah to repentance by allowing them to be taken captive. He knows what is best for individuals as well as nations.

Isaiah, like other Bible writers, was a poet, and most of his book is in poetic form. God has given gifts and talents to each person, and if we allow Him to, He can use these to help others find the way of salvation. When you are reading chapters in the book of Isaiah, it would be good to read them from a version such as the Revised Standard Version, where the verses are laid out in verse form.

PERSON
Isaiah 6

ARE VISIONS REAL?

In the year that King Uzziah died I saw the Lord sitting upon a throne, high and lifted up; and his train filled the temple. Isaiah 6:1.

The Bible clearly teaches that God sometimes communicates to His people on earth through dreams and visions. "If there be a prophet among you, I the Lord will make myself known unto him in a vision, and will speak unto him in a dream" (Num. 12:6). Perhaps some are asking, What is the difference between a vision and a dream? In the Scriptures there is no clear distinction between the two, except that dreams seem to be limited to hours of sleep, while visions may come while the person is awake or in the form of a dream as he or she sleeps.

A vision is a supernatural means by which God communicates His will through prophets. Generally the prophet is unaware of his surroundings as the Spirit of God completely controls him, and he actually seems to enter into the experience that is being revealed in the vision. This is what happened to Isaiah. We know that no one has actually seen God, but the prophet was so much in vision that he said, "Mine eyes have seen the King, the Lord of hosts" (Isa. 6:5).

That vision had a profound effect on Isaiah, for afterward everything he wrote seems to be related to it. The celestial being with six wings, saying, "Holy, holy, holy, is the Lord of hosts" (verse 3), also made a deep impression on the mind of the prophet, and as a result Isaiah uses the phrase "the Holy One of Israel," or simply "Holy One," at least thirty times in his book. We too need to catch a vision of the holiness of God and understand that sin separates God and man.

The gospel prophet was in the Temple court praying when he saw the vision of the Lord sitting upon a throne, and he was concerned about the apostasy and idolatry of God's people. It was also a time of crisis and sadness, because the king had just died after being in seclusion for four years with leprosy. When we are concerned about conditions in the church, community, and our country, the first thing we should do is to pray about it.

PERSON
Isaiah 7

GOD'S SIGN

"Therefore the Lord himself will give you a sign. Behold, a young woman shall conceive and bear a son, and shall call his name Immanuel." Isaiah 7:14.

After the death of King Uzziah, Jotham, who is mentioned only twice in Isaiah, reigned. Ahaz, the king who followed Jotham, had a great deal of contact with Isaiah. The reason for this was that he was a very wicked king who worshiped strange gods, including the fire god Molech.

The kings of Syria and Israel were marching against Judah, and the people of that little country were terrified. Isaiah called on King Ahaz with a message of hope; " ' "Do not fear, and do not let your heart be faint because of these two smoldering stumps of firebrands" ' " (Isa. 7:4, R.S.V.). But the wicked king would not believe that Jehovah could deliver the nation. Unbelieving Ahaz was invited to "ask . . . a sign of the Lord" (verse 11), but he was so stubborn that he would not even do this. The Hebrew word for sign can also be translated "token," "mark," or "reminder." This word is a visible reminder of God's power and was used to describe the first rainbow and the Sabbath.

Isaiah reminded King Ahaz that his (Isaiah's) own children were a sign of God's power. "I and the children whom the Lord hath given me are for signs and for wonders in Israel from the Lord of hosts" (chap. 8:18). These boys were named Shearjashub and Mahershalalhashbaz, meaning "the Lord will save, a remnant shall return," and "speed the spoil, hasten the plunder." Just as the prophet's children's names had special significance, Isaiah declares that the Messiah's names would be special too. Immanuel means "God with us," and a little later Isaiah gave more names of the Messiah, all of which would be reminders of His nature and work.

One of these was "Prince of Peace" (chap. 9:6). Peace is the result of salvation, and is like a beautiful golden cord running through the book of Isaiah. When we have the peace of God in our lives, we have an inward joy in spite of what happens to us. Then we are truly "signs" that God is with us.

PERSON
Isaiah 11

CHILDREN RIDE LIONS?

The wolf shall dwell with the lamb, and the leopard shall lie down with the kid, and the calf and the lion and the fatling together, and a little child shall lead them. Isaiah 11:6.

Leopards and lions are members of the cat family, but we are certainly not able to stroke them. However, in the kingdom to be set up by the Prince of Peace we may ride on their backs! Animals such as the wolf, the leopard, and the lion were peaceful vegetarians when God created them. And more than four thousand years ago Isaiah predicted that in the new earth they will again be peaceable. This description of harmony among the animals is one of the most glorious pictures of the kingdom of God. It certainly creates in us a desire to be a part of that kingdom. We can be if we invite the Prince of Peace into our hearts now.

At the time Isaiah was instructed by God about the peaceful kingdom of heaven, the Assyrian Empire had been likened to a large forest that was cut down (Isa. 10:33, 34), and the kingdom of Judah was compared to a tree stump. Then came the wonderful announcement that from that stump would come a shoot, indicating that there was still life in the roots. In this interesting manner Isaiah describes how Jesus, the Messiah, would come from the line of Jesse and his son David. Although the tree of Judah appeared dead, the promise was that one day it would grow again, and that through this line the Messiah would come.

It is sad to note that when the Messiah did come, the descendants of the kingdoms of Judah and Israel did not accept Him. They were looking for an earthly king to deliver them from the Romans who occupied their country, but they certainly did not get this mistaken idea from Isaiah. This gospel prophet portrayed the spiritual nature of the Messiah. Isaiah stated that Jesus was a king, for indeed He is "King of kings," but he highlights the fact that "the Spirit of the Lord shall rest upon him" (chap. 11:2) and that His kingdom would be in a warless world. Wars in this world have proved that fighting is not the way to bring peace, and we know that true peace comes only when the Prince of Peace dwells in our hearts. All who would be subjects of His kingdom of peace must crown Jesus king of their lives now.

212

PERSON
Isaiah 26

ALIVE FOREVER

Thy dead shall live, their bodies shall rise. O dwellers in the dust, awake and sing for joy! For thy dew is a dew of light, and on the land of the shades thou wilt let it fall. Isaiah 26:19.

No wonder the song recorded in Isaiah 26 has been entitled "A Song of Trust and Triumph." The promise is sure: "Thou wilt keep him in perfect peace, whose mind is stayed on thee: because he trusteth in thee" (verse 3). In the light of all that God has done and will do for us, we certainly have every reason to "trust . . . in the Lord for ever" (verse 4).

It was not the plan of the Prince of Peace that anyone should die. When Adam and Eve were created, it was planned that they would live eternally. However, once they sinned, God could not allow the human race to live forever. We can certainly see what would have happened if men such as King Ahaz had lived on without dying. Although we humans are subject to death, God has made it possible for all to be resurrected. One of the first promises of the resurrection is our Morning Watch text today.

The statement "O dwellers in the dust, awake and sing for joy!" (verse 19, R.S.V.) explains correctly the state of those who are dead. More than forty times Jesus likened death to a sleep, and those who are dead in Christ, as we shall see when we study the New Testament, will rise at the second advent of Jesus (1 Thess. 4:16-18). In Isaiah 25 we find another picture of the resurrection. "He will swallow up death in victory; and the Lord God will wipe away tears from off all faces; and the rebuke of his people shall he take away from off all the earth: for the Lord hath spoken it" (verse 8).

The resurrection outlined by Isaiah will occur at the second coming of Jesus when the righteous dead will be raised. There is a second resurrection when the wicked will be raised, but soon after they will be eternally destroyed. God cannot allow into His kingdom any who do not have the Prince of Peace in their heart, for if He did, sin would rise up again and destroy the heavenly kingdom. In His love God has made provision for all to have a part in the first resurrection or to be translated at His coming. What a happy day that will be!

213

PERSON
Isaiah 35

HIGHWAY 35

And an highway shall be there, and a way, and it shall be called The way of holiness; the unclean shall not pass over it. Isaiah 35:8, K.J.V.

In most countries of the world the main highways are numbered. One day while traveling in the United States, I was interested to hear a radio preacher refer to Highway 35 in the book of Isaiah. Later I discovered our text for today, which states that God has a highway and that it is "The way of holiness." It is so named because only the godly can travel on it. It is the highway to the Holy City, the New Jerusalem.

If the people of Israel had walked God's way of holiness, their land would have been as pictured in Isaiah 35—people from all nations would have traveled to Jerusalem to learn about the true God. However, despite the many evidences of God's leading and the messages that He gave them through the prophets, the chosen people proved unfaithful, and God could not do for them in the Land of Promise all that He wanted to do. His second plan is that Christians will be able to enter into the heavenly land where there will be no desert and no one will be blind, deaf, lame, or dumb (see *The Ministry of Healing,* pp. 159, 160). Heaven will be beautiful, and everyone will be happy there. The description of this heavenly land, as given by Isaiah, is one of the most exquisite pen pictures of the new earth in all of Scripture.

There is only one way to enter the way to the heavenly city, and that is to discover "the narrow way" spoken of by Jesus (see Matt. 7:14). He said there is a broad way that leads to destruction and a narrow way that leads to eternal life. One place where that way is clearly described is in John 14:6: "Jesus saith unto him, I am the way, the truth, and the life: no man cometh unto the Father, but by me." Yes, the way to eternal life is the road that follows in the footsteps of Jesus. It leads in the paths of service and sacrifice. But to those who keep their eyes fixed on Jesus while they walk, it is a way of joy. There will be a wonderful reunion with the redeemed of all ages at the end of Highway 35.

PERSON
Isaiah 37

PRAYER NEEDS PRACTICE

"So now, O Lord our God, save us from his hand, that all the kingdoms of the earth may know that thou alone art the Lord."
Isaiah 37:20.

Abraham prayed, and Lot and his family were saved from destruction.

Elijah prayed, and fire came down from heaven.

Daniel prayed, and he was saved from the lions.

Hezekiah prayed, and Judah and Jerusalem were saved from destruction.

The reign of Hezekiah, the king who followed Ahaz, covers one of the most important periods in Judah's history. Hezekiah loved the Lord, and one of his first acts was to destroy all the idols in the country. In the sixth year of his reign the northern kingdom had been invaded by Assyria. Now in the fourteenth year Sennacherib, the new king in Assyria, surrounded Jerusalem, preparing to take the city. His soldiers had built fires and put their battering rams and stone catapults in position. The bowmen were poised in long lines, waiting for the order to fire their lighted arrows. The situation was so hopeless that Hezekiah tore his clothes, a symbol of deep distress. But Isaiah assured him that the nation would be delivered.

It is pleasing to note that the king went to the house of the Lord and prayed. He recognized that the promises of God were sure and that prayer needed only practice. His beautiful petition is recorded in verses 16-20 of today's chapter, in which he appeals to God to demonstrate to the Assyrians that He is the true God and that there is no power in the gods made by human hands. We should pray that God will be glorified and that He will answer our prayer if it is for our best good and if our requests are according to His will.

In direct answer to Hezekiah's prayer, God sent a message by Isaiah (chap. 37:33-35). God also gave a sign assuring the king that although all agriculture had stopped, the nation would have sufficient food. Hezekiah must have jumped for joy at this cable from space! The people of Judah had no way to defend themselves, but 185,000 Assyrians were dead by the next morning. The defeat of the Assyrian army is only one of the miracles recorded in the Old Testament.

DEATH POSTPONED

"Go and say to Hezekiah, Thus says the Lord, the God of David your father: I have heard your prayer, I have seen your tears; behold, I will add fifteen years to your life." Isaiah 38:5.

Hezekiah's sickness, which happened before the Assyrian invasion and defeat, was so bad that he was at the point of death. While lying on his bed he received a message from God, delivered by the prophet Isaiah: "Set thine house in order; for thou shalt die, and not live" (2 Kings 20:1). Hezekiah wept and prayed that the Lord would heal him. Isaiah had started for home, but he was sent back with the revised message that is recorded in our Morning Watch text.

From this dramatic story we learn many things, and there is one particular point to highlight at this time. God's prophecies and divine judgments, as delivered by the prophets, are conditional. As we have noted, the messages concerning the restoration of the land of Israel depended on the obedience of God's people. And as we see from the story of Hezekiah, a death sentence was changed, and the king lived for fifteen more years.

"Restored to his wonted strength, the king of Judah acknowledged in words of song the mercies of Jehovah, and vowed to spend his remaining days in willing service to the King of kings. His grateful recognition of God's compassionate dealing with him is an inspiration to all who desire to spend their years to the glory of their Maker."—*Prophets and Kings,* p. 342.

We must not conclude from this story that God changes His mind when we weep and pray. Nor should we conclude that He favors some people more than others. In His divine providence, seeing the end from the beginning, He knows what is best for each nation, church, and individual. It could be that Hezekiah was healed because of the impact it made on the surrounding nations, including Babylon (see 2 Chron. 32:31).

We know it was God's original plan for people to live forever, and this will be the privilege of those who choose to be subjects of the heavenly kingdom. Then we will not have just fifteen years added to our lives, but we will live eternally in ideal conditions.

PERSON
Isaiah 40

PREPARING THE WAY

A voice cries: "In the wilderness prepare the way of the Lord,
make straight in the desert a highway for our God." Isaiah 40:3.

When the pasha, a high-ranking official of the Ottoman
Empire, was to visit a certain place, messengers were sent
ahead to have the people prepare the way for him. Their
proclamation, very similar to this one made by Isaiah,
commanded that the cattle and sheep paths be made into roads
on which horse-drawn vehicles could travel. The citizens had to
remove stones from the paths, straighten dangerous bends, and
level uneven ground. Only when we visualize the preparations
that went into preparing the way for a monarch to travel can we
fully understand the force of this declaration to prepare a path
for the coming of the Messiah. Roads for earthly monarchs are
made smooth by works of our hands, but we can prepare a way
for the King of kings only by surrendering our wills and
believing in Him. When Jesus abides in us, He is able to change
our characters so that we become loving and lovable Christians.
"Then with Christ working in you, you will manifest the same
spirit and do the same good works—works of righteousness,
obedience."—*Steps to Christ,* p. 63.

The children of Israel were no doubt pleased when they
heard the words of Isaiah 40 assuring them of comfort and the
coming Messiah. They wanted a Messiah, but they were not
prepared when He came. There was not even room in the inn for
Him. It is very easy for us to say that we want to walk Highway
35 and that we are looking for the Second Advent. But we need
to make sure we are prepared for Jesus' return. Remember, the
Jewish nation knew the signs, but they did not receive the Lord
and find salvation.

The call to prepare the way of the Lord was also made by
John the Baptist, and the words of our text pointed to the work of
this forerunner of Jesus' first advent. We are to be ready to
prepare the way for the Second Coming. "These closing chapters
of the book of Isaiah should be diligently studied; for they are
full of the gospel of Christ. They reveal to us that Israel was fully
instructed in regard to the coming Saviour."—Manuscript 151,
1899.

PERSON
Isaiah 42

THE DIVINE SERVANT

Behold my servant, whom I uphold, my chosen, in whom my soul delights; I have put my spirit upon him, he will bring forth justice to the nations. Isaiah 42:1.

In the days of Isaiah wealthy people employed servants to do menial tasks. The wages were very poor, and these employees often lived in primitive shelters. It is hard to imagine that the Creator of the universe came to this world of sin and lived as a servant. However, because He loved us so much, this is just what He did, and Jesus Himself stated that He fulfilled this prophecy of Isaiah (see Matt. 12:17-21). Part of our Morning Watch text, the words "in whom my soul delights" (R.S.V.), was heard at the baptism of Jesus, revealing that in the person of Jesus we have the promised Messiah and the suffering Servant.

Isaiah 42 to 52 reveals Jesus as a servant of Jehovah. The term "my servant" is used many times in these chapters. At times the word *servant* has a twofold application: first to Israel or to someone God used to do His work; and second, in its wider fulfillment, to Jesus. It was God's original plan that Israel would be a light to the nations and would bring spiritual revival and reformation to "them that sit in darkness" (Isa. 42:7).

Jesus, after whom we are to pattern our service, ministered to those who were hurt and to those who were depressed and weak. ("A bruised reed shall he not break" [verse 3].) The people in Isaiah's time were familiar with reeds, for they used them in building houses and furniture. The reeds that had been bruised by storms or animals were of no use. However, when it comes to bruised people, Jesus ministers to them.

Another beautiful characteristic of the King who became a servant is that "he shall not fail nor be discouraged" (verse 4). Although He became a "bruised reed" Himself, in whom many people saw no value, He faithfully performed His work until He was able to say on the cross, "It is finished." When we are servants of Jesus, we will overcome discouragement and finish the work He has given us to do.

PERSON
Isaiah 53

HE DIED FOR US

*Surely he has borne our griefs and carried our sorrows; yet we
esteemed him stricken, smitten by God, and afflicted. But he was
wounded for our transgressions, he was bruised for our
iniquities; upon him was the chastisement that made us whole,
and with his stripes we are healed. Isaiah 53:4, 5.*

Isaiah 53 is one of the most important chapters in all the
Bible. The chapter division should commence after chapter 52,
verse 12. These few verses contain one of the most perfect Old
Testament pictures of the servant who becomes our suffering
Saviour. The description of Jesus' death is so vivid that it would
be easy to think the account was written by one of the disciples
who was an eyewitness to the crucifixion. This impression is
reinforced by the fact that the description is in the past tense, as
though it had already happened. But it was written by Isaiah
seven hundred years *before* Jesus died on the cross. It is the
climax of the fifty-two preceding chapters, and practically every
phrase is quoted somewhere in the New Testament.

In just five verses (5 through 9) there are nine statements
that Jesus did not die for Himself, but for us. You and I are saved
from our iniquity when we recognize that Jesus died for our sins
and that we are forgiven. Our acceptance of Christ as our
Saviour and Mediator leads us to confess and forsake sin and to
love and serve Jesus. It is at this point that we become children
of God. We can then read verses 4 and 5, substituting "my" and
"me" for "our" and "us." "Christ was treated as we deserve, that
we might be treated as He deserves. He was condemned for our
sins, in which He had no share, that we might be justified by His
righteousness, in which we had no share. He suffered the death
which was ours, that we might receive the life which was His.
'With his stripes we are healed.'"—*The Desire of Ages,* p. 25.

"This chapter [Isaiah 53] should be studied. It presents
Christ as the Lamb of God. Those who are lifted up with pride,
whose souls are filled with vanity, should look upon this picture
of their Redeemer, and humble themselves in the dust. The
entire chapter should be committed to memory. Its influence
will subdue and humble the soul defiled by sin and uplifted by
self-exaltation."—*The Youth's Instructor,* Dec. 20, 1900.

PERSON
Isaiah 65

THE NEW EARTH

"For behold, I create new heavens and a new earth; and the former things shall not be remembered or come into mind."
Isaiah 65:17.

Although we do not know all the details concerning the new earth, the promise that there will be such a place is as sure as the fact that we are now living on this planet. We have also been told by Paul that we cannot imagine how beautiful and enjoyable that new earth will be. The main joy will be that Jesus is there. Walking on streets lined with gold will be a very special experience, but the best thrill will be to have fellowship with the Servant, our Saviour and King.

As we study the pen pictures of the new heaven and new earth outlined in Isaiah 60 through 66, we must remember that many applied first of all to what God wanted to do in the Promised Land for the children of Israel and Judah. When we understand this, the statements in these passages that seem to be out of harmony with new-earth conditions are more clearly understood. The Bible does not contradict itself, and many of its prophecies had this dual application.

There are a number of beautiful descriptions of the new earth that are confirmed in the New Testament, and those who study them soon desire to be in that kingdom. In that sinless place we will have fellowship with Jesus, the angels, and with people of all ages of earth's history; there will be no more sickness, death, or separation; no one will lack land, food, or a house; the animals will all be tame; each month and each Sabbath people will come together to worship God.

God's willingness to help us enjoy the new heaven and the new earth is indicated in these words: "I was ready to be sought by those who did not ask for me; I was ready to be found by those who did not seek me" (Isa. 65:1, R.S.V.). This promise of assistance is repeated in verse 24: "Before they call, I will answer; and while they are yet speaking, I will hear." We certainly have a hot line to heaven, and God is waiting for us to dial for any help we need.

PERSON
Isaiah 66

A MINIATURE BIBLE

Thus says the Lord: "Heaven is my throne and the earth is my footstool; what is the house which you would build for me, and what is the place of my rest?" Isaiah 66:1.

The book of Isaiah has been called a miniature Bible for the following reasons: the Bible is a library of sixty-six books; Isaiah is a book of sixty-six chapters. The Bible has two main divisions—the Old Testament with thirty-nine books and the New Testament with twenty-seven; Isaiah has two main divisions: chapters 1 through 39, largely dealing with the unrighteousness of the people and the success of their enemies, and chapters 40-66, highlighting the righteousness of God and His triumphs in delivering His people. At the beginning of the second part of Isaiah and at the beginning of the New Testament, we have the same statement concerning the forerunner of Jesus, who was to "prepare . . . the way of the Lord."

The miniature Bible (Isaiah) and Genesis both begin with a picture of man and the result of sin's entering into the world. Isaiah and the Bible both conclude with descriptions of a new heaven and a new earth. As we have discovered, the key word in Isaiah is *salvation,* which is the key word of all the Scriptures. No wonder Isaiah is called the gospel prophet and is quoted in the New Testament more than any other Old Testament writer. He has also been called "the fifth evangelist," for his book resembles the accounts of Jesus' life, death, and resurrection as recorded in Matthew, Mark, Luke, and John.

The word *everlasting* is used frequently in the Bible, and Isaiah lists six of the attributes of God that are everlasting: security (chap. 26:4), joy (chap. 35:10), salvation (chap. 45:17), love (chap. 54:8), covenant keeping (chap. 55:3), and light (chap. 60:19). Also, the princely prophet's favorite expression describing God is "the Holy One."

Isaiah died a martyr's death (see Heb. 11:37). He was faithful to his prophetic calling, and his writings call people back to God and point to the coming King. Isaiah is one hero of faith that I want to meet in the new earth, don't you?

221

PERSON
Jeremiah 1

CALLED BEFORE BIRTH

Now the word of the Lord came to me saying, "Before I formed you in the womb I knew you, and before you were born I consecrated you; I appointed you a prophet to the nations." Jeremiah 1:4, 5.

Jeremiah's excuses for not readily accepting God's call to be a prophet are similar to those that young people today give for not serving the Lord. He first of all stated that he did "'not know how to speak'" (Jer. 1:6, R.S.V.), saying that he was only a youth and was therefore inexperienced. The Lord knew he was a young man (about 21), and that he was "naturally of a timid and shrinking disposition" *(Prophets and Kings,* p. 419). God also knew that Jeremiah was not as eloquent as Isaiah. But his tenderheartedness was exactly what was needed for delivering the strong message of judgment that was God's final effort to rescue His people from their idolatry.

The young man Jeremiah had been set aside by God before his birth to take the gospel of *light, love,* and *life* to the chosen people one hundred years after Isaiah. God also called John the Baptist before his birth to herald Jesus as the light of the world. Before I was born, my mother dedicated me to become a minister, and although I did not hear the voice of the Lord speak to me, I certainly had a strong conviction at the age of 12 that God wanted me to be a minister.

From the story of Jeremiah's call we see that God has a plan for every life. "Each has his place in the eternal plan of heaven. Each is to work in cooperation with Christ for the salvation of souls. Not more surely is the place prepared for us in the heavenly mansions than is the special place designated on earth where we are to work for God."—*Messages to Young People,* p. 219.

This shy young man from a small town northeast of Jerusalem was requested not to marry, because of the special work that God wanted him to do (chap. 16:1, 2). Like Jesus, he was not received by his people or family, and he was betrayed, beaten, put in stocks, and imprisoned several times. Like Jesus, he obeyed implicitly. He uses the expressions "Thus saith the Lord," "The Lord said unto me," and "The word of the Lord came," et cetera, many times in the fifty-two chapters of his book.

PERFECTION
Luke 1

PERFECT BOOK

It seemed good to me also, having had perfect understanding of all things from the very first, to write unto thee in order, most excellent Theophilus. Luke 1:3, K.J.V.

Six blind men were introduced to an elephant.

"The first man felt on the elephant's side and concluded that the beast must be like a wall. The second touched his tusk and decided that the elephant must be like a spear. The third took hold of the wiggling trunk and judged the animal must be like a snake. The fourth, taking hold of the creature's knee, decided that the elephant must be like a tree. The fifth, touching a great flapping ear, concluded that the elephant must be like a fan. The sixth, chancing to take hold of the elephant's tail, announced flatly, 'The elephant is like a rope!' "

This old story from India illustrates the fact that mere fragments of information can lead to wrong conclusions. Many people have taken a verse or a chapter of the Scriptures and have come to wrong conclusions too.

But we know that each book of the Bible is inspired by the Holy Spirit. The book of Luke is in harmony with the other books of the Bible, and Luke states that he has carefully checked all the information that he presents.

Luke is first mentioned as a fellow worker with Paul. His background fitted him to write what has been described as "the most beautiful book in the world." Luke was a Greek, an educated man and a physician. He also wrote the book of Acts, and both books are addressed to a fellow Greek, Theophilus, whose name means "friend of God."

Although the book of Luke is a well-written and scholarly account of the life of Jesus, that is not the main reason it is called "the most beautiful" or "the most perfect" book. It deserves these titles because it features Jesus as the perfect example and the Holy Son of God.

The twenty-four chapters of Luke introduce us to a whole library. As we read and study these various books, we will have many glimpses of the perfect Man. Artists have painted more pictures from the book of Luke than from any other book in the Bible. Luke's pen pictures will lead us to say that the book of Luke is "light for my life."

PERFECTION
Luke 2

PATTERN BOOK

And Jesus increased in wisdom and stature, and in favour with God and man. Luke 2:52, K.J.V.

When a young worshiper of Buddha enrolled as a student at a Seventh-day Adventist college in the United States, he agreed to live up to the regulations of the school and to attend religious services.

His roommate was excited at the prospect of having a Buddhist for a roommate. As the young man unpacked his trunk, he took out a little image of Buddha and placed it in the center of his dresser. And though he was faithful in attending worship, every day he prayed to the little idol.

The Adventist roommate thought to himself, What a wonderful opportunity! Now we can see what Christianity does for a person; we can see how it will woo him away from his worship of Buddha. This man is my mission field. One of these days I am going to ask him what he thinks of Christ. I am going to be very careful to do everything I can to live a Christlike life before him.

The college year slipped by quickly, and the Adventist was soon watching the man from the Far East pack to leave. After he had left, the roommate regretted that he had never asked him about the influence of Christianity. So he decided to write him a letter. In it he asked, "Friend, would you tell me, having spent nine months with Christian people, what do you think of Christ?"

The Buddhist replied that he was very pleased with the time that he had spent at the college. "You asked me a tremendous question, What do I think of Christ? Your Christ is wonderful, but why aren't you Christians more like Him?"

The Buddhist's question is one that we all need to answer. Why aren't we more like Jesus? All who claim to be Christians need to be patterns that show to the world what Jesus is like. The *perfect pattern* for all of us is found in the life of Jesus as He lived during the thirty-three years He spent in this world. It is summarized in our text today. In the pattern book of Luke we discover that we are to develop mentally, physically, spiritually, and socially.

PERFECTION
Luke 3

HISTORY BOOK

Which was the son of Enos, which was the son of Seth, which was the son of Adam, which was the son of God. Luke 3:38, K.J.V.

Matthew and Luke both give us an accurate account of the genealogy or birth line of Jesus, but there are several differences between the two accounts. Matthew begins with Abraham and follows the family line down to Jesus; Luke begins with Jesus and traces the line back to Adam, "the son of God." This is because Matthew was writing for Jewish people and Luke was writing for Gentiles. These genealogies also show that Matthew wanted to reveal Jesus as king, and Luke wanted to reveal Him as the perfect man.

We can be thankful that Jesus was both a king and a perfect man. If He had been only our king, we might consider Him to be out of our reach.

Maybe because Luke was a physician, he gives more details concerning the miraculous birth and the boyhood of Jesus. Also, Luke is the only writer who records the shepherds' visit to the stable and Jesus' trip to the Temple in Jerusalem at the age of 12.

Luke's history is not dry and uninteresting, because it is centered in a *Person* whom everyone needs to know. Most history books just record what has happened, but this history book is unique because its main character lived in the past, is living in the present, and will live in the future.

A man in the city of Manchester, England, looked out his window and was amazed to see a sea gull splashing in a dish of water. The weather had been very stormy, and the sea gulls had moved inland. But this poor bird missed the ocean and the feel of water.

It is more pitiful to see a person, who was intended to fellowship with God, trying to find happiness in the shallow dish of worldly pleasures. Just as God intended for the sea gull to fly over the ocean, so He intends for us to have abundant life now and eternal life hereafter. We will find a satisfying life when we discover a personal friendship with the perfect Man, Jesus.

PERFECTION
Luke 4

GEOGRAPHY BOOK

And Jesus returned in the power of the Spirit into Galilee: and there went out a fame of him through all the region round about. Luke 4:14, K.J.V.

How would you like to travel to faraway places? Some of you may already have had this opportunity. I have been privileged to visit about sixty countries, and a region that I particularly enjoyed was Palestine, the land where Jesus lived.

We can learn much about other countries by reading books, listening to those who have been there, and watching films about the area. We can also learn about certain countries by reading the Bible. Luke has a lot to say about Palestine, so we can call his book a geography book.

Jesus spent most of His time in the region of Galilee. Many of His twelve disciples also came from there. Nazareth, where Jesus lived as a child, was in Galilee, and other cities in the area included Capernaum, Nain, Cana, and Bethesda.

Nazareth was situated among the hills of lower Galilee. It was only a small village, and people did not think anything good could come out of it. But many people who have made a valuable contribution to this world have come from small towns and humble circumstances.

We need to do what God wants us to in spite of what other people say or think about us. Luke records that Jesus was rejected in His hometown, Nazareth.

As I visited Capernaum on the Sea of Galilee, I recalled that this was an important town in Bible geography. It was the hometown of Peter and Andrew and was the place where Matthew was called to follow Jesus. And the Bible records that Jesus performed many miracles in Capernaum.

It is not enough for us to know Bible history, though; we must learn to know and accept the *Person* of history. It is not enough to know Bible geography; the towns and countries of this world are only temporary. Soon a better kingdom will be set up, but in the meantime we are to follow the *perfect pattern* and "preach the kingdom of God to other cities also" (Luke 4:43).

PERFECTION
Luke 5

FISHERMAN'S BOOK

"Put out into the deep and let down your nets for a catch." And Simon answered, "Master, we toiled all night and took nothing! But at your word I will let down the nets." Luke 5:4.

"My name is Andrew and I want to tell you about one of the most outstanding events of my life. As long as I live I shall never forget what happened that morning.

"The Sea of Galilee was calm on this particular day, but our hearts were troubled. Peter seemed to be especially upset. We were not only disappointed because we had not caught any fish all night but we were discouraged about other things as well. For one thing, we were concerned that John the Baptist was in prison. And we were tired and hungry, having fished all night.

"There were already people on the beach when our boats came to rest on the sandy shore. Jesus was there and we were glad to see Him, but recognized that He was tired also. He had come there to escape the multitude, but they had followed Him. In order to speak to them, He asked whether He could use our boat. We took it out a little distance from shore and were encouraged by His words that could be heard clearly over the lapping of the water.

"After Jesus finished speaking, He turned to Peter and told him to take the boat out to where the water was deep and to let the nets down there. I can still see the doubtful look on Peter's face. We all knew that it was best to fish at night when the fish could not see the nets.

"Nevertheless, we obeyed. And when the nets were lowered, the boat began to shake and we realized that the nets were full of wriggling fish. We recognized that Jesus had performed a miracle, and motioned for our fishing companions, James and John, to come and help us pull in this amazing catch.

"After the boats had been brought back to shore, Jesus looked at the four of us. There was a smile on His face and love in His eyes as He said, 'I can see that you are amazed and even afraid. There is no need for this. However, I haven't done this that you might get rich. I have done it to show you that I can use you to help men and women learn about the kingdom of heaven. I want you to be fishers of men.'"

PERFECTION
Luke 6

SERMON BOOK

"Give, and it will be given to you; good measure, pressed down, shaken together, running over, will be put into your lap. For the measure you give will be the measure you get back." Luke 6:38.

"Always we hear the plaintive cry of the teen-agers: 'What can we do? Where can we go?' I can make some suggestions. Go home! Hang storm windows. Paint the woodwork. Rake the leaves. Mow the lawn. Shovel the walk. Wash the car. Learn to cook. Scrub some floors. Repair the sink. Build a boat. Get a job. Help the minister, the Red Cross, the Salvation Army. Visit the sick. Assist the poor. Study your lessons. And when you are through—and not too tired—read a book.

"Your parents do not owe you entertainment.

"Your village does not owe you recreational facilities.

"The world does not owe you a living. You owe the world something. . . .

"In plain, simple words: Grow up; quit being a crybaby; get out of your dream world; develop a backbone, not a wishbone; and start acting like a man or a woman. I'm a parent. I'm tired of nursing, protecting, helping, appealing, begging, excusing, tolerating, denying myself needed comforts for your every whim and fancy, just because your selfish ego instead of common sense dominates your personality, and thinking, and requests."

The above protest was written by an obviously discouraged parent and apparently was first published in the *Christian Science Monitor*. It struck such a responsive chord in the hearts of some readers that it has since been quoted in many magazines and newspapers. The message is addressed to those teen-agers who don't know what to do with themselves.

It is significant to note that no one who has ever lived entirely for himself is remembered. The names of the famous men and women of the past and present are those who gave of themselves in unselfish service for others. We also discover from Luke's sermon book that if we give, we will receive blessings. This statement is part of Jesus' well-known Sermon on the Mount. It contains lots of light for our lives.

PERFECTION
Luke 7

WOMAN'S BOOK

And behold, a woman of the city ... brought an alabaster flask
of ointment, and standing behind him at his feet, weeping, she
began to wet his feet with her tears, ... and kissed his feet, and
anointed them with the ointment. Luke 7:37, 38.

Do you think this act was a waste of money? Judas, the
treasurer for the disciples, certainly did. Do you think it was
wrong for this woman, whom Luke says "was a sinner," to touch
Jesus? Simon, who gave this feast in Jesus' honor, thought so.

Judas was not really concerned about the cost of the
ointment or the poor whom he said could benefit from its sale. He
was a thief, and there is reason to believe that it was not the poor
who would have benefited. "The act of Mary was in such marked
contrast to his [Judas'] selfishness that he was put to shame; and
according to his custom, he sought to assign a worthy motive for
his objection to her gift."—*The Desire of Ages,* p. 559.

Simon, quick to question the fact that the woman touched
Jesus' feet, was the host who had omitted to provide the
customary water for his guests to wash their dusty feet. In
contrast, Mary, who had sacrificed to buy the ointment, sought
to anoint Jesus privately.

The Lord allowed Mary to perform this deed because it was
one of the greatest acts of love ever performed. Jesus stated that
"wheresoever this gospel shall be preached in the whole world,
there shall also this, that this woman hath done, be told for a
memorial of her" (Matt. 26:13). As we read this sweet story, we
are reading a fulfillment of Jesus' prophecy.

Also, "as the alabaster was broken, and filled the whole
house with its fragrance, so Christ was to die, His body was to be
broken; but He was to rise from the tomb, and the fragrance of
His life was to fill the earth."—*Ibid.,* p. 563.

This is just one of the stories that Luke records about a
woman. He has more to say about women than do the other
Gospel writers.

W idow of Nain, chap. 7:11-17.

O ther women healed, chap. 8:1-8, 43-48.

M ary Magdalene, chap. 7:36-50.

E ager group at the tomb, chap. 23:27-31.

N oted sisters, Mary and Martha, chap. 10:38-42.

PERFECTION
Luke 8

RULE BOOK

"Take heed then how you hear; for to him who has will more be given, and from him who has not, even what he thinks that he has will be taken away." Luke 8:18.

The kiwi, the national bird of New Zealand, is unusual in many ways. It is about the size of a chicken and has brown feathers and a very long bill. It is the only bird known to have nostrils in the tip of its bill that it uses to smell its food. And the kiwi cannot fly.

The extinct dodo was another flightless bird. Larger than the kiwi, the species lived on the island of Mauritius many years ago. The expression "dead as a dodo" is still used today.

While the dodo's wings were too small to enable the big bird to fly, many people believe that the kiwi lost its ability to fly because it did not use its wings. The kiwi and the dodo both remind us of one of the rules of life that Jesus has given to us. As we consider the natural world and also the people about us, we see that those who use the gifts and talents they have increase their abilities. On the other hand, those who do not make the most of their gifts find that those capabilities become "as dead as a dodo."

This rule in today's verse can be expressed in mathematical terms. Talents that are used are multiplied; talents that are not used are subtracted. We must not look at the talents of other people and become jealous or dissatisfied. There would be few songs of the birds if only those that could sing best were to do so. Let us remember that God made both the crow and the nightingale, and that He likes to hear both of them.

This rule that Luke records applies also to students. The knowledge that we gain must be shared with others in order for it to increase. If we neglect to share what we have been privileged to learn from our lesson books and from the Bible, we may become unable to hold in our memories the many wonderful things that we have learned.

This rule also applies to Christians. If we share our faith, it is strengthened; those who don't share their faith lose it. We certainly do gain by giving and lose by trying to keep what we have.

PERFECTION
Luke 9

PIONEER'S BOOK

"If any man would come after me, let him deny himself and take up his cross daily and follow me." Luke 9:23.

George was tremendously excited as he boarded the vessel with his parents and other missionaries who were sailing from the United States to South Africa. After a long sea voyage, the party arrived in Cape Town and proceeded by train to Mafeking. Here they had to purchase tented wagons and commence a 620-mile trek over desert tracks and jungle trails.

On July 25, 1895, they arrived at Solusi, near Bulawayo, in the country now known as Zimbabwe. Here they founded the first Seventh-day Adventist mission for non-Christians. George's father, Elder G. B. Tripp, was the leader of the group. There were no boys George's age, so he became great friends with Dr. A. S. Carmichael. Until their houses were built, George and the others lived in tents.

Troubles for the missionary band multiplied when fighting broke out among the African tribesmen, and for five months they had to shelter in the town of Bulawayo. Ellen White wrote concerning African missions, "The poverty of the missions in Africa has recently been opened before me. . . . Our brethren have not discerned that in helping to advance the work in foreign fields they would be helping the work at home."—*Testimonies,* vol. 6, p. 27.

It was a happy day when the missionaries were able to return to Solusi. Soon afterward, help arrived, but Elder Tripp, given the opportunity to go on a two-month furlough, decided to stay by the newly formed mission station. A malaria epidemic broke out, and Dr. Carmichael was the first to fall. On the day after his funeral, Elder Tripp became ill and did not recover. He died March 7, 1898, and on April 2 his son George, just 12 years old, was also laid to rest.

As I stood by the graves of these pioneers who had followed in the footsteps of David Livingstone, I realized that we are privileged to follow a noble band of workers. Those who paid the supreme sacrifice to advance the work of the gospel in Africa will one day rejoice when they know that the three angels' messages have spread throughout the world. We need to be prepared to follow the path of duty no matter what the cost.

PERFECTION
Luke 10

MISSIONARIES' BOOK

After this the Lord appointed seventy others, and sent them on ahead of him. . . . And he said to them, "The harvest is plentiful, but the laborers are few; pray therefore the Lord of the harvest to send out laborers into his harvest." Luke 10:1, 2.

Matius (Ma-TEE-us) lived in a small hut in Cannibal Valley, high in the mountains of New Guinea. The people of this area lived in fear and hate. They were constantly at war with one another, often killing and eating their enemies, hence the name of the valley. They wore no clothes and had no furniture, electricity, or tools.

Often Matius would take a load of sweet potatoes to the market four hours down the river. One day a shopkeeper asked him to stay there and work for him. Since the boy's parents were dead, he decided to accept the offer. He was a good worker and followed instructions well.

"How would you like to go to school, Matius?" asked the shopkeeper one day. Matius was delighted with the idea, so the shopkeeper arranged for him to go to a government school many miles away.

While attending school, Matius was adopted by a young Adventist couple. He soon learned to know Jesus, was baptized, and decided to attend the Adventist academy. The boy's life was now completely different from what it had been in the highlands, but he couldn't forget his people back in Cannibal Valley. He wanted them to learn about Jesus too, so he decided to go and tell them that Jesus is coming soon.

"I cannot wait until I am a preacher," Matius declared. "I must go now!"

So the young man returned to Cannibal Valley. He received no pay for his work, but the people loved him and were so glad to have him back that he felt it was worth the effort. In just two months' time he had built a small grass church and a house. About three hundred people were attending Sabbath services, and the children of the valley were enrolled in school.

When W. E. Smith wrote this story, eight other villages wanted Matius to come teach their children and hold Sabbath schools. But Matius cannot go to all the villages himself. More dedicated workers are needed so that many more people can learn about Jesus.

PERFECTION
Luke 11

PRAYER BOOK

He was praying in a certain place, and when he ceased, one of his disciples said to him, "Lord, teach us to pray, as John taught his disciples." And he said to them, "When you pray, say..." Luke 11:1, 2.

In the Gospel of Luke we can find much instruction about prayer. Luke records five occasions when Jesus prayed:

At His baptism (chap. 3:21).

In the wilderness (chap. 5:16).

When He was alone (chap. 9:18).

Up in the mountain (chap. 6:12).

Before the disciples asked Him to teach them to pray (chap. 11:1).

Luke also tells us more about what Jesus taught regarding prayer than do Matthew and Mark. This chapter records the story of the friend who came at midnight asking for food for his children. Recorded only by Luke, this story shows that we need to "ask" and to "knock."

In answer to the disciples' request "Lord, teach us to pray" Jesus gave a perfect model prayer. It is very brief, and can be recited in about one minute. Luke's record of the Lord's Prayer, or the Disciples' Prayer, is not complete. The entire prayer is found in Matthew 6:9-13.

The Lord's Prayer can be divided into two main parts. In the first division God's name, His kingdom, and His will are mentioned. When we pray, we should address God and speak of His kingdom and His will before we make our requests. The second division of the Lord's Prayer contains four petitions. However, note that three of these are for spiritual needs and only one is for material things. And even the one request for physical needs is an unselfish prayer, "Give *us* this day *our* daily bread."

Prayer has been described as the "key to the door in the morning and the lock for the door at night." We need to begin and end each day with God. Let us remember that prayer should not be concerned with what we wish of God, but what God wishes of us.

233

PERFECTION
Luke 12

TREASURE BOOK

"For where your treasure is, there will your heart be also."
Luke 12:34.

On December 21, 1979, five Mercedes Benz cars were discovered buried in the sand of the Sinai desert. These luxury cars, which sell for $40,000 each in that part of the world, were wrapped in plastic. Apparently the thieves who stole them had planned to recover them after the territory was redivided in 1982. As I write this, police are searching in the sand for eighty-one more stolen cars.

This account illustrates the extent to which some people will go in order to get rich. It reminds us of stories of pirates raiding ships and of masked horsemen holding up stagecoaches. All these people have made money their treasure, and they will do almost anything to get it. Unfortunately, many lives are lost as a result of this greed.

Heavenly treasure is the only kind that we can safely seek. Jesus has been described as the Pearl of Great Price, and He is the best treasure to seek after. And He wants each of us to develop a righteous character, which is the only treasure that can be taken to heaven.

The parable of the rich man who was possessed with building bigger barns to hold his harvest reminds us that it is not wise to concentrate on earthly riches. This man thought more of himself than he did of other people, but he died before he could build bigger barns. This parable is found only in the book of Luke, and is a warning to those who selfishly seek for earthly treasure. The parable is preceded by Jesus' solemn warning about covetousness, which is lust for things that belong to someone else.

It is a rule of life that "where your treasure is, there will your heart be also." If we would lay up treasures in heaven, we have to lay down earthly treasures. I want to have my treasure in heaven rather than in the sands of the desert, don't you?

Jesus never asks us to give up anything that is for our good. We never lose out by giving up what the world may count as valuable. When we exchange earthly treasures for heavenly, we are making a good investment.

PERFECTION
Luke 13

GARDENER'S BOOK

"What is the kingdom of God like? . . . It is like a grain of mustard seed which a man took and sowed in his garden; and it grew and became a tree, and the birds of the air made nests in its branches." Luke 13:18, 19.

Francis was born in the Italian city of Assisi. Although his father was wealthy, Francis forsook the treasures of this world in order to serve the poor. He became a missionary and established a religious order known as the Franciscans.

When St. Francis of Assisi was asked what he would do if he were told that he would die at sunset that day, he replied simply, "I would finish hoeing my garden." This man, who died in 1226, wanted to be as faithful in caring for his garden as he was in caring for the poor. God expects us to be faithful in all that we do.

The parable of the fig tree reminds us that we are to be faithful, and like the trees that were created to bear fruit, we are to bring forth good fruit in our lives. The people in Jesus' day were like a leafy fig tree that did not bear fruit, and like a fruitless tree they had to be cut down. This "cutting down" of the Jewish nation occurred in A.D. 70, when Jerusalem was destroyed by the Roman army.

The second parable in today's chapter of Luke's gardening book is more encouraging. Luke states that the kingdom of God would be like a tree that would grow from a tiny seed. Mustard, one of the smallest seeds, can grow into a bush that is from six to twelve feet tall. There were only a few followers of Jesus when He told the story of the mustard seed, but today millions of people claim to be Christians. And from that day on, people all over the world have become subjects of the kingdom of God.

The Bible prophecies also reveal this growth of the kingdom of heaven. In Revelation the last warning message is to go to "every nation, and kindred, and tongue, and people." And we can have a part in spreading these three angels' messages (Rev. 14:6-12).

These verses are a summary of God's warning message for this world. The prediction that they will be heard by everyone echoes the words of Jesus, "And this gospel of the kingdom shall be preached in all the world for a witness unto all nations; and then shall the end come" (Matt. 24:14).

PERFECTION
Luke 14

TEACHER'S BOOK

"He who has ears to hear, let him hear." Luke 14:35.

A young French college student was traveling home by train. Seated opposite him was an elderly man whom the student recognized to be a religious person. The youth struck up a conversation and told the man that it was silly to believe in God and prayer. He stated that he had studied science and that all things came from nature and that there was no God. The old man listened but did not comment. The young man asked his name and address so that he could send him some printed materials showing that there is no God.

The old man put his hand into his coat pocket and took out a card with his name and address on it. The young man was surprised and embarrassed when he read what was printed on the card: "Louis Pasteur, Professor of Science." He realized that this was the famous Dr. Pasteur who had made important discoveries concerning bacteria. Dr. Pasteur had been responsible for helping doctors find cures for many diseases.

The student and the scientist both had ears to hear, but the student had closed his ears to hearing about God.

There were many people living at the time of Jesus who had ears but who did not hear truth. Unfortunately, many of them had, like the young scientist, been brought up to believe in God but had failed to see God in the world around them. In order to help these people to hear truth, Jesus spoke directly. In the fourteenth chapter of Luke are nine teachings that Jesus presented on one Sabbath:

T he Sabbath is a day for sharing our faith (verses 1-4).

E veryone must choose to accept the invitation to heaven (verses 15-24).

A ll should show kindness to the unfortunate (verses 12-14).

C hristians must be careful as builders and soldiers (verses 28-33).

H umility is the way to advancement (verse 11).

I t costs something to be a true disciple (verses 26, 27).

N ever exalt yourself (verses 7-11).

G od's people are to be desirable people and effective witnesses (verse 34).

S ome people have good ears and still don't hear truth (verse 35).

PERFECTION
Luke 15

STORY BOOK

And the Pharisees and the scribes murmured, saying, "This man receives sinners and eats with them." So he told them this parable . . . Luke 15:2, 3.

Twenty-five of the forty parables, or "secret stories," that Jesus told are recorded in the book of Luke, more than are found in Matthew, Mark, or John. Three of the outstanding stories are recorded in today's chapter. Although each deals with something that is lost and each has a lesson, they are not complete in themselves but need to be read together.

The first story is about a shepherd with one hundred sheep. He knew his sheep by name, and they followed him. When one sheep got lost, the shepherd went out to find it. "By the lost sheep Christ represents not only the individual sinner but the one world that has apostatized and has been ruined by sin."— *Christ's Object Lessons*, p. 190.

A woman with ten silver coins searched hard for the one that she lost. The coin was a Greek drachma, and was worth one day's work. No wonder she was happy when she found the coin! She immediately told her friends, and they rejoiced with her. "So in the family if one member is lost to God every means should be used for his recovery. . . . If there is in the family one child who is unconscious of his sinful state, parents should not rest. Let the candle be lighted."—*Ibid.*, pp. 194, 195.

One of Jesus' best-known stories is about the lost son. However, there were really two lost sons in this story, because the older brother was lost in selfishness. When the prodigal son left home, he said, "Father, give me." When he "came to himself" and went back to his father, he said, "Father, make me." Many today have the "give me" sickness. We need instead to say, "Father, make me into what You would have me to be."

These three parables give us three pictures of wrongdoing. It is natural for sheep to go astray, and this is a picture of those who become lost *naturally*. The lost coin is a picture of those who are lost *helplessly*. However, the lost son reveals that there are those who become lost *deliberately*.

PERFECTION
Luke 16

SERVANT'S BOOK

"No servant can serve two masters; for either he will hate the one and love the other, or he will be devoted to the one and despise the other. You cannot serve God and mammon." Luke 16:13.

He was named Man of the Century in 1950. He received the Nobel Peace Prize in 1953. He was awarded the Order of Merit by Queen Elizabeth in 1955.

At 24 years of age he had finished his Doctor of Philosophy degree, and at 38 years of age his Doctor of Medicine. He also received honorary doctorates, and today is remembered as an outstanding missionary doctor and writer on the subject of theology.

Do you think Dr. Albert Schweitzer served two masters? We might conclude that this man lived to make a name in this world. But this is not the case.

Dr. Schweitzer went to Africa as a missionary without any salary. He was not granted a cent for his equipment or his transportation. All he wanted to do was to serve God. Dr. Schweitzer expressed a desire to use his talents to help his fellow human beings, and served more than forty years at a hospital that he raised up in French Equatorial Africa. This hospital became a symbol of Christian service to all missionaries.

"Tell me, Dr. Schweitzer, if you had a chance to speak to all the young people of the world, what would you tell them?" This question was asked by Daniel Walther, and the answer is recorded in *The Youth's Instructor* of June 12, 1956. Would you like to know what Dr. Schweitzer said?

"I would tell them to be more thankful. . . . Yes, there is another quality I would like to see develop in young people everywhere, and that is plain, down-to-earth honesty."

The words and example of Dr. Schweitzer show the wisdom of serving God and others rather than serving Satan and self. We may also see the truthfulness of another statement of Jesus recorded in our chapter today, "He that is faithful in that which is least is faithful also in much: and he that is unjust in the least is unjust also in much" (Luke 16:10).

PERFECTION
Luke 17

LEPER'S BOOK

And as he entered a village, he was met by ten lepers, who stood at a distance and lifted up their voices and said, "Jesus, Master, have mercy on us." Luke 17:12, 13.

Luke recorded not only more of Jesus' parables than the other Gospel writers but also more of His miracles. The Gospel of Luke mentions twenty of the thirty-five recorded miracles of Jesus. The healing of the ten lepers is recorded only in this Gospel.

In Bible times lepers were regarded as outcasts and were not allowed to come into the villages and towns. People believed that leprosy was the result of sin, and Luke says the ten lepers "stood afar off." But the compassionate Jesus loved to heal people. So when these men called out to Him by name and requested that He have mercy on them, He responded.

Luke, who was always interested in details, states that the only one who returned to thank Jesus was a Samaritan. Samaritans were a race of people whom the Jews regarded as inferior to themselves. But this time it was the foreigner who proved to be the only grateful one. Jesus' question "But where are the nine?" reproves all who are ungrateful. Failing to give thanks is a "sin of omission."

Paul has also counseled us against this sin: "In every thing give thanks: for this is the will of God" (1 Thess. 5:18).

A young man rescued nineteen people from icy Lake Michigan. After they were all warm and dry, the hero was asked by a reporter what was the most outstanding thing that he remembered about the rescue. The young man said, "The thing I can't understand is that only one said 'Thank you.'"

People have not changed much through the ages. There was only one in ten who said Thank You to Jesus, and one in nineteen who said Thank you to the man who saved them from drowning. Let us determine to be among those who give thanks.

We certainly need to say Thank you to people who help us or who give us things. However, we also need to express thanks for love, friendship, home, family, church, and the many other blessings we enjoy.

PERFECTION
Luke 18

CHILDREN'S BOOK

"Let the children come to me, and do not hinder them; for to such belongs the kingdom of God." Luke 18:16.

Delson was only 6 years old when he enrolled at the Seventh-day Adventist church school for the Maricopa Indians in Arizona. As the missionary teacher, Hazel Rathbun, recalls, "Delson was a quiet boy. From the very beginning he loved the story of Jesus."

Delson, at 9 years of age, stated, "I'll lead out and see to it that we help our parents learn the story of Jesus." The children marched out to the gate of the school, where Delson lined them up and said, "Teacher, you can depend on us! Every time we put our feet down marching, it means that we will stamp out drinking and will help our people accept Jesus and show them how to march to heaven."

At 17, Delson was still a faithful Sabbath school and church member. And he proved that children are not too young to be true Christians and faithful servants of God.

Bernard and Michael DeBeer earnestly prayed that their father would be baptized, and wept for joy when he stood during an evangelistic meeting to indicate that he wanted to become a Seventh-day Adventist. Now he is a church officer and is giving Bible studies. God used these faithful junior youths to help win their father for the kingdom of heaven.

The verse following our Morning Watch text has another message for us: "'Truly, I say to you, whoever does not receive the kingdom of God like a child shall not enter it'" (R.S.V.).

Everyone who enters the kingdom of God must have the childlike characteristics of simple trust and loving obedience. A little child shows great faith in his parents as he toddles forward to fall into their arms. This is the kind of faith we need to have in Jesus. Before we could understand words we obeyed our parents' commands, and just so Christians are careful to heed their heavenly Father's voice. You can share the story of Jesus with others, for there are many who need to know of the *light, love,* and *life* that people discover when they choose to be Christians. Jesus is counting on us to show others "how to march to heaven."

PERFECTION
Luke 19

LOST-AND-FOUND BOOK

"For the Son of man came to seek and to save the lost." Luke 19:10.

"Help!" The cry was heard above the guns firing in the jungle. Hidden safely behind a rock, a soldier recognized the voice as that of one of his friends. The lieutenant told him that he would be silly to go out, for he would surely be shot and his friend would probably die too. But the soldier did not hear any more. Instead he ran out and dragged his friend to safety. When asked why he had risked his life, he said, "I was called from within to go out. As I reached out to my friend, he said, 'I knew you would come.'"

The courage and love shown by this soldier reflect the love of Jesus. He came to this lost world and was willing to die in order that we might be rescued from sin. Our verse today reminds us of the depth of this love. Zacchaeus was one of the lost who was found by Jesus. Zacchaeus was a tax collector for the Roman government, and thus was regarded as a traitor to the Jewish nation. However, there was some good in this man, for "he sought to see Jesus" (Luke 19:3). Because he was short and there were many people around Jesus, Zacchaeus climbed a tree. It was while this lost man was in the tree that Jesus found him. Our Lord still seeks and finds those who are lost.

Jesus is so concerned about rescuing the lost that He has enlisted all the angels in heaven to help Him. He has also appealed to every Christian to engage in the work of finding the lost. No matter how far we have wandered from God or where we are hiding, Jesus wants to find us.

Zacchaeus invited his friends to meet Jesus, and as a result many others found eternal life. When Jesus finds us, our first reaction should be to tell our friends of this wonderful Person, Jesus. Zacchaeus also repented for cheating the people and gave back with interest everything that he had taken. When we accept Jesus, we must also do what we can to make things right with others.

PERFECTION
Luke 20

QUESTION BOOK

"Tell us by what authority you do these things, or who it is that gave you this authority." Luke 20:2.

The Arabs used to say that there are only four kinds of people: First, those who know not and know not that they know not; they are foolish. Second, those who know not and know that they know not; they are simple and should be instructed. Third, those who know and know not that they know; they are asleep and should be awakened. Fourth, those who know and know that they know; they are wise—follow them.

Although the religious leaders in the days of Jesus asked a lot of questions, it is evident that they were not in the group who knew what to do. They should have been the first to recognize that Jesus had the answers to their queries, but they only questioned His authority. They constantly reminded themselves that He did not have authority from the church to teach.

Using a common form of conversation, Jesus replied to these leaders' question by asking one of His own: Had John the Baptist baptized by the authority of Heaven or of men? They discussed this among themselves but couldn't give Him an answer. If they were to answer that John had baptized only by man's authority, it would make the people angry, since it was believed that John was sent from God. But if they admitted that he had baptized with Heaven's authority, they would be forced to recognize that Jesus was the Messiah, which was what John had preached. They did not have the courage of their own convictions, and they let the crowd influence their decision. This time the crowd was right, for both Jesus' and John's authority was from Heaven, and the leaders had seen plenty of proof of this.

Jesus then told the story of a man who owned a vineyard. The people realized that those who killed the owner's servants and his son represented the leaders of the day, but apparently they were like those who "know not and know not that they know not."

Instead of following the Man who could give them the correct answers to their queries, they just asked more questions. Like some today, they were given good answers but would not humble themselves to admit their mistakes and to accept truth.

PERFECTION
Luke 21

PROPHETIC BOOK

"Look at the fig tree, and all the trees; as soon as they come out in leaf, you see for yourselves and know that the summer is already near. So also, when you see these things taking place, you know that the kingdom of God is near." Luke 21:29-31.

World fairs, or expositions, include large, impressive displays from countries around the world. In 1939, a world's fair was held in New York City. A large American company, Westinghouse Electric, had the most publicized project at that fair. They buried what they called a time capsule, a large, torpedo-shaped shell that contained many things that represented life in the 1930's. Among the items included were a box of golf balls, a Bing Crosby record, a microfilm containing 10 million words of today's English, and a Bible.

The president of Westinghouse, when asked why a Bible had been included, replied, "The Holy Bible, of all the books familiar to us today, will most likely survive through the ages. Therefore the Bible that we placed in the capsule will be sort of a connecting link between the past, the present, and the future."

The Bible has indeed proved to be a "connecting link," linking the centuries before Christ with the centuries after Christ. It also links heaven and earth through the perfect *Person,* Jesus, and our world of the present with the new world of the future.

The twenty-first chapter of Luke contains prophecies that tell us when this world will pass away and the new world order will commence. No, we do not know the day or the hour, but signs that Jesus has given tell us that we are near that event. (See January 24 reading.)

Those who buried the time capsule in 1939 believed that the world would still exist in the year 6,939. As we study Bible prophecies, we conclude that time has almost run out. Every spring as we see the trees begin to leaf, it should remind us that Jesus is coming soon.

PERFECTION
Luke 22

CHRISTIAN'S BOOK

Simon, . . . I have prayed for thee, that thy faith fail not: and when thou art converted, strengthen thy brethren. Luke 22:31, 32, K.J.V.

As predicted, Simon Peter was converted. This means that he became a true Christian. Let's note from this poem how, when, where, and why someone else, like Peter, was converted.

"You ask me *how* I gave my heart to Christ? I do not know.
There came a yearning for Him in my soul so long ago.
I found earth's flowers would fade and die—
I wept for something that could satisfy;
And then—and then—somehow I seemed to dare
To lift my broken heart to Him in prayer.

"You ask me *when* I gave my heart to Christ? I cannot tell.
The day, or just the hour, I do not now remember well.
It must have been when I was all alone;
The light of His forgiving Spirit shone
Into my heart, so clouded o'er with sin;
I think 'twas then I trembling let Him in.

"You ask me *where* I gave my heart to Christ? I cannot say.
That sacred place has faded from my sight as yesterday.
Perhaps He thought it better I should not
Remember where. How I should love that spot!
I think I could not tear myself away,
For I should wish forever there to stay.

"You ask me *why* I gave my heart to Christ? I can reply;
It is a wondrous story; listen while I tell you why.
My heart was drawn, at length, to seek His face;
I was alone, I had no resting place;
I heard of Him, how He had loved me with a love
Of depth so great, of height so far above
All human ken; I longed such love to share,
And sought it, then, upon my knees in prayer.

"He heard my prayer! I cannot tell you how,
Nor when, nor where; only—I love Him now."
                                        —Author Unknown

PERFECTION
Luke 23

MURDER BOOK

And when they came to the place which is called The Skull, there they crucified him, and the criminals, one on the right and one on the left. Luke 23:33.

The title for our reading today is not a very pleasant one. However, it is an accurate description, because Jesus *was* murdered. He was innocent of any crime against the Jewish nation or the Roman government. His trials were not fair, and the one that was held at night was actually illegal. Even Pilate, the Roman governor, said, "I find no fault in this man" (Luke 23:4).

The mob spirit overruled justice, however, and Jesus was nailed to a cross. This method of execution was one of the cruelest that the pagan mind had ever thought of. His cross was thrust into the ground and Jesus was left to die in the heat of the sun.

"If sinners can be led to give one earnest look at the cross, if they can obtain a full view of the crucified Saviour, they will realize the depth of God's compassion and the sinfulness of sin."—*The Acts of the Apostles,* p. 209. If we could fully understand how Jesus died, we would not play with temptation. Instead, we would plead earnestly for power to live lives that emulate the perfect life of Jesus.

One of the key verses in the book of Luke is found in this chapter. The statement from the lips of the Roman centurion accurately describes Jesus: "Certainly this was a righteous man" (verse 47). The centurion was not a Christian, but this declaration is an inspired truth of the Bible. Jesus is indeed our perfect example. His spotless character was seen even when He hung on the cross. While people were spitting at Him and mocking Him, Jesus prayed, "Father, forgive them; for they know not what they do" (verse 34).

Jesus allowed Himself to be killed on Calvary that we might have eternal life. One day those who murdered the Saviour will see Him coming in the clouds of heaven as King of kings and Lord of lords. He is in that kingdom right now preparing a place for you and me, and like the thief on the cross we should pray, "Lord, remember me" (verse 42).

245

PERFECTION
Luke 24

SONGBOOK

And they returned to Jerusalem with great joy, and were continually in the temple blessing God. Luke 24:52, 53.

The song of Mary begins Luke's songbook. It occupies eleven verses in chapter one and is sometimes called "The Magnificat," because it magnifies the perfect character of God. It is a song of gratitude, and is one of the most beautiful in the Bible.

As we contemplate God's goodness and love in giving us His perfect Son as our Saviour, we should also magnify God's character. Through the ages Satan has tried to misrepresent God and portray Him as the author of suffering and death. As Christians, we need to let everybody know that God is love and that He loves everyone.

The song of Zacharias, also found in chapter one, is a song of praise to God for the Messiah to come. Both the song of Mary and the song of Zacharias contain many Old Testament prophecies and phrases. As we see the Old Testament prophecies about Jesus fulfilled, we too can say, "Blessed be the Lord God" (Luke 1:68).

The song of the angels, sung to the shepherds on the hillside, is also recorded in Luke:

" 'Glory to God in the highest,
  and on earth peace among men with whom he is pleased!' "
  (chap. 2:14, R.S.V.).

The shepherds were so inspired by the angels' song that they said, "Let us now go even unto Bethlehem and see this thing which is come to pass, which the Lord hath made known unto us" (verse 15).

As we consider the songs recorded in the book of Luke, we ought to say to one another, "Let us now go and tell others about the peace that the Lord hath made known unto us."

The writings of Luke should lead us to sing, "Glory to God in the highest." The last verse of the book tells us that the disciples were so overjoyed with the resurrection and ascension of Jesus that they sang praises to God in the Temple. The gloom of the tomb gave way to the joy of the resurrection morning, and they had a song in their hearts.

PERFECTION
Job 1

RICHES TO RAGS

And the Lord said to Satan, "Have you considered my servant Job, that there is none like him on the earth, a blameless and upright man, who fears God and turns away from evil?" Job 1:8.

A poet can take a worthless sheet of paper, write a poem on it, and make it worth $3,000; that is *genius*. A businessman can sign his name to a piece of paper and make it worth a million dollars; that is *prosperity*. Your country's treasurer can take metal, stamp an emblem on it, and make it worth a dollar; that is *money*. A tradesman can take five dollars' worth of metal and make it into something worth twenty-five dollars; that is *skill*. An artist can take a piece of canvas, paint a picture on it, and make it worth $5,000 dollars; that is *art*.

But only God can take a worthless, sinful life, wash it in the blood of Jesus, put His Holy Spirit in it, and make it a blessing to humanity; that is a *miracle*.

Job was a miracle man. His worthless, selfish life had been changed until he was perfect and upright. He feared God and had turned away from wrong thoughts and deeds. He had come to the place where he reflected the character of God to his neighbors in the Arabian Desert. Although we are not certain, possibly Job lived at the same time as Moses, who wrote the book of Job. God said of Job that there was "none like him in the earth."

Job was very rich. "His substance also was seven thousand sheep, and three thousand camels, and five hundred yoke of oxen, and five hundred she asses, and a very great household; so that this man was the greatest of all the men of the east" (Job 1:3).

Satan was angry when Job proved that men could, with God's help, become perfect. He charged that Job loved God only because he was rich. So God permitted Satan to persecute Job by touching all that was important to him. Through heathen men, lightning, and a whirlwind, Satan caused Job to lose not only all his animals but his seven sons and three daughters as well.

The perfect character of Job is seen in his reaction to these tragedies. It is recorded that "in all this Job sinned not, nor charged God foolishly" (verse 22). Even when he had lost everything and was left with only rags for clothes, Job remained true to God.

247

PERFECTION
Job 2

COVERED WITH BOILS

So Satan went forth from the presence of the Lord, and afflicted Job with loathsome sores from the sole of his foot to the crown of his head. Job 2:7.

It is evident from the story of Job that because of Adam and Eve's sin in the Garden of Eden, Satan was permitted to continue to maintain his influence upon this world. The meeting between God and the angels—sons of God—and Satan, recorded in today's chapter, most likely did not take place in heaven, since Satan had been expelled from there. When God asked Satan where he had come from, he replied, "From going to and fro in the earth, and from walking up and down in it" (Job 1:7). We can be thankful that because the "second Adam," Jesus, died on the cross, Satan will one day be entirely destroyed.

At this meeting God asked Satan what he thought of Job. The devil replied that Job was serving God only to save his own skin. At that time God gave Satan permission to afflict Job's body, but not to take his life. This good man was covered with sores from the top of his head to the bottom of his feet. We do not know exactly what kind of disease he got, but we do know that he suffered for a long time.

Job must have been a terrible sight and in real agony, because his wife advised him to "curse God, and die" (chap. 2:9). Once again we see the beauty of his character in his reply, which came in the form of a question: "Should we receive all God's benefits as a matter of course, and then complain when He sends affliction?" (see verse 10).

The story of Job needs to be told today when people want to curse God because of trouble. Even some Christians doubt God's love when they suffer or lose loved ones. I believe God agonized with Job just as He did when His own Son died on Calvary.

The story of Job proves God's love and care for His people in the midst of their suffering. Although we will not cover all forty-two chapters of Job in this book, we will see, from the sections that we do study, the evidences of God's care for Job and for all of us.

248

PERFECTION
Job 3

JOB COMPLAINS

After this Job opened his mouth and cursed the day of his birth. And Job said: "Let the day perish wherein I was born." Job 3:1-3.

In just forty-five minutes the lifework of the sculptor Jacques Lipschitz was destroyed by fire in a building in midtown New York. As the artist expressed it, "It's awful, just awful. Part of my life is gone." However, instead of being overwhelmed by discouragement, he bravely and cheerfully said, "I shall simply have to start all over again." There was a strength to his character that rose in this moment of tragedy.

After Job had dwelt on his troubles for some time, he was so discouraged that he asked to die. Wisely, God did not grant this desire, but He did stay with him through the crisis. After some time Job rose above his discouragement and courageously vowed to start again.

"From the depths of discouragement and despondency Job rose to the heights of implicit trust in the mercy and the saving power of God. Triumphantly he declared: 'Though he slay me, yet will I trust in him: . . . he also shall be my salvation.' Job 13:15, 16. . . . Hope and courage are essential to perfect service for God. These are the fruit of faith. Despondency is sinful and unreasonable. . . . For the disheartened there is a sure remedy—faith, prayer, work."—*Prophets and Kings,* pp. 163, 164.

It is easy to complain and become discouraged. However, there is a simple, sure remedy. First we can increase our *faith* by reading the Bible (Rom. 10:17) and by studying the lives of men and women such as Job and Esther. Then we can *pray* for strength to rise above discouragement. And third, *work* was given to us not only to exercise our bodies but also to refresh our minds. Labor is one of the best ways to achieve a bright outlook.

Two men looked out the same window. One of them looked down and saw mud; the other looked up and saw the stars. No matter where we are, we can look up and see Jesus and the stars.

When you and I feel discouraged we should remember that
　　—after every storm the sun shines,
　　—after every sunset there is a sunrise,
　　—after every winter there is a summer.

PERFECTION
Job 2

JOB'S COMFORTERS

Now when Job's three friends heard of all this evil that had come upon him, they came each from his own place, Eliphaz the Temanite, Bildad the Shuhite, and Zophar the Naamathite. They made an appointment together to come to condole with him and comfort him. Job 2:11.

Have you ever heard someone spoken of as a "Job's comforter"? The term is often used to describe a person who comes to give you comfort but who only tells you that what you are suffering is a result of your mistakes or sins.

Eliphaz, Bildad, and Zophar were the original "Job's comforters." They were apparently friends of Job, and they truly wanted to console him. It was unfortunate, however, that they allowed Satan to use them to bring greater trials to their friend.

The dialogue between Job and his friends occupies twenty-nine chapters of Job, the book that many believe to be the oldest in the Bible. Note some of the harsh statements that these comforters made:

Eliphaz said, "'Is not your fear of God your confidence, and the integrity of your ways your hope?'" (Job 4:6, R.S.V.). "'For affliction does not come from the dust, nor does trouble sprout from the ground'" (chap. 5:6, R.S.V.).

Bildad stated, "'Does God pervert justice?'" (chap. 8:3, R.S.V.). "'Behold, God will not reject a blameless man'" (verse 20, R.S.V.).

And Zophar added, "'Know then that God exacts of you less than your guilt deserves'" (chap. 11:6, R.S.V.). "'It is higher than heaven—what can you do?'" (verse 8, R.S.V.).

During this conversation between Job and his three friends, Job speaks nine times, Eliphaz speaks three times, Bildad three, and Zophar two. The speeches are written as poetry, and in the older Bible versions it is difficult to understand what the speakers are trying to say.

There is also a younger friend of Job, Elihu, who makes four speeches. His point is that suffering occurs to keep people from sinning, rather than as punishment.

Our best Comforter is Jesus, who stays closer to us than even a brother or sister. He has also promised that the Holy Spirit will be a Comforter to His people.

PERFECTION
Job 38, 39

GOD ASKS SIXTY QUESTIONS

Then the Lord answered Job out of the whirlwind: "... I will question you, and you shall declare to me." Job 38:1-3.

In one of his speeches, Job complained that God had broken him with a tempest or whirlwind (chap. 9:17). After Job, his three comforters, and Elihu had talked themselves out, God spoke from a whirlwind. He did not attempt to settle the arguments or to explain the reason for suffering. He had a higher purpose, and that was to make Himself known. As God reveals His power, goodness, and wisdom, all Job's questions are answered.

God spoke to Job and his friends, rapidly asking about sixty questions concerning the mysteries of nature. Neither Job nor his comforters could answer them. As Job considered these questions, he forgot the speech that he had planned to make, and gained a new appreciation of God. The questions that God asked Job are good ones for us to study. They are recorded in chapters 38 to 41, and fall into three groups:

Questions concerning Creation (chap. 38:4-15): "Where wast thou when I laid the foundations of the earth?" This question led Job to reflect on God's creative power.

Questions concerning the world itself (verses 16-38): There are questions about the ocean, light and darkness, snow and hail, clouds, the stars, and planets. By these questions God is acquainting Job not just with scientific facts but with his own origin and character.

Questions concerning the mysteries of animal life (chap. 38:39 to chap. 39:30): These questions include such subjects as lions and ravens, goats, donkeys, oxen, birds, ostriches, and the horse. Even the "Ha, ha" noise, or neigh of the horse, is mentioned (chap. 39:25).

There are many scientific truths in the book of Job, some of which have been confirmed only in recent times. It is interesting to read these facts, but we must remember that the real messages of the book are to encourage Job, to show that God is perfect, and to reveal that He is not the author of suffering.

Even though we may not be able to answer God's sixty questions, we know that He loves us as much as He loved Job.

PERFECTION
Job 40, 41

THE BIRDS TELL YOU

"But ask the beasts, and they will teach you; the birds of the air, and they will tell you." Job 12:7.

The Pacific golden plover is a small, beautifully colored bird that nests in the northern part of Alaska and Siberia. Each autumn the plovers fly to the shores of the Pacific, then take off over more than 2,500 miles of ocean to the Hawaiian Islands, and continue on 7,000 miles farther to Australia and New Zealand.

The Arctic tern, however, probably holds the record for migratory birds. The terns nest in Alaska and northern Canada, within the Arctic Circle, and fly to the islands off the tip of South America. Instead of returning by the same route, they make a round trip of almost 25,000 miles.

The white-throated warbler of Central Europe annually strikes out for the eastern end of the Mediterranean, then makes a mysterious change of direction and goes south to the lake country of Central Africa.

Many theories have been suggested to explain the remarkable flight of billions of migratory birds. However, as far as scientists are concerned, they are still among the mysteries of nature. On the other hand, many creationists who believe in the Word of God see in migratory birds another example of the testimony of nature to an all-powerful Creator.

Many animals, birds, fish, and insects migrate each year. Bird migrations are easily observable and have been studied for centuries. More than 2,000 years ago, Jeremiah noted the regular, annual arrival of migratory birds. Said he, "Yea, the stork in the heaven knoweth her appointed times; and the turtle and the crane and the swallow observe the time of their coming; but my people know not the judgment of the Lord" (Jer. 8:7).

Just as the migratory birds of the sky know "their appointed times," so Christians need to be aware of the hour of earth's history in which they are living. We need to warn people that this is the end of time and to share with them the love of God. A star in the heavens heralded the first advent of the Lord Jesus. Likewise, specific signs declare that His second coming is soon.

PERFECTION
Job 42

RAGS TO RICHES

And the Lord blessed the latter days of Job more than his beginning; and he had fourteen thousand sheep, six thousand camels, a thousand yoke of oxen, and a thousand she-asses. Job 42:12.

The story of Job has a happy ending. God is revealed as a God of love, and Job's faith is confirmed and his possessions doubled. He also has seven sons and three daughters. The book began with the description of a man with riches going to rags and ends with his restoration to riches.

But fourteen thousand sheep, six thousand camels, a thousand yoke of oxen, and a thousand she-asses were not Job's main blessings. His greatest gain was that he grew in character as a result of his experiences. Character is all that we will take through to the kingdom of God. And sometimes character can best be developed through suffering and trials.

"God leads His children by a way that they know not; but He does not forget or cast off those who put their trust in Him. He permitted affliction to come upon Job, but He did not forsake him. He allowed the beloved John to be exiled to lonely Patmos, but the Son of God met him there, and his vision was filled with scenes of immortal glory. God permits trials to assail His people, that by their constancy and obedience they themselves may be spiritually enriched, and that their example may be a source of strength to others."—*Patriarchs and Prophets,* p. 129.

This month, in the book of Luke we have seen many pen pictures of the *perfect* Person, Jesus. As long as we keep our eyes fixed on this pattern, we will grow "in favour with God and man" (Luke 2:52). In the book of Job we have caught a glimpse of a man who was perfect in God's sight. God knew that Job would remain true when He allowed Satan to conduct the experiment. Job's faithfulness to God and God's care for Job reveal the beauty of God's character. From these two books we can see the *light* available to us, the *love* that surrounds us, and the eternal *life* that is waiting for us.

It does not really matter whether we have rags or riches. Our main concern is to have Jesus, for He supplies our needs. Remember, He exchanges rags of sin for robes of salvation.

PROVIDENCE
Judges 3

HEROES OF FAITH

But when the people of Israel cried to the Lord, the Lord raised up a deliverer for the people of Israel, who delivered them, Othniel the son of Kenaz, Caleb's younger brother. Judges 3:9.

Abraham was six feet four while he was still a teen-ager. Even when only a boy of 8, he was strong enough to use an ax, which he described as "that most useful instrument." He helped his father build a log cabin, and even though his entire school attendance was less than one year, he read all the books he could get hold of. One of his favorites, which no doubt helped him later in life, was *The Pilgrim's Progress.*

This boy was reared in a humble log cabin, and despite difficulties and reverses became a lawyer and eventually President of the United States. And it was under his leadership that the United States was reunited into one country. Abraham Lincoln was a Christian, and this fact led him to work for the freedom of the slaves, declared in the Emancipation Proclamation, effective January 1, 1863.

From the beginning of this world, God has had men and women who have delivered people from slavery in various forms. One of these heroes was Moses, who delivered millions of Israelites from the slavery of Egypt. Joshua led this same nation to conquer the land of Canaan. Following the death of Joshua, God raised up twelve judges who delivered the Israelites from slavery. The word *judge* does not accurately describe their work, for they were actually generals or chiefs. They were called judges because they ruled the people after delivering them from their enemies.

The book of Judges contains the records of the lives of these heroes. We cannot say exactly how long these judges ruled, but the era spanned more than 350 years, up to about 1050 B.C.

The first judge was Othniel, one of the brothers of Caleb. He was followed by Ehud and Shamgar. Like Abraham Lincoln, most of Israel's judges came from obscure families and did not appear to be outstanding in any way. However, as they answered the call of the Lord to do what He wanted them to, they became heroes. As we give our lives to God and make ourselves available to do His will, we too will become heroes of faith.

PROVIDENCE
Judges 6

GIDEON'S CALL

"The Lord is with you, you mighty man of valor." . . . *"Go in this might of yours and deliver Israel from the hand of Midian; do not I send you?" Judges 6:12-14.*

You can imagine the surprise of Gideon the farmer when an angel called him to be a judge as he was threshing wheat. He did not expect to be selected, and the nation certainly had not considered him to be a general. Gideon protested when told that he was "a mighty man of valor" and that he was to deliver Israel from the Midianites, who were as numerous as grasshoppers. He realized that he was the least-known member of the smallest tribe of Israel. In God's sight, however, Gideon's humility was one of his best qualifications for being commander in chief.

"The Lord does not always choose for His work men of the greatest talents, but He selects those whom He can best use. Individuals who might do good service for God, may for a time be left in obscurity, apparently unnoticed and unemployed by their Master. But if they faithfully perform the duties of their humble position, . . . He will in His own time intrust them with greater responsibilities. Before honor is humility."—*The SDA Bible Commentary,* Ellen G. White Comments, on Judges 6:15, p. 1003.

The selection of Gideon as one of the most outstanding judges of Israel is an illustration of God's providence or guidance. This month we will see God's guiding hand in the affairs of nations through the lives of judges, kings, a queen, and ordinary individuals. We must always remember that God is in control, and that even though events may not seem right, "all things work together for good." As we study God's providence, we will note that what at first glance may seem to be an accident or a defeat could really be a part of God's plan.

In God's providence Moses was rescued from the bulrushes and taken into the palace in Egypt. In God's providence Joseph was sold into slavery. In God's providence a farmer became a mighty general to deliver Israel from seven years of slavery under the Midianites.

"We have nothing to fear for the future, except as we forget the way the Lord has led us, and His teaching in our past history."—*Life Sketches,* p. 196.

255

PROVIDENCE
Judges 7

GIDEON'S ARMY

And the Lord said to Gideon, "With the three hundred men that lapped I will deliver you, and give the Midianites into your hand; and let all the others go every man to his home." Judges 7:7.

If you were a general with the choice of thirty-two thousand soldiers or three hundred soldiers to fight the armies of two nations with more than thirty-two thousand men, which number of soldiers would you choose? I think we would all choose the larger army. Can you imagine how Gideon felt as he looked at the combined forces of the Midianites and the Amalekites that "lay along the valley like grasshoppers for multitude" (Judges 7:12)?

Why do you think God ordered the reduction of Gideon's army from thirty-two thousand to three hundred? The answer is found in verse 2: "Lest Israel vaunt themselves against me, saying, Mine own hand hath saved me."

God's providence and guidance could be seen only if a small group were victorious over an army that could not be numbered.

Gideon's army was reduced in number by a series of tests. First, when he told those who were afraid to fight to go home, twenty-two thousand left. The ten thousand remaining were hot and tired from marching, and as they came to a river God stated that those who quickly took water in their hands and drank as they ran should remain in the army. Those who forgot their mission and took time to kneel and drink were to be sent home. When the test ended, three hundred men remained. With this small group God defeated the huge armies that had hoped to destroy the Israelites.

Israel was victorious only after they destroyed the altars of Baal from among them. We cannot enter upon any work for God while known sin is casting its shadow over our lives. Before the sun rose on the broken altars of Baal and Ashtoreth, Gideon, as instructed by the Lord, had erected an altar to God. It is not enough to do away with bad things in our lives; we must fill the vacancy with that which is right.

And Gideon's army was united—"They stood every man in his place" (verse 21). God wants unity in the Christian army so He can lead His remnant church to victory.

256

PROVIDENCE
1 Samuel 2

THE LAST JUDGE

Now the boy Samuel continued to grow both in stature and in favor with the Lord and with men. 1 Samuel 2:26.

The words of our text are the same as those used to describe the boyhood of Jesus (see Luke 2:52). "Samuel had been placed under the care of Eli, and the loveliness of his character drew forth the warm affection of the aged priest. He was kind, generous, obedient, and respectful. . . . Samuel was helpful and affectionate."—*Patriarchs and Prophets,* p. 573.

As we read the story of Samuel, whose name means "heard of God," we note that he grew in the Christian life despite the evil influences of Eli's sons. Although it is good to be in favorable circumstances and associate with the right people, we cannot blame our behavior on where we live or with whom we must associate. We are all free to choose whether we will do what God wants or what other people tempt us to do. The life of Samuel, another of God's heroes, is light for our lives.

Samuel was the last of the judges. He was also a priest and prophet, with the responsibility to anoint the first king of Israel, Saul. The story of this man whom God used to link the period of the judges and the monarchy covers twenty-five chapters in the book of First Samuel. Samuel was used to bring the people back to God during a time of Philistine suppression. After the ark of God was captured by the Philistines, God used Samuel to defeat them. It was a wonderful day when the ark was returned to Israel.

Later Samuel erected an altar and called it Ebenezer, which means "stone of help." Before erecting the altar, he called on the people to put away their idols. Today God is calling young people to erect Ebenezers. Will you ask Him to help make your home a "stone of help"?

Another valuable contribution made by Samuel was the establishment of the schools of the prophets. "In those schools of the olden time it was the grand object of all study to learn the will of God and man's duty toward Him. In the records of sacred history were traced the footsteps of Jehovah."—*Ibid.,* pp. 593, 594. As we study at home and school, we need to learn what is God's will for our lives.

PROVIDENCE
1 Samuel 9

THE FIRST KING

"Tell the servant to pass on before us, and when he has passed on stop here yourself for a while, that I may make known to you the word of God." 1 Samuel 9:27.

Samuel the prophet made this request of a young man near the gate of the city of Ramah. The youth, son of an important chief, was destined to become the first king of Israel.

The meeting of Samuel and Saul was the direct result of God's guidance. Although Saul was the son of a wealthy man, he followed the custom of caring for his father's animals. One day as he was watching donkeys on the mountainside, they strayed. With a trusted servant the lad set out to find them. For three days they searched in vain. When they neared the city of Ramah, the servant suggested that they ask Samuel the prophet about the lost animals. This was in God's plan, and the prophet was waiting for them at the gate.

Samuel quickly assured them that he would tell them where they could find the donkeys. He then told Saul that he, Saul, was the person the nation was looking for. The young man was surprised, and declared that it could not be, for he was from the smallest tribe and from the least important of all the families of Israel. However, despite his words of self-depreciation, he was given the honored place that evening at a banquet with about thirty leading city officials.

He spent the night in the prophet's guest room, and the next day, as the custom was, their host escorted the visitors to the city gate. At this point the man of God requested young Saul to "'stop here yourself for a while'" (R.S.V.). And there on that dusty road the youth who had set out to find lost animals was anointed as king (1 Sam. 10:1).

There are several lessons in this dramatic story. In the straying of the donkeys we see natural events, but behind the wandering hoofs we see God leading Saul from a secluded country life to be king. It is not strange for God to lead by unknown and different paths. We must not be discouraged by life's detours and strange ways, for God can use these circumstances to lead us to find His plan for our lives.

258

PROVIDENCE
1 Samuel 16

A SHEPHERD TO BE KING

Then Samuel took the horn of oil, and anointed him in the midst of his brothers; and the Spirit of the Lord came mightily upon David from that day forward. And Samuel rose up, and went to Ramah. 1 Samuel 16:13.

Many boys today are named David, which means "beloved" or "chieftain." These two words certainly describe the shepherd boy who became king. David's subjects loved him, and from his psalms we see how much God loved him and how much he loved God. David was one of the chief kings of Israel, and God used him to establish the kingly line through which Jesus was born.

David was only a youth when Samuel secretly anointed him to be king of Israel. He was the youngest of the eight sons of Jesse and would not have been selected if a committee had been responsible for finding a king. The people selected Saul because of his physical characteristics, but God selected David because of his qualities of character.

Although David made many mistakes, he repented, and we have many expressions of his sorrow for his sins, recorded in the book of Psalms. "David was susceptible to the influence of the Holy Spirit, and the Lord in His providence trained him for His service, preparing him to carry out His purposes. Christ was the Master-builder of his character."—*The SDA Bible Commentary,* Ellen G. White Comments, on 1 Sam. 16:7-13, p. 1018.

If we allow God to be "the Master-builder of our character," we too can become subjects of the King of kings. Let's see what is included in character development.

C haracter is what God knows you to be.

H ardships help to mold your character.

A knowledge of Scripture strengthens character.

R equires surrender of self to service to God and man.

A ttained only through Jesus.

C hristian's character seen in daily life in the home.

T ested when we don't think others know what we are doing.

E xample of good character seen in Jesus' life.

R esult of self-discipline.

PROVIDENCE
1 Samuel 17

THE VALLEY OF ELAH

And David said, "The Lord who delivered me from the paw of the lion and from the paw of the bear, will deliver me from the hand of this Philistine." 1 Samuel 17:37.

The Israelites were camped on the eastern side of the valley of Elah, and the large Philistine army was on the western slope. They had been there for forty days, and the Israelites not only were unprepared to fight but were also frightened. The reason for their terror was that each day Goliath, Philistine champion standing about 9½ feel tall, walked down toward the river and shouted insults to God and challenges for someone to come and fight him. His spear weighed at least 13 pounds, and his helmet and armor, gleaming in the sun, were spearproof.

One day, to the amazement of the Philistines and the amusement of Goliath, a shout went out that Israel was sending someone to fight. Goliath became angry when he saw that his adversary was only a young man in shepherd's clothes armed with a sling.

But David was not frightened at the threats of the giant, because he trusted God. " 'You come to me with a sword and with a spear and with a javelin; but I come to you in the name of the Lord of hosts, the God of the armies of Israel, whom you have defied. This day the Lord will deliver you into my hand'" (1 Sam. 17:45, 46, R.S.V.).

You can imagine the shouts of victory when the giant fell as a result of a stone from a shepherd boy's sling! The Philistines fled in panic, and many were killed or captured.

The valley of Elah was a valley of *separation* and *challenge*. However, when David trusted in God, it became a valley of *decision* and *victory*. To be victorious, we need to be separated from the world and refuse to be frightened by the challenges that it gives us. When we make a decision to trust in God's providences, whatever valley we are in will become a valley of victory.

After this incident David was invited to Saul's palace to play his harp, and later he became armorbearer, a captain in the army, and the king's son-in-law. However, Saul became jealous of him, and for years David was forced to flee for his life. After Saul's dishonor and death, David became king of Israel.

PROVIDENCE
2 Samuel 7

SOMEBODY OR NOBODY

Then King David went in and sat before the Lord, and said, "Who am I, O Lord God, and what is my house, that thou hast brought me thus far?" 2 Samuel 7:18.

Why do I get into blue moods?
Why am I doing the things I do?
I like myself; is this wrong?
Am I weird in the way I reason and think?
Why do I sin when I don't want to?
How can I understand myself?
Who am I—somebody or nobody?

If you have been asking questions like these, you will be pleased to learn that you are not alone; many people ask "Who am I—somebody or nobody?" Actually, wondering about ourselves is a part of life.

Jack was uncertain as to who he was and put up false fronts. He pretended to be someone he wasn't in order to have friends. "Before I got into high school I didn't smoke, swear, or drink. Now I do all three, although I don't make them a habit. I do these things because my friends do them. I could resist these temptations, but why don't I?"

Jack didn't want to do the things he believed were wrong. He was not hooked on smoking, swearing, or drinking. But he was hooked on belonging. He had not discovered the importance of making his own choices and setting his own standards.

When we accept Jesus Christ into our lives, we become somebody. We become brand-new persons. And with Christ's help we can have self-acceptance and know who we are. We can also have self-understanding. We can know our true worth and experience self-development because we will know what we can do.

David, king of Israel, at the height of his reign asked the question "Who am I?" As we consider whether we are somebody or nobody, we can remember that it is God who enables us to accomplish good things; it is God who has made it possible for us to have eternal life. As we connect our lives to the King who came in the line of David, the promise made to David that he would "dwell in the house of the Lord for ever" applies to us.

PROVIDENCE
1 Kings 3

YOU CAN HAVE ANYTHING

"Give thy servant therefore an understanding mind to govern thy people, that I may discern between good and evil; for who is able to govern this thy great people?" 1 Kings 3:9.

Have you ever seen a wishing well? I have seen pools of water with hundreds of coins lying on the bottom. These coins have been thrown there by people who believe that by doing so, they can make their wishes come true. If you did have the opportunity of wishing for anything, what would you ask for? Share your wish with those with you or write it down on a piece of paper.

Solomon became king when he was a young man, and God said to him, "Ask what I shall give thee." The young king could have asked for wealth or anything else his heart desired, but he made a very wise decision. A part of what he asked for is contained in the Morning Watch text. After telling God that he was "but a little child" and that he did not know "how to go out or come in," he asked for wisdom. He did not ask for great knowledge, but that he might be able to use his knowledge to make wise decisions.

Every day I pray that my children will be given the ability to make wise decisions. All young people should pray that God will help them to "discern between good and evil" (R.S.V.).

Our chapter for today states that before God asked the king what he wanted, "Solomon loved the Lord, walking in the stature of his fathers" (verse 3). If only Solomon had continued to keep close to the Lord, he would have been an even greater king than he was and would not have made some of the big mistakes that he did! God's promises are conditional on obedience, and Solomon did not always act wisely, in that he did not always keep his heart right with the Lord.

Solomon certainly showed wisdom as a judge, and there are examples of his wisdom in stories written about him and in his books, Proverbs, Song of Solomon, and Ecclesiastes. Reading these books will help us to become wise. Solomon wrote more than three thousand proverbs and one thousand psalms. He was qualified to write these because "God gave Solomon wisdom and understanding beyond measure, and largeness of mind like the sand on the seashore" (chap. 4:29, R.S.V.).

PROVIDENCE
1 Kings 8

THIRTY THOUSAND BUILDERS

"Now the Lord has fulfilled his promise which he made; for I have risen in the place of David my father, and sit on the throne of Israel, as the Lord promised, and I have built the house for the name of the Lord, the God of Israel." 1 Kings 8:20.

If there were 1.3 million men in Solomon's kingdom, one out of every forty-three of them was required to help build the Temple, palace, and courtyard. The arrangement was that each man would build for one month and have two months to do his own business.

It had been David's dream to build the Temple, but because he was a man of war, God had told him that he could not. However, he did begin to collect materials. Fragrant cedar wood was brought from as far away as Lebanon. Costly stones, gold, and silver were also brought from other countries.

The dedication of the Temple was a special day in Israel. The service took place during the seventh month, the time of the Feast of Tabernacles, when everyone came to Jerusalem. The people rejoiced that the harvest was over and because the long-awaited Temple was completed.

Solomon offered the dedication prayer (1 Kings 8:22-53). It included thanksgiving, a pledge of obedience, a request that the Temple be a place of prayer, and that the presence of God would be there. The ark of the covenant was moved from the tent where it had been housed to the Most Holy Place in the Temple, symbolizing the return of God's presence to the sanctuary. God also assured Solomon, "I have heard thy prayer, . . . I have hallowed this house, which thou hast built, to put my name there for ever" (chap. 9:3).

Today a Moslem mosque stands on the site of the ancient Temple on Mount Moriah in Jerusalem. As a tourist, I stood in that mosque and thought of the many events that were associated with that spot. It was here that Abraham demonstrated his willingness to offer his son in obedience to God's command and David offered sacrifices to God.

Many people visit Mount Moriah to see the site of Solomon's Temple. We know that our bodies are "the temple" of God. We should be as careful to dedicate our bodies to the Lord each day as Solomon was to dedicate the Temple.

PROVIDENCE
1 Kings 11

THE KINGDOM DIVIDED

Therefore the Lord said to Solomon, "Since this has been your mind and you have not kept my covenant and my statutes which I have commanded you, I will surely tear the kingdom from you and will give it to your servant." 1 Kings 11:11.

It is hard to believe that the man who in his youth asked for wisdom to discern between good and evil would do "evil in the sight of the Lord." It is hard to believe that a king who while dedicating the Temple would pray, "'Let your heart therefore be wholly true to the Lord our God'" (1 Kings 8:61, R.S.V.), would allow his heart to be captured by women who did not love the Lord. It is hard to believe that the man who had been blessed with so much wealth would come to the place where he forgot that it was God who owns the silver and the gold and gives us power to live.

Although it is sad to read of King Solomon's fall, it is good to have an accurate account of what happens to those who do "evil in the sight of the Lord." We do reap what we sow.

The consequences of Solomon's sin not only cost him the throne of the greatest nation on earth but also led to the division of his kingdom. Because of the unfaithfulness of its first three kings, Israel existed as a nation for only 120 years, with Saul, David, and Solomon each reigning forty years over the united country.

The kingdom was first divided into two parts. In God's providence and for the good of the people in their rebellious condition, ten of the tribes formed the northern kingdom, known as the kingdom of Israel. Jeroboam was their first king, and he was very wicked. Two tribes remained loyal to the house of David, and they became known as the kingdom of Judah. Their first king, Rehoboam, Solomon's son, allowed the people to worship idols. The two kingdoms often fought each other. Eventually they were both overthrown by pagan nations.

During the period of the nineteen kings of Israel and the twenty kings of Judah, God raised up at least fifteen prophets to try to stem the tide of wickedness. This is another evidence of God's love and care for His people.

PROVIDENCE
1 Kings 17

"A MAN OF GOD"

And the woman said to Elijah, "Now I know that you are a man of God, and that the word of the Lord in your mouth is truth." 1 Kings 17:24.

Ahab was one of Israel's most wicked kings. During his twenty-one-year reign, idolatry was openly practiced. One reason for this was that Ahab married Jezebel, the daughter of the high priest of Baal. She brought hundreds of false prophets into the kingdom and organized Baal worship. There were many evil and cruel practices associated with the worship of this idol. "The air was polluted with the smoke of the sacrifices offered to false gods. Hill and vale resounded with the drunken cries of a heathen priesthood who sacrificed to the sun, moon, and stars."—*Prophets and Kings,* p. 115.

In God's providence a courageous and loyal prophet was raised up to challenge Ahab and Jezebel. The wicked king was leading the people to worship the creature rather than the Creator, but Elijah, whose name means "Jehovah is my God," was empowered to show dramatically who was the Creator.

The people who worshiped idols were taught that the elements earth, fire, and water were controlled by Baal and Ashtoreth. The first challenge to this belief came when God shut the windows of heaven and there was no rain for three and a half years. The people also worshiped the sun, and as it beat down on the parched ground, they were reminded that Jehovah is God.

In contrast to the disobedience of most of the kings of Israel and Judah, Elijah the prophet was obedient to the Lord. When God told him to go to Zarephath, he went immediately. It was there that the widow fed him from her last supply of food. God rewarded her faithfulness, and her barrel of oil and jar of flour were never empty.

A Japanese student stayed with a man in a small cottage in Britain. Upon returning to his country, he sent a letter addressed as follows: "The man of God, Monmouthshire, Wales." After some discussion, the village postman delivered the letter to the man with whom the student had stayed. If a letter should come to your town addressed to the "boy or girl of God," would it be delivered to you?

PROVIDENCE
1 Kings 18

FIRE POWER

"And you call on the name of your god and I will call on the name of the Lord; and the God who answers by fire, he is God." 1 Kings 18:24.

A noted French explorer noticed something unusual in the jungles of the Congo, which is now the country of Zaire. Each morning when he came out of his tent he saw piles of wood neatly stacked and ready for a campfire. He did not think members of the exploration party had built these during the night, and one morning he asked the chief guide, "Who does this? What are these piles of wood for?"

The guide replied, "That's done by the chimpanzees. They are all around us in the trees and are always watching us. They saw us build a fire last night; they saw us build a fire this morning. As soon as we leave, they come down from the trees and gather the sticks. They put the little ones underneath, the large sticks on top. They have everything right, except for one thing. They have no fire."

Many Christians act like those chimpanzees. They are piling up Bible knowledge, witnessing experiences, Christian education, and church attendance. They have everything right, except they lack the fire.

We need the flame of the Holy Spirit in our Christian lives. In several scriptures the Holy Spirit is likened to fire. John the Baptist said that the Messiah will "baptize you with the Holy Ghost, and with fire" (Matt. 3:11). Jesus Himself said that He would send fire on the earth (see Luke 12:49). When the Holy Spirit came to the disciples, He appeared to the people as "tongues like as of fire" (Acts 2:3).

Fire is a very good symbol for the Holy Spirit, for we know that He is light and that His influence purifies and spreads rapidly. This Fire power in our lives will consume the dross of pride, the rags of self-righteousness, the leaves of empty professions, the stubble of doubts, the thorns of prickly temper, the roots of bitterness, and the trash of cheap talk.

God was able to answer Elijah's prayer for fire to consume the altar because the prophet had put his all on the altar. God never holds back the "fire" when His people are in tune with Him as Elijah was on Mount Carmel.

PROVIDENCE
1 Kings 18

FIRE FROM HEAVEN

And when all the people saw it, they fell on their faces; and they said, "The Lord, he is God; the Lord, he is God." 1 Kings 18:39.

Have you ever stood alone while everyone made fun of your religion? If you have, you have a little idea of how Elijah felt when he stood on Mount Carmel against 850 idolatrous prophets who had the authority of the king and queen.

The terms for the test had been accepted by both parties. It was decided that whichever god sent fire to consume the sacrifice was the true God. The idolatrous prophets could not object, because Baal was known as the fire god.

The false prophets were earnest and persistent in their prayers to Baal. Imagine 850 voices calling hour after hour, "O Baal, hear us" (1 Kings 18:26). Their earnestness reminds us that we must be sure that we are worshiping the right God in the right way. Also we must not be awed by supposedly miraculous signs, because if God had not prevented it, Satan himself could have sent fire down to consume the heathen sacrifice.

Finally it was Elijah's turn, and the first thing he did was to repair the broken altar of the Lord. When we expect to draw near to God, we should certainly make right any broken vows or anything else that separates us from God.

During the day there had been wild screams and shouting. The priests of Baal had even cut themselves and leaped onto the altar. Now, with reverence and in quietness, Elijah offered a prayer to the God of heaven: "O Lord God of Abraham, Isaac, and of Israel, let it be known this day that thou art God in Israel, and that I am thy servant" (verse 36). Immediately fire came down from heaven and burned not only the wood and the offering but also the stones, and dried up all the water around the altar.

Elijah also demonstrated his faith in God by praying for rain. Six times his servant returned from the mountain and said that he could not see any sign of rain, and six times Elijah told him to look again. As soon as Elijah heard there was a small cloud the size of man's hand, he sent a message to Ahab that the drought was over. "Faith such as this is needed in the world today—faith that will lay hold on the promises of God's word and refuse to let go until Heaven hears."—*Prophets and Kings*, p. 157.

PROVIDENCE
1 Kings 19

DON'T QUIT

But he himself went a day's journey into the wilderness, and came and sat down under a broom tree; and he asked that he might die. 1 Kings 19:4.

It is hard to believe that the man whom God used to bring fire down from heaven would let the fire of enthusiasm burn out of his life. It is hard to believe that the man who was used to raise the dead and bring rain to a famine-stricken land would suddenly go into the desert and ask to die.

Those who have been discouraged know why Elijah "sat down under a broom tree" (R.S.V.). "Into the experience of all there come times of keen disappointment and utter discouragement."—*Prophets and Kings,* p. 162. One reason Elijah was discouraged was that he felt the forces of evil were too much for him to battle. He momentarily forgot God.

God encouraged Elijah by sending an angel to prepare a meal for him and by speaking to him in a still small voice after showing him a wind, earthquake, and fire. When we feel discouraged we must remember that God is as near to us as He was to Elijah. We may sometimes think of excuses to quit, but when we are doing God's work we have no reason to give up.

> When things go wrong as they sometimes will,
> When the road you're trudging seems all uphill,
> When the funds are low and the debts are high,
> And you want to smile, but you have to sigh,
> When care is pressing you down a bit,
> Rest, if you must—but don't you quit.
>
> Often the goal is nearer than
> It seems to a faint and faltering man,
> Often the struggler has given up
> When he might have captured the victor's cup,
> And he learned too late, when the night slipped down,
> How close he was to the golden crown.
>
> Success is failure turned inside out—
> The silver tint of the clouds of doubt—
> And you never can tell how close you are;
> It may be near when it seems afar;
> So stick to the fight when you're hardest hit—
> It's when things seem worst that you mustn't quit.

268

PROVIDENCE
1 Kings 20

TOO BUSY

"And as your servant was busy here and there, he was gone." 1 Kings 20:40.

Our text today was spoken on a battlefield as part of a parable. The disguised prophet, probably Micah, was rebuking Ahab for releasing a notorious prisoner of war.

God had intervened on Israel's behalf, and in the second battle 127,000 Syrian soldiers were killed and the king of Syria, Ben-hadad, was captured. Ahab did not obey God's command, however, and allowed Ben-hadad to escape. When asked how this happened, Ahab said that he was "busy here and there." As a result of the king's disobedience and lies, God allowed him to be killed by the Syrians under the command of the escaped Ben-hadad (1 Kings 22:34, 35).

Vital lessons are presented in this dramatic Old Testament story. There are opportunities in the natural world for planting and harvesting. The farmer may be "busy here and there," but if he doesn't work in the proper way, he won't have a harvest. God also gives us opportunities in the spiritual world. We must not be so busy with the study of *doctrines* that we let our *devotions* go. We must not be so busy following *fads* that we let our *faith* go. We must not be so busy with *campaigns* that we let the *Comforter,* the Holy Spirit, go.

God gives opportunities to everyone, but they are neglected by many. Ahab paid a high price for his neglect. Note the steps in his downfall.

Ahab showed an unworthy sympathy with the heathen monarch, saying, "He is my brother" (chap. 20:32). We cannot have close companionship with worldlings. Ahab also made a "covenant," accepting the terms proposed by Ben-hadad. We have no reason to adopt the standards suggested by worldlings. We are to announce by life and words the way a Christian should live. The third step in Ahab's downfall came when he sent Ben-hadad away, showing disobedience to God's command.

From the parable on the battlefield we see that fellowship with the world leads to companionship with worldlings. Companionship leads to covenants with the world. Covenants with the world lead to disobedience to God's commands. And disobedience to God's commands leads to our own destruction.

PROVIDENCE
2 Kings 2

A DOUBLE PORTION

When they had crossed, Elijah said to Elisha, "Ask what I shall do for you, before I am taken from you." And Elisha said, "I pray you, let me inherit a double share of your spirit." 2 Kings 2:9.

When we are very hungry, we like to have a double portion of food. When we do not have any money, we are thrilled to be given twice as much as we had expected to get. When Elisha, who was to replace Elijah as the prophet of God, was asked what he wanted, he requested a double portion of the spirit of Elijah. This reminds us of Solomon's request for wisdom. Neither Elisha nor Solomon asked for riches or honor. When we pray, we should ask for spiritual blessings rather than the things of this world.

When Elisha asked Elijah for "a double portion of thy spirit," he was really asking to be treated as the spiritual son of the prophet. Elijah could not grant this request, but God could, and He did make him Elijah's successor with the spiritual power that he requested.

"Elisha received a double portion of the spirit that had rested on Elijah. In him the power of Elijah's spirit was united with the gentleness, mercy, and tender compassion of the Spirit of Christ."—*The SDA Bible Commentary,* Ellen G. White Comments, on 2 Kings 2:9, 15, p. 1037.

As the men talked, a "chariot of fire, and horses of fire, . . . parted them both asunder; and Elijah went up by a whirlwind into heaven" (2 Kings 2:11). The prophet who had called fire down was taken up by "a chariot of fire." Do you think it was really a burning chariot? No, horses and chariots are often used in the Bible to represent God's power and glory. In Psalm 68:17 angels are referred to as chariots.

The translation of Elijah to heaven is of tremendous encouragement to us. He represents those living on earth in the last days who will be translated after the righteous dead are resurrected. You will remember that Moses was resurrected, representing the righteous who will be raised from the grave and taken to heaven (see *The Desire of Ages,* p. 422).

What a wonderful day it will be when we can be caught up in the clouds to heaven to meet the King and the heroes of faith such as Moses and Elijah!

PROVIDENCE
2 Kings 4

HE SNEEZED SEVEN TIMES

Then he got up again, and walked once to and fro in the house, and went up, and stretched himself upon him; the child sneezed seven times, and the child opened his eyes. 2 Kings 4:35.

Sometimes when you sneeze, someone says, "God bless you." This phrase could have come from the story of the Shunammite's son, whom Elisha raised from the dead. Earlier in the chapter we read that the boy had been a "gift" from God. His mother and father had not been able to have children, but God had intervened, and as a result of Elisha's prayer, the son was born. One day while the boy was working in the fields, he became sick and died. The parents called on Elisha, believing that God could raise their child to life through the prophet.

Elisha performed sixteen miracles that are recorded in 2 Kings. In verse 43 of today's chapter we read that God gave him the ability to multiply bread as Jesus did. With only twenty small barley loaves, one hundred hungry men were fed, and there was even some food left over.

"The lesson is for God's children in every age. When the Lord gives a work to be done, let not men stop to inquire into the reasonableness of the command or the probable result of their efforts to obey. The supply in their hands may seem to fall short of the need to be filled; but in the hands of the Lord it will prove more than sufficient."—*Prophets and Kings*, p. 243.

Scientists who have studied the structure of the bumblebee say that its wings are too small to enable it to fly. But the bumblebee does not know this. It expects to fly, and it does.

There are many things that seem to stand in the way of our doing God's will. If we dwell on these instead of exercising faith, we will not do what God wants us to do. When God calls you to do something for Him, He gives the ability to do it. Next time you see a fat bumblebee flying, say to yourself, "If that bee can fly, I can do whatever God has designed for me to do."

If there is something worthwhile that you should do, resist the temptation to say "I can't." The word *can't* is easily changed to *can* by dropping one letter. It may not be easy to say "I can," but with God's help you can do all things in harmony with His will.

PROVIDENCE
2 Kings 5

DIPPED SEVEN TIMES

So he went down and dipped himself seven times in the Jordan, according to the word of the man of God; and his flesh was restored like the flesh of a little child, and he was clean. 2 Kings 5:14.

Malamulo is a well-known name on the continent of Africa and in many other countries. A school, hospital, and leprosarium have been operated there for almost eighty years. Malamulo is situated in the country of Malawi, about forty miles south of the capital city of Blantyre. A pioneer missionary, J. C. Rodgers, selected the name, which means "commandments."

On one of my visits to Malamulo I met Kampala, a leper. Although he walked with a stick, Kampala was very grateful for his treatment. A filmstrip entitled "Kampala, the Tenth Leper" was made to show what is being done for the sick people and lepers at Malamulo.

If someone had asked Kampala to bathe seven times in the river near Malamulo, I wonder whether he would have done it. Naaman had to be encouraged by his servants to follow Elisha's instructions to dip seven times in the Jordan. Do you think God planned for the word *seven* to occur so many times in the Bible?

Naaman, commander in chief of the army, would not have been healed had it not been for a captive Hebrew maid. This girl said to Naaman's wife, "Would God my lord were with the prophet that is in Samaria! for he would recover him of his leprosy" (2 Kings 5:3). And the proud Naaman had such confidence in the young woman that he did go to the humble prophet for healing.

Although this girl was in a foreign land, she still believed in God and His prophets. She had no doubt been taken captive during one of the wars between Israel and Syria, and she was loyal to her master. "A slave, far from her own home, this little maid was nevertheless one of God's witnesses, unconsciously fulfilling the purpose for which God had chosen Israel as His people."—*Prophets and Kings*, p. 244.

We must remember that no matter where we live or with whom we associate, our primary purpose in life is to witness to God's love and power.

PROVIDENCE
2 Kings 18

THE SECRET OF SUCCESS

And he did what was right in the eyes of the Lord, according to all that David his father had done. He removed the high places. . . . He trusted in the Lord the God of Israel. 2 Kings 18:3-5.

In April we discovered that the Waldensian Christians endeavored to do what was "right in the eyes of the Lord." Like Paul, they could not be forced to deny their faith. Inside the Waldensians' church in Torre Pellice in northern Italy is a painting celebrating the 250th anniversary of the beginnings of the Waldensian movement. The painting shows a tree rooted in rocks, with a Bible supported in the tree. Inscribed on the Bible are the words that when translated read "Be thou faithful until death." Underneath the tree are the words "We vow and promise in the presence of the living God to uphold among us unity and order. We vow fidelity even to the last drop of blood."

The secret of success is to do what is right despite the consequences and to trust in God. Hezekiah, the thirteenth king of Judah, was one of the few kings of Judah or Israel who endeavored to do this. Despite opposition, he ordered that the heathen temples and altars be broken down. He even destroyed the bronze serpent that Moses had made in the wilderness because the people were using it as an object of worship. His work of destroying idolatry was followed by rebuilding the Temple so that the people could worship Jehovah again.

Hezekiah led the people in offering sacrifices to the Lord. His beautiful prayer offered on behalf of Israel is found in 2 Kings 19. The Passover, which had not been celebrated for many years, was held each year during Hezekiah's reign.

"The reign of Hezekiah was characterized by a series of remarkable providences which revealed to the surrounding nations that the God of Israel was with His people."—*Prophets and Kings,* p. 339. God is waiting to do for the remnant church what He did in the days of these prophets and kings. The nations of earth today will see "a series of remarkable providences," and many millions will be led to prepare for the kingdom of heaven. As they see God's *providence* and *passion,* they will be led to follow the *Pattern*—the Lord Jesus Christ.

273

PROVIDENCE
Esther 1

RULER OF THE WORLD

"Let the king give her royal position to another who is better than she." Esther 1:19.

The book of Esther is one of the most interesting and beautiful stories in the Bible. It is full of drama, for the destiny of the entire Hebrew nation depended on the actions of one girl. If Esther had not done her part in God's plan, the nation, which gave the world the Messiah, could have been destroyed.

You will enjoy reading this story. And as you read, you will note God's protection for this beautiful, courageous girl, as well as for the entire Jewish nation. Esther and Ruth are the only books of the Bible that are named after women.

Act 1, Scene 1 of this play, which has been called *The Romance of Providence,* begins in a palace banquet hall. Thousands of people are present, dressed in gorgeous robes, but the central character is Ahasuerus, king of Media-Persia. The banquet, which lasts seven days, is attended by the nobles and governors of 127 provinces, plus the top military men of the empire. In another banquet hall the attractive Queen Vashti is entertaining the important ladies of the kingdom.

"On the seventh day, when the heart of the king was merry with wine, he commanded . . . to bring Vashti the queen before the king with the crown royal, to shew the people and the princes her beauty: for she was fair to look on" (Esther 1:10-12). In Media-Persia it meant death to disobey the king, but Vashti chose to risk this rather than to compromise. She did not believe a woman should parade in front of drunken men. "She acted in harmony with a pure conscience."—*The SDA Bible Commentary,* Ellen G. White Comments, on Esther 1:9, p. 1139. We should, as did Vashti, determine to do what is right, no matter what the consequences. For her the result was that she was dismissed as queen.

This King Ahasuerus was not the one mentioned in the book of Daniel. However, his name occurs or is referred to 127 times in the book of Esther. Many students of the Bible are concerned that the name of God is not mentioned in the book of Esther, and that the book is not quoted in the New Testament. However, as one Bible commentator, Matthew Henry, says, "If the name of God is not there, His finger is."

274

PROVIDENCE
Esther 2

ORPHAN BECOMES QUEEN

The king loved Esther more than all the women, and she found grace and favor in his sight more than all the virgins, so that he set the royal crown on her head and made her queen instead of Vashti. Esther 2:17.

As the curtain opens on Act 2, Scene 1 of this dramatic story, an orphaned Jewish girl is crowned queen of the Persian Empire. Esther was selected after a nationwide search was made for a queen. Since the death of her mother and father, Esther had been adopted by her cousin Mordecai (Esther 2:7). They were both descendants of the Hebrews who had been taken captive by Nebuchadnezzar more than one hundred years earlier.

Esther's original Hebrew name was Hadassah, which means "myrtle." She was no doubt given the name of Esther, which means "star," when she entered the Persian palace. Esther was a star in several ways. In the first place she was a very beautiful young woman, but her beauty was not just outward; she also had a beautiful character. And she proved to be one of God's stars because she played an important role in delivering the nation of Israel.

At the time of her marriage and coronation Ahasuerus gave another great banquet, at which time he granted a reduction in taxes and gave gifts to all the provinces in his kingdom. More than three years had passed since the banquet mentioned in chapter 1. In that time Ahasuerus, with a great number of his men, had suffered a terrible defeat when he attacked the armies of Greece. He lived for only thirteen more years, and no doubt Esther as queen mother had much influence in the court during the reign of her stepson Artaxerxes.

Junior youth who are orphans or who are separated from their parents can find encouragement from the story of Esther. God used this orphan girl, living in a foreign country, in a remarkable way. We have also noted that Daniel and Joseph, separated from their parents and taken to strange countries, were used by God to do a mighty work. Rather than praying for changes in circumstances, we should ask God for courage to do what is right under any circumstances. God needs modern Josephs, Daniels, and Esthers.

PROVIDENCE
Esther 3

ENTER THE VILLAIN

Then Haman said to King Ahasuerus, "There is a certain people scattered abroad and dispersed among the peoples in all the provinces of your kingdom; their laws are different from those of every other people, and they do not keep the king's laws, so that it is not for the king's profit to tolerate them." Esther 3:8.

As the curtain opens on Act 3 of this exciting drama, we see the villain on stage. He has just been promoted to be the king's chief officer. This new position makes him very proud, and he is upset when the porter at the gate, whose name is Mordecai, does not bow to him as everybody else does.

Mordecai would not bow to this man, because he, Mordecai, worshiped only God. "Satan worked at this time to counterwork the purposes of God. Haman cherished bitter malice against Mordecai, a Jew. Mordecai had done Haman no harm, but had simply refused to show him worshipful reverence."—*Prophets and Kings,* p. 600.

The villain determined to get even with Mordecai by destroying him, along with all the Jews. He cast lots to determine the day they were to die.

All that Haman told the king about the Jews, except the statement that they did not keep the king's laws, was true. This summary in our text, from the lips of the enemy of God's people, is really a tribute to the nation of Israel. Even though they were in a foreign land, they remained separate and were a part of God's remnant. No matter where we are, we are to live according to God's plan for our lives. And it is a compliment when people recognize that we are a distinct people with high principles.

Haman has been called the Judas of the Old Testament. He offered to pay the king ten thousand silver coins to sign a decree to kill every Jewish man, woman, and child. No doubt the war with Greece had drained the treasury, so the king was willing to accept this bribe.

At this time in the drama it appears that the villain will triumph and God's people will be destroyed. However, there is a heroine in the palace. She is the queen, and at this point even the king does not realize that she is a Jew (Esther 2:20).

PROVIDENCE
Esther 4

THE HEROINE EMERGES

"Go, gather all the Jews to be found in Susa, and hold a fast on my behalf, and neither eat nor drink for three days, night or day. I and my maids will also fast as you do. Then I will go to the king, though it is against the law; and if I perish, I perish." Esther 4:16.

As the first scene of Act 4 opens, the villain is laughing because he thinks his plot will succeed. The king has placed his signet ring on a decree that all the Jewish people are to be destroyed. As the curtain opens on another scene in this act, we see thousands of Jews, scattered throughout the country, praying earnestly. Although there is no reference to Satan in the book of Esther, he is really the author of Haman's plot. "Satan himself, the hidden instigator of the scheme, was trying to get rid of those who preserved the knowledge of the true God."—*Prophets and Kings,* p. 601.

At this climactic time in the drama the God of heaven intervenes for the protection of His people. However, what these troubled ones did not know was that He had made provision for their protection and deliverance five years before, when one of His faithful young people was made queen of Persia. "But the plots of the enemy were defeated by a Power that reigns among the children of men. In the providence of God, Esther, a Jewess who feared the Most High, had been made queen of the Medo-Persian kingdom. . . . Angels that excel in strength had been commissioned by God to protect His people while they 'stood for their lives.' "—*Ibid.,* pp. 601, 602.

In God's providence there was another hero in the drama. Mordecai was God's man at the right place at the right time. He kept Esther informed about the Jews and inspired her to risk her life to save God's people.

Although Esther was queen in a pagan king's palace, she did not lose her hold on God. She loved Him so much that she was prepared to give her life to do what He wanted her to do and what He had planned for her to do. Even the queen was not allowed to go to the throne room and ask a favor of the king without being invited. If she did so and the king did not extend his scepter to her, she would be executed. But Esther's reply was immediate. She said that she would go and, if need be, perish in her attempt to save her people.

PROVIDENCE
Esther 5

THE QUEEN'S BANQUET

And when the king saw Queen Esther standing in the court, she found favor in his sight and he held out to Esther the golden scepter that was in his hand. Then Esther approached and touched the top of the scepter. And the king said to her, "What is it, Queen Esther? What is your request? It shall be given you, even to the half of my kingdom." Esther 5:2, 3.

Why did Esther ask the king to come to a banquet? Why didn't she ask him for what she really wanted—a pardon for the Jews? Was she confused by the favorable reception she received? One day we will be able to ask Esther these questions, but as we study the story it seems that this was not the time to ask the favor. Like Esther, we must learn tact and diplomacy. Solomon, the wise man, says that there is a time to speak and a time to be silent.

The queen carefully chose the time that seemed best for her request that the king bring Haman to the banquet. If we live close to the Lord, He grants us wisdom to know the best time to do things. It is often hard to wait, but God wants His people to learn patience, one of the graces of the Christian life.

Proud Haman gleefully told his wife and friends of this new honor—he was going to a private banquet with the king and queen. However, he admitted, "'Yet all this does me no good, so long as I see Mordecai the Jew sitting at the king's gate'" (Esther 5:13, R.S.V.). It seems strange that, with all his riches and honors and people bowing to him, one poor Jew could spoil it all for Haman. Just as a small screw may stop a big machine, so one gate official upset the prime minister of Persia.

In order to remove the black spot in his world of sunshine, Haman built gallows on which he planned to hang Mordecai. He made them about 75 feet high, so that the execution could be seen easily. It is evident from this story that unchecked hatred leads to murder. Solomon said, "As . . . [a man] thinketh in his heart, so is he" (Prov. 23:7).

The best cure for hatred is to pray for the grace to love. It is not possible to love and hate someone at the same time.

278

PROVIDENCE
Esther 6

AWAKE ALL NIGHT

On that night the king could not sleep; and he gave orders to bring the book of memorable deeds, the chronicles, and they were read before the king. Esther 6:1.

Esther had sought an unexpected audience with the king once before in order to tell him that two men were plotting to kill him. At that time Mordecai had warned the queen of the plot against the king's life. You can read the story in the last verses of Esther 2. When Esther appeared to announce the banquet, Ahasuerus possibly thought she was coming to tell him of another plot to kill him. God used this event to prepare the king's mind for the request that Esther was going to make.

From the record books of the kingdom from which the king read when he could not sleep, he was reminded of how Mordecai had saved his life. He called his servants and asked them whether Mordecai had been rewarded, and they said, "'Nothing has been done for him'" (Esther 6:3, R.S.V.). In God's providence, Haman was at that moment entering the palace court, and when the king heard that, he said, "Let him come in."

When the monarch asked, "'What shall be done to the man whom the king delights to honor?'" (verse 6, R.S.V.), Haman thought Ahasuerus was talking about him. He therefore said that the man should be dressed in royal robes, put on the king's horse, and led through the streets. He added that someone should walk ahead and call out, "'"Thus shall it be done to the man whom the king delights to honor"'" (verse 9, R.S.V.).

You can imagine Haman's surprise and horror when the king commanded, "'Make haste, take the robes and the horse, as you have said, and do so to Mordecai the Jew who sits at the king's gate. Leave out nothing that you have mentioned'" (verse 10, R.S.V.). The day he led the horse with Mordecai on it through the streets must have been one of the worst of Haman's life. This part of the story of Esther proves that we reap what we sow.

Apparently Haman had his own wise men, and they told him, "'If Mordecai, before whom you have begun to fall, is of the Jewish people, you will not prevail against him but will surely fall before him'" (verse 13, R.S.V.). This message was delivered to him just as the king's servants took him "in haste to the banquet that Esther had prepared" (verse 14, R.S.V.).

PROVIDENCE
Esther 7

THE VILLAIN EXECUTED

Then Queen Esther answered, "If I have found favor in your sight, O king, and if it please the king, let my life be given me at my petition, and my people at my request." Esther 7:3.

In some countries banquets last for several days. The first banquet we read about in Esther lasted seven days; this one, arranged by the queen, lasted two days. Although the king was interested in food, he was more interested in learning what request Esther would make.

When the queen revealed that the death decree signed by the king included her, Ahasuerus was angry. Apparently it did not matter to him that thousands of his subjects were to be slain, but when he realized that his beautiful, loyal queen was included, he demanded to know who was responsible for this plot. Esther replied, "'A foe and enemy! This wicked Haman!'" (Esther 7:6, R.S.V.).

At that moment, with his life in danger, Haman revealed that he was a coward. He threw himself on his knees close to the queen and begged for his life. However, the king was further angered by this action and immediately commanded that Haman be executed on the gallows he had prepared for Mordecai. Those gallows were standing near Haman's house, and the punishment fitted the crime of this wicked man.

It was a short time between the discovery of Haman's crime and his execution. Apparently one of the king's servants told the monarch of Haman's plot to hang Mordecai. Sometimes it seems that wicked men and women prosper, but their prosperity is temporary. The same justice that led to the execution of Haman will be given to all who have tried to take God from His throne or who have persecuted and killed the subjects of the King of kings. There is a day of judgment for all who have lived on earth.

The story of Haman also shows that we should not be misled by other people's opinions. Those who enjoyed Haman's favor while he was in power did not speak up for him when he was condemned. Some of those who shouted "Hosanna to the Son of David" (Matt. 21:9) when Jesus entered Jerusalem also cried "Away with him, crucify him" (John 19:15) just a few days later. We can expect false friends to desert us when we need help, but Jesus will never leave or forsake us.

PROVIDENCE
Esther 8

THE FINAL ACT

The writing was in the name of King Ahasuerus and sealed with the king's ring, and letters were sent by mounted couriers riding on swift horses that were used in the king's service, bred from the royal stud. Esther 8:10.

The drama is not finished. The plot to destroy Esther, Mordecai, and God's people has been exposed and the villain has been executed. But the decree to destroy all the Jews in one day is still binding.

Historians tell us that the laws of the Medes and Persians, issued by the king and sealed with his ring, could not be changed. There was no way that even King Ahasuerus could cancel his decree to execute the Jews. How were God's people to be saved? What was the message of the second document that was sent out in the name of the king and carried by the couriers on swift horses?

The exact words of the decree are not recorded in the Scriptures. However, we do discover that Queen Esther and Mordecai wrote it themselves. The king said, "'And you may write as you please with regard to the Jews, in the name of the king'" (Esther 8:8, R.S.V.). What do you think they wrote?

Because Esther lived so close to God, she had the wisdom to think of what could be done to save her own life and the lives of the Jews. In verses 11 and 12 of Esther 8 we read that the second decree authorized the Jews to defend themselves.

On the day that they were to be killed, the Jewish people gathered in their cities to defend themselves. "Angels that excel in strength had been commissioned by God to protect His people while they 'stood for their lives.'"—*Prophets and Kings,* p. 602.

This was an unusual change of events for the Jews, and illustrates God's providence and protecting hand for His people. Mordecai, who had been so faithful and had advised and inspired Queen Esther, was given the position that Haman had held, becoming next to the king in authority. The humble keeper of the gate was dressed in a royal robe of blue and white and wore a crown of gold. Sometimes even in this life those who brave the consequences and do right are rewarded. And all will be rewarded in the kingdom of heaven that is soon to be established.

281

PROVIDENCE
Esther 9

THE DRAMA REPEATED

That these days should be remembered and kept throughout every generation, in every family, province, and city, and that these days of Purim should never fall into disuse among the Jews, nor should the commemoration of these days cease among their descendants. Esther 9:28.

The Feast of Purim is still celebrated by Jews today. The Hebrew word *pur* means "lot," and the feast was so named because Haman cast lots to determine when the Jews were to be destroyed. The celebration was authorized by Queen Esther and Mordecai, the new prince of Persia, to remind God's people of Satan's plot and of God's providence to save them.

The fact that the Jews still celebrate this feast also has lessons for all Christians. These lessons are described by Ellen White in the book *Prophets and Kings:* "The decree that will finally go forth against the remnant people of God will be very similar to that issued by Ahasuerus against the Jews. Today the enemies of the true church see in the little company keeping the Sabbath commandment, a Mordecai at the gate. The reverence of God's people for His law is a constant rebuke to those who have cast off the fear of the Lord. . . .

"Satan will arouse indignation against the minority who refuse to accept popular customs and traditions. Men of position and reputation will join with the lawless and the vile to take counsel against the people of God. Wealth, genius, education, will combine to cover them with contempt. Persecuting rulers, ministers, and church members will conspire against them. With voice and pen, by boasts, threats, and ridicule, they will seek to overthrow their faith. By false representations and angry appeals, men will stir up the passions of the people. Not having a 'Thus saith the Scriptures' to bring against the advocates of the Bible Sabbath, they will resort to oppressive enactments to supply the lack. To secure popularity and patronage, legislators will yield to the command for Sunday laws. But those who fear God, cannot accept an institution that violates a precept of the Decalogue. On this battlefield will be fought the last great conflict in the controversy between truth and error. . . . Today, as in the days of Esther and Mordecai, the Lord will vindicate His truth and His people."—Pages 605, 606.

PROVIDENCE
Esther 10

PROTECTION GUARANTEED

And all the acts of his power and might, and the full account of the high honor of Mordecai, to which the king advanced him, are they not written in the Book of the Chronicles of the kings of Media and Persia? Esther 10:2.

This short book, which shows God's providence, opened with the exploits of the ruler of the largest empire on earth at that time and closes with the acts of one of God's princes—Mordecai. King Ahasuerus died in obscurity, and his name is recorded only in history books. Mordecai, an obscure official at the king's palace gate, rose to become prime minister, and he has his name written in the book of life. We will have the opportunity of talking to Mordecai in heaven.

The book of Esther opens with a feast given by the king for the mighty people of the kingdom to plan a military campaign against Greece. It closes with a feast of triumph that was held after a successful spiritual campaign by the people of God. There were two queens mentioned in the book of Esther. One was willing to sacrifice her crown in order to preserve the purity of her womanhood; the other was prepared to sacrifice her life to save God's people, who were also her people. As we consider Esther's willingness to die, we see a revelation of Christ. Jesus was not only willing to but did lay down His life for His people, and those who accept Him will find salvation.

The real villain of the book of Esther is not Haman, but Satan. Satan was the one who masterminded the plan to exterminate God's people so that Jesus would not be born as predicted. The real hero of the book of Esther is God, who altered Satan's plan and saved His people. The dramatic story of Esther is a constant reminder to us that our protection as a church and as individual Christians is guaranteed. The power of God is unlimited. The love of God for His people compels Him to do everything possible to save them. We must not limit God in our thinking. He can do anything. We can trust in His providence.

PRAISES
Psalm 117

THE MIDDLE CHAPTER

Praise the Lord, all nations! Extol him, all peoples! For great is his steadfast love toward us; and the faithfulness of the Lord endures for ever. Praise the Lord! Psalm 117.

The middle chapter of the Bible, Psalm 117, is also the shortest of the 150 psalms. The opening and closing statement of this psalm, "Praise the Lord," is the theme of the whole book.

As we begin our study of Psalms, let us consider what praise to God really is. Is it applause? Is it flattery? Sometimes when people praise us they might not really mean it or we might not deserve it. Our praise to God is more than an expression of approval; it is glorifying and worshiping Him. We have already discovered that God is worthy of praise because of His character, the aspects of which include *light, love,* and *life.*

The psalms are songs of praise that are to be accompanied by musical instruments. In Psalm 33 reference is made to singing songs of praise with a harp of ten strings. Musical instruments in David's time included percussion, string, and wind. In Solomon's Temple there was a very large musical organization, no doubt planned by David (1 Chronicles 25).

As we will discover from the twenty-six psalms we study this month, there are many reasons to praise God. In Psalm 117 we note three: God is the supreme object of worship. He is not worshiped out of fear, but because of "steadfast love toward us" (verse 2, R.S.V.). We also note that His faithfulness or truth endures forever. These are attributes of God that lead us to praise Him. It is very important to pray, but we should also praise God in our prayers and in our conversation with other people.

As predicted in Psalms, one day not only will God's people praise Him, but "all nations" as well. This was one of Jesus' favorite songs. "Before leaving the upper chamber, the Saviour led His disciples in a song of praise. His voice was heard, not in the strains of some mournful lament, but in the joyful notes of the Passover hallel: . . . Psalm 117."—*The Desire of Ages,* p. 672.

PRAISES
Psalm 66

THE BOOK OF PRAISES

Make a joyful noise to God, all the earth; sing the glory of his name; give to him glorious praise! Psalm 66:1, 2.

The Old Testament was written in Hebrew, and the Hebrew word for psalm is *tehallim,* which means "praises." This word is based on the word *halal,* which means "to praise."

Only seventy-three of the psalms are definitely stated in the original manuscripts as being written by David. About fifty others list no author, and David may have written some of these also. Solomon was possibly the author of two, and you may be surprised to learn that Moses wrote one.

There are five major divisions to the Psalms, and each of these sections ends with a doxology and amen or hallelujah. In some Bible versions there are headings at the beginning of these divisions. These are Book 1, Book 2, et cetera. Book 1 includes Psalms 1-41. See whether you can discover the other four divisions. In the songs of praise we have a picture of a powerful God giving relief to man in trouble. "The psalms of David pass through the whole range of experience, from the depths of conscious guilt and self-condemnation to the loftiest faith and the most exalted communing with God."—*Patriarchs and Prophets,* p. 754.

The psalms are as meaningful today as they were when they were first written, because people's basic needs do not change. In these wonderful words we find encouragement and inspiration.

Psalm 66 was intended to be sung by a choir (verses 1-12) and a soloist (verses 13-20). It is a call to praise God for His works on behalf of the nation as well as individuals. How wonderful to know that the One who delivered a whole nation through the Red Sea (verse 6) is interested in us individually. "Come and hear, all ye that fear God, and I will declare what he hath done for my soul" (verse 16). Although there are many evidences of God's power in history, the greatest evidence for Christianity is the personal testimony. When we consider what God has done for us, as expressed in this psalm, we will praise Him and keep our vows. When we become Christians, we make promises to God, and we must keep in close contact with our heavenly Father and mend any broken vows each evening.

285

PRAISES
Psalm 2

A THOUSAND YEARS IN ADVANCE

I will tell of the decree of the Lord: He said to me, "You are my son, today I have begotten you." Psalm 2:7.

Many of the psalms, written as long as a thousand years before Jesus came to earth, contain predictions concerning His birth, life, ministry, death, resurrection, ascension, and future role. These are called Messianic prophecies, because Jesus was the Messiah, which means "anointed one." Our Lord was anointed with the Holy Spirit at the time of His baptism. When we are baptized, we also need to pray that the Spirit will come into our lives in a special way.

Three special titles of Jesus are recorded in Psalm 2: Anointed, King, and Son. From earliest times kings and queens have been anointed with oil, and today when English monarchs are crowned this ritual is still carried out. However, because Jesus was anointed with the oil of the Holy Spirit and was the Son of God, He is the only one who can be "King of kings and Lord of lords." His dominion will soon be given to Him, and everyone will recognize that He is the rightful ruler of this earth. We will be subjects in His kingdom if we allow Him to be king of our lives today. We make Him king in exactly the same way that people honor kings on this earth—we pledge allegiance to Him and are faithful under all circumstances. This can be done only through the power that He grants us, and that power is unlimited.

No other Old Testament book is quoted more in the New Testament than is Psalms. Our Morning Watch text today is quoted in Hebrews 1:5. Similar words were also spoken by God from heaven when Jesus was baptized.

Handel, in his oratorio *The Messiah,* quotes five verses from this psalm immediately preceding "The Hallelujah Chorus," and when that powerful chorus is sung, the audience stands in respect.

Soon everyone will proclaim that Jesus is the rightful anointed king of the universe. However, only those who are His subjects now will be citizens of His kingdom. We can sing "The Hallelujah Chorus" with real meaning if Jesus, the Anointed One, the Son of God, is king of our lives.

PRAISES
Psalm 16

FULNESS OF JOY

Thou dost show me the path of life; in thy presence there is fulness of joy, in thy right hand are pleasures for evermore. Psalm 16:11.

Have you ever stood by a fast-flowing river and watched the water swirl quickly around the rocks and splash over them? This rapid movement typifies the joy and pleasure of our childhood years. Our lives are like rivers, and when we are young, there is real delight in meeting new friends, going on vacation, going to camp, and enjoying hobbies and many other activities. As we grow older, the river slows down, and life becomes more like a deep-water lake. There may not be so many fast-moving events that bring immediate joy, but there is a deepening of experience and an inward peace in spite of the trials we encounter. God in His love has given us a wonderful capacity for happiness. It is His desire that we have "fulness of joy," which is that joy and the pleasures that do not destroy the Christian life. These are found in God's presence. The promise is that we "shall not be moved" (Ps. 16:8) if we keep the Lord before us. We will have joy that is independent of the happenings of life when we put Jesus first. Over the years I have written the following lines in autograph books, on pieces of paper, and in hymnbooks for hundreds of young people in many countries, and I would like to pass this secret of joy on to you:

J esus first,

O thers next,

Y ourself last . . . spells joy.

Psalm 16 is also one of the great Messianic psalms, but the full import of its predictions concerning the resurrection of the Lord Jesus Christ was not unveiled until New Testament times. Peter's words on the day of Pentecost stated that the prophecy made by David a thousand years before, "Thou wilt not leave my soul in hell, neither wilt thou suffer thine Holy One to see corruption," was a direct prediction of the resurrection of Jesus (see Acts 2:25-31). This is another example to us that the Bible is its own interpreter and that we do not need to guess at the meaning of verses.

A PSALM OF THE CROSS

They have pierced my hands and feet . . . they divide my garments among them, and for my raiment they cast lots. Psalm 22:16-18.

These accurate details of the crucifixion of Jesus were predicted about one thousand years before they happened. Our Lord's hands and feet were pierced for you and me, and if we had a clear picture of Jesus suffering the most cruel death a pagan mind could think of, we would earnestly turn away from sin. It is a fact that every time we transgress, we crucify afresh the Son of God (Heb. 6:6). If we had been living when Jesus was put to death, no one could have persuaded us to put nails into His hands and feet. And today no one should be able to persuade us to crucify Him afresh by sinning.

If the Roman soldiers had torn Jesus' garment in pieces and each one kept a piece, this prophecy would have failed. However, it is impossible for the Lord's word to fail, for He knows the end from the beginning. Many people have tried to discredit the Bible, but it stands as the reliable word of God. The blacksmith who used to form horseshoes with a hammer and an anvil wore out many hammers, but he never wore out the anvil. It is the same with the critics of the Bible; the critics themselves become worn out, like the hammers, but the Word of God remains as solid as ever.

There are some statements in the Psalms that apply to David, but many apply only to Jesus. As we discovered yesterday, when we compare scripture with scripture, we interpret the meaning correctly and do not have to rely on the explanations of other people. This is one reason we studied and read the book of Mark first. We need to know the Person of the Bible. Then we will clearly see the purpose, the plan, the power, the praise, and the prophecy, and understand all the other words of *light, love,* and *life.*

The cross is almost the same shape as a plus sign, and it certainly is God's plus sign to our world. Everyone needs to add more love to his daily life, and the best source of love is seen in the cross of Calvary.

PRAISES
Psalm 23

THE BEST-LOVED PSALM

The Lord is my shepherd, I shall not want. Psalm 23:1.

Sometimes called "the pearl of Psalms," the twenty-third has for almost three thousand years been the best-known psalm and one of the favorite passages of the Bible. We have come to appreciate not only the exquisite picture of the relationship between a shepherd and his sheep but also the assurance the words give us of comfort, security, and eternal life.

David was a shepherd boy, and we cannot really understand the beauty of the psalm until we know what it meant to herd sheep on the hills of Palestine. The shepherd actually lived with the sheep, and they soon learned to know his voice and would come to him when he called. When the shepherd walked over the hillside, the sheep followed, for they knew that he would find shade from the burning sun and pools of water from which they could drink. He carried a rod, and with this protected the flock from wolves, lions, bears, and thieves. Sometimes the shepherd would take the sheep back to a protected place at night, but on other occasions he would sleep in a small tent near the flock. When a sheep was wounded, the shepherd would bathe the wound with oil, and even carry the injured one.

The comparison of Jesus to a shepherd is very appropriate. He knows His people by name, and they obey His voice. He has declared that He will be with us until the end of the world, and He is a place of shelter in time of storm. He provides us with the water of life, of which we may drink, never to thirst again. He certainly heals broken hearts and anoints His followers with the Holy Spirit, represented by oil.

We will "dwell in the house of the Lord for ever" if we know the Shepherd's voice. There are many voices calling us to follow, but there is only one true Shepherd. If we accept the Lord as our shepherd, we will not want for spiritual strength or the necessities of life. How wonderful it is that God's goodness and mercy are given to us in such measure that we can say, "My cup runneth over." There is also a challenge in this phrase, because "the cup most difficult to carry is the cup that is full to the brim." We need to stay close to the Good Shepherd not only when things are going wrong but also when everything is just fine.

PRAISES
Psalm 24

THE RIGHTFUL KING

Lift up your heads, O gates! and be lifted up, O ancient doors! that the King of glory may come in. Psalm 24:7.

When we stand on the roof of a tall building or climb to the top of a mountain, we do not look in only one direction. In order to get a complete picture of the scene, we need to look in all directions. It is the same when we study the Word of God. We must not limit our reading to one chapter or even one book of the Bible. As we read the best-loved psalm, we see Jesus as the shepherd caring for His sheep. However, if we look at the psalm that precedes the twenty-third, we see the Saviour dying for sinners. Now as we look at Psalm 24, we see the Saviour and Shepherd being crowned king. This means that if I have accepted Christ as my Saviour and allowed Him to care for me as my shepherd, I can be one of His subjects.

Jesus is the rightful king because "the earth is the Lord's and the fulness thereof; the world, and they that dwell therein" (Ps. 24:1). He is also the sovereign of the universe, for He is the "King of glory" and the "Lord of hosts" (verse 10). He has won these titles, for He has been victorious in the battle over sin.

Psalm 24 was first sung on the occasion of King David's triumphal entry into Jerusalem with the holy ark of God. David saved his people when as a young man he slew Goliath. He was also a shepherd who cared for sheep and the children of Israel. The words of the last part of Psalm 24 were sung by the heavenly choirs when the angels welcomed Jesus, the Son of David, back to the heavenly Jerusalem (see *The Desire of Ages,* p. 833). Both David and Jesus were savior, shepherd, and king. This is an interesting fact, but it is more important for us to learn how we can be subjects of the heavenly kingdom. Just as it was necessary when the ark was going into Jerusalem to know who would "ascend . . . the hill of the Lord" (verse 3), so we need to discover who will enter the heavenly kingdom. According to David, the first prerequisites are that the subjects of the kingdom of God will have "clean hands, and a pure heart" (verse 4), and they will always tell the truth.

PRAISES
Psalm 110

OUR HIGH PRIEST

"You are a priest for ever after the order of Melchizedek."
Psalm 110:4.

Yesterday we discovered that both David in the Old Testament and Jesus in the New Testament stated that only those who have pure hearts will be subjects of the King of glory. It would be interesting to learn more about that kingdom, but the Bible is not a geography book about heaven. It is a guidebook on how to get there. We know that heaven is going to be wonderful, but while in this world we must concentrate on becoming, by the grace of Jesus, subjects of that kingdom.

Psalm 110 is another Messianic psalm, the last of this type we will study this month. It was written more than a thousand years before Christ was born, and the person the psalm describes can be none other than Jesus. The psalm must contain a very important truth, because there are more references to it and quotes from it in the New Testament than from any other portion of the Old Testament.

The most important teaching in this psalm is that Jesus is not only Saviour, shepherd, and king, but He is also the high priest. In the book of Genesis we discovered that Melchizedek was a priest-king of Jerusalem, and the author of Hebrews quotes our Morning Watch text to support the fact that Jesus is the ministering high priest in the courts of heaven (chap. 5:5, 6). The priest in the Old Testament sanctuary ministered on behalf of the people and acted as mediator. Jesus is ministering on our behalf and is the only "mediator between God and men" (1 Tim. 2:5).

Most Christians know that Jesus was a servant, Saviour, and shepherd, and that He will be King of kings and Lord of lords. However, many do not know this very important role that Jesus plays as high priest. Unfortunately, there are many who look to other people as their mediators, or endeavor to find forgiveness for their sins by doing good things. Those of us who know that Jesus is our high priest and mediator and rejoice in the knowledge of sins forgiven, begin every day with confidence, that by the sacrifice and mediation of Jesus, we can have pure hearts and see God. When we know this truth, we must share it with others.

PRAISES
Psalm 113

FAMILY PSALMS

Who makes the woman in a childless house a happy mother of children. Psalm 113:9, N.E.B.

Psalm 113 is the first of five psalms known as "Family Psalms of Praise." Our text today refers to "mother"—one of the few times the word is used in the book of Psalms. Surely one of the great reasons for praising God is the fact that He gives us children. Psalms 113 and 114 were sung by families at the beginning of special feasts, such as the Passover. Psalms 115 through 118 were sung by the family at the close of a meal. They were probably the psalms that Jesus and the disciples sang at the Last Supper (see Matt. 26:30; Mark 14:26).

Mother, mentioned in this first hallel psalm, is rejoicing because she has children. When Samuel the prophet was born, his mother, Hannah, rejoiced: "For this child I prayed; and the Lord hath given me my petition which I asked of him: therefore also I have lent him to the Lord; as long as he liveth he shall be lent to the Lord" (1 Sam. 1:27, 28).

Hannah kept her vow, and when Samuel was very young, she took him to the Temple to help the high priest with his duties. Eli "was awed and humbled as he beheld this mother's great sacrifice in parting with her only child, that she might devote him to the service of God" *(Patriarchs and Prophets,* p. 571).

The joy Hannah experienced is the joy that God intends for every mother to have. It is His plan that mothers dedicate their children to the Lord, that their children, like Samuel and Jesus, might grow in favor with the Lord and with men, and that families will be bound together like a book.

"The family is like a book, the children are the leaves;
The parents are the cover that protective beauty gives.
At first the pages of the book are blank and lively fair,
But time soon writes its memories, and paints its pictures there.
Love is the little golden clasp that binds up the trust.
Oh, break it not, lest all the leaves shall scatter and be lost!"

PRAISES
Psalm 8

STARRY-NIGHT SONG

When I look at thy heavens, the work of thy fingers, the moon and the stars which thou hast established; what is man that thou art mindful of him, and the son of man that thou dost care for him? Psalm 8:3, 4.

Many nights David the shepherd boy, alone with the sheep, looked up into the starry sky. Perhaps he composed Psalm 8 by the campfire. (We note many references to nature in the psalms.) Psalm 8 is the first of four psalms that we will read and study that primarily praise God for His works of creation.

As we look up into the stars and see the greatness of God's universe, we also are led to ask, "What is man, that thou art mindful of him?" Our heavenly Father is very mindful of us. Human beings are the best of all God's creation, for we reflect His image. This truth, first stated in the book of Genesis, is repeated in Psalm 8, verses 5 and 6. Following that glorious thought, it is God's plan that we have dominion over the animals, birds, and fish. However, there is a more important fact that shows our value, and that is that God's only Son, Jesus, died that we might be saved from sin.

There are parts of the Bible that have two meanings. Some people feel that this is true about many verses of the Bible, and while we may not agree in all cases, there are some verses into which God has put two applications, and these are the ones we should study carefully. When God intends for us to see a double application of a passage of Scripture, He makes it evident. Hebrews 2:8, 9 applies the words of Psalm 8:4-6 to Jesus. He certainly was the Son of man, He had dominion, and for a while He became man, who is less than God and lower than the angels. Jesus did this in order to be like us, and it is a tremendous source of encouragement to us now to know that our Lord was victorious and that He has promised us victory.

How wonderful it is to learn this tremendous truth about Jesus in the history and poetry of the Psalms! This "Song of the Starry Night" leads us to praise God for creating the universe. We also praise Him for allowing Jesus to come to this earth as a man in order to save us, and for His power to strengthen us in the hour of temptation.

293

PRAISES
Psalm 19

BETTER AND SWEETER

More to be desired are they than gold, even much fine gold;
sweeter also than honey. Psalm 19:10.

Can you imagine something that is better than gold and sweeter than honey? Gold is certainly valuable, and it's difficult to imagine anything sweeter than honey. However, someone who had a lot of gold and all the honey he needed stated that God's law and His Word are better and sweeter than these things. Since then, millions in every generation, whether they have gold and honey or not, have agreed with David.

There are six different terms used to describe the revelation of God in which David rejoiced. These words—*law, testimony, statutes, commandment, fear,* and *judgments*—are respectively declared to be perfect, sure, right, pure, clean, and true. When we take notice of God's revealed will as stated in the Scriptures, including the Ten Commandments, the results are cause for rejoicing. The perfect law revives us; the sure testimony gives us wisdom; the right statutes are cause for rejoicing; the pure commandments enlighten our eyes; the clean fear of the Lord gives us endurance; and the true ordinances of the Lord, through Jesus, assure that we are righteous. No wonder David was excited about God's revelation through the Written Word.

The revelation of God through nature, so ably described in the first six verses of Psalm 19, is also cause for rejoicing. In many ways "the heavens declare the glory of God, and the firmament sheweth his handywork" (verse 1). Nature has always pointed men and women to God. Unfortunately, some who live close to nature worship idols, but they too may be seeking after truth. When we have our eyes fixed on the Creator rather than the creature who was created, then we will be drawn nearer to God through a study of the natural world. "Nature and revelation alike testify of God's love."—*Steps to Christ,* p. 9.

One of the shortest but finest prayers in the Bible is found in Psalm 19:13, 14. With David we need to pray that we will be God's servants, that we will be kept from willful sinning, and that through our Lord and Redeemer we will be upright.

PRAISES
Psalm 29

SONG OF SEVEN THUNDERS

The Lord will give strength unto his people; the Lord will bless his people with peace. Psalm 29:11, K.J.V.

Exactly one hour after my family and I left Matandani School in Malawi, the mission Land Rover stalled on an isolated road. Leaving my wife and two children, I started walking back to the school. I noticed leopard footprints on the side of the dirt road, and a chill went up my spine. Then, as often happens about four o'clock in the afternoon in Africa, the thunder rolled and the lightning flashed across the sky, and the heavens opened with torrential rain. There was nothing for me to do but to keep walking. And there, alone in the midst of an African thunderstorm, I sang praises to God, even though I did not know whether I could reach a village before dark.

As a shepherd boy David knew what it was to be caught in a thunderstorm, and Psalm 29 is a vivid description of one. In typical Hebrew poetic language he describes the rolling thunder, torrents of water, lofty trees broken, mountains and wilderness shaken, lightning striking the earth, and terrified animals in the midst of the storm. He describes the storm as coming in from the Mediterranean and sweeping Palestine, leaving devastation in its trail.

The psalm is entitled "The Song of the Seven Thunders," because the phrase "the voice of the Lord" is used seven times. And David identifies this with the thunder. He is not describing just a thunderstorm; this is a formal praise to Jehovah for His might, strength, glory, power, and majesty. However, the key verse is our Morning Watch text, which states that the mighty God who controls the thunderstorm is abundantly able to give His people peace in the midst of storms.

The Lord blessed me in the midst of that thunderstorm in Africa, and although I was soaked to the skin and walking in mud, I reached a village before dark, where I found an African pastor with a motorbike. We have all been in spiritual thunderstorms, and we know that God is able to grant us peace in the midst of trials, bereavement, failure, and discouragement.

PRAISES
Psalm 104

POET'S CREATION STORY

Bless the Lord, O my soul! O Lord my God, thou art very great! Thou art clothed with honor and majesty. Psalm 104:1.

Those who believe that the Bible is the Inspired Word of God have clear statements showing that God created the world in six literal days. This fact is not only stated in Genesis but is reaffirmed by Jesus when He said, "Have ye not read, that he which made them at the beginning made them male and female . . . ?" (Matt. 19:4). Also David, in this fourth nature psalm, declares God to be the Creator.

Although this psalm focuses on the Creator rather than the created, it reaffirms the Creation record. As a matter of fact, Psalm 104 is really a paraphrase of Genesis 1. If we compare the first chapter of the Book of Beginnings and this psalm of Creation, we note these similarities:

First day—God created light (verses 2-4; Genesis 1 and 2).

Second day—God created the firmament (verses 2-4; Gen. 1:6-8).

Third day—God made the land, sea, and vegetation (verses 5-18; Gen. 1:9-13).

Fourth day—God created the sun, moon, and stars (verses 19-23; Gen. 1:14-19).

Fifth day—God created the fish, birds, and small creatures (verses 24-30; Gen. 1:20-23).

The psalmist became excited about the wonders of God's creation and did not comment on what happened on the sixth and seventh days of Creation. Instead, he uttered praise to God and stated that he would sing praises as long as he lived. The psalm closes as it opened: "Bless the Lord, O my soul!"

Moses records after each day of Creation that "God saw that it was good." Everything God does is good, but David, in this poetic version of the events of Genesis 1, declares that *God is good.* There is a difference of only one letter between the spelling of *God* and *good,* and each time we see the word *good,* we should sing praises to *God* for His *goodness.*

PRAISES
Psalm 51

WHITER THAN SNOW

Purge me with hyssop, and I shall be clean; wash me, and I shall be whiter than snow. Psalm 51:7.

The "top of the world" has attracted many explorers. One of the first to lead an excursion to the North Pole was Sir George Nares. In 1875 and 1876 he led voyages in the ships *Alert* and *Discovery.* Sailing the wooden ships through the ice pack was dangerous, and many lives were lost in the attempt. One man who sailed with the admiral is buried on the side of a snow-covered hill near Cape Beechey. A stone marks his grave, and on it is a copper plaque with these words: "Wash me, and I shall be whiter than snow."

It is hard to imagine anything whiter than snow, so this is a good illustration of how completely God cleanses those who look to Jesus, repent, and are forgiven of their sins. Today's psalm teaches that we are to confess our sins to God, and reassures us that when we do this sincerely and exercise faith in Jesus, we will be completely cleansed.

David has been called one of the great confessors of the Bible. This is shown by the fact that he wrote five of the seven penitential psalms. Psalm 51, one of the outstanding expressions of repentance, was written by David after he broke the seventh commandment (see *Education,* p. 165).

Although David had sinned, he did not say that he was too bad for God to forgive him. "Do not listen to the enemy's suggestion to stay away from Christ until you have made yourself better, until you are good enough to come to God. If you wait until then you will never come. . . . Make the prayer of David your own: 'Purge me with hyssop, and I shall be clean; wash me, and I shall be whiter than snow.'"—*Prophets and Kings,* p. 320.

Psalm 51 is important because "from it we may learn what course to follow if we have departed from the Lord" (Manuscript 147, 1903). This psalm was a favorite of John Bunyan, author of *Pilgrim's Progress,* and we will progress on our pilgrimage when we pray, "Create in me a clean heart, O God; and renew a right spirit within me" (verse 10).

297

PRAISES
Psalm 92

PALM-TREE CHRISTIANS

The righteous flourish like the palm tree, and grow like a cedar in Lebanon. Psalm 92:12.

"See the weary traveler toiling over the hot sands of the desert, with no shelter to protect him from the rays of a tropical sun. His water supply fails, and he has nothing to slake his burning thirst. His tongue becomes swollen; he staggers like a drunken man. Visions of home and friends pass before his mind, as he believes himself ready to perish in the terrible desert. Suddenly those in advance send forth a shout of joy. In the distance, looming up out of the dreary, sandy waste, is a palm tree, green and flourishing. Hope quickens his pulses. That which gives vigor and freshness to the palm tree will cool the fevered pulses, and give life to those who are perishing with thirst.

"As the palm tree, drawing nourishment from fountains of living water, is green and flourishing in the midst of the desert, so the Christian may draw rich supplies of grace from the fountain of God's love, and may guide weary souls, that are full of unrest and ready to perish in the desert of sin, to those waters of which they may drink, and live. The Christian is ever pointing his fellow-men to Jesus, who invites, 'If any man thirst, let him come unto me and drink.' This fountain never fails us; we may draw, and draw again."—*Signs of the Times*, Oct. 26, 1904.

"Christians indeed may be fitly represented by the palm tree. They are like Enoch; although surrounded by corrupting influences, their faith takes hold of the Unseen. They walk with God, deriving strength and grace from Him to withstand the moral pollution surrounding them. Like Daniel in the courts of Babylon, they stand pure and uncontaminated; their life is hid with Christ in God. They are virtuous in spirit amid depravity; they are true and loyal, fervent and zealous, while surrounded by infidels, hypocritical professors, godless and worldly men. Their faith and life are hid with Christ in God. Jesus is in them a well of water springing up into everlasting life. Faith, like the rootlets of the palm tree, penetrates beneath the things which are seen, drawing spiritual nourishment from the Fountain of life."—*Ibid.*, July 8, 1886.

298

PRAISES
Psalm 27

HELP FOR THE HELPLESS

The Lord is my light and my salvation; whom shall I fear? The Lord is the stronghold of my life; of whom shall I be afraid? Psalm 27:1.

David is a popular name, and there will probably be many Davids reading this Morning Watch book. No doubt some parents who name their children David do so because of their admiration for the long-ago king who bore that name. We all love the story of the young man's battle with Goliath, and we also love his shepherd's psalm.

Although David was a hero, he did sin. However, he repented of his sins, and some of the psalms express his heartfelt sorrow.

During another part of David's life, Saul had attempted to kill him on several occasions. At another time David's son Absalom tried to take over the kingdom. It is sad to note that the king was at one time "a hunted fugitive, finding refuge in the rocks and caves of the wilderness" *(Education,* p. 164). However, it was while fleeing for his life that David wrote Psalm 27.

Often it is in times of helplessness that we sense our need, and trust God the most. In this psalm, David reviews his life and realizes that in troublous times he would have given up had it not been for his faith in God. And as he recalled God's intervention in his life, he was inspired with new hope. In today's Morning Watch chapter David states that even if he were surrounded by a vast army, he could have confidence in the Lord. He said also that, even if his father and mother were to forsake him, he knew that the Lord would take him up.

We too may have this great confidence. Remember, one with God is a majority. David's deepest desire in the time of trouble was to "dwell in the house of the Lord all the days of my life" (Ps. 27:4). God desires that we shall have this intense desire to worship, serve, and live eternally with God. This should be our goal in times of peace as well as in times of trouble.

PRAISES
Psalm 37

ANTIDOTE FOR WORRY

Trust in the Lord, and do good; so you will dwell in the land, and enjoy security. Take delight in the Lord, and he will give you the desires of your heart. Psalm 37:3, 4.

"'It is estimated that more than one million cases of poisoning occur each year in the United States, with about ten thousand deaths. A large percentage of poisoning cases occurs in children, and of these children 80 percent are between the ages of one and four years.'" These alarming figures were quoted by Dr. Harold Shryock in the book *You and Your Health.* In this same volume we are told that the remedy for poisoning is an antidote. However, it is necessary to have the right antidote for the particular poison.

Worry is a poison, and many people suffer physical ailments as a result. Worry certainly robs people of peace of mind, and many are not able to sleep. Although David was not a doctor, he was right when he said in Psalm 37 that the antidote for worry is trust in the Lord. This well-loved psalm tells us how to stop fretting and to delight in the Lord despite adverse circumstances. A companion psalm that we will study tomorrow is also an excellent prescription for positive thinking.

Many people have the same experience as David—they fret over the prosperity of wrongdoers. The word *fret* is the translation of the Hebrew word *charah,* which means to "burn with anger." The mature Christian does not envy the seeming prosperity of the wicked. Theirs is only worldly gain, for if they do not accept the Lord Jesus, they will "soon be cut down like the grass" (Ps. 37:2). The advice in this psalm and the book of Job helps Christians to be content with what they have.

Christians can and do have trials and reverses of life. Remember, God in His love allows the sunshine and the rain to fall on everyone. Some of the reasons given in the psalms as to why the Christian is better off than the worldling include: God Himself upholds the righteous and never forsakes them; their needs are all supplied. They are wise, just, obedient, and secure. The Lord helps them, delivers them, and saves them. Although we may not see all these blessings in this life, these are the sure promises of God, and one day we will say, "All things work together for good to them that love the Lord."

300

PRAISES
Psalm 46

LUTHER'S PSALM

God is our refuge and strength, a very present help in trouble. Psalm 46:1.

Martin Luther, an outstanding Christian leader, lived in Germany from 1483 to 1546. He translated the Bible from Latin into German, which meant that for the first time the common people could read the Scriptures. God impressed upon Luther's mind the fact that people are saved by grace through faith. Because Luther preached this truth, he was persecuted and tried for his teachings.

To encourage the people to remain true to the Lord, Luther wrote the hymn "A Mighty Fortress Is Our God," based on Psalm 46. This hymn has become very popular. Apparently the Reformer himself sang it when he was discouraged. It has become known as Luther's psalm, but it soon may become our psalm too.

As predicted in Matthew 24, Luke 21, and Revelation 16, there will be a time of great trouble on this earth prior to the second coming of Jesus. This will be climaxed by the seven last plagues. There will be not only such things as earthquakes, thunder, and lightning but God's people will be persecuted as well. However, we are assured that the plagues will not touch us and that He will be "our refuge and strength."

Note this description of the time just before Jesus returns: "Through a rift in the clouds there beams a star whose brilliancy is increased fourfold in contrast with the darkness. It speaks hope and joy to the faithful, but severity and wrath to the transgressors of God's law. Those who have sacrificed all for Christ are now secure, hidden as in the secret of the Lord's pavilion. They have been tested, and before the world and the despisers of truth they have evinced their fidelity to Him who died for them. A marvelous change has come over those who have held fast their integrity in the very face of death. They have been suddenly delivered from the dark and terrible tyranny of men transformed to demons. Their faces, so lately pale, anxious, and haggard, are now aglow with wonder, faith, and love. Their voices rise in triumphant song: 'God is our refuge and strength, a very present help in trouble. Therefore will not we fear.'"—*The Great Controversy*, pp. 638, 639.

301

PRAISES
Psalm 73

WHAT TO DO WITH DOUBT

But for me it is good to be near God; I have made the Lord God my refuge, that I may tell of all thy works. Psalm 73:28.

Although we know that God is truly good and that we should trust Him, most of us are sometimes tempted to doubt. Sometimes we can't understand why there is a good God and a bad world. The psalmist also had moments of perplexity when he thought about the life of ease that the wicked lived and of how they became rich. He wondered why those who were trying to be good and to serve God did not prosper in the same way (verses 2-16). It is encouraging to note that Bible writers also had moments of doubt and discouragement.

The psalms often have their conclusion at the beginning as well as at the end. We notice in the first and last verses of Psalm 73 the psalmist's conclusion: "Truly God is good to the upright, to those who are pure in heart" (verse 1, R.S.V.). This conclusion was reached by going "into the sanctuary of God" (verse 17). When problems become too big for us, we too need to seek solutions in communion with God. Psalm 73 is the beginning of the third division of Psalms, and the sanctuary is mentioned directly or referred to in almost every one of the seventeen psalms in this section. These poems are designed for use in worship, and when we go to church we should also be able to say, "How lovely is thy dwelling place, O Lord of hosts! My soul longs, yea, faints for the courts of the Lord; my heart and flesh sing for joy to the living God" (Ps. 84:1, 2, R.S.V.).

"While God has given ample evidence for faith, He will never remove all excuse for unbelief. All who look for hooks to hang their doubts upon will find them. And those who refuse to accept and obey God's word until every objection has been removed, and there is no longer an opportunity for doubt, will never come to the light."—*The Great Controversy*, p. 527.

The doubter sees a tunnel only as darkness, but the person with faith sees the light at the end. The doubter hesitates to take a step unless he can see the future, but the one who has faith looks to Jesus and steps with confidence into the unexplored ocean of life.

PRAISES
Psalm 90

THE FLYING DOCTOR

Let the favor of the Lord our God be upon us, and establish thou the work of our hands upon us, yea, the work of our hands establish thou it. Psalm 90:17.

Sky-wagon A-2 ZGB sped down most of the Kanye, Botswana, airfield before it became airborne. The small blue-and-white Cessna 185 was heavily loaded with medicines, syringes, bandages, and tenting. Dr. Charles Wical, a tall American missionary, was setting out on his flying-doctor trip into the Kalahari Desert to hold three days of outpatient clinics under the plane's wings. Beneath canvas sheeting, one wing would become a consulting room and the other a dispensary.

The first stop for *Sky-wagon* was Sekuma, about 85 miles to the west. As the plane lost altitude, a score of huts could be seen near the landing strip. Before setting the plane down, the flying doctor circled the area to announce his arrival. In no time a large number of people had gathered around for treatment. Some walked; others came on donkeys. Most of the bush people carried bottles and old cans to hold the medicine they hoped the flying doctor would give them.

After setting up the consulting room and dispensary, the flying doctor turned preacher and opened the Word of God to the patients who were waiting for treatment. Dr. Wical said that although he enjoyed flying, he wouldn't be a flying doctor if it were not for the fact that his work was helping people as Jesus had done. He also sees the medical work as an entering wedge, preparing people for the gospel of *light* and *love* that will give them hope of eternal *life*. Like many other flying doctors, Dr. Wical has dedicated the work of his hands to revealing "the beauty [or kindness] of the Lord our God."

After three days of visiting settlements in the desert, Dr. Wical headed back to Kanye Hospital, flying over the station to announce his return. This plane, valuable in Botswana for evangelistic and medical work, was a gift from listeners to a radio program in the United States.

Although you and I may not be flying doctors, we can do work for the Lord. And He will bless what we do and use our hands to bring blessings to others.

PRAISES
Psalm 91

ANGELS GUARD US

For he will command his angels concerning you to guard you in all your ways. Psalm 91:11, N.I.V.

The New International Version is a completely new translation of the Holy Bible made by more than one hundred scholars. It is a modern version that you will enjoy reading.

Psalm 91 contains comfort for all who are passing through times of trouble. In *The New International Version* it reads like this:

"He who dwells in the shelter of the Most High will rest in the shadow of the Almighty. I will say of the Lord, 'He is my refuge and my fortress, my God, in whom I trust.' Surely he will save you from the fowler's snare and from the deadly pestilence. He will cover you with his feathers, and under his wings you will find refuge; his faithfulness will be your shield and rampart. You will not fear the terror of night, nor the arrow that flies by day, nor the pestilence that stalks in the darkness, nor the plague that destroys at midday. A thousand may fall at your side, ten thousand at your right hand, but it will not come near you. You will only observe with your eyes and see the punishment of the wicked. If you make the Most High your dwelling—even the Lord, who is my refuge—then no harm will befall you, no disaster will come near your tent. For he will command his angels concerning you to guard you in all your ways; they will lift you up in their hands, so that you will not strike your foot against a stone. You will tread upon the lion and the cobra; you will trample the great lion and the serpent. 'Because he loves me,' says the Lord, 'I will rescue him; I will protect him, for he acknowledges my name. He will call upon me, and I will answer him; I will be with him in trouble, I will deliver him and honor him. With long life will I satisfy him and show him my salvation.'"

The first verse is the key to this beautiful psalm. Like the remaining verses it teaches that there is a place of safety, security, and point of perfect peace at the center of storms of life. That place, that point, is "in the shadow of the Almighty."

304

PRAISES
Psalm 107

A FLOATING BOTTLE

Let the redeemed of the Lord say so. Psalm 107:2.

Jalad Seyong was strolling along the beach near his home in Malaysia. As he walked, his eyes scanned the sea and his attention was caught by something in the water reflecting the sun's rays. The waves brought the object closer, and Jalad was able to wade to it. He was excited to discover that it was a sealed bottle with a paper inside. Eagerly he opened the bottle to find out whether someone was sending a message of distress.

The paper was a brochure on Christianity, with an invitation to write to an address in Sydney, Australia, for further information. Jalad wrote, and to his surprise received a series of twenty-four The Bible Says lessons and a Bible from the Seventh-day Adventist mission office in Sabah. This young man had been brought up in a Moslem home. However, he had an open mind and was eager to learn, so he studied the lessons. He not only returned the lessons but wrote letters of inquiry. At one time he decided to give up studying, but a Catholic classmate encouraged him to continue.

After completing the lesson on baptism, he wrote and requested that he might be baptized. Having accepted Jesus as his personal Saviour, he changed his name from the Moslem "Jalad" to the Christian name "Paul." The president of the Sabah Mission, Pastor G. W. Munson, visited Paul and explained many of the doctrines of the Seventh-day Adventist Church. Since there wasn't a Seventh-day Adventist church in the town, Paul kept the Sabbath by himself.

At the invitation of the local mission, Paul left his home to enroll at the Sabah Adventist Secondary School. He enjoyed studying at this Christian school and was baptized there during a Week of Prayer.

The person in Australia who put the gospel literature into a bottle is unknown, but it is interesting to note this method of telling others about the gospel and the direct response to what could be called "bottle evangelism." The bread of life was literally cast into the sea, and the angel of God directed its passage so that it was discovered by someone willing to walk in the truths of God's Word.

PRAISES
Psalm 106

A ROAD IN THE SEA

He rebuked the Red Sea, and it became dry; and he led them through the deep as through a desert. Psalm 106:9.

Ever since Moses lifted his rod and God parted the sea, there have been attempts to make tunnels under water, bridges over rivers, and canals connecting oceans. One of the greatest of these achievements was the Panama Canal, which links the Atlantic and Pacific oceans. The canal is approximately fifty miles long, deep water to deep water, and operates on a series of locks.

A ship entering the canal from the Atlantic side sails at sea level. It is then lifted eighty-five feet to Gatun Lake in three steps, and from there sails eighty-five feet above sea level for thirty-two miles. A simple lockage then lowers the ship thirty feet to Miraflores Lake. Another mile south the vessel enters Miraflores Locks and is lowered fifty-five feet to the Pacific Ocean level. After another eight miles it enters the outer harbor.

The lock chambers are 110 feet wide and 1,000 feet long. Each ship going through the canal uses about 52 million gallons of fresh water. The first survey to ascertain the possibility of building the canal was in 1524. Several countries worked on constructing it over a period of many years. The first ocean steamer passed through the Panama Canal in August, 1914, and the waterway was officially opened in July, 1920. The Panama Canal is now open twenty-four hours a day, 365 days a year, and ships can pass through from one ocean to the other in only ten to twenty hours.

As I stood in the canal's observation tower, I marveled at the engineering skill and hard work that had gone into the construction. However, the dry "road" through the Red Sea was a greater accomplishment. In today's psalm we read of other examples of God's power. As you read Psalm 106 you will discover why it begins and ends with praise and prayer.

These verses are a sequel to Psalm 105, and both cover portions of the history of Israel. In the past events of the nation, we see God's guiding hand. This hand still guides us. With the psalmist we can say with enthusiasm, "Praise ye the Lord. O give thanks unto the Lord; for he is good"!

PRAISES
Psalm 103

A FATHER'S LOVE

As a father pities his children, so the Lord pities those who fear him. Psalm 103:13.

The people of the Bemba tribe in Zambia catch fish in baskets made from reeds that grow on the riverbanks. Although Mary was only 10 years old, she had her own small basket. She was a good worker at home, but she liked catching fish best of all.

With the other village children, Mary would go to the river, lay the basket, and wait patiently. It seemed that each time she went fishing she came back with more fish than the other children, and sometimes with more than the adults. So after her repeated requests, her mother finally agreed to make her a larger basket.

Mary could hardly wait for the day when she could take her new basket to the river. At last it was finished, and early the next morning, balancing her treasure on her head, Mary set off with the other children for the river. This day they decided to cross the river in the canoe. In the middle of the stream, however, the water was turbulent. The waves washed over the side of the little boat, quickly filled it with water, and it sank. Men quickly paddled toward the spot to rescue the young people, but one of the crocodiles that lived in the river seized Mary before help arrived.

When the village people ran back to Mary's house and told her parents what had happened, her mother immediately fainted. Her father rushed to the river's edge. "If the crocodile took my daughter, it must take me, too!" he said, and dived into the river. However, some men rushed into the water and were able to save him.

This African father was willing to give his life as an offering for his daughter's death. He expressed his love by diving into the water.

This is an imperfect picture of our heavenly Father's love. With David we can praise God that God loves us so much that He allowed Jesus to leave heaven to save us. Our heavenly Father protects and guides us. When we get to heaven and see the way He has led in our lives, we will see many evidences of our heavenly Father's love.

PRAISES
Psalm 119

A DIFFERENT ALPHABET

Blessed are those whose way is blameless, who walk in the law of the Lord! Psalm 119:1.

Probably one of the first things you learned in school was the alphabet. There are twenty-six letters in the English alphabet, but today we want to introduce you to an alphabet that has only twenty-two letters.

This different alphabet is Hebrew, the language in which the Old Testament was written. These letters would be difficult for us to write or read, but we can see the Hebrew alphabet in Psalm 119.

The twenty-two letters of the Hebrew alphabet, along with their English pronunciation, are used as divisions for this longest psalm. You will notice that there are twenty-two sections, with eight verses in each section. In Hebrew each verse begins with the letter of the section it is listed under. God is a God of order and is interested in details.

You will have noted that in this Morning Watch book I have often used acrostics to explain truth. An acrostic is a way of summarizing facts by using the letters of the word as the beginning of each statement. Psalm 119 is a Bible acrostic.

Although it is interesting to note that today's psalm is centered upon the Hebrew alphabet, it is more important to note what the psalm teaches. The first verse, which is our text for today, is really a summary of the chapter. It assures us that we will be happy when we walk in the ways of the Lord.

Inasmuch as today's psalm is also the longest chapter in the Bible, we have allowed three days to read it. If we read only about seven sections each day, we should still have some time to think about what we read. A hasty reading of any portion of the Bible without meditation does not help us very much. "One reason that there is not more sincere piety and religious fervor, is because the mind is occupied with unimportant things and there is no time to meditate, search the Scriptures, or pray."—*Counsels to Writers and Editors,* p. 125.

Note this ABC for walking in the Christian pathway:

A sk God for the Holy Spirit to guide us.

B elieve that by God's help we can live victoriously.

C ontinue walking in the ways of the Lord.

PRAISES
Psalm 119

THE *BOUNTY* BIBLE

How can a young man keep his way pure? By guarding it according to thy word. Psalm 119:9.

One of the most famous Bibles in the world is the *Bounty* Bible. In December, 1787, the *Bounty,* commanded by Capt. William Bligh, sailed from England. However, in midocean some of the sailors, led by Fletcher Christian, took over the boat and put the captain and eighteen men adrift in a small boat. Christian and eight other mutineers reached Tahiti, and traveled with a group of islanders to the uninhabited Pitcairn Island.

Soon after their arrival, Christian discovered in his sea chest the Bible that had been given him by his mother before he went to sea. He often went to a cave on the tiny island to study the Bible. Sometimes John Adams, another mutineer, went with him. While they were discovering the cleansing power of God's Word, of which David wrote, others on the island were learning how to make whiskey. As a result of fighting, ten years after their landing John Adams was the only man left, along with eleven women and twenty-three children.

One day Adams dreamed that an angel told him to "go and train the children in the way of the Bible." He shared his dream with Fletcher Christian's eldest son, Thursday October. Together they began teaching the children from the Bible and a prayer book. The Scriptures changed the islanders, and Pitcairn soon became a Christian community.

The *Bounty* Bible was kept by Christian's Tahitian widow until 1839, when someone persuaded her to let it be taken to America to be rebound. It was kept by the Historical Society of Connecticut until, after many years, the Pitcairn people requested that it be returned. The fragile and worn Bible was repaired, rebound, and put into a box with the label "The Pitcairn Bible." In Fiji the people made a beautiful wooden box for it, and the Bible arrived back at Pitcairn in 1950.

Although there are only about one hundred people on this tiny island midway between Panama and New Zealand, today there are almost three hundred Bibles. For more than a century the people of Pitcairn have proved that the Word of God keeps our ways pure.

309

PRAISES
Psalm 119

THE SCRIPTURE STACK

Thy word is revealed, and all is light; it gives understanding even to the untaught. Psalm 119:130, N.E.B.

In the city of Lima, Peru, a poor, wrinkled woman distributed portions of the Bible. Every week she went to a newsstand and gave the owner a section of Scripture and said, "Take and read the message; it will help you in your life."

The man was not interested, but politely accepted the pages and put them on a shelf. Every week the old woman presented him with another part, and he added it to the pile. As the stack of scriptures grew, however, so did his problems. He had to spend long hours at the newsstand in order to make a living; then his wife left him, and he had to care for the children. With little time at home, this became a big problem for him. The once-happy man became sad and desperate.

When he was in the depths of despair, he remembered what the old lady had said: "Read the message; it will be of help to you." These words kept ringing in his ears. And since he had nothing more to lose—for he had lost practically everything—he began reading. He read many portions of Scripture and discovered that they did indeed contain a helpful message. Now he waited eagerly for the old woman to come so that he could read more about God's love for him. One day he asked her to bring him a New Testament, and he studied it intently. This introduction to the Word of God brought light to his life.

After careful study he decided to become a Christian, and accompanied the old lady to church. When he began worshiping God, he was able to look at his problems more objectively, and he started living a new life. He walked in the light that he had, and was baptized. Soon he sold the newsstand and began a new job—directing a church mission.

Perhaps the most interesting part of this story is that the old woman was illiterate and had never experienced the joy of reading God's Word for herself. However, as it had been read to her she had accepted it. Although she could not understand the written pages, she was determined that she would do all she could to share the light.

PRAISES
Psalm 146

A HAPPY CHIEF

Praise the Lord! Praise the Lord, O my soul! I will praise the Lord as long as I live; I will sing praises to my God while I have being. Psalm 146:1, 2.

One of the happiest men that I have ever met is Chief Andrew Ekpenyong, who lives in Nigeria. The chief was not always happy, and he was not born a chief. Let me tell some things about him that I discovered when I talked with him in his hometown of Calibar.

Although his parents were Christians, the chief's early attitude toward God is summed up in these words: "I left my parents and went into life forgetting God. For ten years I never entered a church." However, as a result of two dreams, he was led to remember his Creator.

In his first dream the chief saw a huge cup made of pure gold and filled with water. It was suspended in the sky, and although nothing visibly held it, the cup tilted and water flowed out. As the water disappeared, the chief vowed that he would return to God. A man in a white robe appeared in his second dream, telling him to read Psalm 20:1. When he awoke, he read the verse: "The Lord hear thee in the day of trouble; the name of the God of Jacob defend thee."

These two dreams prepared the chief for his visit to a church, where he met Dr. Mullier, a German missionary. The chief studied the Bible, read many books, including *The Great Controversy,* and was baptized by immersion in 1969. Prior to that time he had endured so many troubles that he did not think life was worth living. He did not have a good job or much money. Today he is a prosperous businessman.

Looking back on his experience, he says, "The Lord has been with me, and for this reason I shall always keep my vows to Him. I will not flinch. If I fail God, I am done for. By God's grace I will not compromise. I am fully committed to keeping my vows. I am very happy with my Lord, my life belongs to Him, and He is guiding me."

Chief Andrew Ekpenyong's testimony is similar to King David's. In the Psalms we have noted his praises to God. Psalm 146 is the first of the five hallelujah psalms that brings the book to a close. These are full of prayer, praise, and adoration.

PRAISES
Proverbs 1

SECRET OF SUCCESS

The fear of the Lord is the beginning of knowledge; fools despise wisdom and instruction. Proverbs 1:7.

"There is no branch of legitimate business for which the Bible does not afford an essential preparation. Its principles of diligence, honesty, thrift, temperance, and purity are the secret of true success. These principles, as set forth in the book of Proverbs, constitute a treasury of practical wisdom. Where can the merchant, the artisan, the director of men in any department of business, find better maxims for himself or for his employees than are found in these words of the wise man:

"'Seest thou a man diligent in his business? he shall stand before kings; he shall not stand before mean men.' Prov. 22:29.

"'In all labor there is profit; but the talk of the lips tendeth only to penury.' Prov. 14:23.

"'The soul of the sluggard desireth, and hath nothing.' 'The drunkard and the glutton shall come to poverty; and drowsiness shall clothe a man with rags.' Prov. 13:4; 23:21.

"'A talebearer revealeth secrets; therefore meddle not with him that flattereth with his lips.' Prov. 20:19.

"'He that hath knowledge spareth his words;' but 'every fool will be meddling.' Prov. 17:27; 20:3.

"'Go not in the way of evil men;' 'can one go upon hot coals, and his feet not be burned?' Prov. 4:14; 6:28.

"'He that walketh with wise men shall be wise.' Prov. 13:20.

"'A man that hath friends must show himself friendly.' Prov. 18:24.

"The whole circle of our obligation to one another is covered by that word of Christ's, 'Whatsoever ye would that men should do to you, do ye even so to them.' Matt. 7:12."—*Education*, pp. 135, 136.

Solomon was well qualified to write the Proverbs, because God granted him wisdom that was the wonder of the whole world. (See 1 Kings 10:23, 24.) The wisdom contained in Proverbs is the secret of true success.

PRAISES
Proverbs 6

"ANTELLIGENCE"

Go to the ant, O sluggard; consider her ways, and be wise.
Proverbs 6:6.

One day Royal Dixon, who had spent twenty years as a wandering naturalist, noticed an ant crossing a rough cabin porch. As the insect approached a crack, it hesitated, for apparently the gap between the boards appeared as large as the Grand Canyon does to us. The ant retraced its steps and soon appeared again, dragging a pine needle many times longer than its own body. With some difficulty it pushed the needle across the crack until the ends rested securely on each plank, then it crossed to the other side. Ingenuity is but one of the many interesting characteristics of these insects.

There are "engineers" in each colony of ants. With the aid of these building specialists the ants tackle very hard work. It has been noted that these insects can cut their way through ten inches of solid rock. It seems that each member of the colony has its particular work. Some are best at building; others cut wood; others burrow. Idleness is never seen, for it is punishable by death in the ant colonies.

At least 3,500 kinds of ants have been catalogued. One African species constructs "hills" more than six feet high. Queen ants are larger than the individual workers and their life span ranges from twelve to seventeen years, while workers in the colony have a much shorter life expectancy of from three to four years.

From a study of ants we find that they have strict regulations on sanitation and cleanliness. They not only clean up the streets and the nurseries of the colony but they also practice personal hygiene. Each ant, after eating, will go through a regular cleanup procedure. Many boys and girls would like the ant's comb, for it is attached to its front legs and cannot be lost.

Ants obviously have a high order of intelligence. They have regular hours of work and relaxation. These industrious little creatures have a form of government that we might do well to take as a pattern. As we consider these industrious and fascinating creatures, it is no wonder that God said, "Consider her ways."

PRAISES
Proverbs 14

LITTLE THINGS

There is a way which seems right to a man, but its end is the way to death. Proverbs 14:12.

How many letters are there in the alphabet?
How many tones are there in the major scale?
How many colors are there?

Just think—all the newspapers, books, and magazines written in the English language are made up of just twenty-six letters; most music is based on just seven tones; all the rainbows and sunsets take their hues from just three primary colors.

Twenty-six letters, seven tones, three colors. These small numbers and the following facts remind us that it is often little things that have tremendous influence on our lives.

● An ocean liner on the way from America to England was wrecked off the Irish coast because its compass was deflected by a small piece of steel from a sailor's pocket knife.

● A 220-ton locomotive with sixteen coaches ran off the rails because of the failure of a metal handle only inches long.

● A French submarine, moving off the coast of Tunis, sank and all the crew drowned because a tiny stone blocked a small valve.

Little things, seemingly unimportant, are vital to the mechanical age. The lives of millions who travel daily depend on the proper function of tire valves, compass needles, and gauges on instrument panels. Everything, then, in the construction of cars, boats, and airplanes is important.

Just so, there are really no trifles in our lives. Our way of life and our destiny is influenced by little things. Often there is only a word that stands between success and failure, life and death. As the words of our text today remind us, even though our ways may seem right, they can lead to our destruction.

Little habits that determine the way we go are often dismissed as unimportant. However, it is the daily pattern of our lives that determines life's direction. Someone has expressed this truth this way:

"Sow a thought, and you reap an act;
Sow an act, and you reap a habit;
Sow a habit, and you reap a character;
Sow a character, and you reap a destiny."

314

PEACE
Ephesians 1

SHOOT OR BE SHOT

He has made known to us his hidden purpose . . . namely, that the universe, all in heaven and on earth, might be brought into a unity in Christ. Ephesians 1:9, 10, N.E.B.

Two brothers who were just twenty months apart in age loved each other very much. When it came time for them to attend college, one chose a college nearby in his home country, and the other chose a university in another country, 150 miles away over rugged mountains. The brother attending school far away visited home regularly until World War II broke out.

During the war the two countries were on opposite sides, and the brother who had left home was unable to return. He eventually took out citizenship in the new country, married, and was drafted into the army. As a soldier, he was told that he would have to go to his former country as a spy. He stated that he did not want to do this, but his superiors dressed him in the uniform of his home country and sent him over the mountains.

One night he was surprised by soldiers, taken prisoner, tried, and sentenced to be shot. On the morning of his execution he stood handcuffed by a stone wall and looked at the firing squad.

Suddenly his eyes met those of the officer in charge—his brother. His brother recognized him and hurried to his commanding officer. "I can't give the order to shoot," he said. But his commanding officer replied, "He may be your brother, but he is our enemy. Either you shoot him or you will be shot with him."

The young officer did not need time to make his decision. He went over to his brother and embraced him, and they died together.

We may come from different generations, different nationalities, and even different tribes within a country, but first and foremost we are brothers and sisters in the Lord Jesus Christ. It is time for us to put aside differences and jealousies and to demonstrate love and unity.

The theme of the book of Ephesians, unity, is one of the greatest needs in the Christian church.

PEACE
Ephesians 2

TEN YEARS OF PEACE

So he came and proclaimed the good news: peace to you who were far off, and peace to those who were near by; for through him we both alike have access to the Father in the one Spirit. Ephesians 2:17, 18, N.E.B.

Since the introduction of computers a few years ago, a great deal of information has been gathered and analyzed. By the use of a computer a Norwegian has made the following interesting calculations concerning war and peace: during the past 5,560 years of recorded history there have been 14,531 wars. During 185 generations, mankind has had only ten years of peace.

Peace is sought after by every nation, community, church, school, and home. Because of greed, jealousy, and hatred, there have been, and will continue to be, wars among nations, people, and even families. Peace is possible only when the Prince of Peace is the ruler of every heart. Peace rules the day when Christ rules the mind.

The Greek historian Herodotus, who has been called the father of history, is reported to have said, "No one is fool enough to choose war instead of peace. For in peace sons bury fathers; in war fathers bury sons."

Yes, it is foolish to choose war instead of peace. In order to be truly tranquil, we must invite Jesus into our hearts. As stated in our Morning Watch text today, "He . . . proclaimed the good news: peace." This calm rest makes it possible for us to have fellowship with the three persons of the Godhead—God the Father, God the Son, and God the Holy Spirit. When we have this kind of relationship, we have the peace that "passeth all understanding"—and all misunderstandings, too!

Today let us pray for peace in our home, town, and nation. Let us ask God for the ability to be a peacemaker. Let us pray that the peaceable kingdom will soon be established so that there will be no more war and trouble. The first era of that kingdom is one thousand years of peace. During this period, known as the millennium, the earth will be at rest, and all God's people will enjoy peace in heaven.

PEACE
Ephesians 3

LIVE A FULL LIFE

With deep roots and firm foundations, may you be strong to grasp, with all God's people, what is the breadth and length and height and depth of the love of Christ, and to know it, though it is beyond knowledge. So may you attain to fullness of being, the fullness of God himself. Ephesians 3:18, 19, N.E.B.

Four double-decker buses loaded with students left Avondale College for Cave's Beach for the annual school picnic. No sooner had the caravan stopped than four young men rushed over the sands and into the inviting swells of the Pacific Ocean.

The waters were turbulent at the spot the boys chose for diving, and there was a strong undertow. Within a few minutes three of them struggled out, but the fourth could not be seen anywhere. Strong swimmers searched the waters, and a helicopter circled overhead. Every day for more than a week students and others patrolled the beaches and searched the waters.

Raymond Wilson's body was not found, and about ten days later it was my sad duty to conduct a memorial service for this dedicated Christian young man. Next month I will tell you more about Raymond. At this point I want to stress that although he did not live even 20 years, his was a full life rooted in the firm foundation of God's Word. He knew the love of Christ.

We tend to think of life as being full only if it is long. The earthly life of Jesus proves, however, that the length of life has little to do with its fullness. In just three short years of public ministry and a total of 30 years of life, Jesus attained "fullness of being" (Eph. 3:19, N.E.B.).

Those who have had the sad experience of losing someone who has not lived many years can be comforted in the fact that life does not have to be long in order to be good. An egg cup can be just as full as a milk bottle, and all fruits do not get ripe at the same season. So it is with our lives. Although Jesus did not live beyond 30 years of age, He was able to say at the end of His life, "It is finished," or "It is full."

PEACE
Ephesians 4

LIVE IT UP!

I entreat you, then—I, a prisoner for the Lord's sake: as God has called you, live up to your calling. Be humble always and gentle, and patient too. Be forbearing with one another and charitable. Ephesians 4:1, 2, N.E.B.

To the average young person, the expression "live it up" means to have a good time in this world. Unfortunately, some of those who live in this way are really not living at all; in fact, they are really dying. We have already discovered that we reap what we sow, and those who defy the laws of nature, of health, and of God can reap only sorrow and eternal separation from God.

Those who are really living are those who are in Christ, the secret of abundant living. The phrase "in Christ," or a similar phrase such as "in the Lord" (Eph. 4:17), is used at least seventeen times in the book of Ephesians. Being in Christ does not involve some mystical magic, but a real experience. When we surrender our wills to God every morning and live in an attitude of prayer, we are living in Christ.

Paul lived so close to the Lord Jesus that he said he was a "prisoner of the Lord's." Though the word *prisoner* suggests someone who is bound, Paul is using it to suggest the freedom and victory he experienced when he was united to Jesus.

Paul challenges, "Live up to your calling" (verse 1, N.E.B.), and shows us how we can really "live it up." In our Morning Watch verse he gives us some examples when he says, "Be humble always and gentle, and patient too. Be forbearing with one another and charitable" (N.E.B.).

The secret of living up to your calling is to have Jesus, the Light of the world, lighting up your life. A Greek word for light is *phōtismos,* from which comes our word *photograph.* When we have Jesus, the Light of the world, our lives will be a photograph of His beautiful life. Only then can we truly say that we are "living it up."

"Words alone cannot tell it. Let it be reflected in the character and manifested in the life. Christ is sitting for His portrait in every disciple. . . . In every one Christ's long-suffering love, His holiness, meekness, mercy, and truth are to be manifested to the world."—*The Desire of Ages,* p. 827.

318

PEACE
Ephesians 5

LIVE IN LOVE

In a word, as God's dear children, try to be like him, and live in love as Christ loved you, and gave himself up on your behalf as an offering and sacrifice whose fragrance is pleasing to God. Ephesians 5:1, 2, N.E.B.

The three-thousand-pound truck skidded off the road and overturned on a riverbank. The driver, a young boy, was thrown out of the truck and pinned in two feet of water.

When the truck crashed, the boy's father, who was at a nearby farmhouse, realized what had happened. He was only five feet eight inches tall and weighed 165 pounds, but with unbelievable effort he pushed the truck onto its wheels and released his son. He then administered artificial respiration until a patrolman arrived to assist. The doctor who treated the boy described the father's effort as superhuman.

This father's love for his son provided him with the ability to muster all his strength to lift the truck off his boy and save him from drowning. A parent's love for a child is one of the most powerful of human emotions. It is a reflection of the love of God, and can sometimes be described as superhuman.

One way to "live it up" is to "live in love" (Eph. 5:2, N.E.B.). It is natural for a father to love his child and for a child to love his or her parents. However, the test of our Christianity is that we love those who do not love us. The only way we can love our enemies is if we have God's love in our lives, making our love "superhuman"—a miracle. I want that kind of love in my life, don't you?

We should also remember that God loves us with a love greater than that of any earthly father. God's love is seen in the fact that He "gave himself up on your behalf as an offering and sacrifice" (verse 2, N.E.B.). Yes, Jesus died in order that we might be saved. We are not in danger of drowning, but we are in danger of losing eternal life. However, if we will allow Jesus to take control and if we will "live in love," we will be saved.

319

PEACE
Ephesians 6

LIVE IN OBEDIENCE

You fathers, again, must not goad your children to resentment, but give them the instruction, and the correction, which belong to a Christian upbringing. Ephesians 6:4, N.E.B.

William L. Stidger, an American author and lecturer, stood one day with a Chinese friend in front of the Temple of Wisdom in the forbidden city of Peking. As they admired the exquisite building, the Chinese friend asked, "What is the most beautiful sight in all the world?"

Stidger thought his friend was referring to temples and said, "The Taj Mahal in India, Notre Dame Cathedral in Paris, St. Peter's in Rome, or St. Paul's——"

"No, no, I don't mean temples," interrupted the Chinese. "They are not the most beautiful sight in the world."

"Ah, then, you must mean a glorious sunrise or sunset."

"No, not sunrises or sunsets."

"Well, then, do you mean a beautiful woman?"

"No, no," said the Chinese. "Women are beautiful, but they are not the most beautiful sight in the world."

Mr. Stidger said, "Then you must mean natural scenery. The Yangtze Gorge, Mount Everest, the Grand Canyon, Yellowstone."

"No, not those," insisted his friend.

"Then I give up," said Stidger with a smile. "You tell me what is the most beautiful sight in the world."

To which his friend replied, "Our philosopher Confucius says the most beautiful sight in all the world is that of a little child going confidently down the road after you have shown him the way."

Your father or mother, pastors, teachers, and leaders in the church are endeavoring to instruct you in the ways of the Lord. They do not want to provoke you, but help you along life's pathway. I believe the Lord rejoices to see children going confidently down the road of life after they have been shown Jesus, "the way, the truth, and the life."

As we walk down the road of life, we should follow Paul's instructions to live in obedience: "Children, obey your parents in the Lord: for this is right." Honor your father and mother.

320

PEACE
Philippians 1

A JOYFUL PRISONER

Grace to you and peace from God our Father and the Lord Jesus Christ. I thank my God whenever I think of you; and when I pray for you all, my prayers are always joyful. Philippians 1:2-4, N.E.B.

A certain king had a very unhappy son. The prince had everything he could wish for—a pony, toys, and even a yacht to sail on the lake. But no matter what was given to him, he remained unhappy.

One day the king consulted a wise old man about his son. The old man took a piece of paper and wrote some words on it in invisible ink. He told the king to hold the paper between his eyes in front of a lighted candle at night and he would be able to read what was written on it. That night the king was eager to find out the message, so he lighted a candle and held the paper in front of it. He read: "The secret of true happiness is to do a little kindness to everyone every day."

Many people who have everything material that they could wish for are unhappy. Others who are in prison (as was the apostle Paul) are able to rejoice. Our happiness is not dependent upon the things that we have. It comes from an inner peace that exists when all is right with God and with others. When we do acts of kindness, we show that we have the love of God in our lives.

Paul had spent many years helping others to find the way to the kingdom of God. Now, although he was in prison, he was not dejected. No doubt he had discouraging moments, but he had found the secret of being joyful even under adverse circumstances.

Paul and Silas had been in prison at Philippi. Although they had been beaten, they sang praises to God. When Paul was chained to a Roman soldier, he accepted the bonds as an opportunity to witness. We can rejoice in all circumstances if we love and serve God faithfully.

The book of Philippians, written by Paul from his prison cell, is a letter of joy. It has no definite outline, but is a love letter to church members then and now. The words *joy* and *rejoice* occur at least fifteen times in Philippians. Paul recognized that his rejoicing would influence others to accept Jesus.

PEACE
Philippians 2

TUG OF WAR

There must be no room for rivalry and personal vanity among you, but you must humbly reckon others better than yourselves. Look to each other's interest and not merely to your own. Philippians 2:3, 4, N.E.B.

Tug of war, although it may be called by different names in some countries, is a game that is played all around the world. It is a favorite at picnics, since all the equipment that is required is a strong piece of rope and two teams. A handkerchief or rag is tied around the middle of the rope, and a line is marked on the ground. At the signal to start, the teams on opposite ends of the rope try with all their might to pull the handkerchief over to their side.

Although tug of war is a popular game, it can lead to angry words. Whenever we compete for a single prize or reward, there can be problems. Because of the human tendency to be selfish, there are always conflicts when only one person or team can win the prize. Some people become so eager to win that they will even cheat or purposely injure another person to do so. You may not have thought of it, but it would be well to arrange all games so that everyone can win.

Those who study the workings of the human mind state that when there is only one prize, it is bad for the winner as well as for the loser. The winner is filled with pride, regardless of how high the standard reached, and the loser becomes bitter because he or she was beaten by perhaps only a point or a second in time.

We have already discovered from the books of Ephesians and Philippians that it is in God's plan for us to have unity in our homes, our churches, and our schools. In our text today we are warned that rivalry is one of the things that destroys unity.

"God's plan of life has a place for every human being. Each is to improve his talents to the utmost; and faithfulness in doing this, be the gifts few or many, entitles one to honor. In God's plan there is no place for selfish rivalry. Those who measure themselves by themselves, and compare themselves among themselves, are not wise. 2 Corinthians 10:12."—*Education,* p. 226.

322

PEACE
Philippians 3

DOO TOWN

Brethren, I do not consider that I have made it my own; but one thing I do, forgetting what lies behind and straining forward to what lies ahead. Philippians 3:13.

Doo Town is one of the most unique and quaint townships in Australia. It is situated near the road between Hobart and Port Arthur on the island of Tasmania. The town is unique because the occupants of the homes have continued the custom of naming each house, and each name contains the word *Doo*. Here are some of the house names: "Af-2-Doo," "Doo Nix," "Doo Little," "Gay Doo," "Doo-Us-2," "Didgeri-Doo," "How-Doo-U-Doo," and "Thistle Doo."

The township arose at the time when people traveled to and from Eagle Hawk Neck by ferry. Apparently the first home was called "We-Doo-It," and since then each house erected has been given a name with "Doo" incorporated in it. One of the house names is an excellent motto for this year. It is "Doo More." There are at least four areas of life in which we need to do more.

In the first place, we should *do more pressing on*. It is true that "a quitter never wins and a winner never quits." To be a winner in the race of life, we have to keep pressing on. A statement by the wise man puts the secret of successful living in this way, "Whatsoever thy hand findeth to *do, do* it with thy might" (Eccl. 9:10).

If we are to be successful in the Christian life, we need to *do more praying*. Prayer does not need proof, it needs practice. And when we have the practice of praying daily, we have powerful, victorious living.

Third, we need to *do more preparing*. Heaven is a prepared place, and the Scriptures reveal that only prepared people enter its portals. In a nutshell, to prepare for heaven, we need to love and obey the Lord Jesus Christ.

Finally, we need to *do more practicing of the gospel*. While waiting for our King to claim us as His subjects, let us share the light of the Spirit and practice the golden rule. "Whatsoever ye would that men should *do* to you, *do* ye even so to them" (Matt. 7:12).

How can you do more pressing on, praying, preparing, and practicing practical godliness? The answer is found in Philippians 4:13.

PEACE
Philippians 4

EVERY NEED SUPPLIED

And my God will supply all your wants out of the magnificence of his riches in Christ Jesus. Philippians 4:19, N.E.B.

In most versions of this text it says God will supply every *need*. However, in *The New English Bible* it says that God will supply our *wants*. Which do you think is correct? Does God give us all that we need or all that we want?

Two of the first words a child learns are "I want." As we come to birthdays and Christmas time, we let people know what we want. Many times what we want is not what we need. We certainly need food and water every day; however, we do not need sweets and soft drinks. We need textbooks for use in schools, but we do not need fictitious storybooks. We need time for recreation that will help refresh our minds and build our bodies, but we do not need to spend time being entertained by television or at the theater.

We also differ in what we determine to be needs, depending on where we live. I have been to places where the people did not have houses to live in or many clothes to wear. I have also been to countries where thousands of boys and girls did not have the opportunity of attending school. Those of us who have homes, clothing, and schools should not be selfishly asking for more things when there are so many in the world who do not have even what we consider to be essentials.

God must become rather disturbed when those who have so much ask for more, while there are those who have so little. As we found out yesterday, our happiness is not dependent upon having things, but on being right with God and with other people.

Yes, our text today should read that God will supply our *needs* rather than our *wants*. However, if we are truly converted, we will want only those things that are needful. When our wants are the same as our needs, it can be said that we are mature Christians. As such, we will forget the successes and failures of the past and "press on toward the goal for the prize of the upward call in Christ Jesus" (Phil. 3:14, R.S.V.). Mature Christians also think on those things that are true, honorable, just, pure, lovely, and gracious.

324

PEACE
Colossians 1

SHARING THE SECRET

*The secret is this: Christ in you, the hope of a glory to come.
Colossians 1:27, N.E.B.*

Do you like to have people share secrets with you? If a secret is really exciting news, it is hard to keep it to ourselves. The secret that Paul is sharing with us in the book of Colossians is one that he intends for us to tell everyone.

The secret that Paul wants us to share is the theme of the Bible and the summary of the gospel. If Jesus Christ dwells in our hearts by our invitation, through His power our lives are transformed. We then become Christians, subjects of the kingdom of grace today, which gives us the assurance of being subjects of the kingdom of glory when Jesus sets up His kingdom. But it is not enough to say that we are Christians; we need to demonstrate that Christ is living in our lives.

The book of Colossians has four chapters and was written from Paul's prison cell. Like Ephesians and Philippians, and other writings of Paul, it is a good book to read without stopping at chapter divisions.

While in Rome, Paul learned from Epaphras that the Christians at Colossae needed counsel. False teachings were spreading among the believers, and Paul's response was the best answer that we can give—the truth. We too should spend more time in presenting truth and less time arguing about errors.

Although Paul makes reference to the church and the Christian workers, the main subject of this book is Jesus Christ. Note some of the wonderful truths concerning our Saviour that are presented in this Epistle. These are "secrets" we need to share with as many people as we can:

C hrist is all in all (chap. 3:11).

H ead of all rulers (chap. 2:10-15).

R edeemer of all the universe (chap. 1:20).

I mage of the invisible God (verse 15).

S ource of fortitude, patience, and joy (verse 11).

T he treasure house of all wisdom and knowledge (chap. 2:2, 3).

PEACE
Colossians 3

DO I HAVE TO OBEY?

Children, obey your parents in everything, for that is pleasing to God and is the Christian way. Colossians 3:20, N.E.B.

Johnny and Gerry were very good friends and often played together. One day Gerry went over to Johnny's house and said, "Let's go out in the field and play." Johnny immediately replied, "I can't because my father said not to."

Johnny was surprised when Gerry said that his father had given him the same instruction. Then Gerry said, "Our fathers should have given us a reason why we shouldn't play in the field today. If you don't come, I'll find someone else." But Johnny said that he would not go.

Johnny was playing at home when he heard an ambulance siren. Later he learned that Gerry had been bitten by a rattlesnake while playing in the field. Fortunately, he was taken to the hospital before the poison killed him, and he eventually recovered from the bite.

The two fathers, going separately to work, had seen the snake in the field. Each had shouted back to his son not to play there, but neither had had time to explain why.

Although we do not always know the reason for obeying our parents, it is wise to do so. Most parents love their children and ask them only to do things that are for their good and to stop doing things that are harmful.

The only time you should not obey your parents is if they ask you to do something that God has said we should not do. For instance, there might be a case where a parent who does not know about God will ask a child to steal. Our text today is similar to the one in Ephesians 6:1: "Children obey your parents in the Lord." When our parents love and serve God, we should always obey them.

God has established the father as the spiritual leader of the home, and it is the responsibility of the father and mother to see that their children are trained to love the Lord. God has a chain of command—God, government, father, mother, children. When we follow that chain, the family is linked together, and God can bless it. It is a rule of life that the way we respond to our parents' authority will become the way we respond to God's authority.

PEACE
1 Thessalonians 4

GREAT DAY

For this we tell you as the Lord's word: we who are left alive until the Lord comes shall not forestall those who have died; because at the word of command, at the sound of the archangel's voice and God's trumpet-call, the Lord himself will descend from heaven. 1 Thessalonians 4:15, 16, N.E.B.

The second coming of Jesus is mentioned in every one of the eight chapters in First and Second Thessalonians. It is the main teaching in these letters, and there are at least twenty references to this blessed hope of every Christian. Not all the chapters in Thessalonians are included to be read in our study, but Christians need to read them anyway.

Paul reaffirms the Bible teaching that the people who die before Jesus comes again will wait in the grave until the resurrection. Then, at the command of Jesus Himself, the angels will sound the trumpet that will raise the righteous dead. No matter where they are, our Creator will give them life again.

Jesus will not walk on the earth at this time, for we are told that the righteous dead who are resurrected and the righteous who are living will "meet the Lord in the air." When we studied the prophecies, we discovered that the righteous will remain in heaven for a thousand years, and then return to live on earth (see Revelation 20).

"Our Lord's coming is mentioned 318 times in 260 chapters of the New Testament, occupying one in every 20 verses from Matthew to Revelation. Surely this should be sufficient to show its importance." There is no need for misunderstandings concerning the second coming of Jesus or the whereabouts of the dead. As we study these references, we discover the truth about these two important teachings.

The hope mentioned in Thessalonians can be the hope in the heart of every Christian. And those who have this hope need to share it with those who do not have it. The resurrection morning is going to be the happiest day this world has ever seen. Loved ones who have been separated for years will be joyfully united. All will want to worship the One who has made this possible—Jesus.

PEACE
1 Thessalonians 5

LETTER IN THE TRUNK

Do not quench the Spirit, do not despise prophesying. 1 Thessalonians 5:19, 20.

Stephen Smith lived near Washington, New Hampshire, and in 1850, with his wife and children, became an Adventist. For some time he was a faithful church member, but in a year or two he adopted some strange views concerning the advent of Jesus Christ and became very critical of Ellen G. White.

During this difficult time the Lord showed His love for Stephen Smith by appealing to him to change from his waywardness. This was done through a letter from Ellen G. White. However, when Stephen saw the return address—Mrs. E. G. White, Battle Creek, Michigan—he was furious. When he reached home, he threw the testimony into an old trunk.

Twenty-seven years rolled by, and in 1884, as an old man, Stephen Smith began to read the *Review and Herald.* Several articles appealed to him, and he said, "That's the truth." Turning to the name of the author, he noticed that they were written by Ellen White. His wife and others saw a remarkable change in his life as he continued to read the articles.

Eugene W. Farnsworth, an early Adventist preacher, was conducting a series of revival meetings in the Washington, New Hampshire, church in 1885. Stephen knew Elder Farnsworth and journeyed the twelve miles to Washington to be present for the Sabbath service. At the close of the service he stood up and said, "No honest man can help seeing that God is with the Advent Movement and against us who have opposed it. I want to be in fellowship with this people in heart and in the church."

After this public confession Stephen Smith began to review his past experience. One day he recalled the unopened letter from Ellen G. White in his trunk. For the first time in twenty-eight years he wanted to know what was inside the envelope. With trembling hand he unlocked the old trunk and lifted the lid. Opening the letter, he read a picture of what his life would be if he followed the course that he had pursued. Looking back over nearly three decades of godless living, he realized that the prediction had come true. The following Sabbath he gave another testimony to God's love for the sinner and His guidance of the church through the Spirit of Prophecy.

328

PEACE
2 Thessalonians 3

THE ADJUSTABLE FARMER

May the Lord of peace himself give you peace at all times and in all ways. 2 Thessalonians 3:16, N.E.B.

A Chinese farmer was walking along a road carrying a jar of soup suspended on a stick over his shoulder. As the crowd of travelers jostled him, the jar was knocked off the stick and broken, and the soup was spilled. The complacent farmer walked calmly on his way without even so much as looking back. An interested spectator inquired, "Sir, don't you know that your jar of soup was knocked off the stick?"

"Oh, yes," answered the farmer, smiling, "I know it. I heard it drop."

"Then why don't you stop and do something about it?"

"The jar is broken, isn't it?"

"Yes," replied the surprised man.

"The soup is spilled, isn't it?" the farmer asked.

"Yes, the soup is spilled. But why don't you stop and do something about it?" asked the stranger rather impatiently.

"What could I do about it? The jug is broken, the soup is spilled, and nothing can restore them. At the end of my journey I have a home and a well-set table. I have no time to look back at a broken jug and spilled soup."

This farmer is not likely to have a nervous breakdown or give his family ulcers. He has learned to adjust to life's upsets; he refuses to let reverses spoil his response to living. The man's name is unknown; he is just one of 600 million Chinese, and his whereabouts cannot be traced; but his attitude is one that we would do well to copy.

This farmer's way of life is different from ours. However, he can teach us a vital lesson. And unless we learn this lesson, our journey along life's highway, whether by mule or Mercedes, will be spoiled. Without it, we will lack real peace and will darken the pathway of those who travel with us.

Sometimes up and sometimes down—this is the natural course of life. However, we must not and need not lose our equilibrium during the valley experiences. We can "adjust"; we can live. We can demonstrate that the Lord of peace controls us and makes us adjustable.

PEACE
1 Timothy 3

TO YOUNG WORKERS

I am hoping to come to you before long, but I write this in case I am delayed, to let you know how men ought to conduct themselves in God's household, that is, the church of the living God, the pillar and bulwark of the truth. 1 Timothy 3:14, 15, N.E.B.

Timothy joined the Christian church at 15, and at 22 became one of Paul's traveling companions on the apostle's missionary journeys. It is evident from Paul's writings that he loved Timothy and reported that he was a good Christian worker. The relationship was so close, in fact, that the older man regarded Timothy as his son (see Phil. 2:22).

After Paul was released from his first imprisonment, he visited Greece and put Timothy in charge of the church at Ephesus. The young man was sad at having to say goodbye to his father in the faith, and it was to encourage him that Paul wrote this letter. The two letters to Timothy and the ones to Titus and Philemon are different from other letters that Paul wrote, in that they are written to individuals rather than to churches.

Paul was in his 60s when he wrote these letters, and he gives a lot of good counsel to those who are working for the Lord. These are books that young Christian workers should read often. In the two books of Timothy there is much instruction on church organization, administration, and preaching.

W ork as faithfully as teachers, soldiers, athletes, and farmers (2 Tim. 2:1-6).

O rganize elders and deacons to work in the church (1 Tim. 3:1-14).

R emain loyal despite opposition (2 Tim. 1:8-18).

K eep teaching the true Christian message (chap. 3:14).

E ncourage all to study the Scriptures (verses 13-17).

R eveal the conditions in the last days (verses 1-13).

S eek to be a good example (1 Tim. 4:6-16).

Although you may be young, you can learn how to be a Christian worker. God can use you as He used Timothy to assist those who are working for Him. You can also look for opportunities to witness. One day, if time lasts, you may be a full-time worker for Christ.

PEACE
1 Timothy 4

ANGELS WITHOUT WINGS

Let no one despise your youth, but set the believers an example in speech and conduct, in love, in faith, in purity. 1 Timothy 4:12.

More than fourteen thousand young people from more than a hundred countries attended the world Adventist Youth Congress in Zurich, Switzerland. A representative group of these youth from Czechoslovakia, Yugoslavia, Poland, North and South America, Africa, Asia, and the Far East dressed in national costumes and presented a half-hour program for the legislators and office workers in parliament.

The next day a large Catholic newspaper commented that here was a group of youth who were really different, who had found satisfaction in life without the so-called pleasures of cigarettes, drugs, et cetera. In the same newspaper an editorial cartoonist sketched a picture of a woman cleaning the parliament buildings after the visit of these Adventist youth. The artist portrayed the cleaning lady gathering up angels' wings! These dear young Adventists who visited the parliament would be the first to state that they were not angels, but sinners saved by grace. However, their clean, upright Christian lives were so different from many who had visited the city that the newspaper's artist considered them "angels."

This is a time in earth's history when God is particularly counting on youth and children to be "an example of the believers" (1 Tim. 4:12). In past ages the Lord has been pleased with young men and women such as Joseph, Daniel, Meshach, Shadrach, Abednego, Esther, Ruth, and Stephen. During the time of the Reformation and rise of the remnant church there were young men and women whom God could count on.

We need to consecrate our lives to God every morning and make ourselves available to do the Lord's work through His power, so that He can count on us. Our lives need to testify to the saving power of the Lord Jesus Christ, and people will be influenced to accept our Saviour when they see that we too are "angels without wings."

PEACE
2 Timothy 1

FROM DEATH ROW

Of this Gospel I . . . am not ashamed . . . because I know who it is in whom I have trusted, and am confident of his power to keep safe what he has put into my charge, until the great Day. 2 Timothy 1:11, 12, N.E.B.

The first letter I received from Bill was simply an inquiry for additional information about the Bible. He had been reading *Signs of the Times,* which was delivered to the prison by an Adventist youth society. Inasmuch as I was then writing the youth columns for that publication, his letter, addressed to "Pastor, Seventh-day Adventist Church, Newcastle," was delivered to me. The fact that I received this letter, Bill and I both believe, was a part of God's plan for his life.

That was seventeen years ago, and since then Bill and I have exchanged hundreds of letters. On every possible occasion I have visited him, and on those visits I have noted that here was a man who had found Jesus, learned to love the Bible, and wanted to serve the Lord. Talks with prison officials confirmed my evaluation.

On November 9, 1979, Bill was released from prison and wrote to me as follows: "My greatest wish now is to be baptized, and I can tell you my faith has not wavered. I am still sure where I am going. I went in [to prison] as Bill, and when I left he stayed behind and I am again known by my second name, Paul. For as Paul of old left Saul behind, so those wasted years are left forever. All I want to do is to be ready when Jesus comes. I am now at peace with myself, for I truly believe that God forgives, and I am secure in His love."

When I read those lines, tears came to my eyes, and I praised God for the gospel that changes the lives of men and women. No one who has seen the changes that I have seen in Paul's life could doubt or be ashamed of the gospel of Jesus Christ. Many people who read the Second Epistle to Timothy get tears in their eyes too. It was the last letter from Paul, and it was written on death row.

The confidence of Paul in his Roman prison and that of the new Paul in Australia is the confidence that you and I should have. We should be able to say with certainty, "I know . . . in whom I have trusted."

332

PEACE
2 Timothy 3

THE *PITCAIRN*

All scripture is inspired by God and profitable for teaching, for reproof, for correction, and for training in righteousness, that the man of God may be complete, equipped for every good work. 2 Timothy 3:16, 17.

Pitcairn is not only the name of a tiny island but also the name of a small Seventh-day Adventist mission vessel.

The total cost of the *Pitcairn* in the year 1890 was $22,098.35, and the entire amount was paid for by Sabbath school offerings. On November 25, 1890, the ship arrived at its first destination, Pitcairn Island. The vessel's arrival followed earlier visits there by a Seventh-day Adventist layman, John I. Tay, who had arrived in 1886. In that year all the islanders had decided to keep the seventh day as the Sabbath. When Tay returned to California, he shared this thrilling story. This stirred up interest in South Seas missions and led to the construction of the *Pitcairn*. Mr. Tay and his wife were on the ship when it arrived at the island.

The people of Pitcairn gladly received not only the Word of God as it was shared with them by John Adams and by Fletcher Christian's son but also the truths that were taught by John I. Tay and the missionaries who arrived with him. Since the first eighty-two people were baptized by Pastor E. H. Gates, the ship's minister, most of the citizens of Pitcairn have become members of the Seventh-day Adventist Church. A fifth-generation descendant of Fletcher Christian stated, "I would say that the Bible is the best-read book on Pitcairn."

Although separated from any continent by more than 3,000 miles of ocean, the people of Pitcairn are an integral part of the worldwide remnant church. Almost two hundred years have passed since Christian landed on Pitcairn Island, and 1980 marked the ninetieth anniversary of the arrival of the boat named for the island. The people of Pitcairn in the 1980s still rejoice that Sabbath school members in the 1890s gave their offerings to purchase the ship. A minister who recently served there says, "No, the Word of God will never go out of style . . . especially not on Pitcairn Island, where its influence turned bloodshed to order and sorrow to joy." On Pitcairn the Scriptures certainly proved to be "profitable" for all who read them.

PEACE
Titus 2

SELF-CONTROL

For the grace of God has dawned upon the world with healing for all mankind; and by it we are disciplined to renounce godless ways and worldly desires, and to live a life of temperance, honesty, and godliness in the present age. Titus 2:11, 12, N.E.B.

Charles A. Lindbergh was the first person to fly across the Atlantic Ocean. His solo flight in 1927 took 33½ hours. As a result of this feat he became famous, and as so often happens, many companies sought to use his name to promote their products. It was long before the relationship between smoking and cancer had been established, but Lindbergh refused a large sum of money from a company that wanted to use his picture in a cigarette advertisment.

Lindbergh, who became a colonel in the Air Force and was for a time a technical adviser to Pan American Airways, had learned to discipline himself. His refusal to endorse cigarettes showed that in this area of his life popularity and money could not change his self-control. We are to go further and to follow Paul's counsel to Titus, which will lead us to "renounce godless ways and worldly desires, and to live a life of temperance" (Titus 2:12, N.E.B.).

Robert E. Lee, who refused the offer to become commander of the United States Army during the Civil War, has been considered by some to be the greatest leader of either side of the War between the States. Lee was once offered $10,000 (which would be worth about $50,000 today) to permit his name to be used in connection with a gambling lottery. At this time the general needed the money very badly, but his answer was "Gentlemen, my name is all I have left. It is not for sale."

Is your name for sale? Do money, popularity, and social pressures lead you to sell the name Christian or to do things that you should not do? If you follow the examples of Charles Lindbergh and Robert E. Lee, you will not sell your name. If you follow the advice of Paul to Titus, you will, by the grace of God, exercise self-control under all circumstances.

PEACE
Philemon 18

A RUNAWAY SLAVE

And if he has done you any wrong or is in your debt, put that down to my account. . . . I undertake to repay—not to mention that you owe your very self to me as well. Philemon 18, 19, N.E.B.

Onesimus had a name to live up to, and when he ran away he was not true to his name, which meant "profitable." He apparently had stolen some money from his master, Philemon, and had found his way to the great city of Rome. It is not very likely that in a city of one and a half million people he would find Paul merely by accident. The apostle was in prison, but the Lord used him to persuade Onesimus to become a Christian. Paul also gave him a letter and advised him to go back to his master.

This is the only one of Paul's private letters that has been preserved, but no doubt he wrote many of them. It is the briefest of Paul's Epistles, just twenty-five verses, but its message and presentation are outstanding. The purpose of the letter was to persuade Philemon to forgive his runaway slave, and as we read it we find many beautiful characteristics that should be in our letters—courtesy, tact, generosity, a personal appeal.

Young people today can witness by writing letters. Every youth society and Pathfinder Club could have a letter-writing band. It is a ministry that all can engage in. We can write letters to those who have lost loved ones, to those who are lonely and discouraged, and to those who are unable to attend church.

Paul's love for this repentant runaway was so great that he said he would repay what the slave had stolen. This is a reminder of Jesus' love for us. Although we have done wrong, He stands in the judgment hall and says on our behalf, "If this Christian has done any wrong, put that down to My account." Because Jesus died on the cross and shed His blood, He has a credit account in the books of heaven. His blood is able to cover the mistakes that we have made if we confess and forsake them.

Although we are not told that Onesimus was set free, most Bible students believe he was. When Jesus comes into the heart of a slave of sin, he recognizes his need to make things right with other people. When he does this and returns to his true master, Jesus, he is set free.

PEACE
Hebrews 9

THE FIFTH GOSPEL

For Christ has entered, not that sanctuary made by men's hands which is only a symbol of the reality, but heaven itself, to appear now before God on our behalf. Hebrews 9:24, N.E.B.

The four Gospels, Matthew, Mark, Luke, and John, portray to us the *pattern, person,* and *perfection* of Jesus, and give *proof* of His divinity. In these Gospels we learn about Christ's ministry on earth, and now we discover a book that describes in detail Christ's ministry in heaven. It has been called, naturally, the "fifth Gospel."

The book of Hebrews is important for all Christians to read. Many know about the birth, death, and resurrection of Jesus, and they believe they are going to see Him again. However, not all Christians are aware of the fact that since Jesus' resurrection He has served as mediator, high priest, and judge in the courts of heaven.

Jesus' work as high priest in the heavenly sanctuary plays a very definite part in His atonement for sin. *Atonement* simply means that Jesus has brought God and man "at-one-ment," or together again, by His sacrifice for sin.

In order to understand fully the meaning of the heavenly sanctuary, we need to have a knowledge of the earthly sanctuary built in Old Testament times. That is why we devoted two months to the study of the *plans* and *purposes* of God as seen in the books of Moses. Also, we discovered in the book of Daniel information on the sanctuary and the judgment.

From the study of the books of the Bible that deal with the sanctuary we learn that Jesus commenced His work as high priest in the second apartment of the heavenly sanctuary in 1844, at the end of the 2300-day prophecy.

Isn't it wonderful to know that Jesus is not only our sacrifice but also our high priest? He not only gave His blood to atone for our sins but also ministers in our behalf in the heavenly sanctuary. I am looking forward to the day when Christ says that the work of mediation and judgment are finished, because then He will "appear the second time" (Heb. 9:28).

336

PEACE
Hebrews 11

GOOD, BETTER, BEST

And without faith it is impossible to please him; for anyone who comes to God must believe that he exists and that he rewards those who search for him. Hebrews 11:6, N.E.B.

"Good, better, best.
 Never let it rest,
 Until your good becomes better,
 And your better becomes best."

This little rhyme, known to many of you, contains a lot of truth. There should be continual growth in our lives, particularly in our Christian characters. By God's power we are able to progress through "good" and "better" to the place where we offer Him our "best."

Better is the key word in the book of Hebrews. It occurs at least thirteen times in the King James Version, and is used three times in chapter 11.

"Good, better, best" faith is the subject of Hebrews 11. There is also a definition of *faith* in today's text. We note that faith is essential for all who would please God. In order to strengthen our faith, Paul reminds us of that which was exhibited by men and women in Old and New Testament times. Reading this chapter about the lives of such notable characters as Enoch, Noah, Abraham, and Moses is like walking through a hall of fame. As we study the brief pictures in this hall, we gain confidence to make our good better, then best.

And as we consider these heroes of faith, we are led to ask, How can I have more faith? Paul told us in Romans that we can gain this by reading God's Word every day. When I was a junior youth, one of my leaders gave me the following definition, which contains the secret of strengthening our faith:

F orsaking
A ll
I
T ake
H im.

337

PEACE
James 4

"I SHALL ADVANCE"

Be submissive then to God. Stand up to the devil and he will turn and run. Come close to God, and he will come close to you. James 4:7, 8, N.E.B.

World War I was fought from 1914 to 1918. That is such a long time ago that even your fathers and mothers may not know very much about it unless they have studied history. It is sad when nations fight one another, and we are all looking forward to the time when there will be no more wars.

One of the great generals of that war won fame by this brief message, delivered at a time when his armies were completely disabled. On a European battlefield he said, "My right army is crushed, my left is crumbling, my center is receding. Situation excellent; I shall advance."

Despite the discouraging situation, the general did advance and was victorious. There is a tremendous lesson for the Christian in this message. As we look out in the world, we see the forces of evil coming upon the church on every hand. As we look one way, we see it being crushed by persecution. As we look another way, we see members crumbling because of their desire for worldly things. As we look in yet another direction, we see many members receding because of discouragement. Today God is looking for leaders to stand up and say, "Situation excellent; I shall advance."

Yes, the Christian is on a battlefield, and the devil and his evil angels are lined up in strong columns before us. However, we have the assurance that if we submit unto God and resist the devil, he will flee. Remember that one with God is a majority and say, "I will advance." Thus we will give the devil a fright, and "he will turn and run," and you and I will have peace in our lives.

The nearer we draw to God, the nearer He will come to us. This is the "light for my life" that you and I need today.

PEACE
1 Peter 1

"IT WORKS"

You have been born anew, not of perishable seed but of imperishable, through the living and abiding word of God. 1 Peter 1:23.

During the lunch break the chief astronomer looked for the mechanic who had been called in to repair the turning mechanism of the great telescope; he found him reading a Bible. "What good do you expect to get from that book? It's out of date. Why, you don't even know who wrote it!"

The mechanic thought for a moment, then replied, "Don't you make considerable use of the multiplication tables in your calculations?"

"Of course," replied the astronomer.

"Sir, do you know who wrote them?"

"Why, I guess I don't," admitted the scientist. "I trust them because they work."

"Well," stated the mechanic, "I trust the Bible for the same reason. It works."

Here is the best proof for the truth of the Bible; here is the irrefutable answer to the skeptics' charges against the Scriptures; here is the guarantee that satisfies space-age youth—"It works."

Bible-believing young people rejoice in the tremendous power of the Word of God. They see it in their own lives every day: in victory over temptations that if indulged bring sad consequences; in peace amid the reverses and setbacks of life's journey; in control of temper, although often provoked.

Although the Bible is still a best seller and available in eleven hundred languages and dialects, there are millions who need to know that it is relevant and that "it works."

If you know the power of the Word of God, then do introduce others to the Book of books and share the love of God with them.

If you have doubted or discredited the Bible, why not find out for yourself what it really says? It takes about eighty hours to read, and you have nothing to lose and everything to gain by reading the Bible through and by reading it thoroughly.

PEACE
2 Peter 1

ALL IS POSSIBLE

Grace and peace be yours in fullest measure, through the knowledge of God and Jesus our Lord. His divine power has bestowed on us everything that makes for life and true religion. 2 Peter 1:2, 3, N.E.B.

Au Sable is one of the largest youth camps operated by the Seventh-day Adventist Church in North America. It is located in Michigan and occupies 840 acres. On a recent visit to Au Sable, I noticed this statement in the camp kitchen:
"With God all things are possible.
Nothing is ever too hard to do
If your faith is strong and purpose true.
So never give up and never stop,
Just journey to the mountaintop."
I do not know the author of this handwritten statement, but it echoes the promise, peace, and power stated by Peter in our text today. Both statements remind us that "all things are possible" only when we demonstrate faith and when we are, by the grace of Jesus, endeavoring to be true Christians.

Peter has also outlined a ladder for us to climb to the mountaintop. This ladder has eight rungs, and each one is important for us to rest on. The rungs in Peter's ladder are faith, virtue, knowledge, self-control, steadfastness, godliness, brotherly affection, and love (2 Peter 1:5-7, R.S.V.). Peter states that if we do not have these gifts we are "blind and shortsighted" (verse 9, R.S.V.). On the other hand, he says that if we climb this ladder we "shall never fall" (verse 10).

Peter's Epistles were written near the close of his life. The first one was to encourage the Christians in times of persecution, and the second gives instruction as to how to deal with problems that arise within the church.

To help us do all the things God has asked us to do, we have His prophetic Word. Peter describes the Scriptures as a "lamp shining in a dark place" (verse 19, R.S.V.). He reaffirms that Scripture is sure and reliable. As you let this lamp of God's Word shine into your lives you will be able to say that every day you have "light for my life."

340

PEACE
1 John 1

FIORDLANDER

If we confess our sins, he is just, and may be trusted to forgive our sins and cleanse us from every kind of wrong. 1 John 1:9, N.E.B.

How would you like to attend a youth camp in a park that covers millions of acres of majestic scenery? One Easter I had the privilege of camping with young people in such a place. Fiordland National Park, which was our home and playground during the camp, covers more than 3 million acres. Deep, dense forests run from the shores of huge lakes and fiords to the snowline on the gaunt peaks of high, rugged mountains. One glance at this vast and majestic scenery explains why this region is among the world's greatest tourist attractions. This scenic park occupies the entire southwestern sector of the South Island of New Zealand. It includes many lakes with tongue-twisting names such as Manapouri and Te Anau.

The youth camp was held on the shores of Lake Manapouri, almost six hundred feet above sea level. The lake has often been described as the most beautiful in New Zealand. It covers about fifty-six square miles and is studded with some thirty small, forest-clad islands. On the Saturday evening of the campout, the party boarded the luxury cruise launch *Fiordlander* and traveled on the lake for about two hours. The launch, which had been used by Queen Elizabeth and the royal family of England, stopped several times as the captain pointed out interesting facts and figures.

No doubt the stop that impressed the young people most was the one above the deepest lake water in New Zealand. Below us was 1,455 feet, or about a quarter of a mile, of water. Above us was a dense, dark sky, broken only by myriads of shining stars that reminded us of God's love and His control of the universe. At that moment I remembered the words of Micah 7:19 and 1 John 1:9 and determined to share these statements of God's love with as many people as possible.

We can rejoice that when we confess and forsake our sins, God forgives and forgets. They are as it were cast "into the depths of the sea."

PEACE
1 John 4

NO NEED TO BE AFRAID

There is no room for fear in love; perfect love banishes fear. 1 John 4:18, N.E.B.

Calvyn was a minister's son, but he did not know Jesus as his personal Saviour. He wanted to follow his parents' example and counsel, but he also wanted to be popular with some of his friends who had not given their lives fully to Christ either.

In a remarkable way Calvyn made a decision to go to college. In his first year at the school the struggle went on, but on two occasions he gained the victory over specific temptations. And finally he responded to God's call to give his life completely to Jesus. He transferred to Avondale College to study for the ministry, and after graduation and marriage he became a pastor in Australia.

The call to serve in New Guinea was not one that he had dreamed of. However, he was soon enjoying his work there. In order to reach remote areas, he often had to fly.

U.B.Y.—"Uniform, Bravo, Yankee"—were the call letters of the Cessna 207 that was to take him home after a long walkabout. As the aircraft rose to about four hundred feet from Goroka Airport, the motor sputtered, and the plane crashed within sight of the tower.

Calvyn was unconscious for several hours. He had broken eight ribs and three vertebrae and had a hairline fracture of the skull. He was also paralyzed on one side of his face and had no tears or taste.

After spending two weeks in the Goroka hospital, he was to fly back to Lae by commercial airliner. But as he found his seat in the plane, he was overwhelmed with feelings of fear. At this point a portion of our Morning Watch text came to his mind, "Perfect love casteth out fear." He then prayed, "If Your promises are true and You love me, please cast out my fear." From that moment he was not afraid of the flight. From his home he flew to Australia for further treatment in the Sydney Adventist Hospital. Four weeks later he was back in New Guinea.

During the next four years Calvyn Townend flew confidently in all sizes of planes under all conditions. Yes, we can claim God's promises to banish fear.

PEACE
3 John

LIVING WISELY

I pray that you may enjoy good health, and that all may go well with you, as I know it goes well with your soul. 3 John 2, N.E.B.

A Portuguese monastery perched precariously atop a three-hundred-foot cliff. Visitors were strapped into a huge wicker basket and pulled to the top by a ragged rope. As one visitor stepped into the basket for the descent, he asked anxiously, "How often do you get a new rope?" "Whenever the old one breaks," a monk replied.

In this space age too many people speed on, disregarding rules of health. Many people realize too late that they have no health and no time left. We must remember that when "the rope" breaks, it cannot be replaced. The Creator gave us only one life on this earth.

Review your habits. What are you doing? Are you rusting out, burning out, wearing out—or are you truly living your life out? In order to live as God has planned, we should read His suggestions for healthful living as outlined in the Scriptures.

One of the basic laws of health is to be "moderate in all things." It is not sufficient to refrain from eating and drinking harmful items. We must also show self-control in the good things we do. This means that we need to have a balanced diet, avoid unhealthful food combinations, abstain from eating between meals, and not overeat.

Two other rules of health are to eat wisely of proper foods and to get plenty of exercise. According to Genesis 1, the ideal diet is vegetarian. Because of the prevalence of disease in animals today, it is wise for us to get back to this original plan. And each day we should participate in some form of physical activity.

The relationship between the mind and the body is very close, and we need to avoid bad moods and indulgence in self-pity. As we look on the bright side of life, we will cultivate a happy and cheerful disposition. The Bible, which contains words of life, declares that this attitude is as good for us as medicine.

"A merry heart doeth good like a medicine: but a broken spirit drieth the bones" (Prov. 17:22).

PEACE
Jude

THE CHOICE IS YOURS

From Jude, servant of Jesus Christ and brother of James, to those whom God has called, who live in the love of God the Father and in the safe keeping of Jesus Christ. Mercy, peace, and love be yours in fullest measure. Jude 1, 2, N.E.B.

Where there is faith, there is love.
Where there is love, there is peace.
Where there is peace, there is God.
Where there is God, there is no need.

The choice is ours. If we choose, we can have faith, love, and peace in our lives. The way to obtain them is to have God as the center of our living. When this is achieved, there is no need. On the other hand, if there is a need in our lives today, it is because God is not there.

In this brief letter written by Jude, who was possibly a brother of Jesus, we once again have assurance of faith, love, and peace. Jude assures us that we can be "in the safe keeping of Jesus Christ" (verse 1, N.E.B.).

Keep, the key word in this Epistle, is mentioned at least five times. First, we are kept in the faith—the faith of our fathers (verse 3). Second, we are kept in love of God; and third, the Lord has guaranteed to keep us from falling.

"Now to him who is able to keep you from falling and to present you without blemish before the presence of his glory with rejoicing" (verse 24, R.S.V).

What a guarantee! When someone assures me that he will keep my car and house in good care while I am on vacation, I have peace. When my secretary guarantees to keep my office work up to date while I am away, I am very pleased. And when Jesus Christ, the Creator of the universe, declares that He will keep me from falling and will present me without fault to the Father, words cannot describe my joy. All I can say is, "This is light for my life." I rejoice that this light will keep me in the faith, in the love of God, and in the safekeeping of Jesus. When I think of these blessings, I choose to be a Christian, don't you?

344

PROOF
John 19

WHAT'S YOUR PROOF?

When Pilate heard these words, he was the more afraid; he entered the praetorium again and said to Jesus, "Where are you from?" But Jesus gave no answer. John 19:8, 9.

Several years ago the president of France went fishing on the Seine River. Although his bodyguards were nearby, they left him alone to enjoy a bit of solitude. While they were out of sight a game warden came along. He did not recognize the president and asked him for his fishing license.

The president had left his license at home, but he explained, "It's quite all right. I am the president of France." The game warden smiled and said, "Yes, I know. And I am the President of the United States. Come along."

Just then the bodyguards returned and stopped the warden from taking the president to the police station.

But no one came to rescue Jesus, the Son of God, when He was in Pilate's judgment hall. Because the Jews were asking for Jesus to be crucified and Pilate wanted to please them, the Lord's life was at stake. Pilate first asked Jesus, "What is truth?" And then, "Where are you from?" or, in other words, "Who are you?"

If you had had the opportunity of going into Pilate's judgment hall to identify Jesus, what would you have said? If Jesus were on trial today, what proof would you give as to His identity? Since we have studied aspects of the life of Jesus, including His *pattern, person,* and *perfection,* we should be able to identify Him. Matthew, Mark, and Luke have given us clues as to His identity, and John's book is devoted to giving *proof* as to who He is.

Pilate asked, "What shall I do with Jesus?" It is necessary to know who Jesus is and to be able to prove His identity, but it is more important to know Him as our personal Saviour.

Before studying the fourth Gospel, which is different from the others, we will look at two Old Testament books, Ruth and Jonah, which offer *proof* that there is a God of *passion* and *power* who is planning to establish the kingdom of peace. Both of these books are Christ-centered.

PROOF
Ruth 1

WEARY PILGRIM

But Ruth said, "Entreat me not to leave you or to return from following you; for where you go I will go, and where you lodge I will lodge; your people shall be my people, and your God my God." Ruth 1:16.

"Tell me the truth, Jim. Did you do it?" This question was asked by a mother, who could not believe that her son had committed murder. Jim was frightened as he sat in the prison visiting room with the guard standing by. He answered, "I did not do it."

On the day of his trial the judge said to Jim's mother, "If you'll persuade your son to plead guilty, we will be easy with him." But the trusting woman replied, "Your Honor, he did not do it."

Jim was tried and found guilty anyway, and on the day of his execution the chaplain said to him, "Jim, you are facing eternity; tell me, did you do it?" After a moment's silence Jim said, "I did do it; go and tell my mother."

The chaplain went to Jim's mother and found her with her head bowed low in sorrow. He told her the sad truth, and with tears streaming down her face the mother replied, "Chaplain, go quickly and tell Jim I love him still."

This mother's love for her son was so strong that she was loyal to him even when she knew that he was guilty. The loyalty of love is also illustrated in the story of Ruth the Moabitess. With her husband dead, Ruth had to decide whether to stay in Moab or to return to Judah with her mother-in-law, Naomi. Naomi tried to persuade her two widowed daughters-in-law to stay in their own country. They both wept, and the Bible says, "Orpah kissed her mother-in-law, but Ruth clung to her" (Ruth 1:14, R.S.V.). Although it meant going to an unknown land and an uncertain future, Ruth said, "I will go."

In our family relationships we need to do more than just show outward affection by kissing, as did Orpah. We need to show the passion that Ruth showed, and cling to our family. Those who have Christian mothers can bring joy to them by saying, "Your God shall be my God."

PROOF
Ruth 2

POOR REAPER

And Ruth the Moabitess said to Naomi, "Let me go to the field, and glean among the ears of grain after him in whose sight I shall find favor." Ruth 2:2.

Naomi and her husband, Elimelech, had left Palestine because of a severe famine. While in Moab, Elimelech, whose name means "My God is king," died. It was ten years after that when Naomi decided to return to her homeland, and one of her daughters-in-law, Ruth, accompanied her. When they arrived in Bethlehem, Ruth met a wealthy relative whose name was Boaz. From a study of Biblical genealogy we discover that Boaz' mother was Rahab, who had lived in the days when Joshua led Israel.

In the time of the judges it was the custom for farmers to allow the poor, the fatherless, the widows, and the strangers to gather the grain that his harvesters missed. Ruth labored patiently in the fields in the heat of the day to gather barley for Naomi and herself.

In times of hardship and failure we must be prepared to work hard and patiently. Although we should pray for God's blessings, we must also do what we can to provide what is needed for ourselves and for others. Ruth left a fertile country to work as a poor person in Palestine. Her love for her mother-in-law was so strong that she demonstrated patience and worked hard to support them both.

The story of Ruth up to this time, although very beautiful, seems to be the natural events that followed a tragedy. But then the Bible says, "She happened to come to the part of the field belonging to Boaz" (Ruth 2:3, R.S.V.). This was not by chance. It was in God's *providence* that Ruth selected that field. And later in the story we shall see what God's plan was in bringing Ruth, a descendant of Lot, to Palestine.

"Worry is blind, and cannot discern the future; but Jesus sees the end from the beginning. In every difficulty He has His way prepared to bring relief. Our heavenly Father has a thousand ways to provide for us, of which we know nothing. Those who accept the one principle of making the service and honor of God supreme, will find perplexities vanish, and a plain path before their feet."—*The Desire of Ages,* p. 330.

PROOF
Ruth 3

YOUNG BRIDE

And she replied, "All that you say I will do." Ruth 3:5.

A young woman was busily checking hats and coats in a cloakroom of a large hall in Stockholm, Sweden. It was almost time for the commencement of the program, and she worked without looking at her customers.

As one man put his hat and coat on the counter, she said, "That will be 25 öre." The man said politely, "I'm sorry, I haven't any money." The young lady was impatient as she repeated, "It will be 25 öre anyway." Then someone gave the man the money, and the girl gasped as she glanced up at her customer's face, for standing before her was the king of Sweden!

If this young lady had loved her work and her customers, she would have been courteous to all of them. We can see the word *court* in courtesy, and court is a royal word. As subjects of the heavenly King, we need to show courtly behavior at all times.

I am a little thing with a big meaning.

I help everyone.

I unlock doors, open hearts, banish prejudice;

I create friendship and good will.

I inspire respect and admiration.

I violate no law.

I cost nothing. Many have praised me; none have condemned me.

I am pleasing to those of high and low degree.

I am useful every moment.

I am courtesy.

In the story of Ruth, the wealthy landowner, Boaz, displayed courtesy to the poor reapers, greeting them with "The Lord be with you." And the reapers answered, "The Lord bless thee." Boaz showed particular interest in Ruth and showed her even greater courtesy. When she asked why, he told her it was because of her kindness to Naomi.

It was in God's plan that Ruth should meet Boaz and that Naomi should encourage her to be friendly with him. Naomi outlined to Ruth a custom of that time whereby she could properly show Boaz that she would like to marry him. Once again Ruth demonstrated respect and courtesy to her mother-in-law when she said, "'All that you say I will do'" (Ruth 3:5, R.S.V.).

348

PROOF
Ruth 4

ROYAL GRANDMOTHER

Then the women said to Naomi, "Blessed be the Lord, who has not left you this day without next of kin; and may his name be renowned in Israel!" Ruth 4:14.

The keynote of the book of Ruth is the kinsman Redeemer. The word *kinsman,* or its equivalent, is found more than thirty times in this love story. *Kinsman* means "close relative," and it also had extra meaning in the days of Ruth. Naomi explained to Ruth that Boaz was more than just a relative. He was a kinsman who could redeem her husband's property.

Boaz married Ruth, and apparently they were very happy together. And our Morning Watch text says that the women rejoiced with Naomi that the Lord had provided a next of kin to restore her husband's name and property.

At this point in the story we see God's plan not only for Naomi and Ruth but also for the whole human race. God had led a heathen girl to Bethlehem to become the bride of Boaz. Apparently Ruth had learned of the true God. "All who, like Rahab the Canaanite, and Ruth the Moabitess, turned from idolatry to the worship of the true God, were to unite themselves with His chosen people."—*Christ's Object Lessons,* p. 290.

This beautiful love story does not end with Ruth and Boaz. They had a son whose name was Obed, who was the grandfather of King David. That means that Ruth became the great-grandmother of David, and an ancestor of Jesus.

Boaz is in many ways a type of Christ. He redeemed the name and property of Naomi's husband; Jesus redeemed the name of His people and has given them a heavenly inheritance.

If the Jewish nation had fully understood the book of Ruth, they would have seen that love is lasting and that God is no respecter of persons. Ruth was a heathen Moabite girl and Boaz was the son of Rahab, who had been a harlot. However, because they responded to God's love, they were privileged to become ancestors of Jesus.

As we respond to God's love, He enables us to become "relatives" of the redeemed of all ages. How exciting it will be to meet all these "relatives" in heaven!

PROOF
Jonah 1

FOUND A SHIP

But Jonah rose to flee to Tarshish from the presence of the Lord. He went down to Joppa and found a ship going to Tarshish; so he paid the fare, and went on board, to go with them to Tarshish, away from the presence of the Lord. Jonah 1:3.

When the group of Adventist young people found the ship, it was a near wreck, lying in the docks of Harstad, Norway. It was Norway's oldest schooner, built in 1868, ten years before the first Seventh-day Adventist missionary, J. G. Matteson, arrived in that country. The boat had sailed the seas between Norway, Greenland, and Russia.

It cost more than $345,000 to purchase and restore this tall, elegant ship. It had to be reshaped, repainted, resailed, and fitted with a new engine. Eighty-four feet long, with 480 square meters of sail, it is now white with gold trim, and glides gracefully over the waves with its sails blowing in the breeze. The name of the ship is *Anna Rodge,* and the Adventist youth who found it wanted to witness about God's love in every way they could to as many people as possible.

The *Anna Rodge* is owned by two brothers, Magne and Aage Inndahl, who not only love boats but who dared to put their dreams into reality. Youth directors and young people of Norway are operating this schooner for Christ.

Already the ship has proved to be a tourist attraction, and wherever she docks along the 35,000 miles of Norway's coastline, people crowd on board to view an exhibit of the Adventist Church or to accept an invitation to a stop-smoking clinic, cooking demonstration, or evangelistic campaign being held in the area.

Jonah also found a ship, but at that time he had a different reason for searching than did the youth of Norway. He wanted to escape from God's call to tell the people of Nineveh of His love. So he found a ship going to Tarshish, which probably was on the coast of Spain.

God's love for Jonah was such that He didn't forsake him even when the prophet fled from Him. In order to help Jonah, God sent a great storm on the sea and arranged for a big fish to rescue him when he was thrown overboard.

PROOF
Jonah 2

ABANDON SHIP

"But I with the voice of thanksgiving will sacrifice to thee;
what I have vowed I will pay. Deliverance belongs to the Lord!"
Jonah 2:9.

When the ocean liner *Wahine* was on the rocks off Barrett's
Reef, New Zealand, 12-year-old Stephen O'Neill made a vow
with his father, "If we get out of this, we will serve Jesus for the
rest of our lives."

The *Wahine* had set out from Lyttleton harbor in the South
Island of New Zealand for Wellington, at the tip of the North
Island. The sea between the two islands is known as Cook Strait
and is one of the most treacherous waterways in the world. This
journey was a tragic one for the *Wahine,* as she was battered by
the worst storm in the history of New Zealand. Turbulent seas,
with waves thirty to forty feet high, pitched and tossed the ship
mercilessly.

Cold fear gripped the heart of Clarrie O'Neill and his family
when an urgent voice informed the passengers that the *Wahine*
was on the rocks. Although the ship was badly damaged, rescue
vessels arrived and soon had it in tow to Wellington. Unfortunately, the tow cable broke, and once again the beautiful new
ship drifted helplessly in the raging storm. The cargo of cars and
heavy machinery broke loose and, aided by a gigantic wave,
rolled the ship onto its side, where shortly it sank below the
surface of the boiling sea.

A short while before the *Wahine* sank, the passengers were
put into lifeboats, but many of these also capsized. It is
significant to note, however, that Clarrie O'Neill, one of our
publishing department directors, along with his wife and six
children, managed to get into a small lifeboat that miraculously
reached shore. Had their boat capsized, the family would have
had no hope in the raging sea, with winds gusting up to 137
miles per hour. Of the 730 people on board, 54 lost their lives.

Clarrie O'Neill's comment on the shipwreck is similar to
Jonah's statement after his deliverance: "Through prayer and
singing we were able to witness and bring comfort to many, and
I praise my God for that opportunity. I saw in my children the
result of faithful family worship and continual witnessing of an
all-powerful God in the home, as calmly they endured the
ordeal."

351

PROOF
Jonah 3

RETURN VOYAGE

Then the word of the Lord came to Jonah the second time. . . .
So Jonah arose and went to Nineveh, according to the word of the
Lord. Jonah 3:1-3.

Jonah's return voyage was not by ship, but inside the great fish. Although the King James Version states that it was a whale (see Matt. 12:40), the word literally means "sea monster." This was the first known "submarine ride" that anyone ever experienced.

God's passion for the prophet and for the people of Nineveh was why Jonah was given a return voyage. It would have been just punishment if he had been swallowed by the fish and had never been heard of again. However, God's ways are not man's ways, and His love is beyond the love that we demonstrate. "Yet in the hour of Jonah's despair the Lord did not desert him. Through a series of trials and strange providences, the prophet's confidence in God and in His infinite power to save was to be revived."—*Prophets and Kings,* pp. 266, 267.

The trials that God used to help Jonah include:

T empestuous storm (Jonah 1:4).

R eal discomfort (chap. 2:2).

I nstant plant (chap. 4:6).

A great fish (chap. 1:17).

L ittle worm (chap. 4:7).

S un and wind (verse 8).

After being cast out of the whale and reaching dry land, Jonah went to Nineveh and preached that it would be destroyed in forty days, but he was not at all pleased with what happened. He apparently did not believe that the people would repent, but they did.

What happened in Nineveh could happen in the capital city of your country. In just one day, as a result of the preaching of one man, the whole city turned to God. This was a miracle. But God had to speak to Jonah twice before he obeyed. We need to determine that we will obey God and do His work when He calls us the first time.

PROOF
Jonah 4

RESCUED AGAIN

"For I knew that thou art a gracious God and merciful, slow to anger, and abounding in steadfast love, and repentest of evil." Jonah 4:2.

In 1525 Martin Luther, the great Protestant Reformer, helped some nuns to escape from a convent. One of them was Katharina von Bora, who later became his wife.

One morning at their home in Wittenberg, Luther seemed particularly gloomy. In two countries his followers were being burned for their faith. The people he was now preaching to had Bibles, but they did not seem to be living good lives.

After he went to his study this particular day, his wife dressed herself in black and knocked at her husband's door. He was surprised when he opened it and saw her in mourning dress. "Is someone dead?" he asked. "Yes!" "Who?" Luther inquired. Katharina replied, "God."

Martin was surprised and said, "What do you mean?" His wife replied, "Well, you go around here so mournfully that I have the impression God must be dead, since you trust Him no longer." Luther smiled and said, "Thank you, my dear. You are always my good angel. Of course God is not dead, and we must never forget it."

After the people of Nineveh repented, instead of being happy, Jonah became discouraged. He was angry and asked to die. He certainly acted as though God were dead. The experiences that he had been through should have led him to trust God fully. Instead, he sat under a gourd plant and sulked. The shade had been provided by God, for this plant had grown up quickly. When Jonah continued to feel sorry for himself, however, God allowed a worm to destroy it, and again Jonah prayed to die.

The closing chapter of the book of Jonah highlights God's steadfast love for the prophet, the citizens of Nineveh, and all people. The key verse in the book is our text today, which speaks of God's love. However, God's love for people is also seen in the last verse, where He said that He could not destroy Nineveh where lived many people who were ignorant of His love. God had pity on those who did not "know their right hand from their left" (Jonah 4:11, R.S.V.).

PROOF
John 1

"COME AND SEE"

Nathanael answered him, "Rabbi, you are the Son of God! You are the King of Israel!" John 1:49.

After Philip responded to Jesus' invitation to follow Him, his first act of discipleship was to find Nathanael and tell him that he, Philip, had found the Messiah. His friend was skeptical and said, "Can there any good thing come out of Nazareth?" (John 1:46). But he responded to Philip's invitation to "come and see" (verse 46).

On a dusty road near Cana, the Saviour and Nathanael met. Jesus recognized this young man as a true follower of Jehovah when He said, "Behold an Israelite indeed, in whom is no guile!" (verse 47). Nathanael was surprised and said, "'How do you know me?'" (verse 48, R.S.V.). To this the Saviour answered, "'Before Philip called you, when you were under the fig tree, I saw you'" (verse 48, R.S.V.). The answer so astonished Nathanael that he bowed before Jesus and said, "'Rabbi, you are the Son of God! You are the King of Israel!'" (verse 49, R.S.V.).

There is nothing unusual about Nathanael's being under a fig tree, but the fact that Jesus revealed his exact location is miraculous. The shade of the fig tree is where Eastern families delight to take their midday meal and meditate. Jesus did not say that Nathanael was under *a* fig tree, but under *the* fig tree, indicating a particular location where Nathanael had retired to read the Scriptures and pray.

Christ has knowledge of us before we have knowledge of Him. "He who saw Nathanael under the fig tree will see us in the secret place of prayer."—*The Desire of Ages,* p. 141.

Jesus not only revealed supernatural knowledge about Nathanael's whereabouts but He showed that He knew his character also. He stated that Nathanael was a true Israelite, one who could be trusted.

Can the Lord Jesus say of each one of us, "A Christian, indeed, in whom there is no guile"? We may be foolish at times and even forgetful, but we should never be deliberately false in any area of our Christian life.

Nathanael is one of many witnesses that John introduces to those who are wanting *proof* of who Jesus is. This disciple stated that Jesus was a teacher, the Son of God, and a royal king.

PROOF
John 2

MIRACLES, MIRACLES

This, the first of his signs, Jesus did at Cana in Galilee, and manifested his glory; and his disciples believed in him. John 2:11.

Every 24 hours your heart beats about 100,000 times; your blood travels 168 million miles; you breathe 23,040 times; you inhale 438 cubic feet of air; you eat 3.25 pounds of food; you drink 2.9 pounds of liquid; you lose in weight 7.8 pounds of waste; you perspire 1.43 pints; you turn in your sleep 25 to 35 times; you could speak 4,800 words; you move 750 major muscles; your hair grows .01714 inches; you exercise 7 million brain cells.

These fantastic accomplishments are the result of God's skill in creating us. As we realize what happens in our bodies during each twenty-four hours of life, we agree with the psalmist when he says that we are "fearfully and wonderfully made" (Ps. 139:14). We have discovered that Jesus is the Creator and His power to create is *proof* that He is the Son of God. The human body is a miracle performed by Jesus.

The first recorded miracle that Jesus performed during His lifetime was also proof of His creative power. This miracle was performed at a wedding reception at Cana in Galilee. The father of the bride was concerned because the grape juice had run out before the feast was over. The drink translated "wine" in our Bibles is "the pure juice of the grape" *(The Desire of Ages,* p. 149). Jesus would not have provided alcoholic drink, which is condemned in other parts of Scripture. This act of instantly changing water into grape juice is something that only the Creator of the vine could do.

The guests at the wedding feast had ample evidence that the son of Mary was the Son of God. No doubt many believed, and John records that the miracle strengthened the faith of the disciples also. This is the first of six miracles of Jesus recorded in John's *proof* book. Jesus performed at least thirty-five miracles, which can be compiled by reading all four Gospel accounts of His life.

PROOF
John 3

"RABBI, WE KNOW"

This man came to Jesus by night and said to him, "Rabbi, we know that you are a teacher come from God; for no one can do these signs that you do, unless God is with him." John 3:2.

Nicodemus is the third witness whom John calls on to testify that Jesus is the Son of God. Nicodemus was a prominent religious leader and a member of the leading church group of the day, the Pharisees. He was also a member of the Sanhedrin, the main council of the Jews and the highest court in the Jewish nation. Considering that the Sanhedrin was chaired by the high priest and that there were only seventy-one members, Nicodemus was certainly an important man.

Nicodemus visited Jesus secretly and stated that he believed Him to be "a teacher come from God." He had seen the signs, heard the teachings, observed His life, and he was convinced. "After the Lord's ascension, when the disciples were scattered by persecution, Nicodemus came boldly to the front. He employed his wealth in sustaining the infant church that the Jews had expected to be blotted out at the death of Christ. . . . Nicodemus related to John the story of that interview, and by his pen it was recorded for the instruction of millions."—*The Desire of Ages,* p. 177.

The instruction was recorded for us because it contains a step toward heaven that everyone should know. Jesus said to Nicodemus, "Verily, verily, I say unto thee, Except a man be born of water and of the Spirit, he cannot enter into the kingdom of God" (John 3:5). It is not enough to be baptized by immersion. We also need to experience a change in our life style that can be brought about only through the power of the Holy Spirit. We are to surrender our wills to God every day and ask that the Holy Spirit come in and take control of our lives.

The best-known text in the Bible is found in today's chapter. This verse that speaks of God's love is also a *proof* text. The love of God that allowed His only Son to die on the cross is evidence that cannot be argued against. Those who try to say that Jesus' miracles were natural events and that the Bible is just another book cannot explain away the love of God. John says the *source* of love is God and shows the *proof* of love is Christ.

PROOF
John 4

"COME, SEE A MAN"

"Come, see a man who told me all that I ever did. Can this be the Christ?" John 4:29.

A widely circulated newspaper recently published a list of the most influential persons in history. On the top half of the page were line drawings of one hundred people, and on the lower half was a brief description of each of them. The roster had been compiled by Michael Hart in a book entitled *The One Hundred: A Ranking of the Most Influential Persons in History*. It was a list of the most powerful, though not necessarily of the greatest, people who have ever lived.

Those listed in the B.C. group included Moses, Cyrus of Persia, Alexander the Great, Augustus Caesar, Confucius, Buddha, and Julius Caesar. The list of those in the A.D. period was far longer and included Paul; Johann Gutenberg, who invented movable type; Christopher Columbus, the explorer; Albert Einstein, the physicist; Martin Luther, the Reformer; William Shakespeare, the writer; Thomas Edison, the inventor; Ts'ai Lun, who invented paper; and Alexander Graham Bell, who invented the telephone. The compilation also included many leaders of nations, military generals, and other scientists, inventors, religious leaders, artists, musicians, and authors.

As I studied this page while flying between Europe and the United States, I scanned the list to see if Jesus was mentioned. I was disappointed to find that our Saviour's name was third, and noted the explanation that was given. It stated that if the followers of Jesus had put into practice His wonderful teachings, He would have been at the top of the list of influential people in history.

The woman at the well believed that Jesus was the most influential person she had ever met. When she learned that this Man who had never seen her before knew all about her past life, she was convinced that He was indeed the Messiah. She was also excited about what Jesus told her concerning the water of life and ran excitedly back into the city, saying to everyone she met, "Come, see a man, which told me all things that ever I did: is not this the Christ?" (John 4:29).

357

PROOF
John 5

JESUS IN EVERY BOOK

"You search the scriptures, because you think that in them you have eternal life; and it is they that bear witness to me." John 5:39.

The word *witness* is used more than twenty times in the book of John. In this chapter Jesus states that John and the Scriptures bear witness to who He is. As we have searched the Scriptures this year, we certainly have seen that Jesus is the center of every book. The sixty-six books of the Bible reveal His *coming, dying, saving,* and *reigning.*

In *Genesis* He is the Seed of the woman.
In *Exodus* He is the Passover Lamb.
In *Leviticus* He is the atoning sacrifice.
In *Numbers* He is the smitten Rock.
In *Deuteronomy* He is the Prophet.
In *Joshua* He is the Captain of the Lord's hosts.
In *Judges* He is the Deliverer.
In *Ruth* He is the heavenly Kinsman.
In the *six books of Kings* He is the Promised King.
In *Nehemiah* He is the Restorer of the nation.
In *Esther* He is the Advocate.
In *Job* He is my Redeemer.
In *Psalms* He is my All in All.
In *Ecclesiastes* He is my Goal.
In *Song of Solomon* He is my Satisfier.
In the *prophets* He is the coming Prince of Peace.
In the *Gospels* He is Christ coming to seek and to save.
In *Acts* He is Christ risen.
In the *Epistles* He is Christ at the Father's right hand.
In the *Revelation* He is Christ returning and reigning.

In the *Old Testament,* the Christ of prophecy—*coming.*
In the *Gospels,* the Christ of history—*dying.*
In the *Acts* and *Epistles,* the Christ of experience—*saving.*
In the *Revelation,* the Christ of glory—*reigning.*

PROOF
John 6

"I AM THE BREAD"

Jesus said to them, "I am the bread of life; he who comes to me shall not hunger, and he who believes in me shall never thirst." John 6:35.

The words *I am* are often used in English to describe who we are or where we are going. When someone asks me what work I do, I generally say, *"I am* a youth director," or *"I am* a minister." No doubt when someone asks you what you are going to do during the holidays, your reply commences with *"I am . . ."*

In the next fourteen days you will notice that Jesus also used the words *I am* often. Several books and many sermons have been written about the "I am's" of Jesus. In the first five chapters of John, we are given testimonies from individuals who were convinced that Jesus was the Son of God. Now John focuses attention on who Jesus said He was and who the crowds that followed Him said He was.

The statement "I am the bread" is recorded four times in this chapter. Jesus selected the figure of bread because it was something with which the people were familiar. The multitudes looked to Jesus for bread, and these statements were made immediately after He had fed the 5,000. They said, "This is of a truth that prophet that should come into the world" (John 6:14), and wanted to crown Jesus king right there. But the Lord knew that they did not fully understand who He was, so He said, "I am the bread of life."

As we consider how important bread is, we realize our need of Jesus. We cannot live without bread to strengthen our bodies, and we cannot live the Christian life without "the living bread," Jesus. Bread satisfies the hunger that we experience each day, and if we eat the "bread of life," we will truly enjoy living and will obtain eternal life.

In our Morning Watch verse today we are promised that as we eat the bread of life we shall not hunger, and as we believe in Jesus we shall never thirst. Jesus had just finished talking to the woman of Samaria about the living water, so we know what He meant by the statement about thirst. Bread and water are two essential needs of our bodies. Thus we see that Jesus supplies all our needs.

PROOF
John 7

"I AM SPEAKING"

"If any man's will is to do his will, he shall know whether the teaching is from God or whether I am speaking on my own authority." John 7:17.

Dalmatians, Labrador retrievers, and boxers are some of the breeds of dogs that are used as guides for blind people. They are also called seeing-eye dogs, as they actually become "eyes" for their blind masters. It takes a lot of work to train a guide dog, and they are very valuable animals. They obey the voice of their masters, who trust them completely.

Before people become followers of Christ they are spiritually blind. It is even possible for some to read the Bible and not discover that Jesus is the Son of God, or how to become Christians. One reason for this is that people want proof before they will have faith. However, in our text today Jesus states that first we need to exercise our faith, and then we will discover the proof we desire. Commitment to Jesus must precede assurance, and surrender comes before victory.

"While God has given ample evidence for faith, He will never remove all excuse for unbelief. All who look for hooks to hang their doubts upon will find them. And those who refuse to accept and obey God's word until every objection has been removed, and there is no longer an opportunity for doubt, will never come to the light."—*The Great Controversy,* p. 527.

Even after they had witnessed the feeding of the five thousand and Jesus walking on the water, "There was much murmuring among the people concerning him" (John 7:12). "While some said, 'He is a good man,' others said, 'No, he is leading the people astray'" (verse 12, R.S.V.). Today also there are two opinions concerning Jesus. We need to show by our lives and words that His teachings have changed us.

The officers who were sent to arrest Jesus came back to the Pharisees and said, "'No man ever spoke like this man'" (verse 46, R.S.V.). The reason Jesus' speech was so impressive was that no one had ever lived like Jesus lived. The life and words of Jesus proved that He was not only a "good man" but a "God-man."

PROOF
John 8

"I AM THAT I AM"

Jesus said to them, "Truly, truly, I say to you, before Abraham was, I am." John 8:58.

"With solemn dignity Jesus answered, 'Verily, verily, I say unto you, before Abraham was, I AM.'

"Silence fell upon the vast assembly. The name of God, given to Moses to express the idea of the eternal presence, had been claimed as His own by this Galilean Rabbi. He had announced Himself to be the self-existent One, He who had been promised to Israel, 'whose goings forth have been from of old, from the days of eternity.' Micah 5:2, margin. Again the priests and rabbis cried out against Jesus as a blasphemer."—*The Desire of Ages,* pp. 469, 470.

By using the title "I AM," Jesus made claim to being the Son of God. "I AM" is one of God's titles, and was first used when He was making a covenant with Abraham. This name showed God's superiority over all other gods. Since the time of Abraham and Moses, the Jews had regarded it as the most sacred name of the true God.

As soon as Jesus claimed this as His name, the religious leaders took up stones to kill Him. It was the custom to stone people to death for taking God's name in vain. It is interesting to note that Jesus hid Himself, not because He was afraid or guilty, but because it was not the time for Him to die nor the manner in which He was to die.

Jesus had been asked to state who He was (John 8:53). However, when He told them His true identity, they did not accept it because it did not fit their ideas. Today many people are asking who Jesus is, and when they find out, they do not accept Him as their Saviour. Also, there are others who ask for truth from God's Word but when they find it they do not follow it. This is a good time for us to examine ourselves and to find out whether we really know who Jesus is and whether we are really doing what He wants us to do.

From this chapter we see that we cannot just accept the opinions of the majority or the religious leaders. The leaders in Jesus' time wanted to stone the One who said He was the Son of God. I want to accept Jesus and His teachings no matter what others say or do, don't you?

361

PROOF
John 9

"I AM THE LIGHT"

"As long as I am in the world, I am the light of the world."
John 9:5.

Every four years athletes from many countries gather to compete for gold, silver, and bronze medals during the Olympic games. As each gold medal is presented to the winner of various contests, the national anthem of his or her country is played.

The Olympic games are always opened with a ceremony that includes lighting a flame. Since the first Olympic games were held in Greece, the fire is brought from there, and runners are selected to carry the Olympic torch to the stadium from the ship or plane that has brought it to the host country.

The 1964 Olympic games were held in Japan. The young man chosen as the last runner, with the privilege of carrying the flame into the stadium and lighting the giant torch, was just 19 years of age. He had been chosen for his character, physique, and athletic ability. He ran up the last 163 steps, dipped the torch into the huge bowl, and as the flame shot out, a trumpet sounded. The games had officially begun.

A youth director present at those games asked the young man how he was able to make the run without faltering. He replied, "I trained for this moment. The torch would go out in nine minutes, and everything depended on me. There was no time to stop; I had to run, run, run. I was ready, and I gave everything that I had."

Jesus was chosen as the last runner to bring light from heaven to earth. The prophets had also carried the torch of truth, and John the Baptist was the second-to-last runner. When Jesus came to this earth, He had only thirty-three years to reveal the *love, light,* and *life;* everything depended upon Him. He was ready, and He gave everything that He had. He did not attempt to do it in His own strength, but continually asked the Father for the power necessary to carry the light to Calvary's hill.

Jesus was not only the carrier of the light but also the source of light. In John's Gospel *light* and *life* are closely associated, and when we receive Jesus as the light of our lives, we also have eternal life.

362

PROOF
John 10

"I AM THE GOOD SHEPHERD"

"I am the good shepherd. The good shepherd lays down his life for the sheep." John 10:11.

"Science is my shepherd
I shall not want.
It maketh me to lie down on foam-rubber mattresses.
It leadeth me beside six-lane highways.
It rejuvenates my thyroid gland.
It leads me on the path of psychoanalysis.
For peace of mind's sake.
Yea, though I walk through the valley of the shadow of
The iron curtain, I will fear no Communist.
For you are with me.
The radar screen and hydrogen bomb
They comfort me.
You prepare a banquet before me in the presence of
The world's billion hungry people.
You anoint my head with home permanents,
My tray runneth over.
Surely prosperity and pleasure should follow me
All the days of my life.
And I will dwell in Shangri-la forever."

Shangri-la is an expression that is used to describe a place of peace. Although there are scientists, statesmen, philosophers, and politicians who still dream of this age of Utopia, most people realize that it will never be possible on this earth.

Science is not able to shepherd us into an age of peace, but Jesus can, for He is the Good Shepherd. The greatest news of all time and the biggest announcement is that Jesus Christ, the Son of the living God, is about to come the second time and bring in an age of peace.

In the days of Jesus the sheep that had peace were safely in the fold at night. The shepherd closed the door to keep wild animals out. Jesus says that He is not only the shepherd but also "the door" (John 10:7). Jesus is our door to safety and satisfaction.

PROOF
John 11

"I AM THE RESURRECTION"

Jesus said to her, "I am the resurrection and the life; he who believes in me, though he die, yet shall he live." John 11:25.

Last month I told you a little about Raymond Wilson, a young man who lived a short but full life. Those who knew Raymond believe that, just as surely as Lazarus was raised from the dead, so this young man, who was not even 20 years of age when he drowned, will hear the voice of the Life-giver on the resurrection morning. That day will be a wonderful reunion and a day of joy for all of us.

After Raymond's sudden death, one of the students at Avondale College wrote the following letter to the grief-stricken parents: "The night before Raymond went to the college picnic on Sunday at Cave's Beach, he spent at least two hours with me. . . .

"The major part of our time was spent in discussing the value of Christian education and the worldwide Advent Movement in general. From my precious knowledge of Raymond as a friend and a brother in the Lord, and from his warm and sincere discussion on Christian education that night before his death, I do not doubt for a moment the fact that the Lord had His hands on him.

"I am still feeling the warmth of his answer to my pertinent question that night—Isn't it wonderful to be a Seventh-day Adventist? The response he gave me with his face radiant in the love and knowledge of our Saviour was 'Yes, it is wonderful.'

"In closing we wished each other good night and Raymond said, 'I will see you in the morning.'"

To those who die believing in the Lord Jesus, the next thing they will know will be the resurrection morning at the Second Advent. We do not know when that wonderful event will be, but it is important for us to be ready for that morning whenever it comes. Because of what Jesus has done in conquering death, we will have the privilege of seeing our loved ones "in the morning."

Those who have died in the Lord are "sleeping." The next thing they hear will be the voice of Jesus, "the resurrection, and the life," calling them to rise up and live.

364

PROOF
John 12

"I AM LIFTED UP"

"And I, when I am lifted up from the earth, will draw all men to myself." He said this to show by what death he was to die. John 12:32, 33.

A wealthy family went to the country estate of a friend for a holiday with their children. While there the boys decided to wade in the small lake on the grounds. One of them ventured out beyond his depth, and since he could not swim was soon in trouble. His brother screamed for help, and the son of the gardener, hearing the cries, went to the rescue. Jumping into the water, he soon brought the struggling boy to shore. The parents knew that their son would surely have drowned had it not been for the quick action of the young man, and they were very grateful. They decided to do something for him.

The gardener told them that his son had been wanting to go to college but that he was not able to send him. "He wants to be a doctor," the father said.

"He shall go to school!" the grateful parents declared. "And we shall be happy to pay his expenses."

At the time of the Teheran Conference in World War II, Prime Minister Winston Churchill of England was ill with pneumonia. The king of England gave instructions that the best doctor available should be sent to his bedside. That doctor was Alexander Fleming, the scientist who had been instrumental in discovering penicillin. He was also the young man who had many years before pulled the drowning young Churchill out of the lake.

Said the prime minister to Dr. Fleming, "Rarely has one man owed his life twice to the same rescuer."

Jesus has rescued us twice, because He is both our Creator and our Redeemer. Because He created us, He knows the best way to rescue us when we are struggling in the waters of worldliness. Because He has died for us, He is able to inject His blood to cleanse us when we are spiritually sick.

This statement that Jesus' death on the cross would draw all men to Him is a prophecy. Today, all who look to the cross can find life.

PROOF
John 13

"I AM THE LORD"

"You call me Teacher and Lord; and you are right, for so I am." John 13:13.

Miss Sydney Hall was admitted to the Malamulo Mission Hospital with a suspected case of malaria. However, the doctor soon discovered that she had contracted diphtheria while treating Africans who were suffering from the disease.

The physician did all he could to arrest the disease. Miss Hall told him she was not unwilling to die, but that she preferred to live and do the work God had called her to Africa to do. However, noting her symptoms, she said, "It won't be long now, Doctor."

Miss Hall gave a farewell message: "I have a father and brother living in New York. They are not Christians and strongly opposed my coming to Africa. On the flyleaf of my Bible is their address. Send them the Bible with this message. Tell them that not for one moment have I regretted coming to Africa, nor do I regret it now. Tell them that there is no joy in all the world like the joy that comes from serving and loving Jesus."

An hour later she fell asleep in Jesus. And today she lies in a little cemetery among the bamboo trees at Malamulo. As I looked at Nurse Hall's grave, I realized that she knew Jesus as her Lord, and was prepared to serve and die for Him.

Before Jesus told the disciples that they were right in calling Him Lord, He had washed their feet. This was the work that was normally done by the servant, and although Jesus is our Lord, He is also our servant.

He served as *Servant* when He lived on earth.

He served as *Sacrifice* when He died on the cross.

He serves as *Mediator* in the courts of heaven.

He serves as *Judge* in the heavenly courts.

He will soon serve as *King*.

Those who acknowledge Jesus as *Lord* will serve Him and others.

PROOF
John 14

"I AM THE WAY"

Jesus said to him, "I am the way, and the truth, and the life; no one comes to the Father, but by me." John 14:6.

Along the Mohawk Trail in New York State is a sign with these words:

"Jesus is the way, the truth, the life.
Without the truth there is no knowing;
Without the way there is no going;
Without the life there is no living."

Do you know the *way* through this world's darkness and the problems that you have to meet? Do you know the way to eternal life?

Do you know the *truths* of Scripture, truths that are beyond the narrow confines of men's minds and churches' decrees? Do you know the truth for these tremendous times?

Do you know the truly satisfying *life?* Are you at peace with yourself, your God, and others? Are you really living, or are you just existing for the next round of pleasure?

If you believe you can find a better *way,* learn of other *truths,* and enjoy a better *life,* remember that Jesus is the answer to your quest.

Before Jesus said that He was "the way, the truth, and the life," He told His disciples that He was going away. He knew they would be subject to discouragement, so He said, "In my Father's house are many mansions. . . . I go to prepare a place for you. . . . And the way ye know" (John 14:2-4).

Thomas, speaking on behalf of the group, said what many Christians today might say. He said he didn't know the way. Although the disciples had been with Jesus and had heard Him speak of the heavenly kingdom, they still thought He was going to set up an earthly kingdom.

Today we need to ask ourselves, How many of us are really longing for the heavenly mansions? How many of us truly know the way to the kingdom?

Thomas' question gave Jesus the opportunity to state in a few words what He had spent years trying to explain to them. These are words we need always to remember: "I am the way, the truth, and the life."

PROOF
John 15

"I AM THE VINE"

"I am the vine, you are the branches. He who abides in me, and I in him, he it is that bears much fruit, for apart from me you can do nothing." John 15:5.

A welfare worker found a crippled boy in a poor area of a large city. She had a heart full of love, took an interest in the child, and wanted to see him walk again. She consulted an orthopedic surgeon who agreed to operate, and she said she would pay for the surgery. The operation was a success, and after a long time the boy was able to walk, then run and play like other boys.

Many years later the welfare worker told this story, then said, "He is a grown man now. I want you to guess where he is and what he is doing." The guesses included several worthy vocations: a famous doctor, a minister, a philanthropist, a welfare worker.

At that point the woman interrupted and said, "You are all wrong. He is in prison serving a life sentence for murder. We spent all our time teaching him *how* to walk, but we failed to teach him *where* to walk."

Those of us who are working for the Lord must teach people not only *how* to walk but *where* to walk in the Christian life. First we must show people how to become Christians. Then we must teach them from the Bible where Christians should walk. We need to walk with our eyes fixed on our destination.

The secret of living the Christian life is found in the parable of the vine and the branches, recorded in today's chapter. It can be summarized in three words—"Abide in Christ." There can be no closer picture of union than a branch and a vine. If the branch is separated from the vine, it dies. If it is receiving nourishment daily from the vine, it grows and bears fruit.

To abide with someone means to live in close fellowship. Each day as we give our lives to Jesus, we strengthen our relationship with Him. Then through prayer, Bible study, and witnessing we grow and bear fruit—the fruit of the Spirit.

368

PROOF
John 16

"I AM LEAVING"

"I came from the Father and have come into the world; again, I am leaving the world and going to the Father." John 16:28.

The first Christmas after Linda had learned to read, she was allowed to distribute the gifts on Christmas Eve. According to family custom, the one who handed out the presents could open the first package. After everyone had his gifts, Linda continued looking around the tree and among its branches.

Finally Father asked, "What are you looking for, dear?" To this Linda replied, "I thought Christmas was Jesus' birthday, and I was just wondering where His present is. I guess everyone forgot Him. Did they, Daddy?"

Yes, lots of people forget Christ at Christmas. Millions of presents are put on and under trees to let people know that they are remembered, but the One who hung on a tree for us is forgotten.

Although we don't know exactly *when* Jesus was born, we do know *why* He was born. He came into the world to reveal the true character of the Father and to die that we might have eternal life.

Although we don't know *how* Jesus was born, we do know *for whom* He was born. The Christ of Christmas came to save the human family, to set sinners free, and to give eternal life to you and me.

Jesus said, "I leave the world, and go to the Father." He did this in order to prepare a place for us in the heavenly kingdom. Although there was no room for Jesus in Bethlehem's inn, He is reserving a place for us. All who give Jesus a place in their hearts can live forever in heaven.

When Jesus left the world, He returned to His Father. Can you imagine the welcome He received! Millions of angels sang as they escorted the Christ of Christmas back to His home in heaven. How wonderful to know that we will soon leave this planet and be welcomed home too!

The One who said "I am leaving" also said, "I will come again and receive you." He came the first time as a baby, but this time He is coming as a king.

PROOF
John 17

"I AM PRAYING"

"I am praying for them; I am not praying for the world but for those whom thou hast given me, for they are thine." John 17:9.

Did you know that Jesus prayed for you and me? This prayer of Jesus in John 17 is the longest of His recorded petitions to His Father. In the first part Jesus prays for Himself (verses 1-5). He then prays for the disciples who were with Him (verses 6-19). And in the last part of His prayer (verses 20-26), Jesus pleads for all who would believe on His name.

This prayer could really be called the Lord's Prayer; the more familiar one that He taught His disciples, and that is usually called by that title, is really a model prayer for *us*. The fact that Jesus prayed to His Father is further proof that He is the Son of God.

What was Jesus' prayer for you and me? When Christ prayed to His Father, He asked that His followers to the end of time all "may be one." The reason Jesus pleaded for unity was "that the world may believe that thou hast sent me." Unity in the church is one sign that we are Christ's true disciples. When people see this closeness, it leads many to believe that Jesus is the Son of God.

We cannot just decide to have unity. The only way we can have lasting fellowship is by permitting Jesus to control our lives. We need the power of the Holy Spirit in order to have Christian unity.

In Chicago some visitors were being shown through a factory where train rails were made. In one section were large cranes that traveled overhead and transported vats of hot steel. As they watched, a great vat stopped, tipped gently, and the hot steel flowed smoothly over the molds. The visitors were amazed, as there seemed to be no one operating the equipment. Someone finally asked, "How do they do it?" The guide pointed to the far corner of the room and said, "It's all controlled from up there." As the visitors looked up, they saw a small room where a man sat in front of a row of buttons and levers.

The prayer that Jesus prayed for us will be answered when we are "all controlled from up there." We need to cooperate with God to the extent that we will say, as Jesus said, "Not my will, but thine, be done" (Luke 22:42).

370

PROOF
John 18

"I AM HE"

They answered him, "Jesus of Nazareth." Jesus said to them, "I am he." Judas, who betrayed him, was standing with them. John 18:5.

In a cathedral in Lubeck, Germany, is a stone slab with these words.

"Thus speaketh Christ our Lord to us:
Ye call me Master, and obey me not;
Ye call me Light, and see me not;
Ye call me Way, and walk me not;
Ye call me Life, and desire me not;
Ye call me Wise, and follow me not;
Ye call me Fair, and love me not;
Ye call me Rich, and ask me not;
Ye call me Eternal, and seek me not;
Ye call me Gracious, and trust me not;
Ye call me Noble, and serve me not;
Ye call me Mighty, and honor me not;
Ye call me Just, and fear me not;
If I condemn you, blame me not."

It was Judas who had called Jesus "Master," and had followed Him for three years, who now led the band of soldiers that took Him prisoner. He had seen the *light, love,* and *life* of Jesus during His ministry, and by this act of betrayal Judas experienced *darkness, hatred,* and *death,* as he realized that he had betrayed the Son of God. Jesus still loved him, but Judas hated himself. Instead of enriching his life from the money he was paid, the former disciple committed suicide.

As the soldiers approached, Jesus asked, "Whom seek ye?"

They replied, "Jesus of Nazareth."

Jesus replied, "I am he." The mob fell backward at the sound of His name, another evidence of Jesus' divinity.

And this should also be an encouragement to us. "We cannot save ourselves from the tempter's power; he has conquered humanity, and when we try to stand in our own strength, we shall become a prey to his devices; but 'the name of the Lord is a strong tower: the righteous runneth into it, and is safe.' Prov. 18:10. Satan trembles and flees before the weakest soul who finds refuge in that mighty name."—*The Desire of Ages,* p. 131.

PROOF
John 19

"I AM KING"

The chief priests of the Jews then said to Pilate, "Do not write, 'The King of the Jews,' but, 'This man said, I am King of the Jews.'" John 19:21.

John is the only Gospel writer who records that the Jews tried to persuade Pilate to change the sign posted on the cross. It was the custom to post a notice at executions, giving the name of the accused, where he came from, and his crime. Obviously the Jews were upset that Jesus was called "King of the Jews." Also they realized that if anyone later claimed to be their king, he could well be crucified. The nation was under domination by Rome, and the people were looking for a Messiah-king to deliver them.

On two occasions Pilate had asked Jesus whether He was king of the Jews. Jesus did not answer that He was or that He wasn't. He did say, "My kingdom is not of this world" (John 18:36). Jesus is more than a king in the royal line of David; He is King of kings.

While in this *world* Jesus had no throne, but He has reigned in the hearts of men, women, boys, and girls in every century.

While in *Jerusalem* Jesus had no armies, but in every generation there have been Christian soldiers.

While in *Pilate's judgment hall* Jesus did not take the scepter that was rightfully His, but soon everyone will kneel before His raised scepter.

While in *Nazareth* Jesus had no palace, but today He is preparing palaces for all His subjects.

On the *road to Jerusalem* Jesus refused to be crowned king, but one day the grandest coronation the world has ever seen will be held, when Jesus will be crowned King of kings.

Jesus is the King of peace, the King of glory, the King of this world, the royal King of heaven, the King of kings. I have crowned Him King of my heart, and I believe that you have too. That means that one day we will have the privilege of living with Him in His kingdom. We have discovered from the prophecies that when Jesus comes in the clouds, He will take His subjects to His kingdom beyond the stars. That will be a very happy day for Christians.

PROOF
John 20

"I AM ASCENDING"

Jesus said to her, "Do not hold me, for I have not yet ascended to the Father; but go to my brethren and say to them, I am ascending to my Father and your Father, to my God and your God." John 20:17.

Jesus, our Creator and the One who instituted the Sabbath, remained in the tomb over that holy day. Just before daybreak on the first day of the week, an angel had the privilege of breaking the seal and rolling back the stone from the tomb.

"When the voice of the mighty angel was heard at Christ's tomb, saying, Thy Father calls Thee, the Saviour came forth from the grave by the life that was in Himself. Now was proved the truth of His words, 'I lay down my life, that I might take it again.... I have power to lay it down, and I have power to take it again.' Now was fulfilled the prophecy He had spoken to the priests and rulers, 'Destroy this temple, and in three days I will raise it up.' John 10:17, 18; 2:19."—*The Desire of Ages,* p. 785.

Can you imagine Mary's excitement when she discovered that the One who spoke to her was not the gardener, but Jesus! She must have shouted for joy as He uttered her name. Have you ever been in such a rush to get somewhere that you couldn't run fast enough? That's the way Mary must have felt when she hurried to tell the disciples. Imagine her bursting into the room and saying, "I have seen the Lord!"

The resurrection of Jesus is one of the first significant facts of history. It is also a main teaching of the Bible and is the subject of many prophecies. Jesus Himself predicted that He would rise from the dead and ascend to heaven. The resurrection is conclusive *proof* that Jesus of Nazareth is the Messiah and is the Son of man and the Son of God. It gave power to the disciples and their followers.

In Bernhill Fields, London, inscribed on the tomb of Dr. John Condor, are these words: "I have sinned, I have repented; I have trusted, I have loved; I rest, I shall rise; and, through the grace of Christ, however unworthy, I shall reign." By the grace of Jesus, all those who with Thomas exclaim "My Lord and my God" have the same hope of the resurrection.

PROOF
John 21

"FOLLOW ME!"

Jesus said to him, "If it is my will that he remain until I come, what is that to you? Follow me!" John 21:22.

Tom did not want to work for a witch doctor, but he was only 15 years of age, in a strange country, and needed food and shelter, so he took the job. One of his duties was to gather ten big bags of roots. He then had to cut up the roots, burn them, and make charcoal powder. Tom was frightened when he heard voices telling the witch doctor what to do.

It was the witch doctor who told Tom's uncle that the boy should go to school. Tom was eager to learn, and secretly completed two Voice of Prophecy courses in order to improve his English. Although he really had not learned to know Jesus as his personal Saviour, he was baptized.

Upon completing secondary school, Tom returned to his home country of Malawi and began working as a clerk. As he was riding to work on the first Sabbath, he heard a voice saying, "This is the Lord's day. You shouldn't work on it." This prompted him to tell his boss that he wanted to resign, but he was offered a promotion and continued to work. On the next Sabbath he heard a loud voice telling him that it was the Lord's day.

So Tom resigned his job and began selling Christian books. After making no sales for three months, he spent a night in prayer, asking for the Lord's guidance. When he resumed his work, he sold enough to pay for more than two years of education. And it was while at Malamulo Mission that Tom learned to know Jesus as his personal Saviour and gave his life fully to the Master's service.

Tom spent four years at Solusi College in Zimbabwe, then began working with his wife, Alice, as a Christian teacher in Malawi. Since then he has studied at Avondale College in Australia and at two universities in the United States. Dr. Tom Nkungula has since been appointed education director for the Trans-Africa Division.

Tom was called through a strange set of circumstances to be a Christian worker. Peter, the fisherman, also began to follow Jesus before he was completely converted. Many are called to follow Jesus, but we must be like Tom, Peter, and John, and really learn to love Him.

PROOF
John 1:1-18

"YOU MAY BELIEVE"

Now Jesus did many other signs in the presence of the disciples, which are not written in this book; but these are written that you may believe that Jesus is the Christ, the Son of God, and that believing you may have life in his name. John 20:30, 31.

This year we have had the opportunity of reading and reviewing the Bible story. We now see that to know it is to have light for our lives. To know this light is to love it. To love this light leads us to accept it. To accept this light leads us to live it in our lives. As we live this light in our lives, others will find it too.

As we begin another year of exploring God's Word, let us remember the new dimensions for living we have discovered.

The *pattern,* as found in *Matthew,* is to walk in Jesus' steps.

The *power,* as revealed in *Acts,* is the Holy Spirit.

The *plan,* as seen in *Genesis,* is for all to let the light, love, and life of Jesus flow in blessings to others.

The *purpose,* as found in *Exodus* through *Deuteronomy,* is for God's people to leave the slavery of Egypt and enter into His Promised Land.

The *promises* in Paul's books, from *Romans* to *Galatians,* assure us that all things work together for good to those who love the Lord.

The *prophecies,* found in *Daniel* and *Revelation,* show that God has a timetable for this world. They show that we are living just minutes before midnight.

The *Person,* as revealed in *Mark, Isaiah,* and *Jeremiah,* shows that Jesus went about doing good, for He was good.

The *perfection* in the life of Jesus, as portrayed by *Luke* and *Job,* is the ideal for our lives.

The *providence* of God, seen in the books from *Judges* through *Esther,* leaves no doubt that God is in control of nations and individuals.

The *praises* in the poetry of the *Psalms* and *Proverbs* advise us to trust in God and to rejoice in the knowledge of Jesus.

The *peace,* as seen in the Epistles from *Ephesians* through *Jude,* is beyond anything this world has to offer.

The *proof* of God's love in *Ruth, Jonah,* and *John* shows that Jesus is the Son of God and leads us to say, "I want this *light for my life.*"

GENESIS
1:1	70
2:7	71
3:15	72
4:26	73
5:1	74
6:9	75
7:15, 16	76
8:1, 4, 20	77
9:13	78
10:1	79
11:9	80
12:1, 2	81
13:14-16	82
14:22	83
15:6	84
18:1, 2	85
19:24-26	86
22:7	87
24:63	88
27:29	89
28:12	90
29:4, 5	91
32:28	92
35:3	93
37:28	94
39:2, 3	95
41:39, 40	96
42:6-8	97
45:2, 3	98
49:28	99
50:20	100

EXODUS
1:13,14	101
2:10	102
3:1, 2	103
4:2	104
5:1, 2	105
7:20	106
11:3	107
12:26, 27	108
13:3	109
14:21, 22	110
15:13	111
15:27	112
16:35	113
17:7	114
18:5	115
19:6	116
20:1, 2	117
24:18	118
31:18	119
32:26	120
33:14	121
34:28	122
35:1	123

LEVITICUS
1:1, 2	124
11:44	125
16:33	126

NUMBERS
10:1, 2	127
11:1	128
23:23	129

DEUTERONOMY
18:15	130

JUDGES
3:9	254
6:12-14	255
7:7	256

RUTH
1:16	346
2:2	347
3:5	348
4:14	349

1 SAMUEL
2:26	257
9:27	258
16:13	259
17:37	260

2 SAMUEL
7:18	261

1 KINGS
3:9	262
8:20	263
11:11	264
17:24	265
18:24	266
18:39	267
19:4	268
20:40	269

2 KINGS
2:9	270
4:35	271
5:14	272
18:3-5	273

ESTHER
1:19	274

2:17	275
3:8	276
4:16	277
5:2, 3	278
6:1	279
7:3	280
8:10	281
9:28	282
10:2	283

JOB
1:8	247
2:7	248
2:11	250
3:1-3	249
12:7	252
38:1-3	251
42:12	253

PSALMS
2:7	286
8:3, 4	293
16:11	287
19:10	294
22:16-18	288
23:1	289
24:7	290
27:1	299
29:11	295
37:3, 4	300
46:1	301
51:7	297
66:1, 2	285
73:28	302
90:17	303
91:11	304
92:12	298
103:13	307
104:1	296
106:9	306
107:2	305
110:4	291
113:9	292
117	234
119:1	308
119:9	309
119:130	310
146:1, 2	311

PROVERBS
1:7	312
6:6	313
14:12	314

ISAIAH

1:18	208
5:1	209
6:1	210
7:14	211
11:6	212
26:19	213
35:8	214
37:10	215
38:5	216
40:3	217
42:1	218
53:4, 5	219
65:17	220
66:1	221

JEREMIAH

1:4, 5	222

DANIEL

1:8	162
2:20, 22	163
3:24, 25	164
4:34	165
5:29	166
6:26, 27	167
7:27	168
8:20, 21	169
9:24	170
10:11	171
11:32	172
12:1	173

JONAH

1:3	350
2:9	351
3:1-3	352
4:2	353

MATTHEW

1:1	41
1:16	11
2:23	12
3:2	13
4:10	14
5:14	15
6:12	16
7:7	17
8:27	18
9:9	19
10:1	20
11:10	21
12:40	22

13:10, 11	23
14:14	24
15:32	25
16:13	26
17:27	27
18:5	28
19:21	29
20:16	30
21:9	31
22:15	32
23:12	33
24:3	34
25:13	35
26:29	36
27:22	38
27:29	37
28:7	39
28:19, 20	40

MARK

1:1	192
2:1	193
3:13, 14	194
4:39	195
5:34	196
6:4	197
7:37	198
8:35, 36	199
9:31	200
10:14	201
11:9, 10	202
12:10, 11	203
13:32, 33	204
14:43-72	205
15:32, 39	206
16:6, 7	207

LUKE

1:3	223
2:52	224
3:38	225
4:14	226
5:4	227
6:38	228
7:37, 38	229
8:18	230
9:23	231
10:1, 2	232
11:1, 2	233
12:34	234
13:8, 9	235
14:35	236

15:2, 3	237
16:13	238
17:12, 13	239
18:16	240
19:10	241
20:2	242
21:30, 31	243
22:31, 32	244
23:33	245
24:52, 53	246

JOHN

1:49	354
2:11	355
3:2	356
4:29	357
5:39	358
6:35	359
7:17	360
8:58	361
9:5	362
10:11	363
11:25	364
12:32, 33	365
13:13	366
14:6	367
15:5	368
16:28	369
17:9	370
18:5	371
19:8, 9	345
19:21	372
20:17	373
21:22	374
20:30, 31	375

ACTS

1:8	42
2:1, 2	43
3:6	44
4:13	45
5:18-20	46
6:3	47
7:56	48
8:38	49
9:15	50
10:22	51
11:21, 22	52
12:1-3	53
13:48, 49	54
14:26, 27	55
15:7	56

378

16:9	57	2:14	155	**TITUS**	
17:6	58	4:8	156	2:11, 12	334
18:24	59	5:17	157	**PHILEMON**	
19:19	60	9:8	158	18, 19	335
20:24	61	**GALATIANS**		**HEBREWS**	
21:13	62	2:20	159	9:24	336
22:14	63	5:22, 23	160	11:6	337
23:1	64	6:7	161	**JAMES**	
24:16	65			4:7, 8	338
25:8	66	**EPHESIANS**			
26:29	67	1:9, 10	315	**1 PETER**	
27:6	68	2:17, 18	316	1:23	339
28:30, 31	69	3:17-19	317	**2 PETER**	
ROMANS		4:1, 2	318	1:2, 3	340
1:1, 2	131	5:1, 2	319	**1 JOHN**	
2:4	132	6:4	320	1:9	341
3:23, 24	133	**PHILIPPIANS**		4:18	342
4:20-22	134	1:2-4	321	**3 JOHN**	
5:3, 4	135	2:3, 4	322	2	343
6:4	136	3:13	323		
7:24, 25	137	4:19	324	**JUDE**	
8:14	138			1, 2	344
9:14, 15	139	**COLOSSIANS**		**REVELATION**	
10:9	140	1:27	325	1:3	174
11:22	141	3:20	326	2:1	175
12:2	142	**1 THESSA-**		3:20	176
13:1	143	**LONIANS**		4:1	177
14:11	144	4:15, 16	327	5:9	178
15:13	145	5:19, 20	328	6:2	179
16:20	146	**2 THESSA-**		7:9	180
1 CORINTHIANS		**LONIANS**		10:10	181
1:7	147	3:16	329	11:14	182
2:9	148			13:11	184
3:16, 17	149	**1 TIMOTHY**		13:17	183
7:29-31	150	3:14, 15	330	14:6	185
10:13	151	4:12	331	16:1	186
13:13	152	**2 TIMOTHY**		18:2-4	187
15:58	153	1:11, 12	332	19:11-16	188
2 CORINTHIANS		3:16, 17	333	20:6	189
1:3, 4	154			21:3, 4	190
				22:17	191